Donald Maitland

THE RUNNING TIDE

A VIEW OF
INTERNATIONAL AND
OTHER PUBLIC AFFAIRS
OVER FOUR DECADES

'I must down to the seas again,
for the call of the running tide
Is a wild call and a clear call
that may not be denied'

John Masefield

THE RUNNING TIDE

A VIEW OF
INTERNATIONAL AND
OTHER PUBLIC AFFAIRS
OVER FOUR DECADES

BY

DONALD MAITLAND

UNIVERSITY OF BATH PRESS
2000

PUBLISHED IN 2000 BY

University of Bath Press · Claverton Down ·Bath · BA2 7AY

ISBN 0 86197 126 4

Typographic design and layout: Michael Gray, Monmouth Calotype, Bath
Typeset and PMU: PCS Typesetting · Shepton Mallet · Somerset
Printed by Redwood Books · Trowbridge · Wiltshire

© Photograph of the author courtesy Wessex Newspapers

Foreword by Peter Calvocoressi

Preface *ix*

CHAPTER ONE: THE MIDDLE EAST *1*

I General Survey of the Middle East: Shemlan, Lebanon, 1959 *1*
II Future Relations between the Arabs and the West: Shemlan, 1959 *11*
III The Arabic Language: Shemlan, 1959 *22*
IV War in the Gulf and the Prospects for Peace: Paris, 1991 *26*
V The Demise of Colonialism in the Middle East: London, 1997 *29*
VI Revolution in the Middle East: Marlborough, 1998 *37*

CHAPTER TWO: EVER CLOSER UNION IN EUROPE *49*

I Britain and Europe: The 1961 Application: French Deception or
British Mismanagement: Bath, 1999 *49*
II The State of the Community: Amsterdam, 1976 *61*
III The Construction of Europe: Principles and Beliefs: Brussels 1978 *68*
IV Disturbing Trends: Nuremberg, 1979 *73*
V Europe and South East Asia: London, 1985 *78*
VI European Union and the Arab World: Rabat, 1992 *85*
VII Europe: Who Rules?: Bath, 1996 *93*
VIII Accession of Greece to the Community: Thessaloniki, 1997 *102*
IX The Commonwealth and Europe: London, 1998 *108*
X Decision-Making in the Union: Bath, 1998 *116*
XI Europe: A New Beginning?: Bath, 1999 *130*

CHAPTER THREE: THE GLOBAL CONTEXT *139*

I A New International Order: Chelsea, London, 1974 *139*
II East and West, North and South: New York, 1974 *147*
III The Formulation of British Foreign Policy: Latimer, 1980 *154*
IV Diplomacy in a Changing World: Blakeney, Leicestershire, 1984 *164*
V A Time for New Attitudes: Muncie, Indiana, USA, 1985 *172*
VI Indo-British Relations: London, 1985 *185*
VII The 'Special Relationship': Bath, 1988 *190*
VIII The Christian and the Community of Nations: Wells, 1989 *195*
IX Ring Round the World: Paris, 1990 *203*
X International Order in the Twenty-First Century:
The Role of the United Nations: Bath, 1999 *206*
XI The Nation State and War: Bath, 2000 *217*

CHAPTER FOUR: THE HOME FRONT *231*

I Government and Public: the Problem of Communication:
London, 1971 *231*
II Changing Relations between Downing Street and
Fleet Street: Cardiff, 1992 *244*
III Health Education and Occupational Medicine: Bristol, 1989 *252*
IV The Role of the Pharmacist: Chester, 1991 *258*
V HIV and AIDS: London, 1993 *264*
VI The Health of the Nation: London, 1993 *271*
VII The State of the Nation: A Personal View: Oxford, 1996 *275*
VIII Governance and Decision-Making:
Where Does Power Lie?: Bristol, 1998 *280*

CHAPTER FIVE: THE POLITICS OF ENERGY *291*

I Energy Policy: The Wider Context: London, 1981 *291*
II Energy in International Relations: Harvard, 1982 *297*
III The Significance of Oil to the Middle East: London, 1984 *306*

CHAPTER SIX: SIGNPOSTS TO THE GLOBAL VILLAGE *315*

I Bridging the Missing Link: Nairobi, 1986 *315*
II Communications: A Path to One World: Chelsea, 1988 *321*
III The Prize to be Won: Bangkok, 1994 *331*
IV The New Challenge: Valletta, 1998 *339*

Envoi *345*

Index *347*

PREFACE

Francis Bacon was right when he
wrote: *'Travel, in the younger sort, is a part of education;
in the elder, a part of experience'*.

The posts I have held over the years in various
parts of the world, and in different forms of public service,
have taught me much about other peoples' problems and
aspirations as well as some of the formidable challenges we
face at home. While I have been acquiring experience, I have
frequently been called upon to share my impressions and
opinions with others.

I am grateful to all of those at home and abroad with
whose support and understanding I have been able to observe the
running tide of contemporary history.

FOREWORD

PETER CALVOCORESSI

Sir Donald Maitland has spent most of his working life in the Diplomatic Service in which he reached the highest rank. In 1979 he was chosen by the Foreign Secretary to be Ambassador in Washington but with a general election imminent his appointment was not announced and the incoming Prime Minister did not confirm it. Within the Foreign Office he was a Middle East expert but never in the sense of being appointed to serve nowhere else. He ranged widely with concluding stints as Ambassadorial Representative at the United Nations and the European Community and as Press Secretary to the Prime Minister – the last still a job of unsettled ambience to which he gave a judicious direction (not always followed by his successors).

After retiring from the Diplomatic Service in 1982 he passed with happy ease into other posts and other worlds including energy policy, world wide communications, broadcasting, public health and university government – none of them obviously related to his earlier career. Yet in spite of this diversity Sir Donald's life and this book have a unity. There is first of all his own character. He has a natural gusto for tackling things and getting on with them. He is also – to use a very simple word – uncommonly straight. Not just in his principles and his dealings but in another sense too. He has the incalculable gift of seeing what is not going to happen and so he wastes no time going round and round a problem which, though it be hard, is not in its essentials complex. And when he gets up to talk he goes straight to the point so that the non-specialist, which most of us must be in some at least of his topics, is well rewarded for listening to him.

Finally this selection of Donald Maitland's spoken words defines the meaning of the term 'public service'. The public servant is required to do more than work to the satisfaction of the organisation which employs him and pays him. He has also to explain in plain words what the problems are and what can and should be done about them. This is an essential factor in political and social health and it is one that Sir Donald never loses sight of.

CHAPTER ONE: **THE MIDDLE EAST**

The Middle East Centre for Arab Studies in Lebanon, which I directed for four years, not only taught the Arabic language but also introduced students to the region in which they would be spending a substantial part of their career. The first two lectures in this chapter were part of this latter process. Delivered in 1959, they reflect the impact at that time on attitudes and relationships in the Middle East of the Suez conflict of 1956 and the violent revolution in Iraq in 1958.

I

GENERAL SURVEY OF THE MIDDLE EAST

In many regions of the world the Middle East is seen as a meeting place between the civilisations of East and West. To its own inhabitants it has for thousands of years been civilisation itself. Ever since the most remote antiquity the region has attracted the attention of mankind and the successive civilisations which have flourished within it have made an unsurpassed contribution to human progress. The Middle East has witnessed the empires of Egypt, of Sumer and Akkad, of Assyria, Babylon and Persia. It saw the flourishing mercantile cities of the Phoenicians, the conquering progress of Alexander the Great, the empires of his successors, the Roman conquest and the long reign of Byzantium. These distant episodes are not of special concern today; it is from the time of the Arab conquests that the peculiar characteristics have come into being which distinguish the Middle East, its peoples, its challenges and its politics from other regions of the world.

The main elements in the growth of the Arab empires can be clearly identified. The religion of Islam was revealed to the Prophet Muhammad, an inhabitant of Mecca. Before his death in 632 AD the Hejaz had been united under his rule and the foundations laid for the political unification of Arabia. After his death, full of their zeal for the new religion, the Arabic-speaking tribes of the desert swept out of the peninsula in successive waves and quickly conquered the decadent empires of Persia and Byzantium, exhausted by a long series of wars. In less than a

1

hundred years these tribes had overthrown the Sassanians in Persia and driven back the Byzantine Roman Empires. They had thrust through Syria into Central Asia and India, through Egypt, North Africa and Spain, and even into France, where they were at last checked by Charles Martel near Poitiers in 732.

The Prophet left no instructions as to who should succeed him in his temporal functions. The Faithful accordingly elected a successor as 'Khalifa' – or 'Caliph' in its anglicised form – whose seat was in Medina. Inevitably factions appeared and it was an ill omen that of the first four Caliphs only one died a natural death. In 661 a member of the Ummaya, a leading family in Mecca, seized the Caliphate with the support of a large body of moderate opinion amongst the Muslims, and founded the Ummayad Dynasty which ruled the Empire from Damascus until 750. But a minority had given their support to Hussein, the son of Ali, the Prophet's son-in-law, who had been passed over in the elections of the Caliphs. Hussein and his supporters rose against the Ummayads at Kerbela, south of Baghdad, in 680. Hussein and almost all of his followers were killed, but his partisans, who came to be called the Shi'a, continued their efforts in favour of his descendants.

Under the Ummayads Arab power reached its apogee; but this dynasty was overthrown by a political movement which had its origins in Persia, the success of which signalled the end of Arab racial supremacy in the Empire. Thereafter power passed to the Arabised peoples. A new dynasty, the Abbasids, established themselves in Iraq, founding Baghdad as their new capital. There they reigned until 1258. Under the Abbasids, and especially the much-chronicled Haroun al-Rashid (who ruled from 786 to 809), the Muslim Empire achieved great prosperity and cultural brilliance. Within a century, however, the Abbasid Caliphs had yielded power to the provincial governors, many of them Turkish mercenaries converted to Islam. The process of decline continued and in the 10th century rival Caliphates were proclaimed by the Fatimids, who ruled in North Africa and Egypt, and by the survivors of the Ummayad dynasty, ruling in Spain. A century later the Abbasids accepted what was euphemistically called the 'protection' of the Seljuk Turks, a race of warriors from Central Asia who had been converted to Islam. The Seljuk Empire stretched from India to the Aegean. It was Turkish princes and the Kurdish dynasty founded by Salah al-Din – better known as Saladin – who thwarted the attempt by the Crusaders to establish a frontier kingdom in the Levant during the 12th and 13th centuries.

The invasions of the pagan Mongols – nomadic tribes from Central Asia – disrupted the Seljuk Sultanate. But from its ruins there arose a new Turkish dynasty, the Ottomans, who gradually extended their influence by a series of brilliant campaigns throughout the Middle East. The Ottomans were orthodox, or Sunni, Muslims and through their annexation of Egypt, Palestine and Syria they united practically the whole of Sunni Islam in opposition to Persia which, about 1500, had been re-united under a Shi'a dynasty called the Safavids. For two centuries the two empires struggled for dominion over Mesopotamia, the population of which was mixed Sunni and Shi'a, and which finally fell to the Ottoman Empire.

Authority within the Ottoman Empire was delegated either regionally to local governors or viceroys, or to semi-independent princes in treaty relations with the Sultanate, or to the heads of religious communities. At its best Ottoman rule provided internal security and communications over a vast area and considerable individual and communal freedom, in return for payment of some taxes and a limited degree of personal conscription. For a time this was considered preferable by the subjects of the Empire to conditions under other governments of the time. However, during its period of decay the Ottoman Empire became inefficient, arbitrary and tyrannical. Generally speaking, for the territories which are now the Arab States, the four centuries of Ottoman rule were a period of neglect and stagnation.

Throughout the 18th and 19th centuries the Ottoman Empire steadily lost territory, particularly in Europe. During the same period it was slowly transformed into a nation state, accorded the nominal status of a Power, like those in Europe, with an Empire attached. The decline in the influence of the Empire raised the issue – known as the Eastern Question – of the succession to control over the Dardanelles, the Bosphorus and the Eastern Mediterranean. It was the policy of successive British governments to support the Ottoman Empire in order to prevent Russia from gaining control of these vital sea routes. The issue was complicated, first, by the French attempt to control the route to India by attacking Egypt and, secondly, the rise of a strong dynasty – that of Muhammad Ali – in a virtually independent Egypt, which threatened in the 1830s to carve out a new empire linking Egypt, the Hejaz and the Levant States.

The second half of the 19th century was characterised by the expansion of Britain in the Eastern Mediterranean – Egypt was occupied in 1882 – of France in the western Mediterranean, and by the hopeless indebtedness of the Sublime Porte – the seat of the Ottoman Empire – to foreign interests. Towards the end of the 19th century the unified Germany appeared as a new factor in the politics of the Eastern Mediterranean. German influence in the Turkish armed forces spread rapidly and the Young Turks who, representing exasperation with the tyranny and repression of the Sultan Abdul Hamid, had extracted a constitution from him in 1908, were encouraged in their Pan-Islamic policy by the German Kaiser. It was hardly surprising therefore that when war came in 1914 Turkey, after a month or two of hesitation, should have slipped off the fence on the German side.

*   *   *

Whichever European power held India was bound to take an interest in the Persian Gulf. In addition, the pearl-fishing industry made the Gulf attractive to trading nations. Britain's relations with the Gulf date from 1616, when the East India Company sent ships to trade with Shah Abbas of Persia. Commercial interests were already established there and the British gradually asserted themselves against their European competitors and obtained, by one means and another, the indulgence of the Ottoman and Persian Empires. When Napoleon landed in Egypt Britain was already dominant in the Gulf, but Muhammad Ali's campaigns at one time presented a serious threat to this position – a threat which was not entirely removed until the intervention of the Powers in Syria forced him to withdraw not only from the Arabian Peninsula but from other conquered territories as well.

From then on the British position steadily strengthened, Aden having been acquired principally as a coaling station in 1839. One after another the sheikhs in the Persian Gulf signed agreements putting their territory under the protection of the British sovereign, whose affairs were conducted by the Government of India through a Political Resident and Political Agents. The Residency was moved from Bushire to Bahrain in 1946 and, in the following year, responsibility for the conduct of British affairs in the Gulf passed to the Foreign Office.

British interests in the Gulf were immeasurably enhanced by the discovery of plentiful supplies of oil in Mesopotamia in 1871 and in Persia in 1908 – two events which began the history of those great enterprises – the Iraq Petroleum Company and British Petroleum. The rapid expansion of the oil industry in other parts of the Gulf is unquestionably one of the most remarkable events in the long history of the Middle East.

*   *   *

During the First World War there occurred three events in the Middle East which were decisively to influence the future of the area. The first of these was the revolt of the Hashemite Sherif of Mecca and his sons against the Turks and their guerrilla campaign with T E Lawrence on the right flank of General Allenby's army in Palestine. Many Arabs have argued that this Revolt, which to them signified the re-awakening of the Arab peoples, entitled them to sit as equals with the victorious Allies at the Peace Conference at Versailles. The second event was the conclusion of the Sykes-Picot Agreement, under which Britain, Russia and France agreed on the division of the Sultan's territories into spheres of influence, in spite of specific assurances given to the Sherif Hussein before the Arab Revolt began that large tracts of the territory in question would be granted independence. The third event was the Balfour Declaration which led to the setting up of a Jewish 'National Home' in Palestine.

Following the War Britain was entrusted with mandates over Palestine, Transjordan and Iraq; and France with mandates in Syria and Lebanon. Egypt was declared a Protectorate. The history of the years between the wars is that of the struggle by the growing Arab nationalist movement to end the mandates and to prevent the consolidation of the position of the Jews in Palestine. This opposition culminated in revolts in the 1930s but, during the Second World War, apart from the abortive attempt by a handful of adventurers to overthrow Hashemite rule in Iraq, the political situation remained virtually unchanged. In September 1944, however, an important step was taken when a Preparatory Conference met in Alexandria attended by representatives of seven Arab States. It resulted in the signature of a Protocol establishing a League of Arab States. This Protocol was confirmed by a pact signed in Cairo in March 1945. This defined the purpose of the League as: 'The strengthening of the relations between the member states, the coordination of their populations in order to achieve cooperation between them and to safeguard their independence and sovereignty and a general concern with the affairs and interests of the Arab countries'.

The most important political events of the immediate post-war period were, first, the successful struggle of the Palestine Jews, with the strong support of the United States, world Jewry and a majority of opinion in the United Nations, including the Soviet Union, to establish the state of Israel – at the cost of driving nearly a million Arabs from their homes as refugees. And, secondly, the decline in the region of the power and influence of Britain as a result of the exhaustion of her reserves during the war. The most recent phase has been the rapid spread and increase in influence of the political movement known as Arab nationalism.

* * *

What of the people who inhabit this area? Few of us in our childhood hear the word 'Arab' and remain unmoved. There is some magic in the name which it would be foolish to gainsay. But this very magic creates illusions. Some people still come to the Arab world in search of that flame which once illumined the desert – that ennobling spirit which once sent the Arabs coursing across the world with their own great message. But these people will find, I fear, that that flame has become a will o' the wisp. The traditional Arab way of life – the beduin way of life – formed and shaped in the harsh conditions of the desert, has been eroded by the processes of time, until now it survives only in small pockets here and there in the most forbidding parts of the Arabian peninsula. And even there corrupting influences are at work. Wilfred Thesiger, the latest and surely the last in the line of great Arabian explorers, has said: 'I went to Southern Arabia only just in time. Others will go there to study geology, the birds and plants and animals, even to study the Arabs themselves; but they will move about in cars and will keep in touch with the outside world by wireless. They will bring back results far more interesting than mine, but they will never know the spirit of the land nor the greatness of the Arabs. If anyone goes there now looking for the life I led they will not find it, for technicians have been there since, prospecting for oil. Today the desert where I travelled is scarred with the tracks of lorries and littered with discarded junk imported from Europe and America. But this material dese-cration is unimportant compared with the demoralisation which has resulted among the bedu themselves . . . Now it is not death but degradation which faces them'.

Today under powerful influences, of which perhaps the most potent is Arab nationalism, the word 'Arab' has come to be used to denote people of widely dif-ferent backgrounds, outlook and social status. In view of this it is surely haz-ardous to generalise about the Arabs. Yet there are certain characteristics which may be worth noting, particularly when they have been recorded by men of modesty and sound judgment who have been able to observe the Arabs at close quarters in their own element under conditions of ease and of stress. Foremost among these I should place C M Doughty, whose assertions about the Arabs in his masterpiece 'Travels in Arabia Deserta' are as valid today as when they were written three generations ago. These merit study.

Sir John Glubb felt that some of the Arabs' characteristics were so pronounced that he was justified in noting them in detail. In his book 'A Soldier with the Arabs' he had this to say: 'The Arabs in general are hot-headed, hasty and volatile. They are proud and touchy, ready to suspect an insult and hasty to avenge it. To hate their enemies is to them not only a natural emotion but a duty . . . Politically they tend, like the proverbial Irishman, to be against the government. Of what-ever form or complexion it may be, they are usually ready to change it, though they may later on regret their action and wish to return to their former state. . . . Their mutual jealousies provide their rulers with the means of playing them off against one another, an art which they themselves consider to be of the very essence of politics. But while their hot-headedness makes the Arabs good haters, it makes them also cordial friends. No race can be more pleasant or charming. They are delightful company, with a ready sense of humour. In one quality the Arabs lead the world – it is their virtue of hospitality, which some carry to a degree which becomes almost fantastic'.

The views which we ourselves form will depend on our own character, attitude and experience. It would be imprudent, of course, to allow our private opinions of the Arabs, be they favourable or unfavourable, to influence us in our dealings with them. Nor should we allow ourselves to become obsessed with their short-comings. So many foreigners in the Middle East tend to cry out, in the manner of Professor Higgins in 'My Fair Lady': 'Why can't the Arabs be like us?' This is to pose a question of supreme irrelevance. Not only is it more charitable, but it is also in our interest, to try instead to discover why the Arabs are as they are. If we make this effort we shall inevitably begin to show understanding of the Arabs' problems. And we shall thereby display a sign that almost all Arabs look for in treating with foreigners. It is equally unprofitable to stray too far in the other direction. The foreigner who invariably takes the part of the Arabs in their in-numerable quarrels, or who accepts their point of view uncritically, will gradually lose what standing he may have with all but the extremists.

*   *   *

It may be helpful if I describe a few of the factors which either create problems for the Arabs, hinder their progress in dealing with existing problems, or give rise to revolutionary outbursts.

In the first place, by Western standards the structure of society throughout the Arab world lacks balance. One is impressed by the differences between the nomadic peoples of the deserts, the primitive societies in the small towns and villages, and the highly developed urban communities in the large towns and cities. And one is struck by the obvious inequality between the living standards of the rich and the multitudinous poor. Between these two extremes there exists a group, whose political importance is increasing steadily, of professional men and officials who represent the growing middle class. Many well-to-do Arabs will talk of the need to do something to adjust this unfair distribution of wealth. In some countries much is already being achieved by the intelligent investment of oil revenues to raise the standard of living of the poor. There are signs of the growth of a real sense of social justice which alone can bring about the fundamental changes which the situation requires. But often legislators are drawn from the rich land-owning classes who, understandably enough, see the levelling process simply in terms of raising the standard of the poor and ignore the vast possibilities through action at the other end of the scale – in other words, by taxing their own wealth. Elsewhere new legislators, drawn from the middle class, have in their turn been corrupted by power.

A second important factor is the legacy of Ottoman domination of much of the area for four centuries, followed by no more than one generation of Western Christian rule. There is no tradition of public service and so the outlook even of those now set in authority is neither tempered by responsibility nor matured by experience. They are thus prone to judge others harshly. As T E Lawrence pointed out, it is moreover a characteristic of the Semitic peoples to over-simplify. 'They had', he said, 'no half tones in their register of vision. They were people of primary colours, or rather of black and white, who saw the world always in contour . . . They knew only truth and half-truth, belief and unbelief, without our hesitating retinue of finer shades'.

Another result of Ottoman neglect is the significant lee-way in social and economic development which has to be made up in a short space of time. It is too easy to forget that when the Allied armies occupied the Arab countries in the First World War they found a complete absence, in all but the main cities, of even the most elementary public services.

Yet another consequence of Ottoman rule is the low efficiency of administrations, in many of which, in spite of the short period under European tutelage, corruption is rife. The proliferation of bright lights and flesh-pots in the great cities has bred a generation of officials to whom, for the most part, service in the provinces is anathema, and who are indifferent to the hardships which their fellow countrymen endure in their villages. This is no remedy for a situation in which the peasant's attitude to government is one of fear and resentment – fear of conscription and forced labour, and resentment of taxation, arrogance and neglect.

There are other more or less constant factors whose existence cannot be attributed solely to Ottoman rule. For example, the obsession of all classes with politics, which occupies the thoughts of the Arabs and monopolises their conversation to a remarkable degree; sex is a poor second. And in these politics there is an ambivalence characteristic of the less developed societies. Political parties are tending to disappear from the Middle East and this is largely because they did not take a stand on the great social or international problems of the day; they were in fact personal groupings engaged in an endless struggle for power.

This ambivalence in Middle East politics is one manifestation of the tendency towards occasional inconsistency between word, thought and deed which baffles, not to say, irritates, the newcomer and yet is stimulating when one becomes familiar with the technique. Diplomacy in the Arab world becomes one long guessing game. The most obvious example of this inconsistency is the desire wholeheartedly to adopt Western methods, including occasionally political forms, and at the same time to adhere to locally-rooted and Islamic traditions; or to accept the freedom brought by Western liberalism without at the same time assuming the responsibilities implicit in Western tolerance.

A further factor is the narrow conception of loyalty, which rarely extends effectively beyond the family or tribe. The severity of natural conditions and the precepts of Islam have exalted the family, within which the authority of the head is paramount and, while most Arabs feel loyalty to the notion of Arab unity, the intervening loyalties – to a town, or state, or a service – rarely exist, or tend to take the form of opportunism of the kind which can turn a king's aide-de-camp within six months into a minister of the regime which overthrew and murdered him.

In the economic sphere too there are some more or less constant factors of importance. Industry other than oil is still relatively in its infancy. The position of the Middle East as a staging post on the great route between East and West has encouraged commerce, but has left industry to develop mostly in the form of handicrafts. Thus it is that the overwhelming majority of Arabs are engaged in agriculture. The area of cultivable land is limited and the supply of water exiguous. The agriculturalist is handicapped by other factors. The ancient system of land tenure, carefully but perhaps ill-advisedly preserved by some of the mandatory governments, has produced a mass of holdings which are either too small or too big for economic exploitation. It has destroyed the incentives to increase production and placed many peasants in the power of money-lenders. Again, agricultural productivity per head and per acre is low. This is due not only to out-dated methods of husbandry, or the lack of modern machinery; in many areas the soil is infertile, the water used for irrigation saline, and the crops subject to insect pests, or plant diseases. Under-nourishment among the rural population, poor living conditions and the debilitation caused by endemic disease contribute to the low rate of productivity.

In addition to this, governments of the Arab states have to contend with a rate of increase in the population which promises to consume as much food as can be produced in future years, even if all their best laid and most ambitious plans are successfully carried out. On top of this, some of them are saddled with hundreds of thousands of refugees from Palestine.

All this would seem a sufficient blight on the area. But the strategic and economic importance of the region is such that it cannot escape the attention of the great powers. National governments thus have little time or opportunity to work out solutions to their problems in private.

*   *   *

The prospect throughout the Middle East is not uniformly gloomy. While the factors I have mentioned may apply over much of the region, each state has a character, a history, a tradition and, of course, problems of its own. And it would be wrong to assume that there is no Arab aware of the difficulties of the present and future who is not genuinely anxious to improve the lot of his fellow-countrymen and to permit foreign interests to pursue their legitimate ends in peace. There are many. They deserve our sympathy and understanding; and, failing that, we should at least moderate our criticism.

II

FUTURE RELATIONS BETWEEN THE ARABS AND THE WEST

Few would disagree that the Middle East is one region where Western policies have achieved little success since the end of the Second World War. Some politicians say that the reason for this is that there are too many experts on the Middle East. Some experts argue on the other hand that too little attention is paid to their advice. My own view is that the main reason for the foundering of our policies is the sad lack of understanding on each side of the attitude of the other and the marked unwillingness of each to learn. This state of ignorance might be bliss were it not of special importance that a closer relationship should develop between the two sides in the future.

Those of us whose acquaintance with the Arab world goes back no further than the Second World War cannot fail to be impressed as much by the constant individual kindnesses we receive as by the constant, often official, expressions of hostility, resentment, ingratitude and suspicion towards ourselves, our country and the West in general. We have come to the Middle East on our lawful occasions. We mean no one harm and, in many instances we have come to try to do positive good. Why then are we treated in this way? Is this the fulfilment of the prophecy given to Moses that the iniquities of the fathers would be visited upon the children, and the children's children unto the third and fourth generation (Exodus 34.7).

The truth is that we have arrived among the Arabs at one of those long drawn moments of crisis history – when our interests have come into violent collision with their aspirations. This clash is only part of the great struggle for independence of the peoples of Africa and Asia who have been dominated for some hundreds of years by Christians from Western Europe – a struggle which has been viewed with widely differing degrees of understanding and sympathy by the Western Powers, and one which has been exploited and embittered by the Soviet Union. In due course the dispute between the communist and democratic ways of life may be resolved. But the factors which divide the people of the West from the Arabs are fundamental. These are concerned with race, religion, tradition and manner of thought. Yet – and it is of prime importance if our legitimate interests and their independence are to be preserved that we recognise the fact – it is vital to our common interest that we learn to live and work together in amity and

11

peace. It is profitless for one side or the other to lay down impracticable conditions for cooperation. Tolerance and mutual comprehension must take the place of arrogance and xenophobia. The problem is how to bring about this change and, at the same time, counter the threat of subversion by the Communists, whose aims are to thwart Western policies and to promote instability and unrest with a view to the setting up in the region of pro-Soviet regimes.

Western interests in the Middle East are clear. First, we wish the flow of oil to continue without interruption and indeed to increase. Steps are being taken in Europe to develop alternative sources of energy. Hydro-electric schemes are being implemented and programmes for constructing nuclear power stations in Britain are being accelerated. Exploration for oil is being pursued with vigour and with success in South East Asia, Africa and Latin America. But there is no escaping the fact that the Middle East is now by far the most important source of power for the industry of Western Europe and will remain so for years to come.

Our second interest is that our lines of communication with the countries of South East Asia, the Far East and Australasia should be free from interference. Sir John Glubb has taken this argument further. His view is that, historically, the interest of Europe in the Middle East was solely to be able to traverse the area. In the past the powerful demands of imperial strategy required the British to keep these vital links open – a task we accomplished, first, by a policy of support and friendship for the Ottoman Empire, and then by setting up military bases at various points of importance. There can be no doubt that the Anglo-French intervention in Egypt in the autumn of 1956 has invalidated many of the strategic concepts on which our policies were founded. But there still are military reasons for our interest in keeping open routes through the Middle East, although these may appear less important than the economic and commercial considerations. Large quantities of Middle East oil destined for Europe pass through the Suez Canal, as does the bulk of European exports to East Africa, the Persian Gulf, South East Asia, the Far East, Australia and New Zealand.

Our third interest is to maintain and increase our trade with the Middle East. Industrial production in Western Europe has increased dramatically since the Second War. Oil royalties, grants-in-aid, subsidies, loans from the International Bank and other forms of public and private investment in the region have enabled the appetite for capital equipment and consumer goods to be whetted. The economic conditions are thus outstandingly favourable for a substantial expansion in Western trade with the Arab world, and Western countries look for equally propitious political conditions.

In a word, in order to protect and further these interests, which no one can reasonably stigmatise as aggressive, illogical, immoral, or unjust, we wish to prevent the Middle East falling under the domination of the Communists or xenophobic nationalists.

* * *

In the past Great Britain relied on its military power and its wealth to exert its influence and to preserve its interests in the Middle East. Almost everyone recognises that this is no longer possible. We must adapt our methods to conform to modern trends. If any discussion about these methods is to be profitable, we must first examine the position our country and other Western countries now occupy in the Arab world. The various images of the West in the eyes of Arabs who inhabit widely separated parts of the Middle East and North Africa, who spring from different environments, and who look back on varied stores of experience, contain so many common elements that, in contemplating them, one has the comfortable feeling of having arrived at the threshold of the truth. Our first task in laying a sounder foundation for our future relationship with the Arabs is to recognise those elements which compose the image we project.

In the first place, whether we like it or not, those of us who have come from the West to live and work in the Middle East today have inherited the legacy of a long period of Western influence and rule. It is churlish to argue that this period of foreign domination brought no benefit to the Arab peoples; and it is unrealistic to claim that it did them no harm. In studying the effects of our domination, we should distinguish between what we have done and what we have seemed to the Arabs to have been doing. What the British government intended when they issued the Balfour Declaration was quite different from what the Arabs thought they had intended. Again, what the United States intended when they offered Point Four Aid to Syria was quite different from the Arabs' idea of what they meant.

In the political sphere the West brought to the Arabs the ideas of democratic government and respect for the dignity of the individual, among other aspects of Western Christian liberalism. Nevertheless, in the region itself, the Western rulers tended to practise autocratic rule and, in a few important respects and in many lesser ways which were no less irritating, may have given the impression that they considered that the dignity of man was in some way related to considerations of race and culture. This, of course, is to judge these men by the standards of our day, not theirs.

Our economic impact has also seemed to many Arabs to have been ambiguous. The key to Egypt's prosperity, for example, is cotton. The cotton industry, which was built up by Westerners of skill and enterprise, has made possible a vast rise in the population of Egypt. It is argued, nevertheless, that the founders of the industry were serving the interests of Lancashire and not of Egypt and that Egypt is now left to suffer the consequences of dependence on a commodity of relatively diminishing world importance.

As regards the social sphere, it is sometimes alleged that we interfere too much and sometimes too little with native institutions. This may well be true. The fact that such criticisms are uttered today is a sign that the alleged moral and social superiority of the West is not now accepted. Arabs admire our degree of industrialisation and our technological skills, but they no longer revere the standards by which we judge human conduct. There are various reasons for this – what is seen as the running down of the dynamo of Western civilisation, the spread of education in the Middle East, the growing influence of international public opinion, resentment at the dropping of the atom bomb on Asiatic heads and the exposure by a European regime which employed gas chambers for mass extermination of the myth that Western standards of human conduct are superior.

Our second task in planning the course of our future relations with the Arabs is, I suggest, to clear our minds about the real nature of their ambitions. This is not easy, since the view Arabs take of the history of Arab nationalism depends on who they are, where they are looking from, and when. If they are Christian Arabs from the Levant, they will see the nationalist movement as a counterpart to the encroachment of western civilisation on the countries of the Eastern Mediterranean, which began with Napoleon's invasion of Egypt at the end of the 18th century. They will honour the graduates of the Syrian Protestant College, now the American University of Beirut, who formed a secret society in 1875, the aim of which was not so much the cultural regeneration of their country as the overthrow of Turkish rule. They may also believe that the Arab Revolt in 1916 signified the real awakening of the Arabs.

If on the other hand they are Egyptian Muslims, they may believe that the movement did not begin until the revolt of Arabi Pasha in the 1860s or that it did not really get under way until Gamal Abdel Nasser became its symbol and set it on its road to political success.

If they are Iraqis who consider that the old regime was not wholly bad, they may argue that Arab Nationalism began with the struggle against the mandatory system in the 1920s and 30s. The new Kassimist Iraqis, on the other hand, will say that the movement did not begin until 14 July 1958.

But the Arab who is a devout Muslim living in any part of the world where Arabic is spoken, will rest serenely in the knowledge that the movement began in Mecca in the 7th century AD – the 1st century of the Hejira era.

*   *   *

Another difficulty in the way of understanding the nature of the nationalist movement is that the whole period of political growth for the Arabs from the moment they emerged from the night-time of Ottoman rule to the age of the United Nations, nuclear warfare and rockets round the moon, has had to be compressed into a few years. No wonder then that the ideas of many Arabs today seem muddled and immature. So many ideologies, suggestions and external forces are pulling them in different directions that they have found it simpler to sum up their belief in one word – 'Aruba' – which is something that is felt so strongly that it needs no analysis.

For us with our rational training this is not good enough. We must probe, question and search. I myself think it is one of the greatest shortcomings of Arab nationalism that to understand it perfectly has become a full-time job and one which only those able without difficulty to see the point of view of others can successfully perform.

Arab nationalism is a complex of fears, aspirations, discontents and hatreds. For purposes of analysis the movement can be divided into Arab nationalism on the internal front and Arab nationalism as an external force. The former has been aptly described as a reaction of Arabs to that in their heart which militates against industrialism. This form of nationalism is the desire to accomplish the social reform and economic development so necessary after four centuries of Ottoman neglect – the wish, above all, to end the shame of their backwardness which people as proud as the Arabs find intolerable. But in this regard some Arabs tend towards perfectionism and both to underrate the difficulties of modernising a relatively primitive society and generally agrarian economy and to expect results too soon.

The urge for social reform and economic progress is widespread. Were it not for the picture in our minds of thousands of camels stretching out across the desert as the great nomadic tribes migrate from one pasture to another, one might almost say that this urge is universal. But there is no unanimity as to how the two processes – social and economic – should be effected. There is a tendency, as a first stage, to root out the obvious indications of backwardness, such as the traditional scheme of land tenure or the tribal system, with its paternalism sanctified by a special code of laws, rather than to deal with the real causes of backwardness – ignorance, endemic disease, the scarcity of technical skills, the lack of a sense of responsibility or a spirit of service among government officials.

Sadly, Arab nationalism internally seems to be capable of moving only at one of two speeds – too fast or too slow. The old style regime, such as ruled Iraq until July 1958, is inclined to rely for its power on those sections of the community which believe that change of any kind will work to their detriment – the large land-owning and the rich merchant classes in particular. Through having had it too good for too long, the fibre of members of these classes is often weakened by a degree of moral corruption. However enlightened or progressive individual members of governments may be in countries which contain such a society, they are unable through the inertia of the vested interests, on whose consent they often have to rely for legislative authority for their proposals, to carry through a drastic programme of reform and development. Even if there were no communists poised to exploit this sort of situation in the manner laid down by Lenin, domestic discontent would still mount faster than duly ratified social advance. Many sincere, thoughtful men, with the interests of their fellow countrymen at heart, are forced to the conclusion that the only remedy for such a state of affairs is revolution.

In revolutionary conditions the pace of reform can be too fast. The great estates are broken up overnight and there is no authority ready to assume the functions which, in return for his outrageous profits, the feudalist landlord used to perform. Attempts are often made to legislate the upper class out of existence – attempts which often frighten, destroy or otherwise render ineffective members of the middle class, whose professional or administrative skills played an irreplaceable part in the life of a balanced community.

In some cases revolutionary rule has sanctioned the replacement of the old nepotism and corruption in matters of employment, career or legal dispute by a new favouritism and a new vindictiveness. Justice, whether administered 'in the name of the King' or 'in the name of the people', seems to be arbitrary and capricious.

However, with the maturing of society there was a hope that the trappings of parliamentary democracy might acquire substance. Unfortunately in the post-war years this hope has diminished until it is no bigger than a man's hand; revolutionary regimes have guided democracy into the deep freeze. The reason for this is partly that the old style political parties are thoroughly discredited and partly that the leaders of the revolutionary regimes have so many preoccupations and anxieties that they dare not, in the beginning at least, allow dissentient voices to be heard.

But there may be another explanation. This is the lack of a palpable social objective. I have often felt tempted to ask an eager Arab nationalist to describe for me in general terms a day in the life of a woman in, say, a village in the Syrian Jezira twenty years hence, assuming that meanwhile he had his way. But I have hesitated. To pose such a question would be deemed inconsequent and characteristic of the Westerner's obsession with minutiae. Yet the fact is that, in sharp contrast to Kamal Ataturk, who stipulated in the utmost detail what should be done when, where and how, little planning for a new Arab society has yet begun, except perhaps on the sane fringe of the Baath Party. This in turn may be attributed to the vagueness of the revolutionary leaders' own ideas. They are indeed in a position of real difficulty since they cannot afford to offend the traditionalists or the modernists on both of whom they rely for a measure of support. Furthermore, they may find, when their manifold duties permit them an opportunity for reflection, that they have stumbled into a spiritual no-man's-land, which is neither entirely Islam, whose traditionalism is opposed to their political ambitions, nor Western liberalism, the Christian basis of which they cannot accept.

There are some who argue that Arab nationalism is synonymous with Islam and that its aims, its ethics and its methods are all to be explained in Islamic terms. Others tend to minimise the influence of Islam. Islam provided the Arabs with a divinely inspired book in the Arabic language, but also with criteria for all aspects of human behaviour. To what else indeed can they have recourse in moments of moral or social stress? It seems beyond question that Islam plays a major role in the formulation of Arab nationalist ideas, but the extent to which Arab leaders consciously permit themselves to be influenced by Islamic doctrine is less clear.

* * *

Many people find it curious that in one Arab country after another groups of army officers should manhandle the politicians out of office and seize power. Yet this is not in the least surprising if one understands the position the armed forces occupy in Arab society and if one probes the motives of the young men who choose a military career. The important issue here is the view officers – and particularly those of field rank, that is majors and above – take of their country and its future prospects.

In Western countries young men pursue the honourable profession of arms for a variety of reasons – a desire to serve one's country, a fondness for travel and excitement, an open air life, the chance to exercise authority, or to follow family tradition. The young Arab becomes an officer first of all for reasons of personal prestige and, secondly, in order to earn a decent and steady living in a society in which openings for the mounting number of secondary school graduates are inadequate. After what happened in Egypt and, in particular Iraq, the officer class has become the elite in the Arab world and, to an alarming extent, the future of the Middle East has become bound up with the personal ambitions of service officers whose names may scarcely be known outside their regiments or squadrons. Circumstances have combined to make this so. Instead of preparing for the next war, in the manner of his Western or Communist fellow officers, the Arab officer occupies his time in subjective criticism of the way in which his country is governed. As training for battle occupies comparatively little of his time, he has plenty of opportunity to savour the truth that the armed forces represent the sole alternative to civilian rule and that, in the absence of a strong public opinion, the armed forces have the power to assume control whenever they wish. This realisation, combined with the armed forces' traditional contempt for civilian administrators and their genuine discontent with the often primitive conditions in which many of their relatives live, poses a temptation which may well become irresistible the more repressive and reactionary civilian government becomes.

We have become familiar with Arab nationalism as the force which motivates the Arab states in their external relations. In this sense, for sound historical reasons, Arab nationalism is essentially a reaction to the influence of the west and, to a lesser extent, to the creation of the state of Israel. In its external form Arab nationalism varies from the most passionate desire to remove from the Arab world, and from neighbouring territories, the last trace of Western influence, to the conviction of some Arab leaders that the social and economic regeneration of their countries and people can be accomplished only with the assistance of the industrialised and technologically advanced countries of the West. That there should be a variety of external manifestations of Arab nationalism should not surprise us; we need only to recall how different are the races which comprise the Arab people, how unequally endowed are the different territories of the Arab world, and how varied have been their relationships with the West.

The present crisis in the relationship between Arab nationalism and the West is one of confidence – or rather, lack of confidence. The Arabs are convinced that in any clash between major Western interests and their own, the interests of the Western powers would prevail. Similarly, there is no question in their minds but that, when problems arise which might affect the future of Israel, the Western powers will intervene to ensure Israel's interests are preserved. Whether or not this attitude on the part of the Arabs is justified on political or historical grounds is inapposite. The reality is that no amount of argument will persuade an Arab nationalist that he is mistaken in his belief.

Added to the feeling of mistrust is the resentment of the Arabs at the humiliations they feel they have suffered at the hands of the imperialists. From the moment of Napoleon's arrival in Egypt at the end of the 18th century, the Arabs have been made to consider themselves inferior in almost every field. Of course, the same could be said of many other oriental peoples, but the Arabs' pride and their belief – based largely on the manner in which Islam was revealed – that they are a rather special race of men have made it more difficult for them to swallow their shame. And so they aim to end the 'unequal status', which they regard as an affront to their Arabism, and they dream of recreating a united and powerful Arab empire, stretching from the Atlantic to the Persian Gulf which, it may be argued, never actually existed. By this means Arab nationalist leaders hope to establish a great power capable of dealing with the West, and with the Communists, on terms of equality.

The expressed desire for unity is the main positive element of importance in Arab nationalism in the field of external relations. The Arabs unquestionably have strong feelings of brotherhood one with another, but this arises not so much from a consciousness of community of race as from a common history and, even more significant, the existence of a common language. The spectacular improvement in communications has made it possible for Arabs to speak not only in one language but also with one voice – on a limited number of subjects at least – for the first time since they erupted from the Arabian peninsula with the message that there was no God but God and that Muhammad was his Prophet.

We are all familiar by now with the manner in which Arab nationalism, especially in its extreme form, displays itself. Perhaps the most common is the attempt to remove traces of western influence and power which are reminders of the former 'unequal status'. Arab governments are ready to remove these relics in agreement with the West and by legal means if possible, but in the face of Western opposition and illegally, if necessary. Egypt's abrogation of the 1936 Treaty of Alliance and the nationalisation of the Suez Canal Company are well-known examples of this. At the same time, however, Arab governments may seek to extract from Western governments and enterprises as many financial, economic, military and other benefits as possible, sometimes even holding Western interests to ransom.

Arab attitudes to Israel are predictable. Although the Arab world today is divided into two main camps, the Arabs' fear of Israel binds them closer than at any time since the first stirrings of Arab nationalism. With good reason, most Arabs fear Israel's energy, military skills, organising ability, ruthlessness and vision. They deplore the influence of Jewry throughout the western world, and there are still some who are inclined to heed the warning in the Protocol of the Elders that a state of Israel will one day stretch from the Mediterranean to the Euphrates. The threat of Israeli expansion has given an impetus to the urge for reform of the social system which might enable the Arabs to face the problems of the modern world with more confidence. Many Arabs believe that the creation of a modern and efficient Arab state, or states, must come before a final reckoning with the Israelis.

There is latent in Arab nationalism, as in all nationalisms, an element of extremism. Where it has been kept in check is in those countries blessed with wise leaders who are no less fervent than the demagogues in their attachment to Arab nationalist aims, but who have a more balanced appreciation of the best way of achieving these aims. These leaders, vilified though they may be today, may well be hailed by future generations as heroes of the nationalist movement. Unfortunately, other countries in the region have been less wisely led, and weak and corrupt governments have given in to, or been overthrown by, extremism.

No one who has lived in the Middle East and whose sympathy has been aroused for its people in the difficulties which face them can but be anxious about the future unless and until Arab nationalism, as an international force, acquires a mystique which will encourage it to devote more of its energy to constructive than to destructive purposes. Failing that, the movement will remain prone to exploitation by subversive elements and to outbursts of violence which might, in extreme cases, endanger world peace.

Arab leaders face immense problems. In addition to the social and economic difficulties, they have to contend with certain deep-seated disunities in the Arab world – the historical rivalry between the peoples of the Nile Valley and the Tigris and Euphrates, the divisions caused by the deserts, the schism between Shia and Sunni, and the mutual jealousies of several of the leaders themselves. The best hope may be that the new responsibilities which have fallen on the shoulders of Arab leaders in consequence of the decline of western power and influence in the area will oblige them to moderate their extremism and pursue more realistic aims. After all, blaming the misfortunes of their peoples on the imperialists, or Israel, or treacherous leaders, has never been an adequate substitute for a policy. One might even go so far as to suggest that these new leaders might discover unexpected skills in dealing with the difficulties that confront them. Nearly 800 years ago Gerald of Wales said: 'The hilarity of liberty makes men capable of honourable actions'.

*   *   *

The reconciliation of Western interests in the Middle East with Arab aspirations will clearly call for a change of attitudes on both sides. Only in this way can relations between us develop satisfactorily. If the Arabs can resist the temptation to adopt the most extreme course of action when a choice lies before them, they will go a long way towards getting on to terms with the West. We for our part must hang on. Should there be a general detente between East and West, tensions in this region might relax somewhat. Meanwhile, we must deal with each problem as it arises with all the skill and patience we command. We have already made substantial adjustments. But there are ways in which we might amend our attitudes and conduct. In the first place, we should try at all times to assess correctly the position we occupy in the various parts of the Middle East, neither deluding ourselves with thoughts of former power, nor accepting uncritically assertions that we no longer have any influence to wield. We should endeavour to practise those virtues for which we are respected and to eschew the vices for which we are detested. Secondly, we should bear in mind that our relations with the Arabs will probably depend more on what we can do for them now and in the future than upon our persuading them to take a charitable view of what we have done in the past. Thirdly, we might hasten our own acceptance of genuine international standards. We should realise more fully the common humanity of all societies and the irrelevance of distinctions of colour and culture when compared with the human substance which binds us all together.

If we base our conduct in dealing with the Arabs whom we meet in our daily life on these ideas, we will not only be serving the interests of our own people and the people of this region, but we will also find that these contacts will be both warmer and more rewarding. The future of our relations with the Arabs may well be determined as much by the nature of the thousands of individual contacts we make as by the policies of our leaders.

III

THE ARABIC LANGUAGE

Many visitors to the Middle East Centre for Arab Studies, and especially those who, from 1958 onwards, attended the short background courses on the history, culture and current preoccupations of the peoples of the region, often asked about the specific problems we faced in teaching the Arabic language. The lecture which follows was a response to these enquiries.

The French historian, Ernest Renan, commenting on the intellectual expansion of Arabia in the 7th century, said:

'Of all the features presented by this unexpected appearance of a new consciousness in mankind, the strangest is perhaps the Arabic language itself. This language, unknown before, suddenly displays itself to us in all its perfection, with its flexibility and its infinite richness so completely developed that from that time to our own it has undergone no important change. For it there is no childhood, no old age; once its appearance and its prodigious conquests have been described there is nothing more to be said about it.'

This language was that of the Arabian poets of the sixth and seventh centuries, of the Quran, which emerged in the 7th century, and of the great literature which followed the establishment of the Arab empires. It is today the language of over 60 million people and in their lives it plays a part which is of greater importance than that played by other languages in the life of other peoples. To the Muslim Arab the Arabic language is divine since it was in Arabic that God addressed the Prophet; and to all Arabs the language is the greatest single element in their culture. The script is one of the beauties of the language and, in view of the prohibition on representing the human form, it has played a notable part in Islamic art.

Arabic is one of the survivors of the Semitic group of languages which included Babylonian, Assyrian, Phoenician, Hebrew, Syriac and Amharic. Its peculiarities are for the most part common to all Semitic languages, but it is distinguished by the exceptional richness of its vocabulary which permits a remarkable degree of discrimination and power of extension to express new concepts. In spite of this its vocabulary has remained comparatively free from admixture.

Modern literary Arabic – the form of classical Arabic that is used today through-out the Arab world both as a written language and as a language of formal speech – is used from Iraq in the east to Morocco in the west. This language differs only slightly in morphology and syntax in the various countries in which it is used, but the vocabulary shows considerable variation. A journalistic style has evolved in the modern Arabic of the media. This version is highly standardised and has a relatively limited vocabulary compared with the ancient classical language. This particular style, which some consider to have been influenced by modern European practice, is almost the only form of the classical language read or heard by the less well-educated masses. For this reason it is this journalistic Arabic which is nearest today to a fixed norm for the language.

Like Hebrew and Syriac, Arabic is written from right to left. The alphabet con-sists of 28 characters, whose shape differs slightly depending on whether the letter is at the beginning, in the middle or at the end of the word, or stands alone.

The grammar is essentially logical. There are many rules, but the language is mercifully free from exceptions which make miserable the lives of students of European languages. The basis of the language is the verb which in all but a few cases contains three letters. Various patterns are applied to these triliteral roots to produce variations in meaning. Nouns and pronouns are of two *genders* – mas-culine and feminine. There are three *numbers* – singular, plural and dual. The plural is of two kinds – the *sound plural* which is normally used for persons, and the *broken plural*, of which there are over thirty different patterns. The broken plural is used for both persons and things and is much commoner than the sound plural. There is also a *collective* used to describe animals, trees, plants and so on generically.

A special characteristic of Arabic is the *construct state*, or '*addition*', as the Arab grammarians style it. This indicates possession; for example 'house the man' means 'the house of the man' and 'house man' means 'a house of a man'. A similar construction is used in Gaelic to indicate possession.

The Arab conception of the verb differs from the European. We think in terms of past, present and future, but Arabs comprehend only two *tenses* – the perfect and imperfect which duly denote completed or incomplete actions. It follows that the future tense must be expressed by the imperfect.

The *passive voice* is widely used today in English and other European languages. It is a convenient journalistic device; how often do we read or hear that 'It was reported' that something had happened. In Arabic the passive may be used only if the agent is unknown. One cannot say:'he was injured by the motor car', one must say either: 'the car injured him' or 'it was the car which injured him'.

The verb *to be* does not appear when the English present tense is being used. 'I am here' therefore becomes 'I here' and 'this book is interesting' becomes 'this book interesting' – that is, if one can find a precise Arabic equivalent for 'interesting'.

While the written language is one throughout the Arab world, the spoken language differs from place to place. Major differences in spoken Arabic existed before the Quran was written and these, together with the varied influences to which the spoken language has been subjected throughout the centuries in different parts of the Arab world, account for the variations which characterise the present-day dialects.

There is much confusion, even among the Arabs themselves, about the real nature and extent of these variations. We may hear a Lebanese say on his return from a visit to Baghdad that he scarcely understood what people said to him. In fact the differences are largely confined to the commonest words and expressions. Each country seems to have its own word for 'room', 'table', 'man', 'cup', 'let's do it tomorrow', or 'leave me alone'. The working vocabulary of an uneducated craftsman in the bazaar in Beirut is clearly more restricted than that of a college graduate. His counterpart in Baghdad will have a vocabulary of similar extent but the words the Baghdadi uses for the more common expressions will be different. The first impression of an uneducated Beiruti transplanted to Baghdad would be that Baghdadis speak a language bearing only an occasional resemblance to his own. An educated Beiruti, on the other hand, would have no excuse for reaching the same conclusion were he to mix with educated Baghdadis, since the vocabulary of the educated Arab, regardless of where he comes from, extends far beyond everyday expressions.

This is one factor which aids us in this Centre in teaching spoken Arabic. There is another which is more significant. Improved communications and, in particular, the radio are steadily unifying spoken Arabic in the same way as the *lingua franca* – modern literary Arabic – is being simplified. It stands to reason that if they are going to deal with each other, Moroccans, Egyptians and Saudis must be able to comprehend each other. And so an *intelligentsia*, or *bourgeois colloquial* is coming into being. In effect it means 'speaking proper'.

This *intelligentsia colloquial* is already widely used on the radio and in speech-making. Not long ago I listened to a current affairs programme on the BBC Arabic Service. The commentator, who spoke scrupulously correct modern literary Arabic, was interviewing prominent Arab personalities who happened to be visiting London. The first was Tunisian, the second Sudanese, the third Lebanese and the fourth Jordanian. Each one spoke the intelligentsia colloquial of his country of origin and it was striking how few – and how unimportant – were the differences in their manner of speaking. Of course their accents enabled one to identify their home country. But the most interesting point to emerge was that someone with a sound knowledge of modern literary Arabic would have had no difficulty in understanding what each was saying.

A third factor to our advantage in teaching colloquial Arabic is that those prone to speak *intelligentsia colloquial* belong to the class which is coming to the fore. The cliques of English- or French-speaking aristocrats, whose ancestors subsisted in Ottoman days on the fringes of the Almanach de Gotha, have either been destroyed or are rapidly declining in political importance. Those of us who work today in the Middle East will deal increasingly with a new class amongst whom the need for a *lingua franca* is the most lively.

Our aim in this Centre is to enable those who come here to speak and to understand Arabic in as wide an area of the Middle East as possible. We cannot ignore the fact that the Centre is situated in Lebanon and that our students' first serious opportunities for speaking Arabic will be with Lebanese. We have therefore been obliged to make a compromise which, in circumstances other than those I have described, would be an uneasy one. We have tried to remove the local idiosyncracies from the language spoken by educated persons in Lebanon, Jordan and Syria and, where usage varies notably within this area, we have tended to follow the modern literary language. The result is a language which nobody actually speaks in the Arab world except former students of this Centre, but which enables them to understand and be understood without difficulty in Lebanon, Jordan and Syria and, with minor modifications, throughout the great part of the Arab world from Egypt and Sudan eastwards.

IV

WAR IN THE GULF AND THE PROSPECTS FOR PEACE

The ThinkNet Commission, an international think-tank based in Paris, exists to explore the factors which lead to increasing global interdependence and follows closely all events of major international importance. The text below was circulated in January 1991.

When generals assume responsibility for resolving a dispute, diplomats do not take a vacation. They have three main tasks: to provide political support for the military campaign; to absorb the lessons of past events; and to think creatively about the future.

The Gulf War is an episode of major importance and the diplomatists must perform their task effectively. At present their overriding objective is to preserve the cohesion of the coalition and the clarity of its war aims by every available means. When they come to consider the implications of events leading to the outbreak of war, diplomats could well begin by reviewing the list of victims of the Iraqi invasion of Kuwait.

The first of these was the façade of Arab unity. Arabs know better than anyone how fragile this façade has been. The formation of the Arab League in 1944 was an attempt to re-establish an Arab identity. The creation of Israel in 1948 made the need for unity more urgent. If they thought that Israel would play the role of external integrator, the Arabs deceived themselves. Historical rivalries between the peoples of the Nile Valley, the Fertile Crescent and the valley of the Tigris and Euphrates, ideological disagreements and different political alignments have frustrated every attempt at integration. The most ambitious, inspired by Gamal Abdel Nasser, was the creation in 1958 of the United Arab Republic of Egypt, Syria and, later, Yemen. Within a few years Egypt was the sole component of the union.

The remarkable fact is that, against all the odds, Arabs have persisted in their search for unity. It is not easy for Europeans, Americans, or Japanese to understand the aching desire of so many Arabs to be accorded the respect to which they believe they are entitled. Arabs are proud of their achievements in taking their language, literature, culture and religion half way across the world. Four centuries of Ottoman misrule and a few generations of European colonialism were an affront to Arab dignity. Military humiliation at the hands of the Israelis aggravated their frustration.

The most important cause of Arab resentment is, of course, the injustice and misery suffered by the Palestinians. Other Arabs are deeply affected by their failure to secure redress for them. An Arab foreign minister, explaining why he had kept me waiting for an appointment, told me a Palestinian delegation had arrived unexpectedly to seek his help. Then he said: 'You in the West have no idea how difficult this is for us. These people want us to do so much and there is nothing we can do. How can we explain that to them?' And that was over twenty years ago.

This sense of frustration leads sections of Arab opinion to look for scapegoats – and find them in the West – and to treat as a hero any leader who promises a success-ful campaign against Israel. It was inevitable that Saddam Hussein, once commit-ted to confrontation with the West, would play the Palestine and Arab unity cards. It was equally predictable that this ploy would be effective with sections of Arab opinion, and notably the Palestinians, Jordanians and the more zealous Muslims.

A second early victim of the crisis was the Palestinian cause. Palestinians are intel-lectually and culturally well endowed. Yet, tragically, ever since 1917, when the Balfour Declaration prepared the way for a Jewish national home in Palestine, their political destiny has been in the hands of men who, in the words of Abba Eban, a former foreign minister of Israel, seem never to have missed an oppor-tunity to miss an opportunity. Once again, when Iraq invaded Kuwait, the Palestinian leadership misread the situation. They failed to see the longer term advantage which could flow from an immediate minor change of tactics. By their ill-considered support for Saddam Hussain and his regime, they squandered the important gains they had made over the previous year with influential political opinion in the West.

A third casualty was the credibility of European political cooperation. Right up to the last moment, the world was made aware of the difficulties encountered by the members of the European Community in aligning their approaches to a major issue of unusual clarity – the determination of a newly united international community to oppose a flagrant act of aggression. The reasons for European inco-herence lie in undue attachment to national interest, preoccupation with domes-tic concerns, differing experiences and perceptions of war, and a whiff, here and there, of vanity and ambition.

*   *   *

What of the future? The situation after the war cannot be accurately predicted. Much will have changed. However, planning must take account of certain constant factors. Some of these are obvious. First, economic interdependence between oil producers and consumers in both industrialised and developing countries will endure. Oil is not a dirty word. Oil means heat, light, power, enhanced productivity, mobility, and convenience in place of drudgery. The international community is rightly concerned to see uninterrupted trade in oil on mutually acceptable terms. Secondly, Arabs will continue their quest for international respect. And, thirdly, the need for a just and lasting settlement of the Arab-Israel problem will be undiminished.

The ideal post-war agenda is no doubt being drawn up even now. The diplomatic planners will have in mind a number of questions to which there are as yet no answers. There is now only one super-power; will success in the Gulf exorcise the ghosts of Vietnam and restore American self-confidence? Will the current turmoil in the Soviet Union cause Moscow to abandon its policy of cooperation on international issues with the United States and other permanent members of the UN Security Council? Will the intimate collaboration among members of the coalition outlive hostilities and, if so, in what form? Will the parliaments of Germany and Japan review the constitutional obstacles to their active participation in any future military effort? Will Turkey, nearly seventy years after the Treaty of Lausanne rang down the curtain on the Ottoman Empire, come to be regarded not only by her Arab and Iranian neighbours to the south and east, but also by the disaffected former Soviet republics to the north, as an oasis of stability in the region? Now that East/West rivalry in the developing world has ended, can those countries with large armaments industries agree to desist from supplying potentially aggressive regimes? Can the erstwhile swords at last be turned into ploughshares, to the benefit of industrialised and developing countries alike?

These and other questions constitute a formidable agenda for those whose task is creative thinking about the future. If war is the failure of diplomacy, success lies in exploiting the new circumstances war creates in order to advance where hitherto seemingly insurmountable obstacles stood in the way. This is the benefit the international community stands to gain. And all concerned should combine their efforts to secure this reward.

V

THE DEMISE OF COLONIALISM IN THE MIDDLE EAST

In 1997 the President of the Anglo-Arab Association in London suggested that his members would be interested in my personal account of the changes which had taken place over the years in the relationship between the Arabs and the former colonial powers. The lecture which follows was delivered in June of that year.

Human history has shown that great changes, whether political, social or economic, often follow in the wake of some cataclysm – a destructive war or some overwhelming natural disaster. We have had proof of this theory more than once during the twentieth century.

The depth and pace of change will of course vary according to the circumstances. The months I spent in the Indian sub-continent during the 1940s persuaded me that any continuation of British rule once the war was over would be unjustified. In this respect, when the allies debated the principles on which the post-war world order would be based, I was on Roosevelt's side of the argument, not Churchill's. The emergence of India and Pakistan as independent states in 1947 inspired freedom movements throughout the world.

I was less sure about South East Asia. The Japanese claimed that they were rescuing the peoples of the countries they had overrun from western imperialism. In truth the Japanese were merely replacing one imperialism with another under the guise of the cynically named 'Greater East Asia Co-Prosperity Sphere'. It seemed unlikely that when the Japanese were removed after the war these peoples would willingly accept a return to their previous status. So far as the Middle East was concerned, the future course of events seemed even more difficult to foresee. Anyone hoping to unravel the complexities of that region would face a long and steep learning curve.

Like many of my generation, I had my first glimpse of the Middle East from the deck of a troopship. The date gardens along the banks of the Shatt al-Arab seemed artificially green and the refinery at Abadan underlined the reason for my arrival to join what was known as Persia and Iraq Force. Stalingrad was under siege and I was curious to see the land which would become a major battlefield if the German Sixth Army broke through the Russian defences and descended on the oilfields of Iraq and Persia.

The troopship which brought me and my companions from Bombay to Basra had followed a much travelled route. Kaiser Wilhelm's ambition to build a railway from Berlin to Baghdad and on to Basra – the critical element in his 'drang nach Osten', the 'drive to the east' – had been seen in London and Delhi as a threat to the Jewel in the Crown. In 1912 the Government of India had prepared plans to occupy Basra in the event of war and had undertaken to support the Sheikh of Muhammara against both the Ottoman Sultan and the Shah. The resulting campaign in Mesopotamia shattered the Kaiser's dream, ended four centuries of indifferent Ottoman rule in the land of the twin rivers, and led to the creation of the kingdom of Iraq.

In the early 1940s history was doing its best to repeat itself. The German threat was obvious and the reverses the British suffered in the Mediterranean presented the Iraqi Prime Minister and a small group of ambitious officers with the opportunity to seize power on behalf of their patrons in Berlin and Rome. By the end of May 1941 their venture had failed. Under the terms of the Anglo-Iraqi Treaty, the new Iraqi government agreed to the deployment of a military force of sufficient strength to deter further subversion. Meanwhile, Reza Shah's tolerance of the activities of Axis agents led to the invasion of Persia by British and Russian forces.

* * *

The brigade to which our battalion belonged wisely kept its distance from towns and villages. We moved at frequent but irregular intervals from one site to another and, though we saw much of the country, we had few contacts with the inhabitants. In the autumn of 1943 I returned to India and was in south east Asia when the war ended. In 1946 I had my next glimpse of the Arab world – and not this time in the Middle East. The Mediterraneam coast of Morocco provided relief from the confined environment of Gibraltar. Tangier's international status at that time attracted members of international cafe society. The port of Ceuta was a curiosity. Scarcely any Moroccans were to be seen; one might have been in Andalucía. Tetuan was another world. I admired the way in which the fabric and traditions of a glorious inheritance were being preserved. In September of that year I returned to the Middle East to spend a year at the Middle East Centre for Arab Studies in Jerusalem.

The serenity of the Austrian Hospice, which housed the Centre, was in sharp contrast to the situation beyond the walls of the Old City. From the historian George Kirk we learned of the rivalry among the colonial powers for dominance in the Arab world, the deals of dubious wisdom struck by the victorious allies after two world wars, the growth of Arab nationalism and the steady rise of Zionist influence in Palestine.

The last of these was in the forefront of our minds. A few weeks before our studies began some ninety occupants of the King David Hotel had been killed by a bomb planted by the Irgun Zvai Leumi, the more active of the two Jewish terrorist groups in Palestine. The intractable nature of the problem facing the government in London was evident. The facts emerging about the scale of the holocaust in occupied Europe and the determination of the survivors to make a new life in what they regarded as their 'promised land' steadily undermined Britain's position as mandatory power. It was also clear that the attitude of the United States administration would have a crucial impact on events and that this in turn was susceptible to public opinion. We read with concern that Ben Hecht, a noted New York playwright and film producer, had said that his heart leapt every time he heard of the death of a British soldier in Palestine. Not long after this President Truman pressed for the admission into Palestine of the hundreds of Jewish refugees crowded on to ships arriving unannounced at Haifa.

The situation deteriorated rapidly and, at the end of January 1947, all non-essential personnel were required to leave Palestine. The Centre was closed. The students were dispersed throughout the region until temporary accommodation was found in a tented camp in what was then Transjordan. I spent the intervening weeks in southern Iraq and, after completing the course, joined the Foreign Service in the autumn of that year.

The Egyptian Department of the Foreign Office handled relations with Egypt, what was still the Anglo-Egyptian Sudan, and Ethiopia. The department was also involved in the negotiations to determine the future of the former Italian colonies. I saw the papers relating to the future of Palestine and could sense the burden this problem placed on the shoulders of the foreign secretary, Ernest Bevin. The choices he and his principal colleagues faced were agonising and they were not helped by the behaviour of Richard Crossman and other leading figures sympathetic to the Zionist cause. Those of us in the Middle East departments feared the consequences for our relations with the rest of the Arab world when, as was inevitable, the British mandate came to an end and the United Nations established the state of Israel.

* * *

Towards the end of 1949 I arrived in Amara in southern Iraq to take the place of a former political agent who had ended his career there as consul. The provincial governor and his colleagues greeted me with courtesy and understandable lack of enthusiasm. In contrast, many of the tribal leaders in the area thought I had come to turn the clock back, and it took weeks of patient explanation to persuade them that I was not in a position to intervene with anyone in Baghdad on their behalf. Over the months I learned much about their way of life and about the contribution members of the British administration had made to the creation of the modern state of Iraq. In his masterly work, *The Arab Awakening*, George Antonius, was right to acknowledge the part these men had played in the reconstruction of the country after the First World War.

In the summer of 1950 I was transferred to the British Embassy in Baghdad where I took up the post of oriental secretary. My immediate chief was the oriental counsellor. These somewhat patronising titles implicitly, if not explicitly, evoked a former era. For the next three and a half years I was immersed in the political life of Iraq. In those days many senior Iraqis spoke no English and, for the foreign diplomat, knowledge of Arabic was a passport to their opinions. Fortunately none of the issues in Anglo-Iraqi relations caused serious concern. The attempt to revise the Treaty had failed. The Royal Air Force retained their base at Habbaniya. The Embassy continued to help with economic development. The long-standing Iraqi aspiration to acquire Kuwait was pursued with more rhetoric than vigour, and the establishment of the state of Israel had caused less disturbance than expected. Even the overthrow of the monarchy in Egypt in 1952 and the emergence of an able, ambitious and charismatic leader in the person of Gamal Abdel Nasser were accepted with little obvious enthusiasm. The Nile valley seemed far removed from the twin rivers.

I soon discovered that it was not only the tribal leaders of Amara province who were reluctant to accept that the days of the British mandate were over. The opposition newspaper showed remarkable ingenuity in attributing every misfortune to the machinations of the British. Many others, with no similar axe to grind, were inclined to believe that the British, and the embassy in particular, still wielded important influence not merely in regard to Iraq's foreign policy but also over the country's domestic affairs.

To be saddled with responsibility without corresponding power is never comfortable. But there was a more serious consideration. From our contacts with the moderate opposition leaders, who had no illusions about the limited extent of our influence, we were able to form a picture of the aspirations of the new generation. Their resentment at being persistently excluded from the centres of power was understandable. Nuri Said, who had played a distinguished role in the Arab Revolt against the Turks, was still the dominant political figure. His fault was not his belief that Iraq's interests were best served by close relations with Britain, but rather his refusal to delegate authority. He dismissed the ugly disturbances in the streets as provocations inspired by Iraq's enemies. Sir John Troutbeck, the wise and perceptive ambassador, did his best to convey the need for reform both to the Regent and to Nuri Said himself, but to little effect. His reports to London and his carefully argued advice were noted, but the need for effective defence in the region to counter Soviet ambitions was a prime consideration and London gave Nuri Said the benefit of the doubt.

*   *   *

For most of the next two years I was involved in other issues but, from the sidelines I was able to watch Anthony Eden's efforts to promote peace in the Middle East. Since becoming foreign secretary in 1951 he had been active on the international stage. His successes in securing a settlement of the Trieste problem, in master-minding the Austrian State Treaty and steering the Geneva conference on Korea and Indo-China to a reasonable conclusion encouraged him to seek yet another diplomatic triumph. This would secure his place in history as a great peace-maker. Against the better judgment of his close advisers, he turned his attention to the Middle East.

In his first public speech as Prime Minister in 1955 Eden signalled his sympathy for the Arab cause. However, almost immediately his initiative ran into difficulties. Despite the successful negotiation the previous year which ended the Anglo-Egyptian Treaty, President Nasser announced that Egypt was to purchase arms from the Soviet bloc countries. Confusion followed over a western loan for the construction of the new Aswan Dam. However, this did not justify Eden's violent reaction to Nasser's nationalisation of the Suez Canal Company in July 1956. The most charitable verdict on Eden's conduct must be that at the time he was a sick man.

In October 1956 I took up my new post as director of the Middle East Centre for Arab Studies in Lebanon. The activities of the Centre had to be suspended for some months in 1958 at the time of the first civil war. This sad event highlighted the difficulty of balancing that country's strong links with Europe and the United States with the need to remain in harmony with Arab nationalism. In Iraq, the violent overthrow of the monarchy had wider implications. Apart from ending the country's long-standing special relationship with Britain, it introduced into the region an element of unpredictability. In Egypt other moves of significance were being made. However, the various alliances proposed by President Nasser, which were intended to enhance the international influence of the Arab world under his leadership, foundered not only because of personal rivalries but also because the platform of common interest was too narrow.

During the two years I spent in what was still the United Arab Republic in the early 1960s, I watched a revolution lose momentum. President Nasser acknowledged that the success of the revolution to which he had made the crucial contribution would depend on the leadership's understanding of the conditions they faced. Their original ambitions were admirably clear and clearly admirable. They sought the regeneration of their country within the framework of a re-awakening Arab world. They attributed the parlous state of Egypt, the unequal distribution of wealth, the incompetence of the military and the widespread corruption to the alliance between the monarchy, the landowning class and the imperialists, by which they meant the British. They chose their moments to deal with each of these cancers in turn. In some instances they seemed not to have been in a hurry. It was not until ten years after the revolution that they revealed their social programme.

For the Free Officers 1956 was a critical year. The defeat they feared over the Suez issue turned into a victory. Overnight their leader became not only a popular hero in the Arab world but also a world figure of consequence. This may have persuaded Nasser and his colleagues that other governments in the Middle East, the Muslim world in general and Africa shared their wider aspirations. But this proved not to be so. Early on Nasser correctly identified the key to the success of the revolution. But, in the event, the Free Officers misread the conditions they faced.

*   *   *

The Suez crisis had repercussions in the Red Sea and the Gulf. The disastrous civil war in the Yemen, Kuwait's advance to independence, the British withdrawal from South Arabia, the closing down of the Political Residency in Bahrain, the process of modernisation in Saudi Arabia and the rapid growth of the oil industry along the shores of the Gulf – all these marked the emergence of a new Arabia.

Meanwhile, in western capitals governments were trying to come to terms with the new realities in the Middle East. Attempts to concert reactions were often frustrated by commercial rivalries and, more serious, by the different approaches of the United States and the Europeans to the Arab-Israel dispute. George Brown, the British foreign secretary, saw an opportunity in the Six Day War in 1967. His persistent advocacy of the formula 'Arab recognition of Israel in exchange for the return of territory seized by Israel' led to the adoption by the UN Security Council of Resolution 242, which has been the basis of such progress as has been made since then.

* * *

There remained some relics of the past. Libya had become an independent state in December 1951. Treaties permitted Britain and the United States to retain their bases in Cyrenaica and Tripolitania respectively. Oil was discovered in 1955. Over the next three years more than half of the land area was allocated to fourteen oil companies for purposes of exploration. The western presence, and especially the British, was strong and influential. The head of state, King Idris, was a benevolent ruler, but indifferent to the transformation taking place elsewhere. His entourage had their own reasons for keeping things more or less as they were. However, in 1969, with one exception, they and the royal family made the mistake of taking their normal vacation in August and awoke on the first of September to discover that, after a bloodless revolution, Libya was now in the hands of twelve anonymous junior army officers.

I presented my credentials as British ambassador to Colonel Qaddafi on 9 October 1969. He wore his twenty-seven years with confidence. For him and his young colleagues Nasser was a heroic figure and the world was as it had been portrayed throughout their formative years by the Cairo radio station 'The Voice of the Arabs'. Having secured in negotiation the evacuation of the British and American bases, they turned their attention to the oil industry. They saw no reason why the price of oil should be set unilaterally by the companies and they cut back the production of those which did not accept their demands for a bigger share. Anti-trust legislation in the United States prevented the companies from concerting their responses. The Libyan initiative opened the way for the price increases which led to the oil crisis three years later.

Three years later I was still finding my way around the United Nations in New York when Egypt and Syria mounted their joint assault on Israel in October 1973. An early morning telephone conversation with Henry Kissinger suggested that concerting our response with the Americans might not be easy. So it proved.

However, my French colleague and I found ourselves in total agreement and we kept our European Community colleagues informed of our discussions with the Egyptians and the non-aligned members of the Security Council. Over the weeks the scope of these talks widened. The other European Community representatives joined us and we laid the foundation of the Euro-Arab Dialogue – a new and rewarding exercise in partnership.

The emerging relationship survived the oil crisis. When Soviet forces invaded Afghanistan in December 1979 the British response was immediate. I accompanied Lord Carrington when, in eight days, he conveyed a message of reassurance and support to governments in Ankara, Muscat, Riyadh, Islamabad and New Delhi. A decade later, in the most tragic of circumstances, the fledgling partnership was sealed in blood in the Gulf War.

*   *   *

If in 1945 it was difficult to foresee the future course of events in the Middle East, the question arises: is the crystal ball any clearer today? Threats to the stability of the region remain. Prospects for peace between Israelis and Palestinians are no better than uncertain. The long-suffering people of Iraq await a return to more tolerable government. In the name of religion extremist movements set their own rules which are not those of the Muslim world as a whole. But today there is an important difference. Europe and the Middle East have derived much benefit from the new relationship, based on common interest and common perceptions, which has replaced the old colonialism. The task now is to have the courage to deploy this strength to influence the course of events.

VI

REVOLUTION IN THE MIDDLE EAST

MARLBOROUGH COLLEGE, WILTSHIRE – NOVEMBER 1998

Marlborough College has been teaching the Arabic language for over twelve years and also has a thriving Oriental Society. In 1998 I was invited to share with the Society some of the conclusions I had drawn from my years of service in the Arab world.

This is the story of three revolutions in a region of the world which has played a critical role in world history. The Middle East occupies a strategic position between Europe, Asia and Africa. For this reason it has sometimes been seen as a bridge and sometimes as a barrier. Seldom, if ever, has it been regarded as of little consequence, especially since the discovery of oil. And so it is no surprise that its history has been turbulent.

That history is quite unusually long. As we approach the two thousandth anniversary of the dawn of the Christian era and review the tragedies and triumphs of the intervening centuries, we should draw inspiration from the ingenuity of the human race which has transformed the conditions in which our ancestors have lived and worked, even if we are shamed by the atrocities which have been committed along the way. Life in the early years Anno Domini is hard to imagine. But how much more difficult is it for us to contemplate the world of a man who, according to the historian Manetho, accumulated medical knowledge, greatly patronised literature and built what was said to be 'a house of hewn stones' over five thousand years ago. The house of hewn stones is a euphemistic description of the great monument to the talents, culture and determination of Zoser, a Pharoah of the Third Dynasty – the massive Step Pyramid which stands today for all to see at Saqqara in the Western Desert of Egypt some twenty miles south west of Cairo.

Egypt under Zoser was a dominant world power and it is understandable that, at that time, the people of the Nile Valley should have regarded their rulers as gods. But this did not prevent Egypt from falling under foreign domination in subsequent centuries; this prolonged experience was a factor in the events of the middle of this 20th century. First to invade and conquer Egypt were the Persians in the 6th century BC. They were in turn defeated by the Greeks under Alexander the Great. Next came Byzantium, then the Arabs in the 7th century AD, then the Turkish Mamluks who ruled Egypt from the 13th to the 16th century. In 1517 Egypt was absorbed into the Ottoman Empire. In the 19th century the energetic and ambitious Ottoman governor of Egypt, Muhammad Ali, made himself independent in all but name. The forty years of his rule initiated the history of modern Egypt.

In the days of the Pharoahs western Europe was an uncivilised wilderness. The expansion of the Roman Empire and the spread of Christianity created common interests between the peoples of Europe and the Middle East. But it also sowed the seeds of conflict. The Crusades were an inglorious episode in European history. Rivalry between Britain and France in Asia and Africa led Napoleon to establish a force in Egypt at the end of the 18th century in an attempt to sever Britain's link with its empire in India. Nelson's victory at the Battle of the Nile restored the situation. However, the lesson was learned in London and Delhi and Britain increasingly relied on the Ottoman Sultan to prevent interference with the route to India. The opening of the Suez Canal in 1869 enhanced Egypt's strategic importance and, as the power and influence of the Ottoman Sultan declined, so Britain was drawn into ever closer involvement in the affairs of Egypt. The inevitable happened. The British occupied Egypt in 1882 and, when Turkey entered the war in 1914 on Germany's side, Egypt was declared a British Protectorate. Although some independence was restored to Egypt after the First World War and Muhammad Ali's descendants, Fuad and then Farouk, ruled in theory as Kings of Egypt, power and influence were effectively in British hands. Britain's privileged position was enshrined in a treaty concluded in 1936. So it remained throughout the Second World War, when Egypt was briefly – and decisively – a battleground between the British and German armies.

* * *

The architect of the Egypt of today was born in Alexandria in January 1918. Gamal Abdel Nasser was the son of a post-office worker from Upper Egypt. As a youth he was an enthusiastic student of history and philosophy. His reading instilled in him a strong nationalist sentiment. He organised demonstrations demanding the removal of British forces from Egypt. His studies also persuaded him that the country could be liberated only by the army. In his comprehensive biography, Anthony Nutting, a Minister of State at the Foreign Office in the 1950s, quotes from a letter which Nasser at the age of seventeen, sent to a friend: 'Egypt is in a state of despair. . . But where is the man to rebuild the country so that the weak and humiliated people can rise again and live as free and independent men? Where is dignity? Where is nationalism?'

Nasser's early attempts to win a place at the Military Academy failed and it was only when he made a direct appeal to the Under-Secretary at the Ministry of War, who was shrewd enough to recognise his personal qualities, that he was accepted. Soon after he was commissioned in 1938, Nasser volunteered for service in the Sudan. When he returned to Egypt in 1942 and became an instructor at the Military Academy he gradually assumed leadership of the Free Officers' Movement, whose aim at that time was the eviction of British forces. The only other opposition movement was the Moslem Brotherhood founded in 1928 by a Sheikh of Al-Azhar, Cairo's Islamic university. For years the Brotherhood had advocated a holy war to evict British forces from Egypt. The establishment of the state of Israel changed the situation.

On 15 May 1948, when the last British troops left Palestine and the state of Israel came into being, the armies of Egypt, Transjordan, Syria, Lebanon and Iraq crossed the border to restore the land taken from the Arab people of Palestine. Initially the campaign went well for the Arab armies. But their efforts were undermined by poor coordination, inadequate training and inferior equipment and the Israelis gradually gained the upper hand. When the Arabs eventually decided to seek an armistice in February 1949, they were resisting on only two fronts – the Old City of Jerusalem, held by the Arab Legion of Transjordan, and Falluja in the south, where an Egyptian brigade refused to surrender although surrounded and outnumbered.

Gamal Abdel Nasser was a hero of the siege of Falluja. He returned to Egypt disillusioned with those in authority whom he held responsible for sending an ill-prepared, poorly equipped, untrained army into battle. He decided in the light of this experience that it would not be enough to remove the British presence; a new system of government had to be put in place in Egypt. The lack of effective co-ordination of the Arab military effort also led him to believe that in Arab unity lay the only real solution to Egypt's problems.

Meanwhile tension was rising between Egypt and Britain. In 1951 the Egyptian Government demanded the withdrawal of British forces from the Canal Zone where they had been concentrated for some years. When the British refused, guerrilla attacks on the British bases were mounted by the Moslem Brotherhood with the tacit approval of the Egyptian authorities. Early in 1952, when British forces retaliated and inflicted heavy casualties on Egyptian police in Ismailia, serious rioting broke out in Cairo. Many hotels, restaurants and bars in the centre of the city were burned down. Martial law was declared. Anxious to prevent the overthrow of the monarchy and the government by an extremist organisation, Nasser and his fellow Free Officers decided that they would have to bring forward the revolution which they had been planning. They required a figure-head. They approached General Neguib, who had been elected President of the Officers' Club in opposition to the candidate preferred by the King. He agreed and was elected President of the Free Officers' Executive.

Learning that the King and the Army High Command had been warned of an impending coup, the Free Officers decided to act. By the morning of 23 July 1952 Nasser and his colleagues had achieved their immediate objectives. The Egyptian people were told in a broadcast message in the name of General Neguib that the army had seized power to purge itself and the country of the traitors and weaklings who had brought dishonour upon their country. The Free Officers' Executive became the Revolutionary Command Council. They presented the Prime Minister, Ali Maher, with a short list of demands including the release of political prisoners and the deposition of the King. Farouk was persuaded to sign an Act of Abdication and he sailed from Alexandria with his family in the royal yacht for exile in Italy. This was a quiet and peaceful revolution. No blood was shed until rioting broke out some weeks later near Alexandria, when left-wing workers attempted to take over a textile factory; nine people, including a number of police and soldiers were killed. Despite Nasser's opposition to capital punishment, the leaders of the riot were hanged.

* * *

Until his death in 1970 Gamal Abdel Nasser relentlessly pursued the aims which had inspired the revolution in 1952. He and his colleagues attributed the unequal distribution of wealth, the incompetence of the armed forces and the corruption and nepotism characteristic of the upper reaches of Egyptian society to the alliance between the monarchy, the capitalist land-owning class and those they described as the imperialists. By this term they meant the British, whose troops at that time still occupied strategic areas of their country, and the French, whose interests dominated the Suez Canal Company. High on Nasser's own list of priorities was Arab unity. His appreciation of the geographical position of Egypt and the high intellectual calibre of its people inflated his ambitions. In his 'Philosophy of the Revolution' he painted a picture of Egypt at the centre of three concentric circles – the Arab world, the Muslim world and the African continent.

The Free Officers, now the Revolutionary Command Council, approached their task with cool deliberation. Of course the monarchy had to go at once. The agrarian law, which limited the size of holdings, broke the backbone of the landowners; the influence of the mercantile class was destroyed by nationalisation of major enterprises. Foreign undertakings were sequestrated or nationalised and, after the Suez War in 1956, the British bases were finally removed.

The problem of feeding Egypt's rapidly growing population was addressed partly by the agrarian reforms and partly by irrigating a vast area of the Western Desert which became a major producer of cotton, maize and millet. The most dramatic project was, of course, the High Dam at Aswan, built with Soviet aid, which, by regulating the flow of the River Nile, not only increased agricultural production but, through the generation of electric power, fuelled the industrialisation programme. Curiously, the leaders of the revolution did not reveal their social programme until ten years after the revolution. The explanation for the delay in publishing the 'National Charter' may lie in the modesty of Nasser's own expectation: 'You can build a village in a day, but how long does it take to build a man?'

There is no doubt that this combination of measures severed the link with Egypt's corrupt past and laid the foundations of the vibrant state of today. The passivity with which the people of Egypt had accepted foreign domination for several millennia was replaced with pride in achievement and the recovery of long lost dignity. During the two years we spent in Egypt in the early 1960s, my wife and I were impressed with the self-confidence not only of those in authority but also of ordinary citizens.

In addressing their country's domestic problems the instincts of the Revolutionary Command Council were sound. Their policies responded to the aspirations of the people, they were relevant and the results were appreciated. The same could not be said of the Council's attitude to its external relationships. This was much influenced by the ideas which had formed in Nasser's mind from the moment that he embarked on his youthful study of history and philosophy up to his ordeal at Falluja. He antagonised the west with his opposition to the Baghdad Pact and his arms deal with the Soviet Union; the creation of the United Arab Republic was based on a serious misreading of the intentions of Syria; the war in the Yemen was unnecessary and costly; his call for greater unity of purpose in Africa fell on deaf ears. The mistake Nasser made was to assume that his Arab and African neighbours shared his preoccupations and ambitions.

The victory which Anthony Eden, then a sick and unbalanced man, handed to him over Suez in 1956 established Gamal Abdel Nasser as a world figure of significance and reserved for him an honourable place in history. But in his later years he neglected his own dictum that the success of the revolution would depend on its comprehension of the real conditions facing it. Despite this, Egypt's leadership in recent years has profited immensely from this experience and this has enabled it to contribute significantly to the search for peace in the Middle East.

*　*　*

Like Egypt, the country now known as Iraq has a long history. It too contains monuments to a glorious past. The great civilisations of Sumer and Akkad, of Babylon and Assyria, of the Achaemenian Persians, of Alexander the Great and the Seleucid Greeks, of the Parthians, then the Sassanian Persians – all these flourished in the land of the twin rivers, the Tigris and the Euphrates. The Arab Caliphates established in Iraq after the Arab armies broke out of the peninsula in the 7th century AD were world powers. The Abbasid Caliph, Haroun al-Rashid, renowned for his association with the 'Thousand and One Nights', ruled in the splendour of Baghdad at the end of the 8th century. He regarded Charlemagne as the only ruler of comparable status – and with some justification. However, the seeds of dissension had already been sown. The schism in Islam over the true succession to the prophet Muhammad is sanctified in the tombs at Kerbala in southern Iraq of Hussain, the son of the prophet's son-in-law, Ali, and his half-brother, Abbas, who were killed there in 680 AD fighting for their cause. Kerbala, the nearby town of Najaf and Kadhimain in Baghdad attract thousands of Shi'a pilgrims from neighbouring Iran and further afield every year.

The Mongol invasions in the 13th and 14th centuries left behind more ruins than monuments. In the 16th century what is now Iraq was incorporated into the steadily expanding Ottoman Empire and it remained part of this empire until the First World War. During these four centuries of Ottoman rule Iraq was divided into three 'vilayets' – Mosul in the north inhabited for the most part by Sunni Arabs, Kurds, and Christian Arabs and Assyrians; Baghdad in the centre, inhabited largely by Sunni Arabs; and Basra in the south where most of the population belonged to Shi'a tribes. Inevitably, since the Turks were Sunni, the Sunni Arabs received preferential treatment; it was not until the early 1920s, for example, that Shi'a Arabs in Iraq were admitted to higher education and to the professions.

Ever sensitive to threats to their line of communications with the empire in India, the British had been alarmed by the ambition of the young Kaiser Wilhelm to build a railway from Berlin to Baghdad and on to Basra – a critical element in his 'drang nach Osten' – the drive to the east. Plans were drawn up by the Government of India in 1912 to occupy Basra in the event of war and a commitment was given to the Sheikh of Muhammara to support him, if necessary, against both the Ottoman Sultan and the Shah of Persia. The resulting campaign in what was then called Mesopotamia destroyed the Kaiser's dream and ended four centuries of not especially benign Ottoman neglect.

Iraq became an independent state thanks to the British. A series of treaties negotiated in the 1920s defined the boundaries of the new state which comprised the former Ottoman provinces of Mosul, Baghdad and Basra. The British administration facilitated the negotiations which established friendly relations with the new state's neighbours to the south and east. In 1930 a treaty was signed which came into force two years later when Iraq was admitted to the League of Nations. Among other things this treaty created an alliance under which the British were permitted to establish air bases at Habbaniya in the western desert and at Shu'aiba, near Basra, and had the right to move troops across Iraqi territory. It was this right which enabled a British force to crush the pro-Nazi revolt led by Rashid Ali al-Gailani in 1941.

The British administration of Iraq in the 1920s and early 1930s transformed the country and its prospects. Having acquired this territory more by accident of war than design, the British discovered that they had inherited a major problem. The diversity of the population and the lack of effective communications faced the new rulers with a stark choice – leave the country to its fate or enable it to stand on its own feet. The British chose the latter course. And it was a fortunate circumstance that an outstanding group of administrators was on hand. When I served in Iraq in the early 1950s I heard on all sides tributes to those dedicated men and women who had taken on the task of reconstructing the country. Apart from installing the Hashemite Prince Faisal, who had fought with Lawrence against the Turks in the First World War, as the first King of Iraq, the British had put in place a well-trained civil administration and judicial system, built up the Iraqi armed forces and encouraged the investment of the oil royalties derived from the Iraq Petroleum Company's operations at Kirkuk, and later at Basra, in the development of the economy. On the face of it, these factors seemed to constitute a recipe for progress and stability. However the opportunities on offer were not taken.

The political scene in the years following Iraq's emergence as a sovereign state was dominated by two men. Prince Abdulillah acted as regent until his nephew, the young King Faisal, who was the grandson of the first king of Iraq, came of age. Abdulillah occupied a position of great potential influence, but he lacked both personality and perspicacity. Real power was in the hands of Nuri Said, who had been one of the leaders of a group of dissident Arab officers in the Ottoman army who had defected to the allies during the First World War. Nuri held the post of Prime Minister several times and was widely believed to direct affairs of state even when nominally out of office. His indifference to the fact that Iraqi society was being changed by the emergence, thanks to the reforms of the systems of education and entry to the professions, of a new, modern, educated class was to prove disastrous. Reasonably enough, members of this generation considered that they were entitled to play a part in the government of their country. However, for far too long political power was retained by the professional politicians and their associates among the merchants and landowners. With rare exceptions, the new generation was excluded from positions of influence and power.

During the four years my wife and I spent in Iraq in the early 1950s, we visited every district of every province. The provincial governors, district commissioners, business men, professionals and tribal chiefs we met spoke to us freely about their aspirations and their anxieties. We felt that these people and those they represented deserved far better of their government and, when we left Baghdad in December 1953, we felt that, unless prosperity and political responsibility were more widely shared, discontent could undermine the fabric of the state the British had created a generation earlier. On 14 July 1958 that fabric was destroyed when a little known brigadier called Abdul Karim Qassim carried out a successful coup d'état.

This was an exceptionally bloody event. King Faisal, Prince Abdulillah and all the women and children of the palace were shot in the garden of the Crown Prince. Nuri Said was killed the next day trying to escape disguised as a woman. The bodies of the Crown Prince and Nuri Said were dragged through the streets of Baghdad. The British Embassy was looted and burned.

Qassim charged one of his associates, Colonel Mehdawi, with the task of putting on trial and subsequently executing leading figures of the old regime. The trials, which were televised live, continued for months. Qassim, whom the new British ambassador, Sir Humphrey Trevelyan, regarded as seriously unbalanced, seemed to have no aim other than to exercise supreme personal power. He successfully foiled many plots against him by nationalists, communists and the Baath Party. This was a well-organised political machine based in both Syria and Iraq, whose ambition, as its name suggests, was the renaissance of the Arab world. The unsuccessful conspirators were usually executed but in some cases they were reprieved. This happened after an unsuccessful Baathist coup and one of the ring-leaders, named Saddam Hussain al-Tikriti, escaped with a prison sentence. Eventually, in February 1963, one plot did succeed. Qassim and his henchman, Mehdawi, were killed by sections of the army and air force acting with the Baathists.

None of the successor governments had a long life until Saddam Hussain, who had risen steadily to the post of Vice-President, became head of state in July 1979. In the years that have passed since then, Saddam Hussain and his family and associates from Tikrit and the north have imposed a gruesome tyranny on the people of Iraq. In September 1980 he went to war with Iran. Eight years and thousands of casualties later, and without gaining any advantage, Saddam agreed to a cease-fire. In March 1988 his forces slaughtered several thousand inhabitants of the Kurdish town of Halabja with chemical weapons. In 1991 after the defeat in the Gulf War of the Iraqi forces which had invaded Kuwait, thousands of the Shi'a inhabitants of the marshes in southern Iraq were massacred. This evil regime has survived because of the severity with which it has dealt with its opponents, a deficiency in the UN Charter and the lack of political will in the outside world. Iraq which was once a source of stability in the region is now a menace to its neighbours and an international outcast.

*   *   *

To the Phoenicians of the 2nd millennium BC the coast of North Africa was a valuable guide and an occasional refuge on long voyages. But it also attracted a succession of conquerors – Greeks, Numidians, Romans, Christians, Vandals, Byzantines, Arabs, Normans, Turks and eventually Italians. Until recent years spectacular Roman monuments at Cyrene, Sabratha, Leptis Magna and Tripoli used to attract tourists. Other conquerors, except the Italians, left Libya virtually without trace.

In 1863, the newly established kingdom of Italy conceived the idea of an Italian presence on the southern shore of the Mediterranean in order to prevent the whole of North Africa falling under the domination of the British or the French. The first venture at Tunis failed, but in 1911 a substantial Italian naval force led a successful assault against Turkish and Libyan forces at Tripoli. This was the first step in the colonisation of Tripolitania and Cyrenaica. Under the Italians the main towns, the principal communications and agriculture were skilfully developed.

Fascist Italy's entry into the Second World War in June 1940 on Germany's side posed an immediate threat to Britain's position in the Middle East. Inevitably Libya became a battleground. When in 1943 the German and Italian armies in North Africa had been defeated, Libya came under the authority of Britain and France. In November 1949 the General Assembly of the United Nations resolved that 'Libya, comprising Cyrenaica, Tripolitania and Fezzan, shall be constituted an independent sovereign state'. It was also decided that a UN Commissioner, supported by a Council, should be appointed to assist 'the people of Libya in the formulation of the constitution and the establishment of an independent government'. In December 1951 Libya became an independent kingdom under King Idris, the head of the influential Order of the Sanussi based in Cyrenaica.

In July 1953 Libya concluded a Treaty of Alliance with Britain under which Britain was granted military facilities at Tobruk and El Adem in Cyrenaica. In exchange Britain provided Libya with financial aid and arms. In 1954 the United States, which had been allowed the use of Wheelus air base near Tripoli by the British during the Second World War, concluded a similar agreement with Libya. In 1955 oil was discovered and, over the next three years, more than half of the land area was allocated to fourteen oil companies for purposes of exploration. Libya was transformed. The rapid expansion of the oil industry created undreamt of wealth and this attracted entrepreneurs of all kinds. Before long there was an impressive and influential western presence. King Idris was a pious and benevolent ruler, largely indifferent to events beyond Libya's frontiers. His entourage, on the other hand, had few scruples. For the most part they were ruthless in exploiting their position for their own advantage and saw no need for change. In the community of Arab states Libya had little stature and was regarded, with some justification, as little more than a western colony.

In the summer of 1969 I was appointed British ambassador to the Kingdom of Libya and it was arranged that I would take up my post in the autumn. However, on 1 September a group of junior army officers seized power while the king and all but one of his immediate entourage were outside the country. Initially this was portrayed outside Libya as a coup d'état. In fact it was a revolution – and at the time no blood was shed. On 12 September my wife and I flew to Tripoli which, like the entire country, was under martial law and on 9 October I presented my credentials to the head of state, a recently promoted captain in the Libyan army called Muammar al Qaddafi.

Qaddafi was born to a tribal couple in the desert near to the port of Sirte in Cyrenaica in 1942. He looked older than his 27 years and his face was pitted in the manner often ascribed to infantile malnutrition. His most striking characteristic was an occasional penetrating look. We conducted all our business in Arabic and throughout my time in Libya he treated me with consideration and courtesy.

The aims of the Revolutionary Command Council were clear. They wanted to raise the living standards of their people, to establish their country's independent status and to play a role commensurate with Libya's wealth and potential. These ambitions were widely welcomed in the country; they were seen as an Arab nationalist response to the humiliating defeat of the Arab armies two years earlier in the Six Day War and to the corrupt and pro-western policies of the monarchy. The young officers were inspired by the example of Egypt. Qaddafi was ten years old when Gamal Abdel Nasser mounted his revolution and the view he and his colleagues took of the world had been formed by the propaganda broadcast daily from Cairo by 'The Voice of the Arabs'. Qaddafi himself set out his own philosophy, which he called the 'Third Universal Theory', in his Green Book. Despite the failure of a variety of ill-conceived foreign adventures, he has survived in power for nearly thirty years, thanks to his efficient security service, to the wealth generated by the oil industry, his talent for playing one faction off against another and, above all, the docility and comfortable circumstances of his population.

The United Kingdom broke off relations with Libya in 1984 after the murder of WPC Yvonne Fletcher in St James's Square in London. Relations deteriorated further when a ship was seized in 1987 loaded with Libyan arms and explosives for the IRA who, in Qaddadfi's eyes, were engaged in an anti-colonial struggle, and were further exacerbated by the tragedy of Lockerbie, which led to the imposition of severe sanctions which are still in force.

One is left with the impression that Muammar al Qaddafi is not really of this world. He renamed his country 'The Great Socialist People's Libyan Arab State of the Masses' and, having renounced almost all his official positions, in 1979 he assumed the title of 'Leader of the Revolution and Supreme Commander of the Armed Forces'. His erratic behaviour, the insults he directs at other countries' leaders and political systems and the interference in their internal affairs by agencies of his government have aroused fear, suspicion and contempt. The rest of the world has little choice but to wait until the direction of Libya's affairs is in more rational hands. Until then, Libya, like Iraq, will remain an international pariah.

CHAPTER TWO: EVER CLOSER UNION IN EUROPE

My first experience of the travail of European integration was as a member of the United Kingdom delegation during the abortive attempt in the early 1960s to join the European Community. In the late 1970s I spent four years in Brussels as the United Kingdom's representative and in the early 1990s I acted as adviser to a Member of the European Commission. Throughout this period and since there have been numerous opportunities to speak about this great venture.

I

THE 1961 APPLICATION:
FRENCH DECEPTION OR BRITISH MISMANAGEMENT

UNIVERSITY OF BATH – 28 JANUARY 1999

On 27 February 1961 the Council of the Western European Union held one of its regular meetings in Paris. The United Kingdom was represented by Edward Heath, a member of the British Cabinet with the title Lord Privy Seal. Despite this title Edward Heath was not a Lord but a Member of the House of Commons. The Secretary of State for Foreign Affairs at the time was a Lord – the Earl of Home – and Harold Macmillan, the Prime Minister, thought it right that another member of the Cabinet should be able to answer for the Foreign Office in the House of Commons. Edward Heath was given this task; he also assumed responsibility within the government for European affairs.

This was a deliberate move on the Prime Minister's part. His own background was upper middle class; in the First World War he had been commissioned into an elite regiment, the Grenadier Guards. He served throughout on the Western Front and was wounded no fewer than three times. After the war he married into the aristocracy. Edward Heath's father was an artisan and yet he won a place at Balliol College, Oxford, and was in due time elected president of the Union. In September 1937 he attended a Nazi Party Rally at Nuremberg which was addressed by Adolf Hitler. In 1938 he and a number of his fellow undergraduates accepted an invitation to visit Spain where the Republican Government, hard pressed by the fascists in the civil war, hoped to win them to their cause. In the summer of 1939 he and his closest friend visited Poland and only with difficulty escaped from Germany in time to catch one of the last ferries to England before the Second World War began. As an artillery officer he took part in the liberation of western Europe in the final year of the war. Though separated by a generation, their experiences had driven both Macmillan and Heath to the same conclusion: by one means or another Europe must be saved from another war.

* * *

At the meeting in Paris Edward Heath told his Western European Union colleagues that, if the Common Market countries were able to meet the United Kingdom's difficulties over agriculture and trade with the Commonwealth, the United Kingdom could consider a system based on a common or harmonised tariff on raw materials and manufactured goods imported from countries other than the seven members of the European Free Trade Association (EFTA), which had been formed in November 1959, or the Commonwealth. This was the first public indication that the British government's attitude to the Common Market might be changing. A year earlier, when addressing the Council of Europe, Selwyn Lloyd, Lord Home's predecessor as foreign secretary, had described the British position in these terms: 'We regard ourselves as part of Europe . . . the Channel does not disqualify the United Kingdom from European status'.

Although there had been no meeting of minds when Macmillan and President de Gaulle met in Paris in June 1958 – their first meeting since their encounter in 1943 in Algiers in quite different circumstances – de Gaulle had taken away an impression of British hostility to the European Community. As time passed Macmillan came to realise the risks for Britain in continuing to stand aside. He tried to set these against the demands of the Commonwealth, the EFTA and the domestic agriculture industry. He accordingly asked Duncan Sandys, a founder member of the European Movement and now the Commonwealth Secretary, to assess means of reconciling the European concept with the United Kingdom's obligations to the Commonwealth. Macmillan had astutely appointed another pro-European, Christopher Soames, to the post of Minister of Agriculture.

In the spring of 1960 Macmillan consulted the leaders of the old Commonwealth countries, as well as President Kennedy who made clear his enthusiasm for the great European venture. At a later stage Duncan Sandys and other ministers visited a number of the key Commonwealth capitals seeking and offering opinions. The Prime Minister and his principal colleagues realised that, before the United Kingdom could reach a final conclusion, it would be necessary to convene a full Commonwealth conference. Meanwhile there remained a few sceptics in the cabinet, but Macmillan was able to tell the House of Commons on 31 July 1961 that the government had decided to apply formally for membership of the European Community. The Prime Minister's speech was better received than even his most enthusiastic colleagues expected. The government's decision was endorsed by the House on 3 August. Edward Heath was charged with forming and leading the delegation which would conduct the negotiations.

Following Macmillan's announcement in the House of Commons the Council of Ministers of the Community met to discuss the procedure for the negotiations. To the surprise of his colleagues, Maurice Couve de Murville, the French foreign minister, insisted on two conditions – first, that, instead of appointing a chief negotiator to act on behalf of the Community, the Six should discuss and agree on each proposition to be put to the delegation of the candidate country and, secondly, that the first meeting with the British should be held in Paris, not Brussels, the headquarters of the Community. During that meeting of the Six none of the ministers present raised any objection of principle to the enlargement of the Community to include the United Kingdom.

Edward Heath immediately set about forming his negotiating team. He did so with the care and precision which were to become notable characteristics of his approach to his responsibilities. His invitation to Sir Pierson Dixon, the ambassador in Paris, to take on the additional role of leader of the official delegation was questioned in some quarters; given his duties in Paris, would he be able to devote enough time and attention to this new task? In the event the appointment proved to be sound. The ambassador was highly regarded not only by the French but also in the Diplomtic Service and in Whitehall more generally. His access to French opinion was to prove an important element in the later stages of the negotiations. Dixon's deputy, Sir Eric Roll, was the authority on agriculture. His worldly wisdom and knowledge of languages were major assets. Other members were drawn from the senior and well respected ranks of the Whitehall departments principally involved. The delegation's secretariat was provided by the Foreign Office. The Lord Privy Seal also took the wise step of appointing a young official from the Treasury to work alongside his private secretary at the Foreign Office. I was honoured and excited when, as the deputy head of the Foreign Office News Department, I was invited to be the delegation's official spokesman. In that capacity I attended all the negotiating sessions in Brussels and

Luxembourg as well as the Commonwealth Conference and the delegation's own briefing meetings, at which I reported on press reactions.

The negotiations were opened formally on 10 October 1961 when Edward Heath presented the United Kingdom's application to the Council of Ministers at the Quai d'Orsay in Paris.

It was clear from the reports of British embassies in the member states that these were welcome developments. They had regretted the original British decision not to participate in the enterprise and were now looking forward to a new chapter in the history of the continent. There was, however, one notable exception. When Sir Pierson Dixon called on the French President in July 1961 to convey the news that the British government intended to apply for membership of the Community, de Gaulle 'expressed no pleasure at the news'. Dixon reported that, as he read Macmillan's letter, the General looked 'distinctly vexed'.

*   *   *

Although seven nation states as well as the European Commission were represented in the conference chamber, the negotiations were bilateral. The Six addressed the British delegation through the president of the Council of Ministers for the time being. Occasionally, and by agreement among the Six, other ministers round the table might intervene to complement the president's statement. Under the conditions imposed on the Six by Couve de Murville, the Six met behind closed doors to discuss, and no doubt argue about, their response to any proposition put forward by Edward Heath. This meant that the British delegation had to spend long hours in the offices allocated to them awaiting a summons to the conference chamber to resume the negotiations when the Six had finally agreed on the line they would take. The negotiating sessions normally lasted three days. at the end of each of which the delegation secretaries drafted detailed reports for despatch to London, Commonwealth and EFTA capitals and other interested diplomatic posts. While this work was in hand, I was occupied briefing the international press. Edward Heath himself gave a press conference and radio and television interviews at the end of each round of the negotiations, and followed this with a statement in the House of Commons on the following day.

One of the issues discussed early on was the method by which the United Kingdom would move on to the same external tariff as the Community, given the relationship with the Commonwealth and the members of the Free Trade Area. Much time was spent on such issues as quotas for imports of Indian tea and raw materials and foodstuffs from the colonial and former colonial territories. A major complication was that at this time the Six were still trying to agree on a common agricultural policy. After some delays the policy was adopted in the middle of January 1962 and the question to be decided was how the United Kingdom would adapt to the new policy during the proposed transitional period.

Concerned at the slow pace of the negotiations which he had hoped would be concluded before the summer break, Heath suggested that an overall view of the situation reached should be presented when ministers met on 11 May. This idea was accepted by the Six. Heath already suspected that the French were anxious to draw out the process for as long as possible. The delegation had come to expect an intervention by Couve de Murville whenever agreement on an issue under discussion had been reached and the president was about to move on to the next item on the agenda. These interventions were frequently introduced with the phrase: 'Monsieur le Président, je crains qu'il n'y ait une petite équivoque'. There would then follow a lengthy exercise in obfuscation.

Heath's suspicions seemed to be confirmed by reports from Paris that French officials were concerned at the amount of progress which was being made in Brussels and surprised at the readiness of the British to make significant concessions in order to ensure this. In a despatch addressed to the Foreign Secretary dated 16 May 1962, Sir Pierson Dixon, in his ambassadorial capacity, expressed the view that the French wanted the negotiations to fail. A few days later de Gaulle told Dixon that in his opinion it was too early for the British to enter the Common Market. He stressed the problems with the Commonwealth, while denying that he was formally opposed to British entry.

On 2 June Macmillan arrived in Paris to spend the weekend with President de Gaulle at the Château de Champs. This followed a suggestion made by Macmillan when congratulating the General on his overwhelming victory in a referendum in April. Much of the weekend was spent in discussing the major political and strategic issues of the day, including the questions of alliances, nuclear weapons, the Atlantic Alliance and the role of Europe. No clear conclusions emerged from these talks and Pierson Dixon confessed to being baffled by the accounts he received of the occasion. Macmillan did not find everything baffling. In an entry in his diary for 3 June he summarised de Gaulle's attitude on the British application to join the Community. He did not want us in for two main reasons:

'1. It will alter the character of the Community . . . Now it is a nice little club . . . under French hegemony.

2. Apart from our loyalty to the Commonwealth, we shall always be too intimately tied up with the Americans . . .'

Macmillan's conclusion was that, while he would not openly oppose Britain's entry, de Gaulle would instruct his negotiators to obstruct and delay, or insist on terms on agriculture and the Commonwealth so harsh as to be unacceptable. However, Macmillan acknowledged that it was always difficult to assess the thoughts and emotions of this enigmatic man.

*　　*　　*

Meanwhile the detailed negotiations ground on in Brussels. By midsummer it was evident that Heath's ambition to conclude the process by the beginning of August would not be achieved. While Macmillan was becoming increasingly concerned about the prospects for the Commonwealth Heads of Government Conference to open in London on 10 September, the delegation in Brussels was faced with a dilemma over temperate agricultural products. The French had tabled severe new proposals which were no doubt designed to rule out any possibility of disposing of the agriculture chapter before the recess.

To strengthen his hand with both the Six and London, Heath had arranged for Duncan Sandys and Christopher Soames to accompany him to this session of the negotiations. The immediate issue was whether the delegation should seek to sustain the momentum of the negotiations by accepting the proposals in the hope of amending them at a later stage, or of saying there and then that they were unacceptable. Sir Roderick Barclay, the senior Foreign Office representative, Christopher Audland and John Robinson, the two delegation secretaries, and I favoured the first course; others preferred the latter. The three ministers felt they that did not have the authority to decide and so Heath telephoned to the Prime Minister. Macmillan favoured postponing the question, and Heath acted accordingly.

Suspicions about French motives were strengthened when Couve de Murville asked for the resumption of the negotiations in the autumn to be postponed for a month. However, the general view among the delegations on the eve of the summer break was quietly confident. Although no agreement had been possible on temperate-zone foodstuffs, good progress had been made on manufactured goods from the old Commonwealth, imports from India, Pakistan and Ceylon, and associate status had been secured for the less-developed former colonial territories. All Commonwealth leaders had been informed of the position reached.

The expectation in Brussels was that, with the same determination, the back of the negotiations could be broken by the end of the year.

*   *   *

The next major event was the Commonwealth Conference in September. Shortly before it was due to open, Edward Heath held a meeting at the Foreign Office to discuss the advice he should offer the Prime Minister. One of those present was Macmillan's senior press adviser, Harold Evans. He was in a highly anxious state, reflecting, he told us, the nervousness of the Prime Minister who feared a ferocious onslaught from his Commonwealth colleagues. Given the special pains the delegation had taken to keep Commonwealth governments fully informed, and the largely successful efforts which had been made to safeguard Commonwealth interests and to provide access for their products to a wider market once we had joined the Community, these apprehensions seemed both unjustified and unreasonable, and I said so. After some discussion Evans returned to Number 10 in a better frame of mind. What was worrying however was the light this shed on the mood and perceptions of the Prime Minister. In the event no blood was let during the Commonwealth conference and the heads of government left London moderately reassured.

Steady progress continued throughout the autumn, differences continued to be narrowed and as the Christmas and New Year recess approached spirits rose. Once again the mood among the delegations round the table was positive. With one or two more special efforts in the New Year the great task could be completed. At this point all our best laid schemes suffered the fate immortalised by Robert Burns.

*   *   *

On July 1962 orders had been placed by Britain for the supply from the United States of a number of Skybolt nuclear weapons; this order was accepted by Washington. The Skybolt was an air-launched rocket newly developed by the Americans and was to replace the ground-launched rocket – the Blue Streak. This transaction gave effect to an undertaking given some years earlier by President Eisenhower which included a provision that, in the event of Skybolt proving unsatisfactory, the Americans would instead supply Polaris missiles which would be fitted to Royal Navy submarines. Early in November 1962, after receiving technical reports, Robert McNamara, the US Defense Secretary, recommended to President Kennedy that Skybolt be cancelled. Kennedy arranged for the British government to be informed so that they could prepare the ground before the decision became public. An announcement was made in Washington on 13 December, the very day on which Harold Macmillan travelled to Paris for previously arranged talks with the French President at Rambouillet. It was also intended that, immediately following his meeting with de Gaulle, Macmillan would travel to Nassau for a conference with President Kennedy and senior members of his administration. Both encounters were inevitably dominated by the questions of the supply and ownership of a nuclear deterrent.

At Rambouillet Macmillan informed de Gaulle that he intended to ask Kennedy to supply Britain with Polaris missiles. While de Gaulle accepted that Britain was determined to maintain its own nuclear deterrent, he did not fail to criticise Britain's continuing dependence on the United States. He used this as an excuse for arguing that Britain was not yet ready for membership of the European Community. Macmillan replied that, if this was indeed the President's view, he should have said so at an earlier stage. The conclusions of the Prime Minister's discussions with President Kennedy at Nassau had the effect of providing de Gaulle with yet more ammunition for his attack on Britain's 'special relationship' with the United States.

At any given moment the cancellation of Skybolt would have put the British government in an awkward position. That it should have arisen so close to what was expected to be the successful conclusion of Britain's negotiations to join the European Community was especially unfortunate.

*   *   *

It had been agreed that negotiations would resume in Brussels on 14 January 1963. Edward Heath had spent part of the recess working out a possible solution to the problem of agricultural finance. He arranged to meet Couve de Murville privately over lunch at the British Embassy in Paris on Friday, 11 January. The others present were Pierson Dixon, Eric Roll and Olivier Wormser, Couve's deputy. Over coffee, Heath offered to show his proposed solution to Couve, but Couve said this would not be necessary; he was now satisfied with what had already been agreed. This prompted Heath to ask the leading question: were there any insuperable obstacles to Britain's entry if the negotiations were successfully concluded. Heath repeated the question. On both occasions Couve rejected the possibility. His words were: 'No power on earth can now prevent these negotiations from being successful.' Olivier Wormser indicated his assent to this statement.

In the same week Henri Fayat, the Belgian deputy foreign minister, who was to chair the Council of Ministers for the next six months, went to Paris to discuss procedure with Couve de Murville. As that great Belgian statesman and European, Paul-Henri Spaak, has recorded, Couve, though a hard bargainer, was not intransigent. 'None of us', wrote Spaak, 'had any inkling that a sensation was in the offing. As for Couve, either he knew what was coming and was aware of the coup General de Gaulle was about to spring upon the world – in which case he was a consummate actor – or he knew nothing of the General's plans . . . I believe it is the second of these alternatives that applied. It is out of the question that Couve should have deliberately concealed his intentions and deceived the man due to take charge of the coming meeting of the Six'.

Negotiations resumed in Brussels on 14 January 1963. Optimism pervaded the council chamber. Couve de Murville was absent; it was explained that he had to attend a press conference being given by President de Gaulle. At Edward Heath's suggestion, the meeting proceeded in Couve's absence and was concluded with agreement on all items on the agenda for that day. Immediately after the session ended, news of President de Gaulle's press conference began to reach the delegations. De Gaulle had set out at length and with elegant condescension what he claimed were the reasons why the United Kingdom was not yet fit for membership of the European Community. These reports caused consternation in Brussels. Despite the immediate impression of a French veto in de Gaulle's words, the delegations, with the acquiescence of Couve de Murville's deputy, decided to complete the negotiations. On his arrival two days later in Brussels, Couve was annoyed to find that the negotiations had not been brought to an end. Despite his objections, it was agreed that after a period of reflection the delegations would re-assemble in Brussels at the end of the month.

In the afternoon of 29 January Henri Fayat invited Edward Heath, his two ministerial colleagues and Eric Roll to his office. He said that, with great regret, the member states were prevented from continuing the negotiation. Their regret, he said, would be shared throughout the free world. When the British delegation joined the Six in the Council Chamber, Couve de Murville argued that the negotiations had broken down because of the unwillingness of the British to accept community policies and disciplines. In turn each of the ministers of the Five expressed their regret at the turn of events. Edward Heath refuted Couve's arguments point by point. With his own experience as a young man and that of other members of the British delegation in mind, he concluded his response with these words: 'There have been times in the history of Europe when it has been only too plain how European we are: and there are millions of people who have been grateful for it. I say to my colleagues: have no fear. We in Britain are not going to turn our backs on the mainland of Europe or the countries of the Community'. Later he told the press: 'We entered sixteen months ago into negotiations in good faith. The high hopes of many have been thwarted for political reasons and the will of one man'.

*   *   *

The reasons for the veto have been the subject of much debate. It has recently been claimed that the negotiations failed because they were mishandled by the British delegation. No one who was present throughout the long months of some-times intense negotiation and was privy to the brief from which Edward Heath spoke, could subscribe to such a view. There is, for example, no plausible evi-dence to suggest that British unwillingness there and then to accept the proposals on temperate-zone agriculture tabled at the end of July 1962 had any influence on the subsequent course of events. When I read some of the products of this latter-day revisionism, I am reminded of a cry from the heart of Vicomte Davignon, then a Vice-President of the European Commission, at a meeting of the Committee of Permanent Representatives in the late 1970s. A number of permanent representatives seemed intent on raising minor points on a fairly straightforward issue. Increasingly exasperated, Davignon raised his eyes to the ceiling and said: 'May the Good Lord save us from the complicators.' What was especially poignant about this remark was that, on his day, Davignon could himself be a consummate complicator.

If the British are to be criticised, one or two points could be made. The Prime Minister could be said to have lacked the courage of his convictions. He might have put more pressure on the departments at home to speed up responses to the proposals of the Six. He seemed also to be unnecessarily apprehensive about the attitude of the Old Commonwealth. The Skybolt/Polaris affair put him in an impossible position. This was an unavoidable accident of history.

To my mind the facts show that the reasons for the collapse of the negotiations are to be found in the character and ambition of Charles de Gaulle. In the 1930s, as an up-and-coming middle rank officer in the French army, he criticised his superiors for their failure to learn the lessons of the Spanish Civil War. With great determination he rallied those French servicemen and women who were prepared to continue the struggle after the defeat of France in 1940. As a proud and sen-sitive Frenchman, he resented being received in London, as he saw it, as just one among a number of representatives of countries which had been overrun by the

Nazis. His ambition was to restore the dignity of France and the founding of the European Community was one of the vehicles he chose. Commerce and trade were low in his list of priorities. It was politics and power that enthralled him. He envisaged a Europe assuming control of its own defence and determining its own foreign policies. And of course this would be under the leadership of France. He himself was to be the instrument. Jean Monnet, the inspiration of the Common Market, once told Edward Heath that, in order to understand what was in de Gaulle's mind, one had to realise that on every count he asked himself what would be the verdict of history fifty years on. Further evidence of his conceit is contained in the jottings of Alain Peyrefitte, de Gaulle's spokesman and right-hand man for several years; the manner in which the President rebuked his Prime Minister, Georges Pompidou, for his presumption at meetings of the government at the Elysée Palace recalls Louis XIV's dictum: 'L'Etat, c'est moi'.

The belated British application to join the Community threatened de Gaulle's European concept. As the French agriculture minister said to Christopher Soames: 'It is simple. Now with the Six there are five hens and one cock. If you join, and others too, there will be seven or eight hens. But there will be two cocks. That is not so agreeable'.

In the beginning de Gaulle probably believed that, because of their Commonwealth ties and 'special relationship' with the United States, the British would be unable or unwilling to accept the conditions for entry. This is the only charitable explanation for his allowing his loyal and diligent foreign minister to agree to the opening of negotiations with the British in the summer of 1961. However, as time passed and the negotiations made steady progress, de Gaulle must have begun to realise that they might after all succeed. This could explain his somewhat convoluted remarks in his conversations with Pierson Dixon in the summer of 1962 and his more explicit language when he met Macmillan at the Château de Champs in June. The indications he gave that summer of his opposition to British entry faced the British with a virtually impossible choice. There are some who say now that the French veto was inevitable. That is wisdom after the event. Although warned of his attitude, the British had no alternative but to pursue the negotiations to a successful conclusion and then face de Gaulle with the choice of acquiescing, or defying the will of France's Community partners and causing outrage in the United Kingdom. By the beginning of January 1963 time was running out for de Gaulle. And he may have judged that the Skybolt/Polaris affair gave him a plausible pretext for parading his objections to British membership in public.

Reading today the text of his long, rambling statements at his press conference, one forms the impression not so much of a critique of the British position in the world as of a rationalisation of de Gaulle's own prejudices and a sublimation of his personal ambitions. In a speech at Liverpool on 22 January 1963 Harold Macmillan rehearsed the protest he had made to the President at Rambouillet: 'Recrimination is useless, but the truth should be known. If there was any objection in principle to Britain's entry, we should, surely, have been told so from the start'. Invited a few years ago to comment on this statement, Couve de Murville said: 'C'était une sorte de trahison' – 'It was a kind of betrayal'. It is tragic that a great man, who did so much to restore confidence and pride to his country after the humiliation of 1940 and who wished above all to go down in history as a great European, should have this 'kind of betrayal' attached to his name.

In 1965 after he had been elected Leader of the Opposition, Edward Heath visited President de Gaulle at the Elysée to ensure that he understood that the Conservative Party had not changed its position on Europe since Britain had entered into negotiations to join the Community in 1961. At the end of their meeting de Gaulle said: 'If you become Prime Minister, you will be the man who will lead Britain into the European Community'. On this occasion, at least, de Gaulle's judgment was correct.

II

THE STATE OF THE COMMUNITY

VTH INTERNATIONAL SCHOOL OF THE BUILDING SOCIETIES
INSTITUTE
AMSTERDAM – 24 OCTOBER 1976

Six months ago many hearts and minds were weighed down by quite unjustified pessimism about the European Community. It was being said that the internal integration of the Community was at a standstill; that the Community had lost not only its sense of direction but, worse, its power to decide. The disease that brought disaster to the Prince of Denmark had afflicted Brussels. The European Council had, it is true, patched up a serious quarrel over the way in which the Community should be represented at the Paris Conference on International Economic Cooperation, but it found itself a few months later in deadlock over the distribution of seats in the European Parliament to be directly elected in 1978.

At the end of that European Council meeting the President, Prime Minister Gaston Thorn of Luxembourg, appeared before the European Assembly in a mood of acute depression. He said that he had been experiencing one disappointment after another. He went on: 'It is rather difficult for me to make you realise that the worrying thing after this European Council is that Europe is perhaps in worse shape than is generally thought'. Today, mercifully and wisely, less of that kind of pessimism is to be heard.

So, what is the present state of the Community?

No answer to this question will be intelligible unless one has firmly in mind the principal factors that affect the development of the Community at the present time. Foremost among these is the fact that the economic disparity between the prosperous heartland – most of the Federal Republic of Germany, the Benelux countries and parts of North and Central France – and the periphery is greater now than when the Treaty of Rome was signed in 1957. It is important in this context to recall that, in the Preamble to that Treaty, the High Contracting Parties expressed their concern to ensure the harmonious development of their economies 'by reducing the differences existing between the various regions and the backwardness of the less favoured regions'.

The second factor affecting the Community's development is the recession. This has lasted longer and has cut more deeply than most of us expected. The decline in economic activity and the rise in unemployment have not only increased the disparity between the economically strong and weak areas of the Community but have also brought into focus structural faults of which we were only dimly aware before. The recession has affected our work in another, less obvious, way. In a period of economic stress it is natural that political leaders should have their national preoccupations in the forefront of their mind. This has inevitably weakened – at least for the time being – the will to take collective political action in the internal field.

The third factor is the accession of three new members on 1 January 1973. The process of digesting these states has proved more difficult than many expected, but I believe we are now in sight of the end of the process. The problems of reconciling the material interests of the new members with those of the original Six have been difficult enough. But there has been another dimension to the problem. Many in Europe had exaggerated and, I believe, unjustified expectations of the contribution Britain would make to the Community. Others underestimated – and still do – the influence on the Community of the United Kingdom's special characteristics. For a variety of reasons the British are not easy partners to absorb. Our approach to the law is literal; our Parliament at Westminster is jealous of its powers; our sovereignty has not been compromised by defeat in war for over 900 years; over the centuries we have become intricately involved in continents beyond Europe's shores; and we have evolved our own particular methods of thought and work.

The fourth factor is the oil crisis of 1973. This added a note of urgency to the persistent demands of the Third World for a share of political power and a fair advantage from the exploitation of the world's resources. The Community has been obliged, in the face of this challenge, to develop its political as well as its economic relationship with new areas of the world outside. The 'external integrator' has often been a powerful instrument in evolving political structures. The Heptarchy became England under pressure from the Vikings. More recently, European persecution of Jews led to the establishment of the State of Israel. And the establishment of Israel has brought the Arabs into closer unity than at any time since they broke out of the Peninsula in the 7th century. Similar pressures today are stimulating the process the Community knows as 'political cooperation'.

These four factors are influencing the development of the Community against a background of social unease in each of the member states. Established precepts have been challenged. New ideas have been advanced about religion, morality, crime and punishment, and so on. Our systems based on parliamentary democracy are under scrutiny. In these circumstances it is unreasonable to expect member states of the Community to behave collectively in ways in which they feel unable to behave individually. It should therefore be no surprise that little progress has been made to date in putting into effect the programme sketched out at the Summit Conference in Paris in October 1972. This meeting took place in the euphoria generated by the successful conclusion of the Community's negotiations with the United Kingdom, Denmark, Norway and Ireland and at a time when economies were growing and the full effect of the boom in commodity prices had not yet been felt. Yet the point should be made that the targets set in 1972 were a pale reflection of the federalist ideal which animated the Community's founding fathers in the 1950s.

So what should we do? Weep for a United States of Europe gone beyond recall? Vilify our political leaders for their lack of imagination and political will? Or rail against a fate which has dealt our Europe a fistful of clubs?

I suggest we do none of these things. Instead we should accept that, for the time being, the possibilities for the Community to advance are strictly limited. We should demonstrate our respect for the magnitude of the enterprise Europe is engaged in by assessing without passion the present performance of the Community. We should above all pay close regard to the challenges of the immediate period ahead and consider not only how best these can be confronted, but also whether we cannot turn them to our collective advantage.

*   *   *

Before turning to the future it might be convenient if I were to give some account of the progress we are making today on a few of the more important aspects of our work. These fall into three categories: the Community's relations with the outside world; the further development of common policies within the Community; and the strengthening of the Community's political institutions.

Developments in the field of external relations have been substantial. Since the beginning of this year the Community has signed agreements on aid and trade with Tunisia, Algeria and Morocco. Similar agreements are now being negotiated with the Arab states of the Eastern Mediterranean. The Lomé Convention, embracing 49 African, Caribbean and Pacific countries came into force on 1 April; negotiations with three prospective members are in progress. The

Community has signed Commercial Cooperation Agreements with the four countries of South Asia. It has broken new ground by concluding with Canada an open-ended agreement for economic and commercial cooperation, and it is seeking to bring order into its relations with the Comecon countries. The Member States have increasingly adopted common positions in their dealings with the developing world, for example at UNCTAD IV in Nairobi earlier this year, and in the North-South Conference at Paris. And the Member States decided this autumn to combine in extending their fisheries limits to two hundred miles, and to conduct fisheries negotiations with third countries through the Commission.

Through these and similar actions the Community is becoming – indeed has already become – a major force on the world economic stage. Moreover, through their machinery for political cooperation the member states are increasingly coordinating their attitudes to the major political problems. Last year they voted as a bloc on 83% of the issues raised during the General Assembly of the United Nations at New York. They have devised a special framework for conducting their policy towards the Arab world – the Euro-Arab Dialogue. They are evolving a common view on East-West relations, and on southern Africa. Of course this does not add up to a common foreign policy; the Member States still retain their freedom to act independently where they think fit. Much of what goes on is unglamorous, even ephemeral, and the gradual convergence of ideas is punctuated by spectacular and often public disagreements. But in this field of external relations, reasonable progress is being made.

Internal progress is less obvious. As I have suggested, the times are not propitious for the launch of spectacular common policies such as the Customs Union and the Common Agricultural and Commercial Policies, which were the milestones of the Community's early years. Nor is an early breakthrough likely in energy policy, for example. But this does not mean that the Community is stagnant. On the contrary, new policies are constantly being developed within the existing framework. Previous decisions require practical implementation. The everyday administration of agreed policies throws up new problems which require new solutions.

Steadily and with prudence we are advancing towards a genuine common market within the Nine. The removal of tariffs and quotas was only the beginning. We are now systematically tackling the non-tariff barriers to trade. The going has been and still is hard. Industries in every country find it convenient to shelter behind national standards and specifications which make it more difficult for their competitors to break into their home market. But we have recently had a success: in July the Community agreed on eighteen further measures to remove technical barriers to trade, bringing the total to over eighty. Much negotiation both in Brussels and with the industries and a careful calculation of the swings and roundabouts preceded this agreement. More such agreed measures will be needed before the Community completes the long-term plan it drew up in 1973. We are working to remove barriers in the fields of insurance, banking, company law and public purchasing. And the common standards we are developing reinforce our ability to pursue a common external policy. We can more often present a common front to the Japanese and the Americans about vehicle standards; and the Arabs are interested in basing their common standards on those the Community is adopting. So, as the internal barriers fall, new opportunities open for enterprising firms to exploit not only the extended market, but the market in third countries as well.

A Community which is so active in the external and economic fields can hardly be dead politically, even if it is not striding out towards political union. Indeed, some political acorns have been planted in recent years which could grow into sturdy oaks. Earlier this year the Community decided to hold direct elections to the European Parliament in 1978. This decision still has to be ratified by national parliaments; awkward practical problems have to be solved; and the directly-elected Parliament, when it eventually meets, may not have quite the galvanising effect the enthusiasts would hope. But the Parliament's self-confidence will unquestionably be reinforced and, in due time, it will become a more dynamic political factor in the life of the Community.

A directly-elected Parliament will fulfil one of the ambitions of those who wrote the Treaty of Rome. But they did not intend, and might well have deplored, a further important development – the setting up of the European Council to bring the Nine Heads of State or Government together three times a year. Federalists fear that this body will usurp the Commission's role as the motor of the Community's development. My own view is that this development was inevitable. It has already proved its worth as a flexible instrument for settling disputes, overcoming obstacles, and generating new ideas. Its emergence demonstrates once again that the Community is a living political organism, perhaps the first wholly original political institution to emerge since the eighteenth century.

The activities I have described may be unspectacular. They may seem boring, even petty, to the outsider. But they are the stuff of everyday life. I see no cause for pessimism here. There are those who lament that what they call the 'construction of Europe' has halted or is even in reverse. They should remember that great edifices are built from the ground up, brick upon brick, not from the roof down.

*   *   *

The Community does not exist in a vacuum, and external challenges to its development and its integrity may arise which cannot be foreseen today. Little can be done to prepare for these. But there are two clearly visible challenges to which the Community must respond if its progress is to continue. The first is the challenge of the increasing economic disparity between member states to which I drew attention earlier. The second is the challenge of the further enlargement of the Community to embrace Greece and, no doubt in time, Portugal, Spain, and perhaps other Mediterranean countries which pass the tests specified in the Treaty. This further enlargement is, in my view, both historically inevitable and politically desirable.

There is an obvious connection between these two challenges. Further enlargement on the lines now envisaged will bring into the Community substantial territories along the northern shore of the Mediterranean where the income per capita is low by present Community standards; where a high proportion of the working population is engaged in agriculture – in Greece 34.1%, in Portugal 28% and in Spain 26.5%; and where agricultural methods are relatively backward and where the structure is such that agriculture must be regarded more as a social system than an industry. The accession of Greece, followed by that of Portugal and Spain, which will add a further fifth to the Community's population, would greatly increase the disparity between the prosperous heartland and peripheral areas of the Community.

There is another significant consideration. The accession of these southern European states is likely to take place in circumstances that are unpropitious for a particular reason. If current estimates of growth and of productivity are correct, the wealthier countries in the Community will no longer be able to absorb substantial numbers of migrants from the poorer countries and regions whose agricultural and industrial structures will begin to change in response to the disciplines of the Common Market. Over the first fifteen years or so of the Community's existence there has occurred a massive exchange of migrating labour in one direction and of financial remittances in the other. This exchange has been not only one of the motors of growth but also an equalising factor not merely within the Community, but also between the Community and its Mediterranean neighbours – witness the large numbers of Turkish workers in the

Federal Republic and of North Africans in France and the Benelux countries. This great tide is now on the ebb.

In the Regional and the Social Funds and other arrangements the Community has to hand instruments relevant to the problem I have outlined. The attempt at economic and monetary union, which might appear to be the final stepping stone of economic approximation, has awakened the Community to a problem that already existed: a consequence of economic and monetary union could well be an even stronger attraction of investment capital and other resources towards the main centres in the Community. Since, for many obvious reasons there is no probability that the Community will establish an economic and monetary union in the near future, the main emphasis meanwhile must be placed on closer co-ordination and further development of the existing instruments so that they become effective and sufficient tools for the purposes in hand.

A concentration of effort and resources on the problems of agricultural under-development on the southern periphery and of industrial decline on the north-ern periphery would entail according a lower priority to other problems. One can hear in anticipation the anguished protests of the sacred cows. However, realities once again have to be faced. The Community cannot for the time being address itself to some general scheme of social security, whether by harmonising existing national schemes or even through massive support for farm incomes in the less developed parts of the Community. This would merely finance the production of even greater agricultural surpluses. And the still serious problems of agricultural structure and under-employment, or of regional de-population in the richer areas would have to take second place.

In my view it is reasonable to conclude that the Community can continue on the path towards economic unity only if it concentrates the means at its disposal on those sectors which are critical today. A viable approach is available. This takes account of available resources and could produce results that are both effective and relevant, and will prepare the Community to face the challenges of the future. In the Community's present circumstances surely this is a reasonable ambition.

III

THE CONSTRUCTION OF EUROPE:
PRINCIPLES AND BELIEFS

CROSSROADS FOR EUROPE, BRUSSELS – 25 SEPTEMBER 1978

I have been invited to offer you a personal view of some of the crucial issues affecting the European community – in its wider sense – and to suggest how the Christian faith might influence our response to some of these issues.

The issues before the European Community today are complex, difficult and, in some cases, unfamiliar. Yet they touch us all and it is important that they should be properly understood. This implies, in the first place, acknowledging the context in which we are trying to construct Europe.

The most significant factor is the economic recession. The oil price rises of 1973 and 1974 not only shifted the terms of trade against the industrialised world for as far ahead as one can foresee, but they also drove the world economy, in the space of a few months, into the deepest and longest recession we have experienced since the 1930s. Economic growth and the expansion of trade have both been checked. The recession has coincided with the arrival on the international scene of the super-competitive; Taiwanese, Korean and Brazilian radios, shirts and shoes began to outsell our own products in our own markets.

Other factors are equally relevant. For example, the experience of recent years has invalidated many of the comfortable assumptions on which was based the remarkable recovery of the world economy from the devastation of the Second World War. There is, as a result, much scepticism today about contemporary economic theory. More serious, there is more general distrust of political dogma. And one finds in sections of the younger generation an iconoclastic attitude to long established institutions and, indeed, to authority in general. This, in turn, has led to unprecedented social experiments and new adventures in cultural expression. Apart from this, there is widespread impatience with, and even revulsion against, bureaucracy and against centralism in general. Many citizens want government to wear a human face. Then again, the sectional interest has been glorified. Lobbies advocating this or protesting against that have proliferated beyond imagining. These and other factors have combined to generate a mood of pessimism in the Western world.

None of the trends which we accept today as part of the scenery were apparent when the Treaty of Rome which established the European Economic Community was signed in 1957. European society was more cohesive and confident twenty years ago. So it was in quite different circumstances that the signatories of the Treaty of Rome proclaimed in the preamble their clear political objective when they expressed their determination 'to lay the foundations of an ever closed union among the peoples of Europe' and coined the imaginative title 'Community'.

Despite the changed context, substantial progress has been made with the work of construction. Little remains to be done to complete the common market. The Community has a common commercial policy and a common agricultural policy and, in numerous other fields, the policies of the Member States have been aligned. In 1973 the Community of the original Six was enlarged to become Nine and the process of digesting these three new members is virtually at an end.

The work of the Community touches almost every aspect of public affairs, with the notable exception of defence. Those of us involved in this work accordingly have a wide range of preoccupations. However, there are at present three which cause particular anxiety.

The first is the problem of economic and social divergence as between one part of the Community and another. In the same preamble to the Treaty of Rome which set out their overriding ambition, the signatories expressed their concern 'to strengthen the unity of their economies and to ensure their harmonious development by reducing the differences existing between the various regions and the backwardness of the less favoured regions'. Article 2 of the Treaty itself is more specific and committal. It reads:

> 'The Community shall have as its task, by establishing a common market and progressively approximating the economic policies of Member States, to promote throughout the Community a harmonious development of economic activities, a continuous and balanced expansion, an increase in stability, an accelerated raising of the standard of living and closer relations between the States belonging to it'.

From any point of view this is a laudable objective. But in no other sphere of its manifold activities has the Community failed so spectacularly. The divergence in economic performance, and therefore in living standards, within the Community is now greater than in 1957. One has only to contrast the prosperity of the so-called 'Golden Triangle' with the deprivation of parts of the periphery, for example in Ireland and southern Italy. It is only fair to add that the passages in the Treaty of Rome which I have quoted may well have raised expectations that the European Community would in some way be more successful than individual Member States in removing disparities of wealth. 'Size equals success' was a popular slogan in the 1950s. But this has since been replaced by 'small is beautiful'.

If such expectations were raised, they were surely unreasonable. Much thought and imagination has been applied to this problem of divergence. The Regional Fund, the Social Fund, the Common Agricultural Policy and the European Investment Bank are all mechanisms designed to help us towards a solution of this most intractable of problems. At Bremen last July the European Council devised yet another approach through the establishment of a Europe Monetary System and accompanying policies designed to make this durable. Despite all these efforts the problem has proved virtually impervious to treatment and remains an obstinate stain on the reputation of the Community.

The second great challenge is the forthcoming enlargement of the Community to include Greece, Portugal and Spain. The signatories of the Treaty of Rome, after stating their resolve to preserve and strengthen peace and liberty, called upon 'the other peoples of Europe who share their ideal to join their efforts'. The Treaty thus imposed a legal obligation on the Community to accept the candidature of the three new applicants. Strategic self-interest imposed a moral obligation. Accordingly, the second enlargement of the Community is a political imperative. At the same time, this further enlargement from Nine to Twelve Member States is bound to some extent to be disruptive. Given that the economies of the three candidate countries are less developed than those of the existing members, important and difficult adjustments will be required and a further strain will be placed upon the Community's machinery. But these disadvantages have to be set against the gains, many of which are incalculable.

The third challenge – and to my mind the most important – is the identification of Europe's role in the world.

From the early 1960s, when I was first involved in the European enterprise, I have had in my mind an image which has seemed to me to represent the European Community. This is an image of groups of five- and six-year olds setting off in the morning for school in their smocks, blazers or frocks, or, I suppose, nowadays their jeans, with their satchels on their backs. There they begin their instruction not only in the story of their own nation, but also in our European heritage which one day it will fall to them to preserve and adorn – a heritage which, while it owes much to the democratic idea developed in Periclean Athens, has been above all influenced by the Christian ethic.

The European heritage is not merely to be contemplated with eloquent pride. Unless we allow it to influence our contemporary actions and attitudes it will ossify. We must make of it a continuum. This heritage imposes on Western Europe, in partnership with the United States, the other legatee, a number of obligations towards the rest of the world. It was no part of the intentions of those who established the Community that it should be a fat men's club. Early in its life the Community accepted its obligations towards the Third World; these are political, economic and social in character. If it is unacceptable that within the Community itself there should be disparities in living standards between the prosperous heartland and the periphery, it would be all the more intolerable if, again in the words of the Treaty of Rome, the member states of the Community were to 'ensure the economic and social progress of their countries' and constantly to improve 'the living and working conditions of their peoples' without regard to the plight of the great mass of our fellow human beings in the developing world.

The Community is entitled to say that it has paid more than lip service to its obligations in this respect. A network of relationships with countries of the Third World has been established. The Lomé Convention, through which 53 countries in Africa, the Caribbean and the Pacific are associated with the Community, is the most spectacular example. But there are also the Generalised Preference Schemes and other specific arrangements which give tangible benefits, including the transfer of resources and technology, to developing countries.

But this cannot be the end of the story. It is indeed no more than the beginning. The distribution of largesse is the easy part. Difficulties arise when developing countries seek outlets for the products of the industries they have established with European aid. We have to accept the logic of the situation. But when these products undercut the products of our own industries which may already be in difficulty, the logic of the situation, expressed in human terms, can spell heartbreak on the one hand and frustration on the other. How can we satisfy the legitimate aspirations of the developing countries when an increasing number of our own young people – those who set out ten or twelve years earlier with their satchels on their backs to discover their European heritage – find that they have no secure future? No less than 37% of the unemployed in the Community are under 25 years of age and the unemployment rate in the 16 to 20 year age group at 17% is three times the Community average.

This seems an over-long prologue to my answer to the question I was set – namely, how might the Christian faith influence our response to the issues of today? May I comment first in vicious terms? If, in facing the challenges I have described – the divergence in living standards, the absorption into the Community of the three candidate members and the definition of the Community's role in the world – we are animated by avarice, envy, complacency, selfishness and indifference, we will make no progress and, in due time, the sins of the fathers will be visited upon another generation. This point hardly needs making. If on the other hand, we have in mind the second of the two commandments on which hang all the law and the prophets, we can at least begin to see the way forward.

Apart from this, we should pay less regard to the day-to-day detail of life and work in the Community and focus our attention on the underlying principles of the founding fathers. They believed, no doubt subconsciously influenced by Karl Marx, that the Europe of tomorrow had to be constructed on an economic base. This explains the presence of the word 'economic' in the original title of the Community established by the Treaty of Rome and why the preamble seems to be preoccupied with Mammon. But their purpose, as I have said, was political. They wanted Europe to realise her full potential and to regain the power and influence she had lost through two crippling wars. By this means they hoped Europe could assume a role in the world consistent with, and worthy of, our heritage. Lest we become preoccupied to the point of obsession with the economic problems which face us, we should more often remind ourselves that the economic objectives set out in the Treaty were no more than a means to an end. It is incumbent on its present leaders to hand over the European Community to the next generation in a condition which will enable its higher principles to be achieved. 'I am come that they may have life and that they might have it more abundantly'.

May I therefore end on a virtuous, and I hope, a practical note? The issues we face in the European Community are complex, difficult and, in some cases, unfamiliar. Those who wrestle with them in the European Council, the Council of Ministers and the Commission have an unenviable task, particularly since the context in which they work is today so different from the 1950s. If public opinion in the Member States of the Community can be encouraged to regard their efforts with more tolerance, patience and understanding, I believe they would more readily produce beneficial results. Each one of us can make a personal contribution which would help them.

IV

DISTURBING TRENDS

DEUTSCH-BRITISCHE GESELLSCHAFT
NUREMBERG – OCTOBER 1979

The environment in which the founding fathers took the first steps towards the integration of Western Europe was far more amiable than that which exists today. The processes of reconstruction and reconciliation after the cataclysm were far advanced. The rate of economic growth, stimulated by actions of unparalleled magnanimity on the part of the United States, was high. Inflation was under control and the prospects for employment were good. Communist expansion westwards had been checked and the North Atlantic Alliance had successfully withstood its first challenge – the blockade of Berlin. The immense task of dismantling the colonial empires – a task which was not only politically desirable but also morally just – was well under way. These various factors induced in the governments and peoples of Western Europe a justified self-confidence and optimism. Success would breed success. The rosy dawn held the promise of brilliant perspectives.

The context in which the institutions of the Community operate today could scarcely be more different. The international political environment is seriously troubled, if not positively hostile. The Warsaw Pact countries continue to build up their military strength. Events in Africa, South-East Asia and elsewhere demonstrate that the Soviet Union, which spends up to three times as much of its GDP on defence as we do, continues its opportunistic exploitation of other peoples' conflicts. Human rights are violated across the world. In scores of countries governments systematically practise physical torture. Terrorism has become commonplace in states which adhere to the principles of parliamentary democracy and freedom within the law.

In the economic sphere too conditions are unpropitious. Inflation gnaws away at our hard-won prosperity. The high rate of unemployment, especially among the young, is a constant reproach. The developing countries, who put us on notice at Bandung in 1955 that they would want a fairer share of the world's wealth, pursue their demands for more say in the management of the world economy, for better access to our markets, and for a more generous flow of technology. There has emerged recently from their ranks a number of so-called 'super-competitives' whose exports, notably of textiles, put our own already sorely-pressed industries under special strain.

There are other contemporary phenomena unfamiliar to the founding fathers. Our people, and especially the young, are concerned to check the desecration and pollution of our physical environment. Then again, in most of our countries, many essential tasks are performed by immigrant labour. The presence of this labour force in our society is indispensable to the smooth running of many enterprises and our public utilities in particular. But the different customs and traditions these immigrants bring with them raise delicate social issues which call for tact, understanding and tolerance.

The characteristics of the context in which the Community operates today are, for the most part, the product of trends which cannot be reversed. There will be no return to the comfortable, reassuring circumstances of the 1950s. And we should be wise to expect the problems that confront us to become even more complex and less tractable.

*   *   *

In the Preamble to the Treaty of Rome the founding fathers identified areas where progress had to be made if the ambition of ever closer union among the peoples of Europe was to be achieved. These included the elimination of the barriers which divided Europe; the constant improvement of living and working conditions; balanced and fair competition; a reduction in the differences between the different regions and in the backwardness of the less favoured; the progressive abolition of restrictions on international trade; and increased solidarity between Europe and countries overseas. They also called on like-minded peoples of Europe to join in their endeavour.

Many of these aims have been accomplished. There is a success story here of which the Community can be proud. But other objectives have not been attained, for example as regards the Community's response to the energy crisis. The rates of growth and inflation and the state of employment are all causes for concern.

However, there is another field where the Community's failure is even more marked. Today regional imbalances within the Community are as great as ever. Of course, each member state has the prime responsibility for solving its own economic problems. Nor would anyone claim that persistent regional and structural problems can be solved by indiscriminate use of taxpayers' money, either at national or Community level. Community resources through the Regional and Social Funds have a role to play; and it is arguable that these Funds are still too small. The British Government does not seek massive transfers of resources from the Community, for instance for the regeneration of some sectors of British industry. Nor do we seek large increases in the Community Budget. But we cannot accept that the efforts of any Member State to tackle its economic problems should be rendered more difficult by the budgetary problems within the Community.

Yet that is precisely the situation in which the United Kingdom finds itself. By 1978 the UK would already have been the largest net contributor to the Community Budget but for the transitional provisions of the Accession Treaty. You will recall with what vehemence the view has been expressed in this country that Germany, as the paymaster of Europe, should have a major say in the way Community money was spent, or not spent. By next year the United Kingdom, not the Federal Republic, will be the largest net contributor to the Budget, paying over £1 billion – that is some 49% more than the Federal Republic. By 1982 the United Kingdom's net contribution could be as much as £1½ billion.

Opinion in the United Kingdom is unanimous that this situation is inequitable and unacceptable. I have heard it argued that, with North Sea oil, the United Kingdom is too well off for this large net contribution to be a problem. North Sea oil is no more relevant to the argument than any other resource, agriculture, for example. Is Mexico with its abundance of oil to be regarded as rich and Japan or Denmark poor? In terms of Gross Domestic Product per head, the UK is seventh out of the Nine. For the Community to treat the UK as its biggest single source of finance, and on an increasing scale each year, is manifestly unfair and invites a crisis.

The problem arises from the way the Community raises its revenues and the way it spends them. The revenues are the Community's own resources – the proceeds of nationally collected customs duties and agricultural levies, plus up to 1% of the Value Added Tax – VAT. Of the Community's expenditure no less than 75% goes to agriculture; less than 10% is distributed amongst other Community policies, the rest being used to meet administrative and other expenses. Far and away the most serious cause of the trouble is the disproportionate provision for agriculture in the Community Budget and the fact that the UK benefits so little from this agricultural expenditure; less than 8% is disbursed in the UK. One example will illustrate my main point. In 1977 the UK received £20 million from the Regional

Fund; in that same year the UK contributed £23 million as its share of support for the olive oil regime alone.

Nowhere are the excesses of the CAP more readily condemned than here in Germany. The last major stocktaking of the CAP in 1975 was the personal initiative of Chancellor Schmidt; sadly this led nowhere. The problem is complex. For all its faults the CAP has contributed to social stability in Europe and has preserved a way of life and a countryside which are important for the wellbeing of future generations. But individual Member States – and especially the richer – must ask themselves whether the substantial subsidisation of their farming communities, through the unrequited transfer of wealth from the poorer Member States, can be justified on social or political grounds.

Changes in the Common Agricultural Policy are needed not simply because of the manifest absurdities which arise from the present arrangements, but also because the future health of the Community requires this. It is surely against common sense, against the interests of our peoples and bad for the Community's reputation and future development that so high a proportion of the common budget of so many of the industrialised nations of the world should be spent on agriculture. This distortion stultifies the evolution of other Community policies and ultimately undermines confidence and credibility.

*   *   *

The balance sheet of the European Community's successes and failures reflects the history of the past two decades. Nothing, however, can diminish the achievement of the representatives of the original Six in so rapidly reaching agreement on the Treaty of Rome. Yet it is worth recalling that they did not start with a blank page. A major step in the process of European cohesion was the proposal by the French foreign minister of the day for a coal and steel Community. Here I have in mind not the Schuman Plan of 1950, but rather the suggestion made by Louis Loucheur in 1927 which formed part of that movement for European cooperation which drew so much of its inspiration from French statesmen such as Aristide Briand and Edouard Herriot in the 1930s. The course they followed had already been charted in, for example, the pan-European Union of the early 1920s which looked to what the Treaty of Rome, in the first phrase of its Preamble, was a generation later to proclaim as the foundation of an ever closer union among the peoples of Europe. The Europeans of the 1950s had this lead to follow. And when they chose as their instrument a common market and a community based on a customs union, they were drawing on the historical and empirical experience of the binding force – both economic and political – of a Zollverein, as well as the perceived economic benefits of other forms of trade liberalisation, as in the Organisation for Economic Cooperation and Development and the Benelux.

Establishing a common market and constructing a community on the basis of a customs union were the tasks of the first hours, and the founding fathers fashioned the appropriate instruments. And they did so at a time when NATO was a shield from which the pristine brilliance had not yet faded. The security the Alliance afforded reinforced our social and political self-assurance.

The complexity of our societies today and the fact that, with economic interdependence, the solution to many of our problems is beyond our control, oblige us to proceed with the construction of Europe patiently – brick upon brick. By the same token, it is obvious that a common market and a community based on a customs union constitute an inadequate response to the challenges of today. That is why we have long since had to venture into uncharted territory. That is why it falls so often to the European Council to provide the motivation for our work.

The empiricism of the Community's present-day approach to the problems we face – whether it is the energy crisis, the threat to our environment, how we are to pay our way in the world in years to come, the demands of the developing world, or the numerous other issues on which we concert our attitudes in Political Cooperation – this empirical approach has much to commend it. But it too may prove inadequate.

It may be that, over time, the European Council will identify the substance of the next phase of the construction of Europe, just as the architects of the Treaties of Paris and Rome did for the earlier stage. It is perhaps too soon to speculate as to what the substance might be. But certain factors are clearly relevant. We must not, for instance, allow our concern with money and jobs – and it is this concern which, reasonably enough, underlies many of our problems – to create the impression of a Community preoccupied with the material. Nor should we ignore our many strengths: the stability and freedom of our institutions and our respect for the individual – strengths which we tend to shroud with unbecoming modesty. Could we not articulate a message of confidence in these priceless attributes of our way of life and link with this a practical expression of our determination to defend them? In this way we might add a new dimension to the construction of Europe and thereby inspire other groupings of nations who may wish to follow our example.

V

EUROPE AND SOUTH EAST ASIA

SEMINAR ORGANISED BY THE SCHOOL OF ORIENTAL AND AFRICAN STUDIES AND THE FOREIGN AND COMMONWEALTH OFFICE: LONDON – DECEMBER 1985

When, in November 1977, the Ambassadors of the members of the Association of South East Asian Nations (ASEAN) sat down for the first time with the Committee of Permanent Representatives of the European Community in Brussels to institute a dialogue, the political importance of the occasion was evident to all of us. The ASEAN representatives pressed for a meeting at ministerial level. This took place a year later. Apart from the economic and commercial benefits to which each side was looking forward, the mere fact that ministers of the two regional groupings met was acknowledged to be significant. The ASEAN Ministers made it clear that they did not regard the process of integration in Europe as a model for South East Asia; the differences between the two situations were too great. But at least the European enterprise could serve as an example, perhaps even an inspiration. In individual conversations I found my ASEAN counterparts especially interested in the Community's methods of reconciling differences between member states. Experience in their own organisation had underlined the importance of political motivation if national interests were to be subordinated to collective interests.

This is of course the key to all effective cooperation between states, as the history of alliances and coalitions through the ages testifies. The European Community is the most ambitious, sophisticated and complex enterprise of this kind the world has seen and the prospects for the next period ahead should be assessed in the light of shifts in the balance of national interests within the Community.

*   *   *

1985 has been a year of achievement for the European Community. The way is now clear for the accession of Portugal and Spain next year. The problem of British contributions to the budget has been disposed of, at least for the time being. A timetable has been set for the removal of all the Community's internal barriers. Following the bold measures taken in 1984 to deal with surplus milk production, the Commission has drawn up a comprehensive plan for re-shaping the Common Agricultural Policy; this contains proposals which many have regarded hitherto as heresy. A long-overdue attempt is being made to improve the Community's working procedures. In the Community generally productivity and profits have risen, inflation has declined and most member states enjoy a surplus on their current accounts.

All who wish the European enterprise well will hope that 1985 will prove to be an important milestone in the Community's development. It appears, on the face of it, that the problems raised by the accession of the United Kingdom in 1973 have at last been settled to the general satisfaction and that the Community is now well placed to confront the challenges of the present and future.

For those not involved day by day in the work of the Community, it must seem extraordinary that these problems should have persisted for so long. The truth is that all processes of integration take time. The thirteen American colonies which declared their independence in 1776 did not settle the main elements of their future relationship until 1789 – and how uncomplicated were economic and social issues in those days compared to our own. The Community's experience, while it should be seen in historical perspective, has lessons not only for the future evolution of the Community itself but also for other regional groupings.

I have no doubt that that the difficulties the Community has had to contend with over the past twelve years stem from three major political errors committed in the 1950s and 60s. The first of these occurred in 1954 when the French National Assembly rejected the Treaty establishing the European Defence Community. The second was Britain's decision to stand aside when the European Economic Community and Euratom were being created. The third was President de Gaulle's veto on the entry of the United Kingdom in 1963.

One consequence of the last of these regrettable decisions was foreseeable at the time. Neither Britain and the other three candidate countries on the one hand, nor France's partners in the Community on the other, were willing to accept de Gaulle's veto as the last word; sooner or later the Community was bound to be enlarged. Yet in the interval the Community could not stagnate, and it was likely to develop in ways which would make the accession of new members more rather than less difficult. And so it proved. In the ten years between the veto and the entry of the United Kingdom, Denmark and Ireland in 1973, the Six adopted three policies in particular – the Common Agricultural Policy, the Own Resources System and the Common Fisheries Policy – in forms which, reasonably enough, accommodated their interests but were highly disadvantageous to Britain. Had there been no French veto and had these policies been constructed with the full participation of the United Kingdom, a different balance would have been struck.

It was inevitable therefore, that, regardless of the terms of entry, much time would be spent after Britain's accession on adjusting the balance. Nobody can tolerate indefinitely a situation he believes to be unfair and he will persist until the burden is eased. This explains much of Britain's effort over the past several years. In 1983 a new and more equitable fisheries policy was adopted. This year the grievance over contributions to the budget has been removed. If it is a correct appreciation that the painful process of absorbing the United Kingdom into the Community has been completed, then the Community's energies can be devoted to other immediate challenges. These include not only the budget for 1986, the completion of the common market, the restructuring of the Common Agricultural Policy, but also the question of the way in which decisions are taken in the Community.

In facing these challenges, the Community will also have to absorb two new members. For fifty years, when it was under dictators, Europe beyond the Pyrenees was a separate entity. Now, the enlarged Community of representative democracies, with a population of 320 million, will export three times as much as the United States and seven times as much as Japan. The United States and Japan will each have one language; the Community will have nine. Mediterranean interests will be powerfully represented and the cost of supporting Spanish and Portuguese farmers after the transitional period will place yet another strain on the Community's finances. Spanish and Portuguese links with Latin America will fortify the Community's interest in that continent to their mutual benefit.

* * *

In every move towards the integration of sovereign states, those who carry the prime responsibility have to accept that interests do not lie. Of course, a nation's interests change from time to time – and attitudes change with them. The achievements and disappointments of the past year have emphasised certain differences in approach to the Community of the member states. Italy, the Benelux countries and Ireland still display their attachment to the idealism of the founding fathers. Public opinion in Denmark – the only Scandinavian member of the Community whose centre of gravity has shifted steadily south towards the Mediterranean – is still deeply divided about the Community; this is reflected in caution over suggestions for institutional or constitutional advance. Greece, not as favourably disposed towards the United States as the rest of the Ten and more ready to condone Soviet misconduct, is a special case. The United Kingdom, rid at last of the tedious budget problem, is adopting a more positive attitude towards Community affairs; London has produced an abundant crop of proposals designed to prepare the Community for the tasks ahead. Characteristically, these are severely practical, inspired as they are by traditions of case law rather than the Code Napoleon, and they eschew the rhetoric which is unremarkable in the Romance languages but tends to cause Anglo-Saxon toes to curl.

* * *

The close partnership between France and Germany has been the critical element in the Community's development regardless of which political party has been in power in Paris and Bonn. The original balance of interests on which the Community was founded has been continuously updated. However, over the past several months anxieties have been expressed over the attitude of the Federal Republic. These have been prompted partly by political developments inside Germany and partly by the painful reaction there to the fortieth anniversary of the end of the war in Europe and to Soviet charges of revanchism. The passage of forty years has produced a new generation which accepts no responsibility for the past, but is no less conscious that the German nation is divided. The reconciliation which the creation of the European community achieved is a fact of life and what the Community offers today becomes more important than what it represents. The German refusal to accept this year's agreement on cereal prices added to existing anxieties. Until then the Federal Republic had been relied upon, even on matters which touched important national interests, to accept the majority view at the end of the day.

It is not only in Germany that questions are being asked about the role of the Community in the 1980s and 90s. In the past the answer has been clear. The founding fathers and their contemporaries, who had had personal experience of two European wars, were convinced of the need for Franco-German reconciliation. The succeeding generation was equally committed to removing the possibility of a renewal of Europe's civil war. But they had another ambition. They wanted Europe to recover the influence it had lost with the emergence of the two super-powers. This ambition has not been fulfilled and there is little prospect that it will be in the short term. The youth of today have other preoccupations – the future of work, the protection of the environment, disparities in standards of life within advanced societies, and between industrialised and developing countries.

If the European Community is not seen to be acting effectively in fields which concern them, the young will question its relevance.

Those on the political fringe – the racists of the extreme right, the hard left, the 'greens', the so-called peace campaigners – have a clear idea of the kind of Europe they wish to see. For those who occupy the middle ground of European politics there is today no obvious guiding light, especially since change is the order of the day. Within the Community the process of change has been striking. With the decline of those industries which used to be the engines of economic growth, unemployment in some areas has risen to unacceptable levels. Economic activity is being undertaken by more, and generally smaller, enterprises. The state has moved out of large sectors of manufacturing industry and of many utilities. Trade unions are uncertain about their role in the new circumstances. World wide, prosperity has followed in the wake of higher productivity made possible by technological advances. The gap between richer and poorer nations has widened. No clear structure has replaced the world economic system based on the dominance of the United States which came to an end in the early 1970s. The United States has not yet accepted the consequences of the relative reduction in its power, and neither the Europeans nor the Japanese have recognised that they have an enhanced role to play if a more equitable and relevant balance is to be struck in the democratic world between the United States, Europe and Japan. If European leaders were prepared to assume this responsibility on behalf of the Community and encourage the necessary changes of attitude in the United States and Japan, the younger generation might come to regard the Community in a more positive light.

* * *

A fair and mutually beneficial economic and commercial relationship with Japan is only one of many interests which the ASEAN and the European Community share. Both attach importance to economic and social progress, to political stability, the free trading system and the encouragement of investment. Consultation at regular intervals has made it easier for each side to see the problems from the point of view of the other, and each can carry the benefit into its own consultations within the Organisation for Economic Cooperation and Development on the one hand and the Group of 77 and the Non-Aligned Movement on the other.

None of this could have been foreseen when Mr Edward Heath, then the British Prime Minister, visited Paris in May 1971 to discuss with President Pompidou the terms for the entry of the United Kingdom into the European Community. The talks between the two leaders covered not only specific problems such as access for New Zealand butter and the role of sterling, but also the way in which each wanted the Community to develop. Both were determined that the Community should play an active world role and they accepted that France and the United Kingdom carried a special historical responsibility for promoting the Community's relations with the developing world. Mr Heath's host on that occasion was Sir Christopher (now Lord) Soames, then the British Ambassador in Paris. It was fitting therefore that, when the United Kingdom joined the Community in 1973, Sir Christopher should become Vice-President of the Commission with responsibility for external relations. In this capacity he visited South East Asia in 1973 and 1974. He took back to Brussels the message that the members of ASEAN preferred to develop their relations with the Community on a regional basis; this entailed waiting until ASEAN's internal arrangements enabled it to think in terms of a Cooperation Agreement between the two regions.

This proved to be a wise decision, but not only for the reasons which led to it. In the intervening years the European Community has come to regard cooperation between geographical regions or groupings of states as the surest way to economic progress. This view is confirmed by a glance at the multilateral forums in which North-South relations have been debated. Neither successive United Nation Conferences on Trade and Development, nor the Special Assemblies convened to discuss a new international economic order, nor the Conference on International Economic Cooperation called by President Giscard d'Estaing in 1975 to discuss energy and development, nor the Committee of the Whole which undertook the so-called Global Negotiations in 1981 – none of these has produced the results developing countries desired. The same is true of those international agencies which have strayed from the technical issues which are their stock-in-trade into the field of development. There are various reasons for this. The demands of the developing country participants in international conferences often represent the more extreme point of view. Developed countries, preoccupied with the effects of industrial adjustments and recession, have not been in a generous state of mind these past ten years or more. Apart from this, the size of these conferences is a disadvantage. The highest common factor among 150 participants is likely to be depressingly low. Practical progress is more likely when attendance is restricted to those directly concerned, when precise proposals are discussed and all concerned are prepared to contribute on the basis of shared interest. The European-ASEAN forum fulfils these requirements.

Since the Joint Cooperation Agreement was signed in 1980 valuable progress has been made in the commercial, economic and development fields and the two groups have been able to align their foreign policies on a number of important issues. Both sides are entitled to regard the relationship as a success. But it must remain dynamic. It needs to be nourished. Cooperation should become not only deeper but wider as well. Efforts must continue to be made to improve access to markets and to attract investment. Cooperation in other fields can be fruitful, for example in research and development, and the transfer of technology. Indonesia has concluded agreements with three members of the community – France, Germany and the United Kingdom – on scientific and technological cooperation. This is a good example to follow. Then there is the whole field of training. The ASEAN's most priceless asset is its people. Their immense talents need to be further developed. The Community can help over training at all levels, and especially at the level of managers for both the private sector and the public service. Ideas for new fields for collaboration are to be put forward, such as the recent suggestions for joint efforts in culture, social development and health. These should be sympathetically considered.

The time may well have come for the Community and the ASEAN to think in terms of collaborative efforts in some less developed countries, where the achievements of ASEAN countries in devising solutions to their own problems and adapting Community technologies to their own circumstances could be relevant. Joint actions of this kind would give practical expression to the value of the relationship. Just as, at an earlier stage, the European Community served as an example and perhaps an inspiration to the architects of the ASEAN, so might the relationship which has evolved between the two groupings inspire other regions of the world. The example ASEAN and the Community have set should be a major contribution to economic and social progress in the developing world.

VI

EUROPEAN UNION AND THE ARAB WORLD

CONFERENCE OF ARAB CHAMBERS OF COMMERCE, INDUSTRY AND AGRICULTURE – RABAT, MAY 1992

In his film *Rashomon* the great Japanese director, Akira Kurosawa, tells a tragic love story from the point of view of each of the three individuals involved. Of course the three stories differ in significant respects. The conclusion Kurosawa wishes us to draw is that truth has many facets. And so it is with the European Community. Depending on whether one is a citizen of one of the members states, or a candidate member, a trading partner, or a commercial rival, one will form a particular view about the Community. So it happens that, at one and the same time, the Community can arouse pride, admiration, apprehension – even envy. In the light of this, it may be helpful if, at the outset, I recall certain facts about the Community which may make some of its activities and policies more comprehensible.

The motive for the creation of the European Community lay in the widespread determination to end for ever the civil war which, over several centuries, caused so much misery, death and destruction in Europe. First the Spaniards, then the French, then the Germans had attempted to establish their hegemony over the continent. From time to time the British left their island fastness to intervene, successfully as it turned out, to prevent this. But the cost in lives and treasure was enormous. After the Second World War a handful of wise and ingenious men discussed various means of breaking the vicious circle of violence. They concluded that, by combining in a single entity the heavy industries which had fuelled the military machines, further war in western Europe would be rendered impossible. The Schuman Plan, which brought into being the European Coal and Steel Community in 1952, led inexorably to the Treaty of Rome which established the European Economic Community of six members in 1958.

The notable aspect of these events is that, though they were political acts, the instruments chosen to achieve the political objectives European leaders had in mind were economic and commercial. This reflected the conviction of the founding fathers that economic integration was the only sound basis for political unity, even though this meant that the process would be difficult and long-drawn out. The outstanding Belgian and European statesman of the immediate post-war period, describing the negotiations which led to the signature of the Treaty of Rome, told Edward Heath: 'We started out to build a new Europe and we finished up, months later, in a smoke-filled room arguing about the tariff on bananas'.

The European Community as it is today has been constructed by placing brick upon brick. Some of these bricks have been small – but no less essential to the structure.

The second important fact about the Community is its evolutionary character. The Treaty of Rome and the Treaty of Maastricht both refer to 'ever closer union among the peoples of Europe'. In this sense the Community is a political concept without precedent in human history. Each new stage in the development of the Community – the successive enlargements of its membership, first in 1973 (which brought in Denmark, Ireland and the United Kingdom), then in 1981 (which added Greece) and, most recently, in 1986 (which added Spain and Portugal); the adoption of the Single European Act, which entered into force in 1987 and provided for the creation of a Single Market by the end of this year; and the decision at Maastricht last December to establish a European Union and to move towards monetary union – all of these advances were the product of agreements patiently, and sometimes, painfully, negotiated among the governments of the member states. Acute observers will have noted that, whatever the aspirations of some sections of European opinion, the Community's ultimate destination – if indeed there is one, has, quite deliberately, never been precisely defined in any of these arguments.

The other notable characteristic of the Community is the creative tension between the European Commission in Brussels, which represents the point of view of the Community as a whole, and the Council of Ministers, representing the interests of the member states.

One of the strengths of the Community is that, despite its size and complexity, its institutional framework is remarkably simple. Each of the four main institutions is able to exercise its authority, which is clearly defined and real, not notional, throughout the Community. Any other grouping of states which may be tempted to regard the European experiment as a model for their own closer integration will wish to take careful note of this essential characteristic.

Over the years its gradualistic approach has enabled the Community to widen the scope of its responsibilities – known in the Brussels jargon as 'Community competence'. From the early days of customs union and common commercial and agricultural policies, the Community has raised its ambitions and now seeks to act as one over a wide range, notably in what might be described as the social sector. Political cooperation – the effort to align the foreign policies of the member states – which had operated since 1970 on the basis of intergovernmental agreements, was given legal status in the Single European Act and security cooperation was added at Maastricht.

Progress has been possible because each member state, on acceding to the Community, accepted voluntarily that consensus based on compromise offered the only realistic way forward. In practice this means that national concessions have had to be made for the sake of the greater good of the Community. This, in turn, means suffering an immediate disadvantage in order to achieve a longer term advantage; and tolerating pain in one sector of the national economy in exchange for some compensating benefit in another. This process of give and take calls for political courage; all decisions of the Council have to be defended by individual ministers when they return to their capitals and have to justify their actions, including any concessions they may have made, before their own parliaments and public opinion.

On the face of it the Community is a success story. Europe is still and will long remain a grouping of separate nations. Each speaks it own language. All cherish the customs and traditions they inherited from the tribes from which they were originally created. Despite this, the relationship between the peoples of western Europe is closer today than ever before. The younger generation have a strong sense of their European identity and little patience with nationalist prejudices. The platform on which relative prosperity and favourable prospects rest is, of course, the fact that the Community has become a major economic power and a market of prime importance.

Not surprisingly, beneath the surface there are problems to address. The Treaty of Maastricht did not end the debate about sovereignty; it merely changed the context. The notion of 'subsidiarity', which is one of the most appropriate definitions of federalism, was accepted last December. This means in theory that sovereignty – in the sense of authority to decide – is to be divided horizontally into layers and that, in consequence, decisions will be taken at the lowest effective level, whether this be local, regional, national, or at the level of the Community. In practice, however, this may not totally discourage tendencies towards centralism in Brussels. The efficient functioning of the Commission services and the political accountability of the Community institutions are other issues which deserve careful attention. And it is clear from the shameful turn of events in what was Yugoslavia that the Community's political cooperation is not yet an effective diplomatic instrument.

None of these problems, however, is a prime cause for concern. By far the most serious challenge facing the European Community is how best to respond to the new international situation created by the end of the Cold War.

* * *

From its earliest days the European Community has given high priority to its relations with other regions of the world and its close neighbours in particular. A process will soon begin which will lead to the accession to the Community as full members of Sweden and Austria. In due course other countries in western and central Europe will also join when the necessary conditions have been met.

The proximity of the Arab world has made it a region of special concern to the European Community. Arab countries are a valuable market for European goods and expertise and a vital source of oil. Instability, political upheaval and conflict in the region can threaten these interests. It follows therefore that the Community should consider it a matter of common prudence, as well as good neighbourliness, to contribute constructively to the stability and prosperity of the region. Specifically, it is an aim of Community policy to encourage cooperation both within and between the region and the Community.

The framework within which the Community has been conducting its relations with the Arab world consisted originally of two elements – the Euro-Arab Dialogue, instituted after the Arab-Israel war and oil crisis of 1973 and 1974, and the network of bilateral cooperation agreements which form the major part of the Community's so-called 'overall Mediterranean policy', first developed in 1971 and 1972.

The first of these has unfortunately not met the aspirations of its initiators, partly because each side had its own perception of the nature and purpose of the Dialogue and partly because political considerations interfered with attempts to identify areas where practical progress could be made. Since the Gulf War, efforts have been made to revive the Dialogue and it is to be hoped that the specialised working committees which are meeting this year will produce positive results.

The cooperation agreements with Morocco, Algeria, Egypt, Syria and Jordan contain two distinct provisions: development assistance (consisting of direct grants and loans from the European Investment Bank) and preferential trade arrangements under which the Arab countries' exports enjoy a measure of access to the Community market. The financial resources allocated to the Arab world were increased as a result of a review of the Community's 'overall Mediterranean policy' in 1989 and specific funds have been reserved exclusively for regional projects.

The results of the Community's Mediterranean policy so far have been modest. It is a sad fact that the facility available through financial protocols for regional cooperative projects for the five-year period 1986 to 1991 has not been used and, as a result, not a single project involving two or more countries of the region was financed by the Community.

The shortcomings of the existing policy have prompted the Community to shift the emphasis away from purely bilateral agreements towards arrangements with sub-regional groupings of states. Welcome progress is now being made in devising an institutional framework for relations between the Community and the Gulf Cooperation Council. The Community would welcome a similar arrangement at some stage with the Arab Maghreb Union.

Two other cooperative projects have been suggested. The first is a proposal put forward by Spain and Italy in 1990 for a Conference on Security and Cooperation in the Mediterranean. The second is known as the 'Five-plus-Five' – an arrangement devised in 1988 for identifying areas for cooperation between five southern members of the Community and the five states of the Maghreb. The agenda includes debt, migration, technological development, and transport and communication.

*   *   *

It must be admitted that, from the point of view of the European Community, the results of efforts to promote cooperation with and within the Arab world have fallen short of expectation. Rather than speculate about the reasons for this it would be more profitable, in my view, to consider what policies might yield better results in future.

There are several reasons for such an approach. In the first place, while the end of the Cold War removed many of the factors which, for forty years, had inhibited action at the international level, it will be some time before the components of any new world order can be identified. At the same time, new uncertainties have

arisen, especially through economic hardship and the revival of nationalist sentiment in the former communist empire. Meanwhile there must be a danger that
the attention of the European Community and other OECD countries will focus
on the new democracies in central and eastern Europe to the disadvantage of
developing countries. Such a tendency would not serve the interests of the wider
international community and must be resisted. And, finally, the Gulf War
reminded us all that inter-state rivalries in the Arab world can still threaten world
peace.

None of these factors should be allowed to impair cooperation between the
European Community and the Arab world. On the contrary, a robust political
relationship, underpinned by strong economic, commercial, social and cultural
ties, is today an even more important common interest. The present is therefore
an appropriate moment to consider the future shape of this relationship.

In this conference hall there is a wealth of experience and wisdom. You will have
your own ideas, both general and specific, about the best way forward.
Nonetheless, I hope you will not think me impertinent if I offer a few personal
reflections on how the relationship between the Community and the Arab world
might be enhanced. In doing so I assume that, for practical purposes, the Arab
world should be considered as having four main dimensions – the Gulf; the Arab-
Israel dimension; the Mashriq; and the Maghreb. I also assume that the closer
economic integration of the Arab world, which the Community regards as highly
desirable and to which the Arab League has aspired for over forty years, is most
likely to be achieved through sub-regional integration in the first instance.

I believe that, when presenting their new ideas for Community policy towards the
Arab world to the Council of Ministers behind the closed doors of the
Charlemagne Building, the hand of the Commission would be immeasurably
strengthened if they could say, for example, that the countries of one of the Arab
sub-regions were embarking on a bold policy of economic development, integration and diversification. In answer to questions from sceptical Ministers round
the table as to what this bold policy consisted of, the Commission would need to
offer convincing replies. It happens that an organisation with which I am associated has recently been examining these issues and has put forward a number of
concrete ideas of the kind the Commission would be glad to quote as evidence in
support of their proposals. I cite these as personal suggestions which you might
wish to consider:

first, a programme of trade liberalisation both within the sub-region and

towards the outside world in preparation for the creation of a free trade
area and, eventually, a customs union;

second, as a complement to trade liberalisation, a plan to harmonise
social and economic policies;

third, preparation for free movement of capital and labour within the
sub-region;

fourth, a plan for gradual convergence of fiscal policy, tax structures and
systems of monetary control; and

fifth, a study of mechanisms, similar to the Community's structural
funds, for compensating sectors which suffer as a result of progressive
economic integration.

Against the background of such a positive programme, the Commission would be
well placed to propose to the Council the kind of contributions the Community
itself might make to a re-invigorated relationship.

I have little doubt that in the circumstances I have envisaged the Commission
would already have been asked by representatives of the sub-region to provide
from the Community's resources technical and administrative advice for those
charged with the tasks of economic development, diversification and integration.

Inevitably the Commission would also have been urged – and reasonably enough
– to secure improved access to the Community's markets for Arab products. Here,
may I make a general observation: pressure to open its markets is likely to be
more effective if the Arab world can increase its attractiveness to the Community
as a trading partner. This can be achieved in a number of ways. First and foremost, the more Arab countries cooperate one with another the easier it is for the
Community to enter into a mutually beneficial relationship with them. But this
is not all. Conditions can be created which will encourage more joint ventures
with the European private sector. These have several advantages: they bring in
additional investment capital; they help to disseminate management skills; and
they foster valuable personal relationships at working level. More specifically,
investment in communications, and especially telecommunications, is seen as evidence of serious intent, not only to develop and diversify, but also to participate
actively in the fastest growing sectors of the world economy.

There are other ways, apart from better access to markets, in which the Community might be prepared to contribute to the effectiveness of a new policy. As part of a combined effort, the Community's Arab partners might therefore look for an increase in Community resources devoted to the region. They might expect the Community to streamline procedures for the provision of advice, technical assistance and the delivery of funds. I should also hope that such contributions by the Community would be enhanced by a programme of cultural and other exchanges designed to remove misunderstandings, to allay apprehensions and to promote relationships of mutual confidence and respect, especially among the young.

Such a programme of work would keep the diplomats of the two sides busy for some years to come. But the rewards would more than justify their efforts.

* * *

A final word. Four years after *Rashomon* was first shown, Kurosawa produced his masterpiece. In *The Seven Samurai,* as you will recall, he tells how a group of anxious farmers seek the help of professional warriors in protecting their families, their crops and their village from brigands. The samurai train the farmers to use their existing weapons more effectively; they show them how to plan their defence and concert their actions; and then they join them in their struggle. In the European Community over the years we have acquired high skills in the processes of integration. It is in our interest, as good neighbours to offer to others the benefit of our experience. As a European and a long-time admirer of the Arab peoples, I hope that your governments will feel able and willing to profit from what your northern neighbours have learned along the path towards European Union.

VII

EUROPE – WHO RULES?

CHARTER 88, BATH – NOVEMBER 1996

The defeat of communism and the demolition of the Berlin Wall in 1989 seemed at the time to herald the dawn of a new, more prosperous era. The reality proved to be different.

While the threat of nuclear war originating in Europe has virtually disappeared, weapons of mass destruction in the hands of unstable regimes in various parts of the world cause concern. The international community has failed to respond effectively and in time to crises and disasters in parts of Africa and South East Asia. The United States, the sole remaining super-power, is unsure of its role. The peoples of the former Soviet Union, unsurprisingly, are finding it far from easy to adjust to their unfamiliar circumstances.

Meanwhile, in many regions of the world economic recession has taken its toll. The casualties, as always, have been the basic rights and prospects of the citizens and especially those least able to fend for themselves. The exceptions are south and east Asia and parts of Latin America. India and China are steadily acquiring the strength they will undoubtedly exploit in the twenty-first century. At the other end of the scale, the poorest regions of Africa have the least chance of escaping from their wretchedness. Population growth, especially in the developing world, has reached new levels and is still rising.

Not everything over the past forty years has changed for the worse. There have been great advances. Methods of travel taken for granted today were not imagined forty years ago. Innovations in medical treatment and care have added years to life and life to years. The information society and, more recently, the Internet have made a reality of Marshal McLuhan's vision of the global village. But it has also raised questions about the international division of labour, the nature of society and systems of governance.

*   *   *

It is against this changing background that more and more people have been re-examining their political systems and asking whether these still respond to the needs and wishes of the citizenry. The indifference of a large proportion of the electorate during the recent presidential election campaign in the United States speaks for itself. In the United Kingdom, which has prided itself hitherto on its reputation as 'the mother of parliaments' the standing of the House of Commons has declined in recent years. Apart from allegations of sleaze, this reflects two particular concerns. First, our electoral system has achieved an unintended result. Since the end of the Second World War no British government has been voted into office by a majority of the electorate. Secondly, the relentless concentration of political power in Westminster and Whitehall has stimulated the demand in Scotland and Wales for the establishment of assemblies with significant authority and responsibility in regional affairs and has caused resentment at local government level elsewhere in the United Kingdom.

This is the domestic context in which the notion of federalism has been introduced into the political debate in the United Kingdom. The wider debate about federalism in Europe became more intense after the signature of the Maastricht Treaty in December 1991.

European leaders could reasonably have expected to be congratulated when, after long and contentious negotiations, they eventually settled the terms of the grandly named Treaty on European Union and European Monetary Union. After all, they had passed another milestone on the road to the ever closer union among the peoples of Europe which the founding fathers had set as the overriding ambition when they signed the Treaty of Rome in 1957.

Since those early days much had happened. The Community had become a customs union in 1968. The three states – the United Kingdom, Denmark and Ireland – excluded in 1963 by what his foreign minister has now admitted was an act of treachery by President de Gaulle – had eventually joined ten years later. The European Monetary System had begun to operate in 1979. Greece and, later Portugal and Spain, had joined and the Single European Act, designed to create a single market, had been adopted in 1986. In the eyes of most of those who had put their names to the Treaty, their achievement at Maastricht was not merely a diplomatic triumph but also an historical inevitability.

Public reaction to the Treaty of Maastricht must have been an unpleasant surprise. This revealed the extent of popular disillusion with the Union. The negative vote in the first Danish referendum and the close result in the French referendum showed how deeply opinion was divided. Polls at the same time in

Germany indicated strong popular resentment at the apparent assumption that Germany would be the permanent paymaster of the poorer regions of the continent. Attitudes have changed little; it was only by a small margin that the Swedes voted, late in 1994, to accept the terms for their membership of the Union. More recently, industrial unrest in Germany, France and Italy has revealed another political miscalculation: the social impact of the economic measures needed to enable states to qualify for membership of the single currency by 1999 has been more severe than some governments expected.

* * *

Popular criticisms of the Union, whether justified or not, are aimed variously at the lack of transparency of decision-making in the Council of Ministers; the tendency of the European Commission to interfere unnecessarily in the affairs of the citizenry; the cost and effect of certain Community policies – notably the common agricultural and common fisheries policies; and the relative ineffectiveness of the European Parliament. It is easy enough to say that the Council of Ministers and the European Commission should share the blame for allowing these resentments to build up over the years. But it is less easy to understand why this situation has come about.

The formula in the preamble to the Treaty of Rome which defined the ultimate purpose as 'ever closer union among the peoples of Europe' had no precedent, as Jean Monnet recognised from the beginning. In 1943, when contemplating the situation which would arise in Europe when the war eventually ended, he wrote 'The real change we are after is not the free flow of goods. It is a change in the relation between people, and this change comes about because these people are no longer thinking in terms of their national, limited responsibilities. . . They are now thinking about common, joint responsibilities. This is the revolutionary character of the process of change that we are trying to set in motion. That process is a revolution, and should be never-ending.' Three decades later, in 1973, Andrew Shonfield captured the essence of Jean Monnet's concept in the title of his Reith Lectures – *A Journey to an Unknown Destination*. As we look back from this distance we realise how remarkable it was that, in the darkest days of the Second World War, Jean Monnet should have devised an original evolutionary concept for the relationship between peoples.

The other unique characteristic of the European adventure is that the treaties confer on the Commission not merely guardianship of the Treaties but also the obligation to propose. It is the Council which disposes. This is the process by which the whole corpus of European Union law has come into being.

The citizens of Europe should be proud of this constitutional innovation. Instead a majority feel alienated from the process of progressive European integration which they find opaque, complicated, intrusive and under anonymous direction. They ask themselves: Who rules Europe? Who is in charge? Concerns vary; of course, from one member state to another. In the United Kingdom any form of federalism is seen in some quarters as an assault on our sovereignty. Utterance of this word can arouse passions usually associated with defence of a maiden's honour. As we know, an excess of emotion can cloud the vision and this may explain why so few protagonists in the Europe debate have penetrated to the heart of the matter. Some, of course, may prefer not to. The issue which deserves the closest attention is not simply the relevance of this or that structure, but rather the real seat of power in Marshal McLuhan's global village.

*   *   *

Modern dictionaries of the English language define 'sovereignty' as 'supreme and unrestricted power as of a state'. This definition begs the question whether it is possible, even if desirable, for a modern state to exercise supreme and unrestricted power in every field of human activity.

Through the ages notions of sovereignty have been influenced by some of the greatest thinkers. For Aristotle law was the seat of sovereignty; and law, in this instance, meant not only the edicts of rulers, but also an impersonal natural law encapsulating rational principle. The emergence of the nation state and the development of secular philosophy undermined the idea that the ruler should be under God and the law. Machiavelli's Prince sought to exercise absolute power by all possible means, without regard to the traditional and moral judgments normally attached to them. The effect of this was to reduce government to a technical calculation of expediency; the basis of the state was to be the sovereign will of the ruler. Hobbes saw the ruler as unlimited in authority. His subjects were accorded only one right – the right to defend themselves against him. Inevitably the philosophical pendulum swung and later definitions seem more relevant to modern circumstances. In *Le Contrat Social*, Rousseau placed sovereignty in the community; what he called 'popular sovereignty' rested on the general will. The growth of nationalist self-consciousness in the nineteenth century, together with parliamentary reform in the United Kingdom, raised questions about the legitimacy of monarchies. The theory of constitutionalism evolved and, in more recent times, the rival merits of federalism and confederalism dominated the debate.

The British have hitherto shown their readiness, when circumstances so require, to accept limitations on their sovereignty by sharing or pooling it. When national survival is at stake it is natural that the demands of any alliance to which the state has subscribed should predominate. During the Second World War cooperation between the United Kingdom and the United States reached unprecedented levels. But this was not a new experience for Britain. For centuries Britain had worked with others to prevent the domination of continental Europe, first by Spain, then by France, then by Germany and, most recently, by the Soviet Union. Over the years the British learned much about the machinery of alliances and of the concessions which have to be made to one's partners in order to sustain the coalition. The Duke of Marlborough's letters to his beloved wife, Sarah, from his headquarters in the Low Countries during the war of the Spanish succession abound with references to actions forced on him by the need to placate his Dutch allies.

The period immediately following the Second World War was remarkable for the extent to which nations were prepared to pool aspects of their sovereignty in facing the problems of reconstruction, reconciliation and the need to secure the peace. Bretton Woods, the signature of the Charter of the United Nations and, later, when the division of the post-war world became a reality, the North Atlantic Treaty, were all based on the conviction that only by collective action could agreed objectives be attained. The European Union, formerly the European Community, is without question the most notable, as well as the most original, experiment in pooling sovereignty in order to serve the collective and individual interests of a grouping of nations.

In the early years of the European venture European leaders were concerned above all with developing what Jean Monnet had defined as common, or joint, responsibilities. The creation of the Coal and Steel Community, the European Economic Community and the Single Market were successive expressions of this ambition. For many years the rightness of this approach was not questioned. It was not until 1975 that a warning note was sounded. In proposing a constitution for a 'European Union', François-Xavier Ortoli, then President of the Commission, said 'European Union is not to give birth to a centralising super-state . . . the Union will be given responsibility only for those matters which the Member States are no longer capable of dealing with efficiently. . .' [The Union's] 'fields of competence will be specified in the Act of constitution, other matters being left to Member States'.

This cautionary language was echoed two years later by Ortoli's successor, Roy Jenkins, in a lecture in Florence. He argued that the Community should concentrate on those 'functions which will, beyond doubt, deliver significantly better results because they are performed at Community level', while leaving to member states 'those functions which they can do equally well or better on their own'.

In speaking in these terms, Ortoli and Roy Jenkins may have drawn unconsciously on a courageous statement made in the heart of Fascist Italy by Pope Pius XI in 1931. He said then that it would be 'an injustice, a great evil and a disturbance of the right order for a larger and higher association to arrogate to itself functions which can be performed efficiently by smaller and lower societies.'

In the European context, the importance of this doctrine, to which the accurate but awkward title 'subsidiarity' has been given, has been recognised at various times since the 1970s. The preamble to the European Parliament's draft for a Treaty on European Union; inspired by the distinguished Italian parliamentarian, Altiero Spinelli, included the following words: 'Intending to entrust common institutions, in accordance with the principle of subsidiarity, only with those powers required to complete successfully the tasks they may carry out more satisfactorily than the States acting independently . . .' This unequivocal injunction was written twelve years ago, in 1984. Three years later Jacques Delors, who had become President of the Commission in 1985, set in train a study of the implications of creating a single market against the background of an expanding Community. The report of this inquiry recommended greater decentralisation of Community policies, more systematic selection of Community responsibilities, while according stronger powers to the Community in monetary policy, competition and budgetary control. It went on to urge that relentless harmonisation should be checked, even in social policy. The Community should act only if the cost/benefit analysts showed that this was appropriate; in general, the inquiry concluded, the Community should frame the actions of member states, not replace them.

Jacques Delors' response to these recommendations was to write the principle of subsidiarity into the Maastricht Treaty. This Treaty prescribes that the 'Community shall take action, in accordance with the principle of subsidiarity, only if and insofar as the objectives of the proposed action cannot be sufficiently achieved by member states and . . . can be better achieved by the Community.' Subsidiarity figures elsewhere in the Treaty. For example, the preamble stresses the need for decisions to be 'taken as closely as possible to the citizen' and extends the application of subsidiarity 'to the achievement of all the objectives of the Union'.

When it met in Edinburgh in December 1992 the European Council drew up guidelines for the application of the principle of subsidiarity. Although since then proposals for some Community measures have been withdrawn, there has been no large-scale repatriation of European Union law. An indication of why this is so is contained in the conclusions of the Group of Reflection, which spent much of 1995 preparing for the Intergovernmental Conference. While insisting that subsidiarity should not be construed as a justification for the inexorable growth of European powers, the Group also warned that it should not be used as a pretext for undermining solidarity, or the achievements of the Union.

The compromise in this language reveals the crux of the dispute which will have to be settled over the next few years if the great European enterprise is to survive the challenges of the next decade. Today the question 'who should rule Europe?' receives two conflicting answers. There are those who look forward to a United States of Europe — what Peter Jay, the BBC's ostensibly impartial economics editor, dubbed 'a country called Europe'. And there are those who advocate a looser structure, based on a realistic definition of sovereignty in today's world, strict application of the principle of subsidiarity; and respect for the diversity of the nations of Europe.

Italy (with a population of 58 million), Belgium (with a population of 10 million), and Luxembourg (with a population of 400,000) are among those member states of the Union who believe that a fully centralised European system would best serve their interests. It is to be expected that many of those who work in the institutions of the European Union will support this aim. After all, their métier is the brick-upon-brick construction of Europe and they are constantly on the lookout for new bricks to add to the structure. Their reluctance to see the principle of subsidiarity rigidly applied is instinctive.

More important than this is the current attitude of the government of Helmut Kohl. He and his colleagues know as well as anyone that from the beginning the main purpose of ever closer union has been to accommodate the size and strength of Germany at the heart of the continent. However, they underestimated the problems which would follow the end of the cold war and are now grappling with the economic, social and political consequences of reunification while anxiously monitoring developments in central and eastern Europe. Their anxiety is understandable, but the wisdom of their response is debatable. With the support of the French who, for sound historic reasons, attach special importance to their relationship with Germany, Helmut Kohl and his colleagues, in according absolute priority to the achievement of a common currency, are seeking to apply a European solution to essentially German problems without adequate regard for the priorities of other member states.

This is not a healthy situation and it is important that the question 'who rules Europe?' should receive a clear answer. If, as we approach the new millennium, there is to emerge a European Union which will achieve the ambitions of its founders, which will recognise that the strength of our continent lies in its rich historical, linguistic, religious and cultural diversity; and which, at the same time, will command the respect and support of its citizens – if these objectives are to be achieved, then a convincing alternative to a United States of Europe will have to be advocated without delay.

Formulating and articulating such a message is a task tailor-made for the architect of grand alliances, the pragmatist, the objective arbiter – the other corner of the triangle of forces which, with France and Germany, must lead the Union into the new century. Unfortunately, for reasons of which we, our partners and the wider world are only too well aware, the United Kingdom has for the time being disqualified itself from playing this role. However, we should not lament. There are encouraging signs. The main political parties have a similar approach to the question of a single currency. And, behind the rhetoric and behind the scenes, the competing think-tanks are preparing policies for the next parliament. They would be well advised to pause and reflect on the advice offered by Lord Nolan in his First Radcliffe Lecture at Warwick University on 7 November. After identifying the reasons for the decline in the standing of Parliament, he suggested that 'if the world around Parliament is changing, Parliament must look at how it can best contribute to and influence good government in Britain in that changing world and should not rule out the possibility of radical changes in its role and procedures.' Well spoken, M'Lud.

In this coincidence of constitutional challenges – British and European – lies an opportunity to be seized. Should measures be taken following the next British general election to reverse the centralisation of power, then issues of sovereignty and subsidiarity beyond the borders of Scotland and Wales would inevitably be raised. This could lead in due course to delegation of authority to Northern Ireland and to regions in England. We might see in the United Kingdom a relationship developing between regions and the centre similar to that enshrined in the German Basic Law of 1948 which has proved outstandingly successful in the Federal Republic.

Radical changes of this kind would strengthen our hand in fashioning the future

European Union. In undertaking such a role we should allow our thoughts to soar. Why should we accept that existing systems of governance represent the limit of political evolution? Why assume that the architects of political systems from Pericles to Jefferson, from Karl Marx to the English reformers of the nineteenth century exhausted the constitutional possibilities? In today's interconnected world fewer elements of sovereignty remain within national boundaries. In practice sovereignty is divided horizontally into layers, beginning at global level and descending through national and regional levels to the level of the parish. The intellectual effort of the think-tanks should be applied not only to reforming the British constitution, but also to devising for Europe a new system for ordering relationships between peoples or different cultures, traditions and faiths relevant to the circumstances of the new millennium.

The basis would be ruthless application to the functions of all the Union's institutions of the principle of subsidiarity, and continuous, rather than spasmodic, attention to the concerns of the citizens of the Union. This would entail determining with the utmost objectivity at which level decisions should be taken to achieve agreed aims, and ensuring that this was in practice the lowest effective level. This would also entail opening up the proceedings of the Council of Ministers to the extent that this is consistent with good governance; reconstructing the Commission; enhancing the powers of the European Parliament, perhaps in association with representatives of national parliaments; auditing more effectively observance of Union law; rooting out the fraud and errors which amount to more than 5% of the Union's budget; and consolidating the steady progress being made by member states in the fields of foreign policy and defence.

Such a programme of reform would take time and call for patience and persistence, but it would persuade the citizens of the Union that their concerns were being addressed. They would be further encouraged if the ambition of the founding fathers were re-stated in terms appropriate to an enlarged European Union in the global village. If it were proposed that the objectives of the Union in the new circumstances should be, first and foremost, to seek peace, stability, prosperity and social justice for all its citizens and, secondly, to play an effective role in the world in the interests of the people of Europe and humanity as a whole, then citizens of the Union, faced with the question 'Who rules Europe?' might feel confident enough to say: 'We do.'

VIII

ACCESSION OF GREECE TO THE COMMUNITY

INSTITUTE FOR BALKAN STUDIES, THESSALONIKI
NOVEMBER 1997

It was not until I took up my post as United Kingdom Representative in Brussels in 1975 that I became directly involved in Greek affairs. Two years earlier the United Kingdom, together with Ireland and Denmark, had at last joined what was then the European Economic Community, raising membership from the original Six to Nine. Among the numerous dossiers with which I was to become familiar was one which concerned what the Community termed its 'Mediterranean Policy'. This was an integral part of the relationship the Community sought to establish with the rest of the world.

The Mediterranean Policy had a clear objective. The member states were sensitive to the charge that the Community was a 'rich man's club'. After all, the title 'European Economic Community' given to the new entity by the founding fathers at a time when it comprised only part of one half of the continent, was regarded by some not merely as visionary, but as bordering on the arrogant. As seen from Brussels, the countries of the Mediterranean were neighbours and significant trading partners, and some as future members. Mutual interests should therefore be fostered. This was to be achieved by means of a series of individual Association Agreements, each of which took account of the special circumstances of the Mediterranean partner.

The Association Agreement between the Community and Greece had been signed in July 1961 and had come into operation in November of that year. This was not simply a trading arrangement, important though this aspect was. More important were those elements which explicitly aimed at paving the way for Greece's eventual full membership of the Community. Full membership was also the stated objective of the Association Agreement the Community had concluded with Turkey.

Sadly, events in Greece in April 1967 obliged the Community to suspend the Association Agreement. Only the specific obligations relating to routine matters continued to be honoured. The end of military rule and the restoration of a democratic system in July 1974 enabled the Community to resume operation of the Agreement and, on 12 June 1975, Greece formally applied to join the Community as a full member.

The Council of Ministers of the Community had its first opportunity to discuss the Greek application when it met on 24 June 1975. On the following day, Dr Garret Fitzgerald, the foreign minister of Ireland and, at that time, the President of the Council, told the Greek delegation that the application would be more fully considered by the Council in September; meanwhile, he added, as required by the laws of the Community, the Commission had been invited to give its opinion. Dr Fitzgerald explained that the average time for consideration of applications for full membership was three years.

This was the situation when I arrived in Brussels in the autumn of 1975. I found that reactions to the Greek application were mixed. The British government and the Danes were instinctively in favour of the enlargement of the Community. Apart from this, British military intervention during and after the Second War in efforts, one unsuccessful the other successful at least for a time, which reflected long-standing admiration for the people of Greece, disposed the British to favour moves to bolster democracy in that troubled country. For various reasons other member states were somewhat daunted by the prospect of absorbing Greece; their own economic interests would be directly affected. The predominance in the Greek economy of agriculture and the relatively weak industrial base would necessitate structural changes. Apart from the fact that progress towards agricultural harmonisation before the suspension of the Association Agreement had been limited, it was appreciated that the cost of the changes required would be a charge on the Community's finances. The increase in expenditure could amount to some 6% of the budget of the existing Community of the Nine. One of my colleagues – the representative of one of the original Six – who was noted for his sometimes caustic wit, suggested over one of our weekly informal lunches that, while we should certainly sing 'God Save Greece', we might also sing 'God Save Our Community'.

Although proceedings behind the closed doors of the Commission were normally treated with discretion, my colleagues and I learned that the drafting of the Commission's Opinion raised serious problems and that there was even a possibility that the Commission might recommend rejection of the application, at least for the time being – and this despite the explicit aim of full membership set out in the Association Agreement.

Apart from the economic considerations, there were important political implications. In the first place, disagreements between Greece and Turkey, its neighbour, fellow Associate and potential member of the Community, faced the Community with an unprecedented difficulty. Neither the Community itself nor any of the existing member states was willing to take sides in these disputes. At the same time, it was only realistic to acknowledge that the Community's ability to oblige two countries to resolve their disputes themselves was limited. In any event, it would be important to assure the Turks that the accession of Greece would not affect the rights they enjoyed under their Association Agreement.

On 28 January 1976 the Commission, having completed its task, submitted its Opinion to the Council of Ministers. In recommending that the Community give a 'clear positive answer to the Greek request' for membership in the light of the avowed aim of the Association Agreement and Greece's return to a democratic form of government, the Commission also suggested how the problems raised might be addressed. The Commission expressed the view that time should be allowed, even before the beginning of the normal transitional arrangements came into effect, to enable Greece to accelerate the necessary structural reforms and to develop a closer working relationship with the institutions of the Community. The Commission also recommended that the existing member states should take steps to advance the process of internal development of the Community in the period leading up to enlargement.

*   *   *

On 9 February 1976 the Council of Ministers, after considering the Commission's Opinion, announced that it was in favour of the Greek request for accession and would arrange for talks to 'take place as soon as possible in a positive spirit' in order to establish a common basis for negotiation. It instructed the Permanent Representatives Committee to prepare its discussions to this end, with the assistance of the Commission. However, the Council did not accept the Commission's proposal for a preparatory period before accession. It considered that, as in previous cases, there should be a transitional period after Greece's accession. Questioned by the ever enthusiastic press corps after the meeting, Gaston Thorn, the foreign minister of Luxembourg, who had taken the chair, stressed that no political conditions had been attached to Greek membership. 'The application will be judged on its merits', he said. In answer to a specific question, he emphasised that it would be wrong to link Greek membership with the dispute over Cyprus.

None of the ministers attending the meeting was insensitive to the problems posed by the Greek application. The British foreign secretary, James Callaghan, was certain that one of the main reasons for rejecting the Commission's suggestion of a preliminary waiting period was the unfavourable reaction this would provoke in Athens; it was of political importance that the Community should show solidarity with the new democratic government in Greece.

While reaction in Ankara to the news of the Community's acceptance of the Greek application was predictably one of dismay, it was greeted with satisfaction in Athens. For Greece the Community represented a source of much needed capital, an incentive to foreign investors, access on privileged terms to a large market, and a stimulus to the social policies the new democratic government favoured. The task now was to translate these aspirations into reality.

*   *   *

The events of 9 February 1976 initiated a period of detailed negotiation of the elements which would eventually constitute the provisions of the treaty of accession. At regular intervals over the following years reports were presented to the Council of Ministers about the progress of the negotiations and its members had time to contemplate the implications of the forthcoming enlargement of the Community. The Community of Nine, soon to become Ten, would become the Community of Twelve when, in due course, negotiations with the Spaniards and Portuguese who had applied for membership in 1978, had also been concluded. Reaction to these two further applications had been similar to attitudes in the early stages towards the Greek application. Public opinion in Germany was reported to be nervous about a possible influx of cheap labour and, while Italy and France saw further erosion of their advantageous position in agriculture, the integrationists feared yet more dilution of the Community spirit.

The anxieties of the German public were not shared by Chancellor Schmidt. In a conversation with Roy Jenkins, the President of the Commission, in November 1977 he demonstrated 'remarkable enthusiasm for enlargement'. He regarded it as a central duty of the Community to assist Greece, Spain and Portugal. A month later, addressing a meeting of the Council of Ministers in Brussels, Papaligouras, the Greek foreign minister, voiced his dissatisfaction with the state of the negotiations. The Community's informal response was a commitment to break the back of the negotiations by the end of 1978. Although the term 'breaking the back' in Community parlance meant settlement of the main issues without necessarily tidying up all the less important details, this was a bold undertaking. But it did not prevent Papaligouras from once again expressing his exasperation in even more dramatic terms when he confronted the Council of Ministers in April 1978.

By the early autumn of 1978 substantial progress had been made. The credit for this was due in large measure to the Greek Prime Minister, Konstantinos Karamanlis. For twenty years he had devoted himself to what he called Greek Europeanism. He understood the difficulty of integrating Greek agriculture into the Community system and appreciated that, if the Greeks were to demand either a short or even no transitional period at all, this could provoke the Italians and the French into proposing an even longer period than was then contemplated. A reasonable timetable began to emerge. The back of the negotiations would be broken by Christmas 1978. The process of drafting the necessary agreements would then begin and would be completed in time for signature in the summer of 1979.

Two surprises were in store. The crucial negotiating sessions took place during the German presidency of the Council of Ministers, Hans-Dietrich Genscher being the principal Community negotiator. At the meeting in Brussels in the days immediately before Christmas 1978, the few remaining points of disagreement, notably agriculture and the length of the transitional period, were addressed in turn. When the Council had considered or reconsidered its position on a particular issue, Genscher would leave the Chamber to convey this to the Greek delegation led by the new foreign minister, Rallis, in an adjoining room. In due course he would return to the Chamber to report the Greek response. He took full advantage of his position as president of the Council. He pressed his colleagues to reduce their demands, but refused to adopt a more lenient attitude to the right of Greek families to work in the Community. Members of the Council expected to resume their meeting at 2.45 in the morning of 21 December to discuss two more requests by the Greeks on the subject of Community aid for the production of cotton and sugar and were surprised when Genscher returned to the Chamber accompanied by the Greek delegation to announce that agreement had been reached and, in particular, on agriculture. Although the concessions made were minor, Genscher had exceeded his brief. I admired the way in which his colleagues contained their resentment. When news of the agreement reached Athens, Karamanlis welcomed the outcome as 'the starting point for a better and more secure life for the Greek people'. From the point of view of the British delegation the sentiment he expressed was satisfaction enough.

France assumed the Presidency of the Council in January 1979. When the French foreign minister, Jean François-Poncet, chaired the final working session of the negotiations in April 1979, he in his turn sprang a surprise. It had been the custom that new entrants would sign their treaty of accession at the headquarters of the Community in Brussels. Francois-Poncet announced without warning that his President, Valery Giscard d'Estaing, had agreed with the Greek government that the signature of this treaty would take place in Athens on 28 May 1979. A member of the French repesentation, as surprised as everyone else by this disregard of precedent, suggested *sotto voce* that his President believed that the mantle of Greek civilisation had fallen on his shoulders.

I was privileged to be among those, alongside the new British foreign secretary, Lord Carrington, who signed this treaty in the splendid modern rotunda between the Parliament and the Acropolis. President Giscard was present but did not speak. He sat somewhat apart from the other representatives, looking, in Roy Jenkins' words, 'like the mother of the bride'. The final event was a brilliant reception in the garden of the Old Royal Palace hosted by President Tsatsos. But the day and the glory belonged to Konstantinos Karamanlis.

All that is history. What of the present? It is for each member state to determine whether it has taken full advantage of its membership of the European Community, now the Union. If there are reservations or hesitations in Greece, then these are understandable. Greece has several serious preoccupations. The antagonism of the neighbour to the east persists. Not all the former members of the Soviet bloc are finding it easy to adjust to their new status. An end to the crisis in former Yugoslavia seems as remote as ever. And to the south, Cyprus continues to fester. However, the people of Greece should take comfort from the prospect of important developments in the coming years which could enhance their role in the Union.

*　*　*

IX

THE COMMONWEALTH AND EUROPE: 1960–1973

EUROPEAN INSTITUTE: SOUTH BANK UNIVERSITY
APRIL 1998

When touring Australia in 1884 Lord Rosebery, who was later to become British foreign secretary, made a speech in Adelaide in which he referred to 'the British commonwealth of nations'. This is believed to be the first use in public of the term 'commonwealth' in the context of a grouping of nations. It was not until 1926 that this concept was more precisely defined. Lord Balfour, a former Prime Minister, who had returned to office in 1922 as foreign secretary, described Britain and the dominions as 'autonomous communities within the British Empire, equal in status and in no way subordinate one to another in any aspect of their domestic or external affairs, though united by a common allegiance to the Crown and freely associated as members of the British Commonwealth of Nations'. Five years later – in 1932 – this relationship was enshrined in the Statute of Westminster, an Act of the British Parliament which conferred on the dominions of Canada, Australia, New Zealand, South Africa, Newfoundland and the Irish Free State the power to repeal or amend Acts of the British Parliament which applied to them. It was this Act of Parliament which created what came to be known as dominion status.

At the time of Lord Rosebery's tour, Britain regarded itself as a dominant imperial power and Lord Rosebery's intention was to suggest a way of linking Britain – the mother country – with the new nations created in other parts of the globe by waves of emigrants from the British Isles. Imperial sentiment at the highest political level had been fostered by Disraeli, whose idea it was that Queen Victoria should be made Empress of India – a title she assumed in 1876.

Europe had meanwhile been enjoying a prolonged period of peace inaugurated by the Congress of Vienna in 1815. The Crimean War in the mid-1850s, which was the product of one of the misunderstandings which have bedevilled relations between Turkey and its Slav neighbours, was of marginal importance in political terms.

The main preoccupation of the British in the second half of the 19th century was competition with other powers over colonisation, particularly in Africa. This may explain why, in the early years of the new century, the British government of the day was slow to appreciate the danger posed by the irascible, ill-educated, impetuous German Kaiser. Wilhelm II built up the German navy and frustrated attempts by his rivals elsewhere in Europe to keep his ambitions in check. In the summer of 1914 German armies marched into Belgium and the world slid into the 'war to end all wars'. A generation later, in 1939, hostilities with Germany were resumed. The war which followed – the most destructive in human history – changed the world. But, as the story of the years which have passed since then has shown, not all attitudes have changed with the times.

*   *   *

Like the course of true love, the process of integration in Europe over the past fifty years has not run smooth. There have been notable successes, such as the binding together by the Treaty of Paris in 1952 of the coal and steel industries in western Europe and the decision in 1986 to create a single market. Along the way there have also been serious errors. The first of these was the decision by the British government of the day to stand aside when the negotiations began which led to the signature of the Treaty of Rome in 1957 and the formation of the European Economic Community.

With the benefit of hindsight the attitude of those in authority in London at that time seems to have been remarkably obtuse. The advice from British embassies in the capitals of the six countries which were to form the new Community was clear; this was indeed the start of an important process which would directly affect British interests. It was also their view that the determination of the six governments was such that they could be expected to make every effort to ensure the success of the venture. In the event this advice was ignored.

The political miscalculations of the late 1940s and the 1950s undoubtedly damaged British interests. However, it is only fair to judge those decisions in the light of the circumstances of the time. Alone among the countries of western Europe, Britain had been neither defeated nor occupied. For over five years the British had sustained their resistance to Nazi Germany in close alliance with the United States and supported by the countries of the Commonwealth. British and Commonwealth forces played a major part in the liberation of Europe in 1944 and 1945, repeating their success in the North African and Italian campaigns. In South East Asia, the main instrument of victory over the Japanese was the Indian Army, officered largely but not exclusively by British officers, but manned by every race from the sub-continent.

The strategic direction of the allies' war effort was essentially in Anglo-American hands. Collaboration between the United States president and the British Prime Minister, between their military commanders, between the State Department and the Foreign Office and the respective treasuries reached unprecedented levels. The intimate working relationships established during the war persisted into the immediately following period, when the problems of reconstruction, reconciliation and securing the peace were addressed.

Several British ministers and their senior advisers in the key Whitehall departments had been personally involved in these events and the habit of consultation and, where possible, cooperation with the United States was deeply ingrained. If the word 'mindset' had been in vogue in the 1940s and 50s, it would have neatly and succinctly described the attitudes which had become instinctive. In the same way, the view London took of the Commonwealth was coloured not by delusions of imperial grandeur, but by grateful recognition of the contribution forces from the Commonwealth had made during the struggle for survival. The Commonwealth relationship had stood the test and deserved to be nourished and adapted to changing circumstances. It was understood that the withdrawal from the Indian sub-continent marked the end of colonialism and this raised important questions about the future of the Commonwealth and the colonial empire. This was recognised by the substitution of the name 'Commonwealth Relations Office' for 'Dominions Office' in 1947.

The critical error at this time was the failure once again of the political leadership in London to heed the warning uttered early this century by the American philosopher, George Santayana, in his monumental *Life of Reason* when he wrote: 'Those who cannot remember the past are condemned to repeat it'. In facing the challenges of the post-war world in the 1940s and early 50s, political leaders in London seem to have been so determined to preserve the platform of common interest and shared objectives from which the victory of the allies had been launched that they neglected the critical lessons to be drawn from the events of the 1930s which had led to the war. At Zurich, Amsterdam and elsewhere Winston Churchill, as leader of the opposition, had advocated the need for unity in Europe but, when he returned to power as Prime Minister in 1953, he showed little enthusiasm for the idea he had so eloquently propounded. Anthony Eden, his foreign secretary, showed similar indifference to developments across the Channel, so absorbed had he become in his self-selected role as peacemaker in Trieste, Austria, Indo-China and, finally, and disastrously, in the Middle East.

For those who had suffered under the German occupation, analysis of the causes of the war was a main preoccupation. As early as 1943 Jean Monnet had set out his conclusions and his prescription. He was determined that the allies should not only win the war but also the peace. His overriding aim was to find a peaceful way of containing the size and strength of Germany at the centre of the continent and his proposals were designed to this end. His formula was not simply the free flow of goods, but a change in the relationship between peoples, who would no longer think in national terms but in terms of shared responsibilities.

*   *   *

The steady progress being made by the members of the European Economic Community following the signature of the Treaty of Rome in 1957 persuaded Harold Macmillan, who had succeeded Anthony Eden as British Prime Minister in that year, to consider a reversal of Britain's attitude to the Community. In the summer of 1960 exploratory talks were held in their capitals with the leaders of the Six member states. Commonwealth representatives were also consulted. The lack of enthusiasm of the older members of the Commonwealth – Australia, Canada and New Zealand – was expected, but the opposition of the major Commonwealth countries in the developing world, and notably Nigeria, was a surprise, since they stood to benefit from the Association Agreements contained in Section 4 of the Treaty of Rome.

These soundings persuaded the British Government to test the ground with the members of the Community as a whole. The meeting of the Western European Union on 27 February 1961 provided the opportunity. Edward Heath, who had been appointed Lord Privy Seal to act as deputy to the foreign secretary, Lord Home, and spokesman on foreign affairs in the House of Commons, said then: '. . . if the Common Market countries can meet our Commonwealth and agricultural difficulties, the United Kingdom can then consider a system based on a common or harmonised tariff on raw materials and manufactured goods imported from countries other than the Seven' (the members of the European Free Trade Association) 'or the Commonwealth'. The ministers from the member states of the Community present at that meeting, as well as the international press, recognised that this statement represented a significant advance on the previous British position.

British embassies in the capitals of the Six reported a general desire for Britain to join the Community. In some member states it was hoped that, given Britain's world wide interests, her accession would check any inward-looking tendencies within the Community. Reactions in the Commonwealth were predictably less enthusiastic and members of the British cabinet visited a number of Commonwealth capitals in order to explain the general advantages which would flow from British membership of the Community. However, in Australia and New Zealand in particular this message was ill-received. Despite this, the cabinet endorsed Harold Macmillan's proposal that negotiations to join the Community should be opened. This decision was announced in the House of Commons on 30 July 1961 and was broadly endorsed. Such misgivings as were expressed related to the impact on the Commonwealth and on the sovereignty of the United Kingdom.

Edward Heath was charged with the conduct of the negotiations. He formed two delegations to support him – one resident in Brussels to monitor events in the Community and the other, a high-level peripatetic team, which would advise him at the negotiating table. Among their other duties these two delegations were required to ensure that Commonwealth countries and other interested parties were fully briefed on the progress of the negotiations through their representatives in Brussels and London.

*   *   *

Even before the formal negotiations began, a number of prominent personalities in member states of the Community recommended privately that the best course for the United Kingdom would be to accede to the Treaties of Paris and Rome at once and negotiate the appropriate terms afterwards from within. Though well-intentioned, this advice was unrealistic. The problems affecting the Commonwealth and agriculture in particular were not minor and acceptance of the provisions of the treaties in advance would have seriously reduced Edward Heath's room for manoeuvre. Apart from this, there was no prospect of Parliament endorsing such a course of action.

As soon as the negotiations began the nature of the issues to be resolved became clear. In accepting the principle of a single external tariff the United Kingdom assumed an obligation to reduce most existing tariffs. This, and the imposition of quotas, created problems for Commonwealth countries as well as some of the colonial territories. On behalf of the countries of the Indian sub-continent, for example, Edward Heath put forward a strong case for unlimited entry for tea – a commodity in direct competition with coffee – and at the end of the day this was agreed.

Although the trade of colonial territories was safeguarded under the Treaty of

Rome, for reasons which were never explained a number of the larger colonial territories declined to take advantage of the privileges on offer. In due course the Lomé Convention provided essential assistance to the Commonwealth countries among its seventy-odd beneficiaries.

The agricultural trade of the old members of the Commonwealth was the subject of hard negotiations and reasonable terms were agreed in the spring and summer of 1962. However, immediately before the summer recess the French tabled new proposals for a tariff on imports of temperate zone agricultural producers which would have had the effect of maintaining the price of domestic products. This formula seemed to contradict what had already been agreed. This was not a good omen but, when negotiations resumed after the summer break, steady progress continued to be made.

During the interval in the negotiations a Commonwealth Conference was held in London. On the eve of the Conference Edward Heath discussed tactics with his senior advisers. Also present at this briefing was the press secretary at 10 Downing Street who disclosed that the Prime Minister was not looking forward to the expected onslaught from his fellow heads of government. When the Conference opened the Indian Prime Minister put forward the case for special treatment for tea and the Australians asked for parallel treatment for currants from Victoria. However, the principal objections were political. Harold Macmillan argued that the days of the Empire were over and that Britain would acquire more political and economic influence as a member of the Community than outside it; this would be of direct benefit to the Commonwealth. On the main economic issues, he was able to satisfy his colleagues that the best possible terms for their trade in the wider market which would become available to them when Britain joined the Community had been secured and they left London reasonably reassured.

The arguments were overtaken by President de Gaulle's veto in January 1963 and the files were put into the pending tray until Harold Wilson, who had become Prime Minister in 1964, and his foreign secretary, George Brown, embarked on their tour of the Six member states in the early months of 1967. At a meeting of the Council of Western European Union in July of that year George Brown submitted a second application on behalf of the United Kingdom for membership of the European Community. This application was no more successful. In November of that year it too was vetoed by President de Gaulle. The files went back into the pending tray.

*   *   *

The arrival at the Elysée Palace of President Georges Pompidou in 1969 altered the situation and offered Edward Heath, when he became Prime Minister in June 1970, the opportunity to pursue his ambition. One of his first acts was to register the determination of the new government to pursue the effort to join the European Economic Community. With the bitter experience of 1963 in his mind, the Prime Minister decided that the first step should be to persuade the French of the good intentions of the United Kingdom. A confidential link was established with the Elysee through which ideas and preoccupations could be discussed in parallel with the formal negotiations with the Council of Ministers of the Community.

On the United Kingdom side these negotiations were conducted by a team led by Geoffrey Rippon, the Chancellor of the Duchy of Lancaster. In the different atmosphere that now prevailed, the points of difficulty were steadily reduced. For its part, the United Kingdom was willing to accept the system of Community finance provided that an adequate transitional period could be agreed, but it was anxious to ensure that the legitimate needs of dairy farmers in New Zealand and Commonwealth sugar producers were accommodated. In the end access to the enlarged market for New Zealand butter and cheese was agreed on terms acceptable to New Zealand. Likewise, members of the Commonwealth Sugar Agreement approved the terms negotiated for their exports. By the middle of May 1971 sufficient progress had been made through both channels to justify a meeting between the Prime Minister and the French president. This took place in Paris on 20 and 21 May.

President Pompidou told Edward Heath that, for historical reasons, France and Britain carried a special responsibility in regard to developing countries. Those in the Commonwealth would enjoy the same preferential treatment as the former colonies of existing members of the Community. Pompidou's main anxiety was the position of sterling as a reserve currency. It was a basic principle that the currencies of the member states should enjoy equal status. The ultimate goal of economic and monetary union set out in the Treaty of Rome could not otherwise be attained. Edward Heath agreed that every effort would be made to reduce the sterling balances, provided that the interests of those holding the balances were not harmed and that no unacceptable burden was placed on the United Kingdom's balance of payments. It was also important that the rate of the pound should be maintained. The understandings reached during these critical discussions at the Elysée were subsequently endorsed by the Community Council of Ministers on 7 June 1972.

When their talks had ended President Pompidou led Edward Heath into the Salon des Fêtes where his predecessor had pronounced his veto in 1963. The press were already assembled. When the president made clear that there were no longer any obstacles to Britain's entry into the European Economic Community, everyone present understood that they were witnesses to a moment of historical importance. Neither Europe, nor the United Kingdom, nor the Commonwealth would be the same again.

*   *   *

In the years that have passed since then the producers of temperate foodstuffs in the Commonwealth have found new markets and have forged new relationships. The developing members have taken full advantage of the Lome Agreements and defend their interests in the councils of the World Trade Organisation with vigour.

What, then, of the future? The European Union will pursue its way along the path that does not run smooth. The Commonwealth will continue to develop its unique personality and to exercise its influence for good in every corner of the world. The international community as a whole will be the beneficiary. So there is no reason today for the noble and worldly-wise Lords Rosebery and Balfour, or any other architects of the Commonwealth in ages past, to turn in their graves.

X

DECISION-MAKING IN THE UNION

UNIVERSITY OF BATH – NOVEMBER 1998

An event earlier this year of special importance for the future of the European Union attracted too little attention. On 8 June the then German Chancellor, Helmut Kohl, and the French President, Jacques Chirac, addressed a letter to the British Prime Minister, who at that time was President of the European Council. In this letter they urged that, when it meets in Vienna in December, the Council should have before it proposals for enhancing the Union's ability to act and for bringing it closer to its citizens. They insisted that the principle of subsidiarity should be more strictly applied in order to ensure that decisions are taken at the closest possible level to citizens of the Union. In this respect the two leaders were echoing an appeal by the British foreign secretary in November 1997 that 'Europe should be given back to the people'. However, the Chancellor and the President went further. They also advocated substantial improvement of the working methods of the Council of Ministers and a thorough reform of the structures of the Commission and its services. In support of their appeal Chancellor Kohl and President Chirac uttered a truth which has been neglected by many of those who work in the institutions of the Union. They stated without equivocation that 'The objective of European policy has never been and cannot be to build a central European state, that is a centrally organised Europe.'

In sending this letter the two leaders were in fact doing no more than focus attention on certain decisions of the Treaty drawn up in 1997 at Amsterdam which not only settled a number of issues left over from Maastricht in 1991 but also charted the way ahead. Existing rules for applying the principle of subsidiarity were written into the Treaty of Amsterdam as a Protocol.

For most citizens of the European Union the way in which the decisions which affect them are taken is a mystery and they should welcome this initiative. I had my first exposure to the process in the autumn of 1961 when formal negotiations began between the United Kingdom and the Six Members of what was then the European Community on Britain's belated application to join the great European adventure. These negotiations had a formal character. When Edward Heath, who led the British delegation, had presented a proposition on a particular subject, the minister acting for the time being as president of the Council of Ministers would seek clarification of a few points and then invite our delegation to leave the chamber while the Six and the Commission considered their response. This could take half an hour or the best part of the day. In due course we would be summoned to the Council chamber to hear the response of the Six. By the end of 1962 the consensus among the delegations was that a successful conclusion to the negotiations was in sight. But that proved optimistic. No member of the British delegation was present in the Salon des Fêtes at the Elysée Palace on 14 January 1963 when President de Gaulle committed what his then foreign minister, Maurice Couve de Murville, has in recent years admitted was an act of treachery – *un acte de trahison* – when he vetoed Britain's entry into the Community.

I *was* present however when Georges Pompidou, the President of France, led Edward Heath, now British Prime Minister, into the same Salon des Fêtes on 21 May 1971 to announce the readiness of France to welcome the United Kingdom into the Community. Everyone in the Salon on that day felt privileged to have attended a significant moment in history.

In October of that year – 1971 – the British House of Commons voted in principle that the United Kingdom should join the Community and in January 1972 Edward Heath, together with his Irish and Danish colleagues, signed the treaties of accession.

In today's interdependent, inter-connected world, when an overnight flight can transport one to almost any part of the world, serious bilateral diplomacy is often conducted at ministerial level. However, it is still the principal duty of ambassadors to further and protect the interests of the country they represent in the country to which they are accredited and to ensure that their government is kept fully and accurately informed about developments of significance. It is also their duty to recommend when contact at ministerial level would be appropriate. The clips one sees on television of ministers being greeted by heads of protocol at the foot of aircraft steps indicate when such advice has been offered and accepted.

For professional diplomats multilateral diplomacy offers a different, more substantial challenge. Having served as the United Kingdom Permanent Representative to the United Nations at New York, I was pleased to be invited to assume an equivalent position with the European Communities. My arrival in Brussels in October 1975 coincided with a series of meetings of the Council of Ministers in Luxembourg, a session of what was then the European Assembly in Strasbourg and a meeting with the Soviet-dominated Council for Mutual

Economic Assistance — COMECON. In between these commitments I had to establish the first essential contacts and, despite the meticulous briefing I had received before leaving London, begin to define to my own satisfaction the role I was to play over the years ahead.

The office of which I took charge was called a Permanent Representation. The convention is that diplomatic missions which work with international bodies such as the United Nations and the North Atlantic Treaty Organisation are known as 'Missions' or 'Delegations'. The term 'Representation' in the case of the European Union was adopted for legal reasons; a state cannot accredit a delegation to a body of which it is an integral part. The use of the word 'permanent' is also deliberate. This indicates the non-political character of the staff of the mission in the same way as the term 'permanent secretary' is used to describe the senior public servant in a British department of state. In other countries the title 'secretary-general' serves the same purpose of denoting continuity and political neutrality. For convenience, however, representatives of the member states of the Union are given the rank of ambassador.

The staff I inherited came partly from the diplomatic service and partly from home departments. Diplomats and their families are used to moving house at frequent intervals and treat a posting to Brussels as a normal event in their career. However, a secondment to Brussels poses problems for members of the home civil service. In many cases the wives have jobs in Britain and must either detach themselves from these, or commute.

My deputy expected to return before long to his London base — the Department of Trade. Other officials seconded from home departments occupied most of the other senior posts. The structure of the mission reflected the diversity of the work of the Community. Not surprisingly, the agriculture section, headed by an undersecretary from the Ministry, was the largest. Other sections dealt with economics and finance; external trade; industry and energy; social affairs and regional policy; the environment and transport; and the Community's relations with developing countries. Other members of the staff, drawn mostly from the Foreign Office, served the needs of the entire mission, for example the legal adviser and the head of press and information. Coordination was assured by a senior counsellor from the diplomatic service, whose role was the equivalent of chief of staff. It was his task to ensure that what had to be done was done, done properly and on time.

The role of the mission was not merely to represent the United Kingdom at various levels of the continuous negotiation, but also to advise others with a stake in the European enterprise. These included members of the European Assembly, and of the Economic and Social Council. Individuals and groups with business and other interests in the Community also sought our guidance and we did our best to ensure that at all times the media were fully briefed about the policies we were advocating.

At the earliest opportunity I called on François-Xavier Ortoli, the President of the Commission, and introduced myself to his fellow Commissioners over the following weeks. Another immediate task was to establish a working relationship with the permanent representatives of the other member states, alongside whom I was to labour in the Community vineyard. At the time of my arrival in Brussels Italy held the presidency. My Italian colleague was a veteran diplomatist who explained some of the conventions observed by the Committee of Permanent Representatives, known by the acronym COREPER. This is derived from the French rendering of the name of the committee. The calls I paid on my other colleagues impressed me in two ways. Each one, drawing on personal experience, stressed the essential purpose of the process of European integration. My French colleague, another veteran diplomatist, was explicit; everything we did in Brussels had to do with Germany and the need to accommodate its size and strength in the heart of the continent. He stressed that, in this critical task, France and Britain carried a special responsibility. Even my melancholy German colleague, who still bore the psychological scars of long years in a Soviet prisoner-of-war camp, wanted me to understand the vital importance to his country of the success of the Community and the need for the support of Germany's partners.

The second impression these calls made on me was the personal quality and distinctive talents of my colleagues. This indicated the importance governments of member states attached to the work done day after day on their behalf in Brussels. This perception was reinforced over the following months when I saw their staff at work. As one of the more experienced journalists put it: governments do not send idiots to Brussels to look after their interests.

* * *

The Committee of Permanent Representatives – COREPER – is divided into two parts. Part I, which is composed of the deputy permanent representatives, handles the more technical issues which are to come before ministers. Part II, composed of the ambassadors, handles the rest, including those which are more sensitive politically. Agriculture is the province of the Special Agriculture

Committee; its members are representatives of national ministries of agriculture seconded for the time being to their permanent representations in Brussels. Senior members of the Commission staff attend meetings of both Parts of COREPER and of the Special Agriculture Committee.

COREPER normally meets twice a week, the ambassadors on Thursdays and the deputies on Fridays. The principal function of these committees is to prepare material for meetings of the Council of Ministers. Under the treaties it is the duty of the European Commission to propose and the right of the Council of Ministers to dispose. The whole corpus of Community, now Union, law has come into existence by this process. The role of COREPER is to scrutinise proposals put forward by the Commission and, where necessary, to challenge and, where appropriate, amend those aspects which might prove unacceptable to governments of the member states. Of course, the arguments put forward by members of COREPER are based on initial reactions to Commission proposals in their respective capitals, which in turn will have taken into account comments and advice from the permanent representatives themselves. In most cases Commission proposals, whether amended or not, are agreed at this level and the resultant draft legislation is presented to the next convenient meeting of the relevant Council of Ministers as what are known as 'A points'. These figure as such on the Council's agenda and are usually adopted without comment. The remainder of the Council agenda consists of 'B points' – items on which COREPER has been unable to agree. More recently another category – I points – has been introduced. These are virtually agreed, but not quite.

The dossiers which come before the two parts of COREPER are the result of examination in the appropriate working groups. The composition of these groups matches that of COREPER and the Council of Ministers. For the most part, the members of the groups are the experts seconded to Brussels for the time being from their parent departments in their capitals. Once again the Commission is represented and the chairmanship is assumed by the member state which holds the presidency of the Council.

What sounds like bureaucratic self-indulgence and a procedural extravagance is neither. When a problem arises or an opportunity is perceived which requires swift attention, the issue can pass from Commission to working group to COREPER in quick time and the Council of Ministers can then be presented with a proposition which has undergone all the usual checks and will have been refined and no doubt improved on the way. The weightier and more complex issues which require meticulous attention inevitably take time.

When Italy held the presidency in the mid 1970s an astute member of the Italian Representation called Antici saw the need for a small group to process the dossiers which were to be considered by COREPER. Signor Antici's perspicacity is immortalised in the name of the modest institution he created. Over the years the Antici Group has saved the ambassadors valuable time by ensuring, on the eve of each meeting of COREPER, that the agenda and papers are in order and that all the required legal and other opinions have been obtained.

The Council Secretariat is responsible for the proper conduct of the business of the Council of Ministers and its subordinate bodies and the Secretary-General, the legal advisers and their staff are the arbiters of Council procedure and custodians of Council lore.

Of special importance is the ambassadors' Thursday lunch. The time appointed for the start of meetings of COREPER Part II is invariably set at 10 am. It is an equally invariable practice that proceedings actually begin between twenty minutes and half an hour later. The chairman will adjourn the meeting as near to 1 pm as possible in the hope of reconvening the session soon after 3 pm. It is a strict rule that the exchanges across the lunch table between the ambassadors and the senior member of the Commission in attendance are neither recorded nor reported to capitals. During the years I spent in Brussels I was not aware of this rule being breached on any occasion. The reason is clear. The ambition the permanent representatives share is to work out ways of serving the wider European interest while taking the fullest possible account of the interests of individual member states. The ambassadors are exceptionally well placed to identify both sets of interest and they understand that nothing is to be gained by devising policies which cause unnecessary detriment to one or more member states; on another occasion their own country might find itself in the position of potential victim. For this reason ambassadors seek ways on this informal occasion of helping the colleague who might, because of his instructions, have difficulty in rallying to the majority view without compromising the position of his government.

The framing of the instructions for meetings of COREPER needs careful attention. It is not difficult for the United Kingdom Representation to establish in advance the attitude of the Commission and the other member states towards the various items on the agenda and to report these to London. The initial examination in the relevant working groups provides the first evidence. This can be expanded through bilateral discussion with other representations in Brussels, or through contacts between our embassies and the relevant ministries in member states' capitals. This information, together with the Representation's own recommendations about the handling of the various items on the agenda, has an important influence on the instructions sent from London. What the ambassador wants to receive is not so much a detailed critique of Commission proposals as a clear statement of the outcome London wish him to achieve. Should he welcome the proposal? Should he oppose it? Should he seek to amend it and, if so, in what respect? Should he seek to delay a decision? At one stage I attempted to formalise this procedure. I suggested to London that the first paragraph of my instructions on each item of the agenda should state our objective in the briefest possible terms. This was readily accepted, but someone in London failed to understand the purpose I had in mind; the first telegram of instructions I received in the new format began with the following words: 'Objective: to consider the Commission proposal'.

When COREPER's business is concluded, which is often late in the evening, the ambassadors return to their respective offices to finalise the reports their staff have been drafting on the day's proceedings. A one-page summary of the conclusions of the meeting embodying the ambassador's own impressions is a convenient way of bringing the ministers concerned in capitals up to date.

Each Friday I caught the first flight from Brussels to London. Thanks to the time difference, I reached Whitehall at the start of business for the day. My first call might be on a minister due to represent the United Kingdom at a meeting of one of the Councils during the following week. I would then attend a meeting in the Cabinet Office of senior officials concerned with European affairs. I would supplement orally the written reports on the previous day's COREPER meeting which had been sent overnight to London. In the light of this, the meeting would then attempt to finalise the recommendations in the briefs to be submitted to the ministers concerned.

Meetings of the Council of Ministers often take place on Mondays. Ministers and their advisers arrive from their capitals the previous day. My wife and I regularly accommodated three or four of our London visitors overnight. We would arrange a working dinner, preceded and followed by discussion by the London and Brussels teams of the agenda for the morrow. On these occasions I would begin by reporting the latest news about likely attitudes round the table. The minister would follow with an explanation of any last minute amendments he had made to the briefs. We would then discuss tactics – which of the minister's colleagues might usefully be lobbied in advance; what alliances might be forged; what trade-offs might be considered when the negotiation became serious.

In recognition of the role it had played in the early days, Luxembourg is host to the Council of Ministers in April, June and October. No matter where they take place and whatever the formation – Councils of Foreign Ministers, Agriculture Ministers, Finance Ministers, Development Aid Ministers, or any other group of ministers – these meetings can range from the momentous to the humdrum; from the global to the parochial; from the productive to the frustrating; from the benign to the acrimonious. They consume much time and energy. Yet, because so much is at stake, inconveniences are willingly endured by all the participants.

The prestige, if not the role, of the Council of Ministers and the Commission was affected by the decision in 1974 that the heads of state and government of the member states – only France is represented by its head of state – should meet regularly in what was to become known as the 'European Council'. It was agreed at that time that the advisers who normally attend meetings of the Council would be excluded from meetings of the new European Council. Those present, in addition to the heads of state or government would be foreign ministers, and occasionally other ministers, and the president and vice-president of the Commission. More recently the secretaries-general of the Commission and the Council have also been admitted. Somewhat naively, a demand was made at the outset that the purpose of the new body should be clarified; was it to be the supreme decision-making body, or an occasion for a fireside chat? Inevitably it became both and, since its establishment, any problems over implementation of the European Council's decisions have been resolved.

* * *

The extent to which meetings of the European Council and the Council of Ministers in its various forms advance the process of ever closer union among the peoples of Europe depends on a number of factors – for example, the nature of the agenda, the extent to which the interests of member states are in conflict, and the domestic political situation which each of the participants has for a few days left behind. For this reason, even if he succeeds in securing concessions from this or that member state, the president of the Council cannot always produce agreed solutions. In many cases consideration of intractable issues has to be postponed to a later meeting. But the proper management of the business of the Council depends on the skills of the president.

In January 1977 the United Kingdom assumed the presidency for the first time. For the next six months we took the chair at all meetings – from the working groups to the European Council. Until his untimely death late in February of that year, when he was succeeded by his deputy, David Owen, Anthony Crosland was chairman of the foreign affairs Council. James Callaghan chaired the European Council.

The member of my staff who had now assumed charge of the Antici Group accompanied me on my Friday visits to London. These assumed even more importance. Round the committee table in the Cabinet Office we had not only to prepare advice for the ministers who would speak for the United Kingdom, but also the briefs for the ministers who would chair the Council meetings. Preparations for the presidency had been in hand for several months and the officials specially recruited to assist the process in London had been thoroughly briefed. All of my staff had been in post long enough to observe how representations of other member states had managed the presidency and to draw appropriate lessons. Even more important, since meetings without interpreters are conducted in the lingua franca of the Community namely English *and* French – they and their spouses were all competent in French, thus exploding the myth that the British, as a people, cannot learn foreign languages. The preparation proved invaluable. The conduct of meetings under British chairmanship was widely commended. Unfortunately, similar thought had not been given at political level to issues of substance and our partners were disappointed at the lack of Community initiatives we were willing to encourage.

In preparing for the meetings of COREPER which I was to chair, I was briefed by the staff of the Council Secretariat. In the Council chamber the Secretary-General sat at my side and was able to offer occasional guidance on matters of procedure or precedent. Likewise, the Legal Adviser, who sat behind me, was able to assist when the precise definition of texts was raised. At my first briefing meeting with the Secretary-General and his staff, I caused some surprise when I asked, in regard to the first substantial item on the agenda, what outcome it was suggested I should work for. This, I was told firmly, was not the business of the Secretariat; this was a political not a procedural matter. I said that in that case I would prepare my own list of desirable outcomes. As the weeks passed the Secretary-General and his colleagues became more and more curious about this technique. Eventually I was asked how often I had achieved my intended outcome. I replied that I thought this was regarded by the Secretariat as a political matter but, if they wanted to know, the answer was 100%. Cooperation between us became even closer.

After six months of intense effort and deep involvement in the affairs of the European Community, all of us involved in managing the presidency, whether in

London, Brussels, or the capitals of the other member states, felt that, in terms of the new Europe, we had helped the United Kingdom to come of age.

It is the custom in the diplomatic service that one of the last acts of an ambassador before leaving his post is to address a valedictory despatch to the secretary of state recounting the main events during his mission and setting out any conclusions he may have drawn. This I did in the autumn of 1979. Ten years later I was invited to advise one of the Spanish members of the European Commission on the Community's relations with developing countries other than those belonging to the African, Caribbean and Pacific Group. During my occasional visits to Brussels I had an opportunity to refresh my memory and to update my knowledge of the ways of the European Community. Nothing I learned then caused me to modify in any important respect the impressions I took away with me after four years in the most challenging and demanding post the diplomatic service has to offer.

So, what view have I formed in the light of these experiences?

Immediately striking is the commitment of everyone involved in this great European enterprise. Compared with many other bureaucracies in national and even local administrations, European institutions are modestly staffed. The pressure of work is severe; staff both in the institutions and the representations of the member states work long hours, long days, long weeks. The breaks at Christmas, Easter, Ascension and during the month of August, when all but emergency activity comes to a halt, are more than well merited.

Equally impressive is the way in which common purpose and shared experience breed camaraderie. Many enduring friendships are forged in the heat of the Brussels cauldron. The debating style adopted in formal meetings can give innocent pleasure. While the behaviour of ministers, commissioners and ambassadors at the Council table is for the most part courteous, this does not inhibit indulgence in an elegant form of hypocrisy. In the 1970s a member of the Commission became notorious for his frequent and prolonged absences on foreign trips. When his director-general submitted an important and long-awaited Commission proposal to COREPER on his behalf, the chairman asked that the appreciation of the Committee be conveyed to the commissioner 'next time he is passing through Brussels'. French-speaking members of the Council exploit the richness of their language to the full. It did not take the newcomer long to understand that 'comprehensive' means 'far too long'; 'imaginative' means 'unrealistic'; 'adventurous' means 'unacceptable as it stands'; 'conceptual' means 'vague and pretentious'; 'original' means 'I wish I had thought of that'.

These linguistic gymnastics lightened the atmosphere. But another impression had more serious implications. Initial reactions to Commission initiatives seemed to expose significant differences of approach and I spent some time seeking an explanation. Eventually I concluded, with less than total confidence, that these differences had their origins in history, tradition and, in particular, the legal inheritance. I did not find it easy to come to terms with the confidence, even the idealism, exhibited by those who had lived for centuries within the framework of Roman Law and the derivatives of the Code Napoleon. On the other hand, British empiricism induced London to include in their instructions the most detailed critique of every proposal emanating from the Commission, as well as any amendments proposed by other member states. London's attitude seemed to be that, since the law was supreme and had to be obeyed, the law must be as robust as possible. Every effort had therefore to be made to anticipate all possible contingencies. Some of my colleagues in the Council chamber seemed to treat the same Commission proposals as representing an aspiration, an ambition, which everyone should strive to achieve. For them, identifying the objective was what mattered; whether the path to achievement would prove too arduous or prone to rock falls was a secondary matter which would be addressed, if necessary, in due course. But this did not prevent the Council setting deadlines for attainment of the objective, however unrealistic these might prove to be in practice.

My experience during the abortive negotiations in the early 1960s had prepared me for the detailed nature of the work of the Council. Paul-Henri Spaak, the eminent Belgian statesman, had told Edward Heath then about the negotiations at Messina which prepared the way for the creation of the Community. 'We set out to build a new Europe,' he said, 'and we ended up arguing about the tariff on bananas.' This, I soon discovered, was still a valid comment. For two reasons this disturbed me. In the first place, while those of us behind the closed doors of the Council chamber could understand the rationale for the brick-upon-brick construction of Europe, this was not obvious to the man and woman in the street. Of course, it is no easy task to depict decisions of the Council, which are often of concern only to limited sectors of society, as major contributions to ever closer union among the peoples of Europe. However hard they try and however worthy their intentions, the media can make few headlines out of the tariff on bananas.

I had a more serious concern. Preoccupation with the minutiae, especially at ministerial level, induced the age-old malady of not being able to see the wood for the trees. This led me to doubt whether the common market, even with the subsequent extensions of Community competence into the fields of energy, industry, transport and economic and monetary policy, was an adequate base on which the new Europe should be constructed. Was Europe, to adapt Napoleon's notorious remark about the English, merely a continent of shop-keepers? I therefore recommended in my valedictory despatch to the foreign secretary that the base could be made more solid and the whole enterprise more intelligible to the citizenry if there were closer cooperation in the fields of defence and foreign policy. This suggestion was noted politely in London and ignored.

Since I left Brussels events of major historical importance have changed the lives and prospects of millions of our fellow Europeans. The end of the cold war and the removal of the Soviet tyranny from central and eastern Europe released national and ethnic tensions in some cases with tragic results. The people of the former Soviet Union are finding it hard to adjust to their new circumstances and their situation is not helped by the volatility of their president.

Meanwhile, the construction of the new Europe has been driven forward with untiring dedication. The Community of Ten has become the Union of the Fifteen. Several more candidates for membership wait impatiently in the wings. The European Assembly has become a directly elected Parliament. The Single European Act, the creation of the European Union and the programme for Economic and Monetary Union have significantly advanced the process of closer European integration. However, the results of the referendums on the Maastricht Treaty in 1992 and other soundings of opinion demonstrated the widespread sense of alienation among the citizenry of the Union. Many complain that the proceedings of the Council of Ministers lack transparency; the Council is seen by some as a latter-day secret society. The Commission is accused of interfering unnecessarily in the affairs of citizens. The enhanced powers granted to the European Parliament give the appearance rather than the reality of democratic accountability. The cost and effects of certain policies – notably the common agricultural and fisheries policies – are widely resented. And, despite the recommendations of successive Presidents of the Commission and distinguished members of the Parliament at regular intervals since the mid-1970s, it was only in 1991 at Maastricht that the principle of subsidiarity was embodied in a European treaty. And it is alleged, with some justification, that since then little more than lip service has been paid to this principle.

The Maastricht Treaty foreshadowed an Intergovernmental Conference which would carry forward the process of integration. The result was the Treaty of Amsterdam. Although this Treaty represents progress on a number of issues such as policies to stimulate employment, preparing for the introduction of Economic and Monetary Union, making the proceedings of the Council of Ministers more transparent and increasing the powers of the Parliament, it is disappointing that agreement could not be reached on the reforms of the institutions of the Union which are an essential preliminary to the further enlargement of the Union. In particular, the questions of the size of the Commission and the system of voting in an enlarged Union were unresolved.

In July 1997, one month after the Treaty of Amsterdam was initialled, the European Commission, under the eye-catching title 'Agenda 2000', published its proposals for the development of the Union and the policies it should adopt as it enters the next century. The most notable item in this document is the recommendation that, after reviewing the applications of ten countries for accession to the Union, negotiations should open with the Czech Republic, Estonia, Hungary, Poland and Slovenia, in addition to Cyprus. If in due course these negotiations succeed, the membership of the Union will rise from fifteen to twenty-one.

*   *   *

Today the European Union faces formidable challenges. Turbulence in the financial markets adds urgency to the search for effective responses. First and foremost, the introduction of the single currency must be handled with skill and patience. By itself the single currency will not solve another pressing problem. The dynamic economy on which the prosperity of the citizens of the Union must be based cannot be achieved so long as half of the Union's budget is earmarked for support for food production. Then again, on grounds of security and common interest, the Union must open its doors to those states in eastern and central Europe which qualify for admission and are prepared to accept the obligations of membership. These two problems overlap. Unless it is reformed the common agricultural policy will collapse under the weight of further enlargement. Apart from this, subsidies have to be reduced if the Union is to meet its obligations as a member of the World Trade Organisation.

During its Presidency of the Union in the first six months of this year, the United Kingdom made special efforts to stimulate debate about the governance of the Union in the new millennium. The response from a number of other member states was encouraging. So this brings me back to my first point, namely the need to reform the structures and working methods of the institutions of the Union and, thereby, to 'give Europe back to the people'. The time is ripe for new – even radical – thinking about Europe's future. It is now widely recognised that, by its very nature, a Union of twenty-one, twenty-five, or even thirty states, each with its own history, culture, traditions and beliefs, cannot be governed in the same way as the original Community of Six, or today's Union of Fifteen.

It is encouraging that those who will meet at the Summit in Vienna in December are already looking forward to setting in hand reform of the institutions and methods of the Union and rigorous application of the principle of subsidiarity. If the disaffection of so many of the Union's citizens is to be dispelled, it is imperative that the authority of the Union should be exerted only where this is essential. By devolving authority the Union will demonstrate its respect for the sense of national and regional identity in both the larger and smaller states. After all, there is no reason to suppose that the architects of political systems throughout human history have exhausted the constitutional possibilities. The 'journey to an unknown destination' must continue. And we should allow our thoughts to take wing. It cannot be beyond our collective wit to devise an original system of ordering relations between peoples of different culture, traditions, race and faith which is relevant to the circumstances of the new millennium and acceptable to those whose well-being matters most – the citizens of the Union.

European leaders would regain the respect and confidence of the citizenry if they were to re-state the objectives of the European venture in terms which set the tariff on bananas in its appropriately insignificant context. They should make it clear that the Union is not merely a means of accommodating the size and strength of Germany in the centre of Europe. The Union should also set itself the task of assuring the safety and prosperity of all the peoples of Europe, and undertake to play a more articulate and effective international role in the interests of the people of Europe and of the wider world.

XI

EUROPE: A NEW BEGINNING?

UNIVERSITY OF BATH
25 NOVEMBER 1999

The process of European integration in the second half of this century has been inspired by a vision and frustrated by a series of political errors.

The vision was first articulated by Jean Monnet, a remarkable Frenchman who, when much of Europe was occupied by the armies of Hitler's Germany, devoted his time and energies to trying to persuade otherwise preoccupied political leaders to focus on the problems which would arise when eventually the war ended. Monnet was conscious of the mistakes made at Versailles which contained the seeds of the second cataclysm, and was persuaded that a completely different approach to the long-standing and deep-seated problems of Europe would be needed. In 1943 he wrote: 'The real change we are after is not the free flow of goods. It is a change in the relation between people, and this change comes about because these people are no longer thinking in terms of their national, limited responsibilities . . . They are now thinking about common, joint responsibilities. This is the revolutionary character of the process of change that we are trying to set in motion. That process is a revolution, and should be never-ending'.

The first application of Monnet's formula was the decision of France, Germany, Italy and the Benelux countries in 1951 to establish what they called, with common sense and an engaging lack of modesty, the European Coal and Steel Community – the brainchild of Robert Schuman, the Foreign Minister of France at the time. The logic was impeccable. If the two basic industries which had provided the wherewithal to make war were placed under joint, rather than national, control, the inclination to resort to force to settle disputes would be thwarted.

The creation of this novel Community was a first step. However, it may be judged today that Jean Monnet's most significant and enduring legacy was his inspiration of the definition of the ultimate purpose of the great enterprise in the Preamble to the Treaty of Rome signed in 1957; this was: 'ever-closer union among the peoples of Europe' – a form of words which was neatly paraphrased in 1973 by the journalist Andrew Shonfield, who gave his series of Reith Lectures for the BBC the title: *Journey to an Unknown Destination.*

* * *

The first critical error – in 1954 – was the decision of the then French Government not to present to the National Assembly in Paris the Bill to establish a European Defence Community. The precise reasons for this remain unclear. In the summer of that year an international conference was held in Geneva. The intention was to put a formal end to the hostilities in the Korean Peninsula and to bring peace to Indo-China. 1954 was a difficult year for France and the morale of the members of the French delegation in Geneva, led by the Foreign Minister, Georges Bidault, was low. The war in Indo-China had taken a turn for the worse. After months of gallant resistance the French garrison at Dien Bien Phu had been obliged to surrender. Soon after this Bidault was replaced by Pierre Mendès-France, the new Prime minister.

Meanwhile the countries of Western Europe faced a new challenge. A way had to be found to integrate the armed forces of the new Germany into a larger entity. The creation of a defence community in Western Europe seemed to be an appropriate solution. However, this gave rise to difficulties over the respective roles of NATO and the new entity. With patience these could have been resolved, but the opportunity was not seized. The decision to abandon what had been originally a French initiative meant that, when the leaders of the Six Members of the Coal and Steel Community met in Messina in June 1955 to plan the Economic Community, there was no counterpart in the defence or political field. To paraphrase Napoleon Bonaparte's sarcastic comment about England, the participants ran the risk of creating a community of merchants.

The second political error was the decision of the British to stand aside while these steps towards closer cooperation in Western Europe were being planned. The view in London was that the process of closer integration would founder sooner or later. The only point that one can make in mitigation is that decision makers in London and their senior advisers had spent the critical years of their service to their country at a time when Britain stood alone in Europe and had established with the United States one of the closest military and political alliances in history. The habit of working together had become instinctive – and not only on this side of the Atlantic. Yet it is regrettable, to put it no higher, that the opinion of those of the next generation, who saw the potential in the process of progressive integration in Western Europe, was not given more weight.

When, four years after the Treaty of Rome was signed and the foundations of the Common Market were laid, the British had second thoughts and applied to join the European Economic Community, President de Gaulle committed what his then Foreign Minister, Maurice Couve de Murville, has recently admitted was a kind of betrayal – 'une sorte de trahison'. Despite the fact that sixteen months of intense negotiation had resolved virtually all the problems raised by Britain's application, the French President vetoed Britain's entry. This – the third major political error – was compounded by the enactment by the Council of Ministers over the following ten years of three Community policies – on agriculture, the financing of the Community, and fisheries – in forms which would have been unacceptable to the United Kingdom. This ensured that, when Britain did join the Community in 1973, much ministerial time and goodwill was expended over several years on efforts to moderate the impact of these policies.

* * *

In October 1972 the French President, Georges Pompidou, chaired a conference in Paris to which were invited the heads of government of the existing six members of the Community and of the three states, the United Kingdom, Denmark and Ireland, which were to join at the beginning of the following year. The purpose was not merely to provide an opportunity for the nine future colleagues to get to know each other. More important was the need, in the period immediately before the accession of the new members to focus attention on the future direction of the enlarged Community. At the conclusion of the conference the nine heads of government adopted as their objective the transformation of their relations into a European Union, which would include Economic and Monetary Union, by the year 1980. The idea of creating a European monetary system had come to the fore following the decision by the United States in August 1971, without any consultation with its allies, to abandon the Bretton Woods system negotiated in 1944. This threw currencies across the world into disarray.

In the years that followed much thought was given to the form a European Union might take. In 1975, François-Xavier Ortoli, the President of the Commission, presented a proposal for an eventual European Union. In this document he said: 'European Union is not to give birth to a centralising super-state . . . the Union will be given responsibility only for those matters which Member states are no longer capable of dealing with efficiently.' Two years later, in a lecture in Florence, his successor, Roy, now Lord Jenkins, argued that the Community should concentrate on those 'functions which will, beyond doubt, deliver significantly better results because they are performed at Community level', while leaving to Member States 'those functions which they can do equally well, or better, on their own'. No less than fourteen years were to pass before this doctrine, which we now know as 'subsidiarity', passed into European Union law. It was Jacques Delors, then President of the Commission, who insisted on including a commitment to this principle in the Maastricht Treaty in 1991. However, in correcting one error the newly created Union committed another by not providing effective means to ensure observance of his principle.

Meanwhile, substantial progress had been made towards achieving the aim of Economic and Monetary Union. This owed much to the enthusiasm of Helmut Schmidt, the German Chancellor, and Valery Giscard d'Estaing, the French President, and to the persuasive powers of Roy Jenkins. In 1978 the European Monetary System came into existence, triggered in the end by the fall in the value of the US dollar. To the surprise of no one, the United Kingdom decided not to participate – at least for the time being.

During his term as President of the Commission Roy Jenkins had become increasingly aware of certain inadequacies in the functioning of the Commission. This led him to secure the agreement of his colleagues in January 1979 to appoint an Independent Review Body with the task of examining 'how the Commission's organisation and staff resources can best be adjusted to meet future needs, and thus cope with a rapidly changing workload in the light of defined priorities'. Dirk Spierenburg, a distinguished Dutch diplomat who had served as a member of the Coal and Steel Commission, chaired the Review Body, which had four other appointed members. In October of the same year Spierenburg presented his refreshingly candid Report to the Commission. This drew attention to the many gaps which remained in the implementation of the Treaties; to the disproportionate effort, in terms of energy, time and money, that seemed to be needed to produce even a rather modest output; to the multiplication of meetings of the Council of Ministers without any corresponding increase in the business concluded; and to the 'general phenomenon of an excessive load of business aggravated by slow and confused handling'. The Review Body went on to recommend a set of measures for dealing with these internal weaknesses. First, in future the Commission should be composed of only one Member per country. Secondly, the structure of the Commission should be slimmed down and rationalised at all levels; this would entail reducing as rapidly as possible the number of Directorates-General in order to relate these to the number of portfolios. Thirdly, the College of Commissioners should deliberate collectively on major policy questions. Fourthly, administrative coordination within the Commission must be strengthened. Fifthly, there was a need for better personnel management. And finally, the Commission must exercise its role of initiative with greater coherence, within the framework of the priorities agreed at the European Council. This Council was a formalisation of an ad hoc arrangement whereby the heads of state and government met from time to give political guidance on specific issues to the Council of Ministers. With nine members instead of six and a range of severe problems, for example in the energy and employment fields, it was felt by the mid-1970s that regular, carefully prepared meetings at the highest political level were needed.

At first the verdict of the Review Body and its recommendations were not welcomed by all of Roy Jenkins colleagues, but in due course they accepted the wisdom on which they were based. Roy Jenkins noted in his diary that, when he reported the Spierenburg conclusions to senior members of the Commission staff, they reacted with fairly limited enthusiasm, resignation and some complaint. He added the comment that a lot of the senior staff, but not all, 'hate doing anything which in any way shakes them out of their ruts'.

*　*　*

Progress continued at a steady pace towards the objectives set at the Summit in Paris in October 1972. Eventually, in December 1985, the Heads of Government signed the Single European Act, which created a single market of over 370 million consumers. And, in 1990, the United Kingdom decided to enter the Exchange Rate Mechanism, but did so at a moment when the exchange rate of the pound sterling placed it at a competitive disadvantage.

The Treaty of Maastricht in 1992 represented an important staging post. The challenges posed and the opportunities offered by the end of the cold war reinforced the need for further integration in the Western half of the continent. The Maastricht Treaty was intended to be the Union's response to this seismic development. The most eye-catching decision was the abandonment of the name 'Community', conceived at Messina in 1955, in favour of 'Union'. But the real significance of the Treaty lay in the detailed plans laid down for Economic and Monetary Union, including the introduction of the Euro in those Member States which considered that they were ready and willing to adopt it. The subject of the single currency dominated the proceedings and tended to exclude detailed examination of other pressing matters. However, time was taken to focus attention on the need for a modern trans-European infrastructure and common social and environmental policies. Other issues of importance were bequeathed to a further Inter-Governmental Conference to be held four years later. These included the democratic credibility of the Union and preparations for its further enlargement, including the amendment of existing procedures which were already under strain and would be impractical in a Union of twenty-one members. It was of little help that in this way the Maastricht Treaty added further complications to the already unwieldy decision-making process of the Union.

The conclusions of the Maastricht Treaty were greeted with little enthusiasm. European leaders had failed to appreciate the extent of popular disillusion throughout the Union – the irritation with what was widely seen as unnecessary and sometimes arrogant interference by the Commission in the lives of ordinary citizens; the allegations of waste, profligacy and fraud amounting to over 5% of the Community budget; the cumbersome nature and lack of transparency of the decision-making process; and the relative impotence of the European Parliament in Strasbourg. Preoccupation at Maastricht with economic and monetary union did nothing to dispel this unease.

The Intergovernmental Conference charged with completing the business left over from Maastricht set out its conclusions in 1997 in the Treaty of Amsterdam. These were useful in a limited sense, but some of the more difficult issues, such as the system of qualified majority voting and the size and structure of the Commission in the light of the forthcoming further enlargement of the Union, were yet again left unresolved. This latter subject was discussed by representatives of twenty-six European states at a conference in London in March 1998 and in November of that year it was decided that negotiations would be opened with six of the candidates – the Czech Republic, Estonia, Hungary, Poland, Slovenia and Cyprus.

The situation in the Union was about to change. Allegations of malpractice by individual Members of the European Commission early this year prompted Members of the European Parliament to assert themselves. In January 1999 the Parliament appointed a team of experts to investigate allegations of fraud. The Commission responded by agreeing a timetable for internal reforms. This proved insufficient to satisfy the Parliament and, faced with the disgraceful refusal of those Members of the Commission who had been singled out for criticism to give up their posts, the entire Commission, including the President, Jacques Santer, resigned on 15 March.

* * *

Since then events have moved fast. Early in May the Parliament approved the appointment of Romano Prodi, a former Prime Minister of Italy, as the new President of the Commission. On 9 July the nominations for the new Commission by the Member States and the President-designate were announced at a press conference. Romano Prodi used this occasion to make clear his determination to make a fresh start. He said: 'I am painfully aware that, as Europe grows in importance in people's lives, their trust in the Commission has slipped. We need nothing less than a revolution in the way the Commission works.' Two weeks later he told the European Parliament that fundamental review and reform were needed to make the Commission a world-class administration that leads by example. The policy agenda must address those issues which affect people's daily lives – jobs, growth and sustainable development which balances wealth creation, social justice and quality of life – these must be the priority. He intended to set up a high-level group to prepare for the Inter-Governmental Conference scheduled for December 1999 to pave the way for the enlargement of the Union and overhaul its institutions. Institutional reforms should be put in place by the end of the year 2002, by which date negotiations with the most advanced candidate countries would be coming to a conclusion. Implicit in this programme is a radical reform of major policies, and especially the Common Agricultural Policy, and resolute application of the principle of subsidiarity.

On 1 September Romano Prodi followed the example of Roy Jenkins twenty years earlier when he invited a small team of experts to give their independent views by the middle of the following month on the institutional implications of the enlargement of the Union. The leader of the group was the former Belgian Prime Minister, Jean-Luc Dehaene; the other two members were Richard von Weizsacker, the former President of the Federal Republic and Lord Simon, a former British Government minister.

The three wise men presented their report on 18 October. Their conclusions were concise and trenchant. In the first place, they considered that the political and historical importance of enlargement was such that it could not be delayed or postponed just because institutional reform was incomplete. They were firmly of the opinion that the forthcoming Intergovernmental Conference had to be concluded by the end of the year 2000. As regards the pressing issues of the size and composition of the Commission, the weighting of votes and majority voting, which were highlighted by the European Council when it met in Cologne in June 1999, they took the view that, since enlargement would increase diversity, flexibility in the institutional framework was even more important than at present. As for the procedure at the forthcoming conference, they believed that the Commission should submit comprehensive and concrete proposals in the form of a draft treaty at the very beginning of the conference.

The new Commission held its first formal meeting on 18 September and a month later proposed that accession talks should be opened next year with six more countries – Bulgaria, Latvia, Lithuania, Malta, Romania and Slovakia. This recommendation is likely to be endorsed by the European Council when it meets in Helsinki towards the end of this year. The Commission also recommended that henceforth Turkey should be regarded as a candidate country.

*　*　*

Injecting urgency into the reform of the institutions of the Union was not the only achievement of the European Council at Cologne last summer. European leaders took a major step towards correcting the first error in the process of European integration – the failure to establish a European Defence Community in 1954. The Council accepted that, in order to achieve the objectives of the Common Foreign and Security Policy which had been the subject of seemingly endless debate, the Union had to have 'the capacity for autonomous action, backed up by credible military forces, the means to decide to use them, and a readiness to do so, in order to respond to international crises without prejudice to actions by NATO'. The Council believed that this would increase the Union's ability to contribute to international peace and security in accordance with the principles of the UN Charter. The serious intent in these words was confirmed by the Council's decision to appoint Javier Solana Madariaga, then about to retire from his position as Secretary-General of NATO, to the new post of Secretary-General of the Council and High Representative for the Common Foreign and Security Policy.

*　*　*

Future historians may well see the forced resignation of the European Commission in the spring of 1999 as a decisive event in the story of Europe's journey to an unknown destination. Those who wield power and influence in the institutions of the Union, having acknowledged that the causes for popular disenchantment have to be removed without delay, have committed themselves to ambitious and urgent programmes of reform and innovation. We must now hope that the commitments entered into by our political leaders and by those who serve the Union in its institutions will be speedily and effectively fulfilled. The present is a moment for renewed vision and resolve to commit no more errors. Throughout our continent citizens wish to see emerge from the processes of the next few years a secure and prosperous Europe able at last to wield the influence in world affairs that our human, economic, intellectual and cultural assets deserve. Should this ambition be achieved, we may yet see the names of Romano Prodi and Javier Solana Madariaga adorn the European Hall of Fame alongside those of Jean Monnet and Robert Schuman. *¿Quien sabe?*

CHAPTER THREE: **THE GLOBAL CONTEXT**

The Yom Kippur War in the autumn of 1963, the rise in oil prices and the subsequent demand for a new international economic order brought to the fore the disparities between the industrialised and the developing nations. This issue and its implications remain high on the international agenda.

I

A NEW INTERNATIONAL ORDER

CHRIST CHURCH, CHELSEA – OCTOBER 1974

It is not altogether reasonable, at a time when so many nations are preoccupied with their internal problems, to expect public attention to be engaged by the challenges facing the international community. That we shall be devoting the coming week to prayers for the peace of the world is, therefore, an entry on the credit side of the balance sheet.

In every corner of the world those who do stop to take stock of our international condition are anxious and perplexed as seldom before. Assumptions which gave us a comfortable sense of security and offered the prospect of measured progress towards wider understanding and cohesion are being invalidated every day. We can sympathise with the individual citizen who wonders whether the pace of the changes taking place across the world is not altogether too rapid; and who perceives in this process threats to his own security and to the complex structure of international arrangements we have built up over the past generation. We may find less justification for the despair of those who fear there will be no secure haven from the tidal wave of international anarchy which they believe is about to overwhelm our system.

If pessimism on this scale is not justified, it is surely right that we should examine the more substantial grounds for anxiety about the state of international relationships.

First, there is a fear of domination by the super-powers. The notion is widespread, especially in the so-called Third World, that in some way the United States and the Soviet Union might seek to establish some kind of condominium over the rest of us. There is an emotional basis to this fear. Yet it is as easy to respect power as to resent it. The wise course is to recognise it.. And the indisputable fact is that each of these two great states wields military power unmatched by any other state or group of states. At the same time there is no shred of evidence to suggest that the two super-powers have any grand design, nor that they have received some privileged revelation as to how the world's affairs should be ordered. On the contrary. In my view, what the superpowers are engaged in is no more than an attempt to reduce tension between east and west, to isolate and remove sources of friction, and to identify and enlarge areas of common interest.

We can all be thankful that the mutual deterrence of the super-powers has saved the world from nuclear war on a global scale. Yet this very condition of mutual deterrence appears to have granted a kind of licence to smaller powers to wage bilateral wars with limited objectives. When the causes of such wars lie in a deep sense of frustration at the failure of the international community to remove some festering injustice then, as we have seen three times in the past three years, there seems to be some degree of international tolerance for such resort to force. Limited wars may succeed in redressing a grievance. But they almost always alter the situation in ways other than those intended. Sudden shifts in the balance of power can create new instability and sow the seeds of new tension and disturbance. The objections to limited wars are political and economic as well as humanitarian since as always happens when violence is the instrument, death, destruction, waste and misery follow. The innocent victims reproach the international community for its failures. And more often than not the reproach is justified and unanswerable.

A second ground for anxiety is the steady increase in the military strength of a certain number of the medium powers and the spread of the capacity to make nuclear weapons. If those states concerned have been led to follow such policies through fear for their own security, then they are doing no more than exercising an acknowledged right of self-defence. But in taking steps to enhance their own security they can stimulate corresponding fears in the breasts of their neighbours, and so another vicious circle is brought into existence.

A third source of anxiety is the widespread disregard for human rights of which new evidence is continually coming to light. This takes many forms. In many countries the flow of information is controlled in such a way that facts are withheld from the people, or they are otherwise wilfully misled. Dissenting voices are silenced. The citizens of many countries are not free to leave should they wish to do so. Others are so oppressed that they choose exile. In scores of countries, as a recent investigation showed, torture is practised systematically by government authorities. In other equally unacceptable ways millions of our fellow human beings are denied basic human rights.

But it is not always the state apparatus that oppresses the individual. One scourge of the 1970s is international terrorism. The terrorist deprives whole communities of freedoms which for centuries have been the hallmark of civilised society. It is a contradiction of all that civilised society means when the innocence of the bystander, whether in Santo Domingo or a public house in Guildford, is exploited as a means of pressure on those responsible for our security.

The observer of the international scene is perhaps most perplexed by developments over the past few years in a different sphere – the relationship between the countries of the industrialised North and the developing South.

The problems involved in this relationship are especially sensitive. Since they bring into opposition people of different races, cultures and historical experience, they have undertones of prejudice and resentment, envy and fear. In character these problems are both economic and political. But the central issue can be simply stated. As a whole the nations of the developing world aspire to a higher standard of living, a superior quality of life, and greater influence on the major decisions affecting international relationships. Their complaint is that we in the industrialised world enjoy more than our fair share of political power and derive more than our fair advantage from the exploitation of the Earth's limited resources of raw materials. Indeed some of them argue that we are improvident in our consumption of them. The states of the Third World note that while the technology to exploit is for the time being the monopoly of the industrialised nations, a higher proportion of these raw materials is to be found in their own countries. They therefore seek a more equitable distribution of the benefits of the Earth's resources and adapt their policies accordingly.

Now, nothing could more clearly serve the common interest than that the natural resources of the Earth and the products of man's ingenuity, enterprise and industry should be exploited for the benefit of the maximum number of the Earth's inhabitants.

This is an easy enough principle to articulate. But the question arises: how can this principle be applied effectively and in an orderly fashion?

Since the industrial states repaired the devastation of the Second World War immense wealth and a vast amount of technology and much skill has been transferred to the developing world. There are few corners of the Earth where the tangible results of these great programmes of aid are not evident. Yet, despite this transfer of treasure and expertise, the industrial world has been achieving a rate of economic growth which has left the developing world even further behind in the march towards material prosperity.

The attempt of the nations of the Third World to secure an improvement in their relative position has been one of the main characteristics of the period since the end of the second world war. As early as 1952 the Government of Chile introduced into a discussion of human rights the concept of permanent sovereignty over natural resources. Ten years later, in 1962, the General Assembly of the United Nations adopted a Declaration which asserted that –

'The rights of peoples and nations to permanent sovereignty over their natural wealth and resources must be exercised in the interest of their national development and of the well-being of the state concerned.'

The new states of the developing world had, of course, achieved nominal sovereignty over their natural resources when they won their independence. But in practice no substantial change occurred in the balance of economic power.

Whenever they have had an opportunity to do so the nations of the Third World have advanced their claim. It has been reiterated at every General Assembly of the United Nations since 1962, at the Sessions of the UN Conference on Trade and Development, at the bi-annual meetings of the Economic and Social Council and, in perhaps the starkest terms, at the Conferences of the Non-Aligned States. But all to little real effect.

In the autumn of 1973 a new element was introduced into the North/South relationship. Only now, a year later, is the international community beginning to calculate the dimensions of the new problems created by the sudden and immense rise in the price of oil. In the first place, the division of humanity into three worlds – the democratic, the communist and the developing – is no longer appropriate. The oil producers now have before them the prospect of unimaginable wealth. But at the same time they have acquired a financial power which they realise they will have to exercise with prudence if the world's monetary and trading systems are not to collapse. Such a collapse, apart from bankrupting many enterprises in the industrial West would bring even greater hardship to those members of the developing world – particularly in Africa and South Asia – who neither have oil of their own nor other raw materials with which to buy oil at the new high price. These countries now constitute a new category of hardest hit states.

The suddenness of the energy crisis and the ferocity of its impact should not blind us to the other problems of global compass which are already visible on the horizon. Poor harvests in North America and two inadequate monsoons in the Indian subcontinent remind us how vulnerable are our future supplies of food, and especially of grain. And knowledge that every year across the face of the Earth there are more mouths to feed can only increase our anxiety on this score.

As he surveys developments in all these various fields the individual observer is bound to wonder whether there is any way in which so many trends, each one of which contains a threat to the stability of the international system, can be controlled. Should he assume that the coincidence of so many changes affecting international relationships means that control of our affairs has passed from our hands?

In the past major changes affecting relationships between nations and individuals have generally followed in the wake of some catastrophe. For several centuries up to 1914 the concept of the nation-state dominated international relations. Disputes were settled either by diplomacy or, when that failed, on the battlefield.

Seeking an alternative, the nations determined to order their relations in accordance with a Covenant to which all members of the League of Nations would subscribe. But the United States turned its back, and Europe failed to unite. And so that project foundered. Following the Second World War a further attempt was made to regulate international relationships. I believe that we in Britain have had from the beginning rather fewer illusions than others about what the United Nations can achieve. There were those who had high hopes, when the organisation was formed in the wake of the Allies' victory, that the world was entering upon a period of permanent peace. But at that time we in Britain were still counting the cost of the failure of the League of Nations and we knew it would be unwise to expect too much. We recognised that, just as a computer can only give out information which is first fed into it, so the United Nations could not be expected to exercise more responsibility than individual states were prepared to vest in it.

Has the United Nations met the challenge? Were our hesitations and reservations about its competence justified?

It must be said that the United Nations has a membership today which no-one foresaw in 1945. And it is charged with tasks which, equally, were far from the minds of the founding fathers. In 1945 the aim of the victorious Allies was to prevent a third world war. They gave little thought to the political and economic claims of the colonial peoples.

Yet the Charter of the United Nations has proved to be an infinitely superior document to the Covenant of the League. It has stood remarkably well the test of time. Indeed, few of the weaknesses of the United Nations can reasonably be attributed either to the Charter or to the form of the Organisation which it brought into existence. It is in the attitudes to the United Nations of member states that one finds the causes of the Organisation's shortcomings.

Outside the political field the United Nations has solid achievements to its credit. Important international agreements which will produce practical effects have been concluded in the recent past on the care of refugees and on disaster relief. Work is far advanced in codifying international law. Systems of law are now being worked out for what are sometimes called the 'new frontier' subjects, such as the exploration of outer space and the exploitation of the seabed. 80% of the staff of the United Nations as a whole, and 90% of its budgets (which total nearly one thousand million dollars a year) are devoted to social and economic questions. Through the United Nations development programme, which began in 1966, the international community has mounted a co-ordinated attack on economic and social underdevelopment. The World Food Programme, which began its operation in 1963, has set up procedures for dealing with emergency or chronic food shortages anywhere in the world.

The value of the General Assembly of the United Nations has been steadily undermined in recent years by its tendency to pass quite unrealistic resolutions which have no practical effect. The risks in this to the standing of the United Nations have been more widely acknowledged and the membership is showing some preference for proceeding wherever possible by consensus. But if it is to have any value in practice such a consensus must be a true one and not a spurious consensus which obscures serious differences of principle.

The history of the Security Council, which is the highest international body charged with responsibility for maintaining international peace and security, is quite different. If the Council has not yet learned to make peace it has at least a notable record in keeping it. United Nations emergency and observer forces have been effective, notably in the Middle East, in separating combatants and observing a ceasefire or a truce often in conditions where the will on each side of the line to observe it was negligible. The Council's discussions, whether in private or in public, are for the most part serious, relevant and realistic. Members of the Council take it in turns to preside for a month at a time. There is an admirable custom whereby the President for the month gives a lunch to which he invites the Secretary General of the United Nations and the 14 other members of the Council. As one looks round that lunch table and sees one's colleagues who represent every continent, every race and a variety of political ideologies, one is conscious not of the factors which divide the members of the Council but of the responsibilities which bind them together. This gives grounds for hope that man will in the end decide to settle his differences by peaceful means.

We are left to draw the conclusion that for the time being there will be no single system capable of regulating our affairs as the imperial centres did in the past. We can look for no dominant authority, no world policeman, no universal aunt.

Meanwhile, as it moves towards universality, the United Nations will provide the principal forum where the main issues of the day can be debated by the representatives of the world community on the basis of sovereign equality. The United Nations remains, in the words of Dr Kurt Waldheim, our key, if not our lifeline to a better human society.

How, then, if, the United Nations is still only capable of performing this limited function, can we hope to establish some kind of international order out of the current welter of changes and shifts of balance? With the proliferation since the Second World War of centres of power, responsibility too has been fragmented. We are living in a multi-polar world. The main decisions, whether in the defence, political, economic or social fields, will continue to be taken by the states directly concerned. The military alliances which already exist will continue for the time being. So will other groupings of states which serve the political or economic interests of their members. More such groupings may well be formed to take account of new coincidences of interest. So, if the international community is to make orderly progress, we will have to settle for a whole series of interlocking arrangements, while we continue to advocate wider acceptance of the interdependence of states and argue the irrelevance of the habits of nursing resentments and regretting past grandeurs.

I return to my first point. How should the responsible but bewildered individual citizen face the tumultuous developments of our times? The answer must be the same as it has always been. Our salvation when disaster threatens has invariably depended on the courage, resolution and sacrifice of responsible individuals and on their faith that the human spirit will prevail. 'Throughout time,' Teilhard de Chardin wrote from the trenches in 1917, 'a task greater than individual lives is being achieved . . . It is we who constitute the active part of the universe; we are the bud in which life is concentrated and is at work and in which the flower of every hope is enclosed.'

I have no doubt that this same conviction will enable us to meet the challenges of our time.

II

EAST AND WEST, NORTH AND SOUTH

PILGRIMS OF THE UNITED STATES: NEW YORK, JANUARY 1974

At the same time as wrestling with the demand by developing countries for a new international economic order in the autumn of 1973, the superpowers were seeking to build on the policy of detente. And less than a year had passed since the United Kingdom had joined the European Community.

A few months earlier I had taken up my post as the British Representative to the United Nations in New York. An invitation to speak at the annual lunch of the Pilgrims provided an opportunity to comment on these events.

*   *   *

Henry Wadsworth Longfellow observed that 'all nations must change to something new, to something strange'. I wonder if his language would have been as restrained today. We are in the midst of a process of change as comprehensive as any since the Flood.

In the international sphere there have been two major developments since the end of the Second World War. The first has been the emergence of the two super powers, offset more recently by the coming into existence in Western Europe and Japan of units of great economic strength. The second has been the political emancipation of hundreds of millions of inhabitants of the developing world. Scores of new states have been created with a proliferation, almost overnight, of centres of political power. All of us who work in the United Nations are acutely conscious of the far-reaching character of these changes.

During this period aspects of behaviour in the advanced societies have been subjected to critical scrutiny. The result has been a ferment of new ideas about authority, religion, morality, crime and punishment, education, and so on. Traditional notions about almost every form of human relationship have been put in the crucible. Social experiments have been carried out which earlier generations could not have imagined. The limits of artistic expression have been thrust far beyond what was generally acceptable only a few years ago.

For many people – and indeed for society as a whole – change can provide stimulus and refreshment. But most of us find it unsettling. And the more radical the change, the greater the disturbance. Some believe that the international system with which we have become familiar is on the point of collapse and that Western society is disintegrating. Confusion and bewilderment have combined to produce a wave of pessimism. In my view this is quite unjustified. And I shall seek to explain why.

*   *   *

For centuries up to 1914 the concept of the nation state dominated international relations. Princes met to confer. Their success or failure in reconciling their conflicting ambitions by diplomacy determined whether the aristocracy of the day should aspire to brilliance in the salon or glory on the battlefield.

That system was destroyed in the mud of Flanders. In search of an alternative, the nations decided to order their relations in accordance with a Covenant, to which all members of the League of Nations would subscribe. For two main reasons that project foundered. First, America turned her back and, secondly, Europe, disastrously as it turned out, remained disunited.

Following the second cataclysm a further attempt was made to establish a system for regulating international relationships. The Charter of the United Nations is an infinitely superior document to the Covenant of the League. It has stood well the test of time. Indeed, few of the weaknesses of the United Nations can be attributed either to the Charter or to the form of the Organisation it brought into existence.

Another significant product of the Second World War was, of course, the harnessing of atomic power for destructive purposes. It was simply no longer open to the great powers to overturn the international chessboard with impunity when the game was going against them in order to make a fresh start. Who would voluntarily precipitate a global holocaust? The international community has to find another way of adjusting and adapting international relationships and behaviour.

*   *   *

How should we set about this? We should begin by analysing the problems which confront us.

Two issues are of special concern to Pilgrims. East/West relations have preoccupied the Northern Hemisphere for over a generation. We have lived through different phases – from cold war (at its coldest during the blockade of Berlin), through 'peaceful co-existence' to detente. The question today is whether the nature of the challenge to the Western way of life has changed with the passage of time.

The tone of the exchanges between East and West has certainly improved. Important agreements have been freely entered into by both sides. The existence of common interests is openly acknowledged. The range of official contacts has increased. Negotiations are in progress aimed at improving security and cooperation and achieving a balanced reduction of military strength in Europe. These developments deserve to be given their full weight. But other factors must be put in the balance. We are bound to ask certain questions. Why, for instance, have the forces of the Warsaw Pact been substantially increased to the extent that they far outnumber the NATO forces facing them in Europe? What purpose is the immense Soviet fleet intended to serve? And what did the leader writer in Pravda mean when he said last August that peaceful co-existence 'does not spell an end to the struggle between the two world social systems. The struggle will continue up to the complete and final victory of Communism on a world-wide scale'? Surely this is not what Mr Brezhnev had in mind when he said that peaceful co-existence was gradually becoming the generally accepted standard of international life.

How then should we proceed? We must build patiently on such agreements as have already been concluded with the East. We should respond to any genuine advance on their part, make no unrequited concession and, for the foreseeable future, remain vigilant. Today's generation owes this to the generation which preceded it and which, in the aftermath of the Second World War, took a stand against further encroachment by the Communists. Real detente, in the terms in which we understand it, will be the product of the prescience, courage and steadfastness of those who led us then. These were indeed famous men whom it is right to praise; but future generations will not be able to do so unless we too display these qualities.

*   *   *

Another current pre-occupation is the trans-Atlantic relationship.

The construction of Western Europe is, first and foremost, an act of reconciliation – an ending of the civil war which has racked and ravaged the continent since the collapse of the Roman Empire and disturbed the peace of the world far too often.

Our second aim is to restore to our continent the influence in world affairs of which our disunity has deprived us. In recent months on a number of issues we have been able to speak in unison, and on most of the others in harmony.

The main vehicle for restoring our influence is economic integration. This will provide the broad home market essential for the development of our industries. The European Community, which is the largest trading group the world has known, has particular relationships with a high proportion of the countries of the Third World. We have no intention of becoming a closed shop. As trading nations we must play our European role on the world stage.

Nor is it any part of our purpose to confront or to subvert. The articulation of a European identity is neither an anti-American nor an un-American activity. Who should know better than the American people, as you approach the bicentenary of your nationhood, what it means to join one's destiny to that of one's neighbour? We look for your understanding of what we are about in Europe. Indeed we have every reason to expect it. We drew courage and inspiration from the support successive US administrations gave to the concept of a strong united Western Europe working in the closest concert with the United States.

The sentimentalists are inclined to ask whether the emergence of the European Community means that the trans-Atlantic relationship, and especially the Anglo-American relationship, will be better or worse. With no disrespect to the nobility of the sentiment, I must say that this question strikes me as irrelevant. The fact is that the relationship will be different.

Why should this cause dismay? One of the strengths of the relationship is that it has always been dynamic. On each side of the Atlantic we accept it as a duty to adapt the alliance to changing circumstances. Nevertheless, the basis of common interest and shared ideals and instincts about human affairs is solid and of infinitely more importance than the temporary stresses inevitable in any process of change.

*   *   *

If there were no better reason for close consultation within the Alliance – and indeed among the industrialised nations in general – it would be sufficient to point to an issue infinitely harder to handle than those I have mentioned, and one which dominates our work in the United Nations. This is the relationship between the nations of the industrialised north and the developing south – between the affluent and the deprived.

The problems which arise in the North/South relationship are especially sensitive. Since they bring into opposition people of different races, cultures and historical experience, they have undertones of prejudice and resentment, envy and fear. In character they are both economic and political. But the central issue can be simply stated. The nations of the developing world aspire to a higher standard of living, a superior quality of life and greater influence on the major political decisions affecting international relationships. They believe that we in the industrialised world enjoy more than our fair share of political power and derive more than our fair advantage from the exploitation of the earth's limited resources of raw materials. Indeed some argue that we are improvident in the way we comsume them. The developing states note that, while the technology to exploit them is at present a monopoly of the industrialised nations, these raw materials are for the most part to be found in their own countries. They therefore seek a more equitable distribution of the benefits of the exploitation of the earth's resources and adapt their policies accordingly.

The sudden and immense rise in oil prices has produced a third category of states and, in the process, created a new set of problems for the industrialised world, for those developing countries which have no oil and only limited natural resources of other kinds with which to pay for it, and for the now financially powerful oil producers themselves.

Nothing could more clearly serve the common interest than that the natural resources of the earth and the products of man's ingenuity, enterprise and industry should be exploited for the benefit of the maximum number of the earth's inhabitants. How can such a principle be applied effectively, rapidly and in an orderly fashion?

Despite the immense wealth and technical and other knowledge transferred since the Second War to the developing world, the gap between the affluent and the deprived is growing wider rather than narrower. The majority of the nations of the Third World wish to see the problem handled in an orderly way, through consultation and the bending of a common effort. There are others, of course, who are not interested in an orderly application of the principle of fair shares; who may question the right of the industrialised nations to be prosperous and even the legal framework within which we would choose to defend this right. There will always be those who prefer to seek their ends by confrontation rather than partnership.

If this diagnosis is correct, what are the lessons for our own approach?

First, we have to accept the new realities. Changing patterns cannot be wished away. It follows then that the arrangements which regulate the world's monetary and trading relationships have to be brought up to date to take account of these new realities. We must press on vigorously with the negotiations in both these fields. The joint stake in a successful outcome is so clear that there can be little doubt that in the end the conflicts of interest which are bound to arise will be overcome.

Secondly, we must sustain our programmes of aid and technical assistance to the developing world to the extent that we can afford this. This is not to suggest that our attitude in the industrialised world should be submissive. Whenever necessary, we must stand out against attempts to deal with these problems by methods which disregard the principles for the orderly conduct of relations between states enshrined in international law and the UN Charter.

A solution of North/South problems in the economic field will not be achieved through confrontation but rather through dialogue and cooperation. Just as the well-being of our industrialisd economies depends on a healthy world-wide economy, so do the developing countries – and not least the oil producers – look to us for markets for their produce, for contributions to their development programmes and for investment and technological skills. We are all in the same boat. The lesson of recent history is that while extremist measures on either side may bring a momentary advantage, the benefit is short-lived and such conduct in the end damages the interests of those who resort to it. Our world has become too small for any of us to avoid the damaging repercussions of selfishness; nor can any of us any longer ignore his neighbour. The course we in the industrialised world must follow is clear. We must seek to work out in partnership with the developing countries, and particularly the producers of primary products, arrangements for an economic exchange which will serve both their and our legitimate interests.

*　*　*

This brings me back to my first point. The collaborative effort of the industri- alised nations in handling our contemporary problems will have a greater chance of success if we set pessimism aside. Why should the questioning of aspects of our political, social and economic systems be regarded as a sign of weakness? It could equally well be a sign of vigorous health. And when did we last stop to count our blessings, or to compare our condition with that of others?

With a few important exceptions the new countries are one-party states. Many are military dictatorships. This is their choice. They may well believe that dictatorship is an appropriate political system given the nature of the problems they face. In many countries the flow of information is controlled in such a way that facts are withheld from the public, or they are otherwise wilfully misled. The citizens of many countries are not free to leave should they wish to do so. In scores of countries torture is practised systematically. In other equally unacceptable ways millions of our fellow human beings are denied basic human rights.

For our part, we are parliamentary democracies. We have an informed electorate; an independent judiciary; and that most precious of possessions in any community – a free press. We are ingenious, inventive and tolerant. We are privileged people. And if we can re-assert our self-confidence we will be ready to face any challenge of the future.

III

THE FORMULATION OF BRITISH FOREIGN POLICY

NATIONAL DEFENCE COLLEGE, LATIMER – MARCH 1980

We all know broadly what is meant by the term 'British foreign policy', but equally, most of us would be hard put to define it. Foreign policy has some of the characteristics of the piece of soap in the bath.

Some of our partners chide us from time to time for our lack of a comprehensive and coherent plan – a *gesamtkonzept* – for the attainment of our specific goals in the external field. Our standard reply is that we are content with the empiricism which has stood us in good stead for centuries. What lies behind this standard answer is that if one tries to enumerate the general objectives of our foreign policy one produces only truisms, e.g., to protect British interests abroad; to safeguard the security of our people; to promote their prosperity; to honour our commitments and obligations; and to work for a peaceful, democratic and more equitable world. The cynic would ask: why not add that we are all for motherhood?

Those who are responsible for conducting Britain's foreign policy are aware of these general objectives. But they spend little time in contemplation of them. What preoccupies them is what our interests are, where they lie and how best to strike the right balance when perceived short and long term interests come into conflict. They have to determine how much we need to invest in our security, bearing in mind the economic constraints. They have to allot the right priority to the United Kingdom national interest where this may conflict with Community or Western policy, or even an objective assessment of the international good. It is for them to decide what part, if any, altruism should play in our foreign policies; or should these be based solely on enlightened self-interest. They also have to consider case by case which of the various instruments to hand can be used to best effect.

With the dismantling of the British Empire and the consequent decline in our international standing, it has become more apparent than ever before that a so-called foreign policy cannot be distinguished from the policies pursued in the given domestic sphere. Moreover, given the increasing complexity of modern life and growing economic interdependence, domestic actions have international economic and political repercussions. The reverse is also true. British energy policies, for example, have to be formulated in the light not only of our own indigenous resources but also of likely developments in the Middle East, in the oil producing countries and in our relations with our major partners in the European Community, the International Energy Agency and the Organisation for Economic Cooperation and Development.

Another trend is worth mentioning; heads of government are far more involved today in the conduct of foreign affairs than in the past. This is not simply further evidence of the tendency for decision-making to be pushed ever upwards. This is rather another product of the complex character of public affairs in advanced societies. It is only at head of government level that all the various considerations affecting the issues of the day can be brought into clear focus. We have advanced a long way since the turn of the century when Sanderson, the then Permanent Under Secretary wrote to the then Foreign Secretary, Lord Salisbury, when the Prime Minister was temporarily in charge of the Foreign Office in the following terms: 'I am a sort of standing dish at Arthur Balfour's breakfast. When his attention is divided, as it was this morning, between me and a fresh herring, there are alternately moments of distraction when he is concentrating on the herring, and moments of danger when he is concentrating on foreign affairs'.

I hope that I have said enough to persuade you of the difficulty of defining a foreign policy in the abstract. We have to think in specific terms. First and foremost, we have to recognise the dramatic change which has taken place in our position since the end of the Second War. Then we were without question one of the Big Three. We still ruled the largest Empire history has known. More than that, we felt ourselves to be great even though we had in fact already lost the capacity to sustain the role of a great power. The Suez crisis of 1956 brought this truth home to the British people who have accepted the gradual and painful withdrawal from east of Suez and come to acknowledge our much reduced importance in the world.

*   *   *

British foreign policy today has to be formulated within certain clearly defined limits. First is our relative economic weakness. Our comparatively low productivity and our indifferent industrial relations have kept our growth rate down during the past two decades. In consequence, we negotiate with an economically weak hand and our foreign policy options are fewer than those of other medium-size

155

powers. In addition to are this we are more than others dependent on trade and on imports for our raw materials and food.

Our membership of the North Atlantic Treaty Organisation (NATO) is the principal way in which we provide for the security of our people. This carries with it strict obligations and entails heavy costs, including payments across the exchanges. The American commitment is the keystone of the Alliance and our policies must nourish rather than undermine the Trans-Atlantic relationship.

Our membership of the European Community can provide us with new opportunities and widen our range of options in the foreign policy field. But it also imposes constraints. Indeed the full implications of membership of the European Community may not have been fully accepted.

*   *   *

There are a number of other commitments and particular influences on our foreign policy. These include, first of all, those responsibilities which derive from the world role we played in the past. Our obligations so far as Rhodesia are concerned are now coming to an end. But we retain particular responsibilities in regard to Cyprus, Berlin, and the remaining colonial territories – the Falklands, Gibraltar, Belize, Hong Kong and so on.

Further commitments derive from our permanent membership of the Security Council; the maintenance of our independent nuclear capability; the major role we play in the Commonwealth; and the fact that we are now oil producers.

*   *   *

The British Government of today has to formulate its policies in an international environment entirely different from that which obtained in 1945. Current policies cannot be understood unless these changes are recognised.

Two inter-related phenomena have transformed international affairs since the end of the Second World War: the proliferation of centres of power, and the development of interdependence.

Although it may not have seemed so at the time, the world was a relatively simple place in the years immediately following the War. The process of dismantling the empires had scarcely begun and the United Nations was a comparatively small and coherent body. Outside the Soviet Union and Eastern Europe, international politics and the world economy were regulated by the industrial democracies of the West, of which the unquestioned leader was the United States. Military power was concentrated in the hands of the United States. The bi-polar nature of the world was epitomised in the mutual hostility of the Cold War.

That simple, clear-cut situation has changed. In 1949 there were 59 members of the United Nations. Today there are 151. Decolonisation, and with it the creation of numerous independent states, have brought in their wake a progressive diffusion of political, military and economic power. And here there is a paradox. The development of a multi-polar world has coincided with the emergence of the concept of the super-power. Yet, while we have devised this label for the United States and the Soviet Union — the two countries whose political and military status sets them apart from the rest of the international community, it has recently become clear that the super-powers, though obviously highly influential, are not all-powerful in international affairs.

A few years ago there were high expectations of what détente between East and West could achieve. There was talk then of a condominium of the United States and the Soviet Union in world affairs. However, long before Afghanistan it was realised that there was insufficient common ground between the two super-powers to promote such a high degree of collaboration. Another fact has become clear. Overwhelming economic or military strength on a global scale cannot necessarily be converted into overwhelming political influence at regional level. One example of this can be seen in the Middle East. Over many years the Russians offered moral, military and other assistance to the Arabs. Yet their position in the area is far less firmly entrenched than they would wish. Again, in the Horn of Africa their involvement with Ethiopia and Somalia has had mixed fortunes. On the other side, the Americans were unable to bring the full weight of their military power to bear in Vietnam and they were obliged in the end to withdraw militarily from South East Asia.

World peace still depends on the relationship between the United States and the Soviet Union. But the 150-odd states of the world have the capacity, either individually or collectively, to take independent decisions and, in some cases, to constitute their own poles of regional influence regardless of the wishes of the super-powers.

This multi-polarity is as significant in the economic field as in the political. The emergence of Japan and Germany as major economic powers, the decline of the dollar and the collapse of the Bretton Woods system are symptomatic of the changes which have taken place. But the process of change is not restricted to the advanced industrialised countries. It was inevitable that the newly independent states would not be satisfied with the achievement of their political sovereignty. For many of these countries the aim of economic sovereignty has been just as important. And so what they call the struggle against neo-colonialism has been directed not so much against the residual political influence of the former metropolitan powers as against Western economic influence. Mossadegh's nationalisation of Iran's oil industry in 1951 and Nasser's nationalisation of the Suez Canal Company in 1956 were early examples of the drive for greater control of national economies which gathered momentum in the developing world during the 1960s.

But this was not enough. Many developing countries felt that the benefits they received through controlling their economies were largely negated by what they regarded as an inequitable world economic system, devised by the industrialised democracies to serve their own interests. While world trade expanded almost without check in the 1950s and 1960s the developing states were aware that the gap between the richer and poorer states was none the less widening. The power demonstrated by the oil producers, first in the late 60s, and then exerted to the full in 1973 and 1974, suggested to other developing countries for the first time that it could be within their means to force a refashioning of the international economic system to suit their needs. This stimulated the demand for a 'New International Economic Order' which, despite the slow progress of the various discussions and negotiations, remains one of today's pressing international problems.

Over recent years the balance of economic power has shifted from a narrow circle of industrialised Western nations towards some of the developing countries. This trend, though important, should not be exaggerated. The developing countries are a varied group and only certain of them — probably only the oil producers — actually have the capacity to inflict serious economic damage on the West. The developed world, and notably the United States, Canada, Australia and South Africa, itself produces too high a proportion of the world's raw materials to make cartels in other commodities practicable.

The ability of the developing countries to compel our attention to their demands illustrates not only the diffusion of power but also the world's interdependence.

This term 'interdependence' states a present day truth in shorthand. No nation in the world is able fully to guarantee its prosperity and security in isolation from the international community. This applies even to the super-powers. From time to time we hear talk in the United States of isolationism. Sometimes the purpose is to send shivers down the European spine. It is the fact however that no one of any weight in either of the two main parties in the United States regards isolationism as a realistic or desirable option.

It is an open question to what extent even the Soviet economy can still be described as autarkic. Soviet economic progress is increasingly bound up with imports of Western technology and thus with the well-being of Western economies. Indeed the indebtedness of the Soviet Union to the West has reached unprecedented levels. Moreover, the economic advance of some East European countries is equally dependent on trade with the West.

More specifically, interdependence means that the economies of the industrialised and developing worlds are so closely interconnected that neither can afford to allow the present dialogue to degenerate into confrontation. We in the United Kingdom are highly exposed to the play of world economic forces. Our exports represent some 30% of our Gross National Product. We are second only to the United States in the volume of our overseas investments. We import nearly half our food and even more of our raw materials.

But there is another factor in the equation. If we and the other industrialised democracies depend on developing countries for many of our raw materials, they in their turn depend on us for capital equipment, technology and financial resources.

We cannot supply these unless our own economies are prosperous. And our prosperity depends on expanding world trade. World trade cannot expand unless there is some stability in the international economy and, above all, in the supply and prices of essential commodities. The five-fold increase in oil prices in 1973 and 1974 – which was itself preceded by an unprecedented rise in commodity prices – was a direct cause of the economic recession of the past few years. It is too early to say whether the most recent rise in oil prices will prolong or deepen the recession.

If it is on balance unlikely that we would be held to ransom by the developing world, the pressures on industrialised countries to do something for them will be sustained and will probably grow. It is in our interest to do what we can. Developing country exports may threaten particular sectors of our industries. Textiles are the obvious example. But these exports are also the means by which these countries can buy our exports and generate the growth of their own economies. This is essential if world trade is to increase – to the benefit of all. Of course the process of adjustment is immensely difficult and all the more so in a time of recession and high unemployment in the West. The economic, industrial and social issues involved are politically sensitive. Not the least important reason for stimulating the growth of the world economy is to create conditions which will facilitate economic adjustment to technological change and legitimate competition from newly industrialising countries.

*   *   *

From this enumeration of the particular influences on British policy and my description of the environment within which this policy is formulated, you will have discerned three dominant themes on which we are obliged to have a policy. The first is the East/West relationship. The relationship between the super-powers remains the most important single factor in the preservation of world peace. The Soviet invasion of Afghanistan – only the latest example of Soviet meddling in the Third World – has cast a cloud over détente. For the present British Government détente is not dead, but it must be indivisible and it entails reciprocal obligations.

If the East/West relationship is of paramount importance then we must also take account of the attitude of the two thirds of the international community who belong to the Non-Aligned Movement. They reject this division into blocs and, as I have mentioned, place their emphasis on the establishment of a new international economic order. We for our part are ready to discuss evolutionary change in which our main instruments are aid and trade. The main preoccupation here is how to strike the right balance between opening our market to the developing industries of the Third World while avoiding damage to our own economy. In extreme terms it would be paradoxical to help the establishment of industries in the Third World whose products we shut out of our markets through protectionist measures.

The solution to this problem depends on the third theme – the world economy. Here the problems are familiar – persistent inflation; monetary instability; slow growth rates; rising unemployment. No one really understands how the macro-economic system works today. Nor do we have to hand the instruments to regulate it even if we did understand its functioning. The problem is rendered infinitely more complicated by the pace of technological change, and in particular what *Private Eye* calls the Miracle of the Micro-Chip. The United Kingdom plays its part in trying to tame this monster – and incidentally protect our own national interests – through the continuous process of consultation and negotiation at the economic summits, the meetings of the OECD, the International Monetary Fund and so on.

These three themes — the East/West relationship, the North/South relationship and management of the world economy interlock. But an analysis in as broad terms as these ignores crucial factors. The most serious omission is China, which is populated by one-quarter of mankind and which is now opening up to the rest of the world in a manner we could not have imagined ten years ago. Here it is our policy to develop our relationship at all speed; but only with appropriate prudence. The regime in China is an oppressive communist system, and while our short-term interests may coincide, the same may not be true of our long-term objectives. We must also be careful not to stir the Sino-Soviet pot.

* * *

I turn now to now to the way in which we reach policy decisions on these and other issues.

The process is complex. One must distinguish first between the formulation of national policies on the one hand, and European Community or Western policies on the other. Having reached a national position, we may need to modify this in consultation with our European partners. This takes the form of what is called Political Cooperation, or PoCo for short. In each of the Nine capitals a senior member of the Foreign Ministry is the Political Director and it falls to him to represent the views of his Ministry in discussions amongst the Nine. From time to time the Foreign Ministers of the Nine also meet in the framework of Political Cooperation. They may discuss and adopt proposals prepared for them by the Political Directors or they may spontaneously reach conclusions on an urgent matter which there has been no opportunity to prepare.

Our national position may also have to be modified as a result of discussion in NATO. On certain issues and notably East/West questions, the need for Trans-Atlantic coordination is obvious.

In both forums — the Political Cooperation amongst the Nine and NATO — difficulties can arise because national perspectives differ and because the membership of these groupings does not coincide. This explains in part why so often either the Europeans or the members of the Alliance appear to be in public disarray.

On particular issues there are other frameworks within which policies have to be coordinated. A topical example is the Five in Namibia. At the other end of the scale is Anglo-French cooperation over the New Hebrides — one of the world's few condominiums.

National policy making is itself also complicated. Ministers lay down the broad lines of our policies. Specific issues are examined in the Foreign and Commonwealth Office (FCO) and are the subject of discussion in Cabinet Committees at both official and ministerial level, where account can be taken of the views of Whitehall as a whole. The more important issues are decided by the Cabinet where the Foreign Secretary plays a key role. Parliament adds its voice. The recently established Select Committee on Foreign Affairs will enhance the influence of Parliament on the day-to-day conduct of our foreign policy. Then there are the various think tanks. The value of the Central Policy Review Staff (CPRS) is that it is independent of all government departments. But there are also think tanks or planning staffs within ministries, and influence can also be applied by outside institutions such as Chatham House and the universities.

Within the FCO we try to maintain a flexible structure, adapting the administration to meet changing needs. We make frequent use of emergency units and Task Forces. Two current examples are the teams which have been running the electoral process in Rhodesia and the Afghanistan crisis.

Party politics also have an influence. On many issues the approach is bi-partisan. But there are frequent differences of emphasis, and in foreign affairs the balance can be important. For example, the present Government is more deeply committed to the European Community than its predecessor, and differences of rather more than nuance can be discerned in the attitudes of the two main parties to South Africa, Chile, aid policy and even détente.

* * *

I have made passing references to some topical issues, but I have covered none in detail. In the discussion which will follow, we can perhaps deal with some of these in detail. But there is one subject on which I should like to say a few words before I conclude. The European Community is central to our policies and frequently misunderstood.

The community is the largest trading group in the world — indeed the largest trading group the world has ever known. Whatever the members may think about it, to the rest of the world the Community is an entity of great economic and growing political significance. No individual Western European country can carry the same weight in today's world. Through the Community, the nine members have concluded mutually beneficial trading agreements with states and groups of states in all parts of the world. Through the Community, our aid programmes are more effective. And we have begun in recent years to develop political dialogues which would not have been open to us had we acted individually. There have also been negative advantages. Through the Community we have been able to shield our steel and textile industries from the competition of emerging industrial powers such as Korea and Brazil. This we could not have done alone.

Yet the Community is highly unpopular in this country. There is an image of a vast impersonal bureaucracy which threatens individual liberty and the national identity of the member states. The United Kingdom's huge net contribution to the Community budget is seen as an inequity which must be ended. No wonder people ask what is the point of membership of the Community if we lose both on the swings and the roundabouts.

Of course the Community has problems. The current balance of policies does not serve the aims of the founding fathers as set out in the Treaty of Rome. The Common Agricultural Policy, whose aims are unexceptionable, functions in a way which has become a disgrace. On fisheries, we are still trying to correct the error made by the original Six in pushing through on the eve of our entry a Common Fisheries Policy they must have known was highly detrimental to our interests.

These weaknesses are well understood. Solutions to the problems facing the Community will require in some cases patience and time, and in all instances the exercise of political will, which is the Brussels euphemism for readiness to compromise. It is in the interest of all member states that we settle the budgetary problem once and for all so that the Community can concentrate on the important challenges not only within the Community, such as the forthcoming enlargement to include Greece, Spain and Portugal, the problem of economic convergence and the European monetary system, but also those which face us on the international scene.

No slogan, no key can reduce international affairs to a readily comprehensible whole. The balance of power formulae no longer apply. The role Britain plays in the world is dictated by our perception of our interests and the challenges we face from day to day. In recent years our self-confidence has lapsed, and it has been fashionable to denigrate our international performance. I do not suggest that we should swing to the other extreme and seek to play a role beyond our capacity. But we have a clear role to play. Others wish us to play it. And we should do so with due confidence.

IV

DIPLOMACY IN A CHANGING WORLD

LEICESTERSHIRE FAR AND NEAR CLUB
BLAKENEY – OCTOBER 1984

Several years ago, soon after becoming British Ambassador to Denmark, a friend of mine was invited to address an audience in one of the larger towns. When his staff submitted a draft for his speech containing a review of Anglo-Danish relations from the time of the Vikings, he objected. Despite their protests he prevailed upon his staff to omit the historical allusions and concentrate instead on the numerous contemporary links between Britain and Denmark. The morning after delivering his speech he looked to see how the local newspaper had reacted. Halfway down the second page there was indeed an accurate report of his speech. But what caught his attention was the headline. This read: 'British Ambassador fails to mention Vikings.' I tell this tale in order to convey a polite request that, when I discuss the changes which have been taking place in the nature and practice of diplomacy and suggest the implications of these for the role of ambassadors, you will not be disappointed if I fail to mention the work of the sixteenth century German painter, Hans Holbein the Younger.

In the spring of 1959, as a junior member of the African Department in the Foreign Office, I was surprised to be summoned one afternoon to the Secretary of State's office. When I entered his room I found Mr Bevin standing by the fireplace with Amr Pasha, the Egyptian Ambassador. Mr Bevin turned round and said: 'We've done it'. I was then caught up in a kind of tripartite bear hug which was, on that occasion at least, Ernest Bevin's way of expressing his satisfaction.

What we had done was to agree the terms on which the Government of Uganda could build a dam over the Owen Falls where the waters of Lake Victoria spill out to become the White Nile. The main purpose of the dam was to generate electricity, but it could also be used for holding back the waters of the Lake for storage. Britain and Egypt had agreed in 1929 that states upstream would not interfere with the flow of the waters of the Nile without the permission of the Egyptian Government. Against this background, negotiations took place in London and Cairo over several months and a solution began to emerge on the basis of which Egyptian engineers would be stationed at the dam to monitor the flow of water. In Cairo the file had been submitted to King Farouk and Amr

Pasha had called on the Foreign Secretary to convey the King's agreement. With characteristic thoughtfulness, Ernest Bevin asked me, as the junior working on the file, to join him in savouring the good news.

The Nile Waters negotiations of 1949 were in the classic mode. The interests at stake were precise; the issue was finite. In practice only two governments were involved. The course of the diplomatic exchanges followed the traditional pattern – exploratory discussions in the course of which the main elements of a solution were identified, and then intensive negotiations leading to the striking of the final bargain. A generation later, in my last diplomatic post abroad as the United Kingdom Permanent Representative to the European Communities, my time was occupied otherwise. Across the Channel in Brussels my colleagues from the eight other member states and I found ourselves in a state of permanent negotiation – with each other and with the European Commission, which represents the personality of the Community as a whole. The subjects we debated were disparate. At one of our Thursday meetings as the Committee of Permanent Representatives we might discuss the next phase in our relations with the developing world; the future of the European steel industry; the validity of nuclear safeguard measures; commercial relations between the Community and China; the problem of unemployment, especially among the young; and research into the treatment of sewage sludge. Few of the issues we handled were finite; their diversity seemed limitless; interests of all kinds apart from those of the nine governments and the Commission were involved; and the negotiating process seemed interminable.

This was a far cry from the comparatively straightforward problem of the Owen Falls Dam. But before I venture an explanation as to what had happened in between, I should make the point that the objectives of diplomacy have not changed. The diplomatic relationship continues to be the normal channel through which one nation communicates with others. The Congress of Vienna laid down certain basic rules for the conduct of diplomatic relations and clothed them with an elegance and a courtesy which, even to this day, mislead some observers as to the hard-headed, if not ruthless, affair diplomacy usually is in practice. The cynic who said that the art of diplomacy is to let somebody else have one's own way was not too wide of the mark.

The rules devised by the Congress of Vienna provided a framework for the dialogue between states which remained relevant for a hundred years. The world which the European leaders of 1815 envisaged disappeared on the Somme, at Verdun, in the mud of Flanders and the assault on the Winter Palace at Petrograd. The full effect of the events of 1916 and 1917 was not felt until a generation later. The decision of the United States not to participate in the League of Nations and the Soviet Union's preoccupation with the internal consequences of the Revolution nourished the illusion in the 1920s and 30s that Western Europe was still the fulcrum of the modern world. The renewal of Europe's civil war in 1939 and the attack on Pearl Harbour revealed the reality. Since 1945 the implications of these events have been all too clear, even if they have not been universally accepted.

The dominant factor has been the emergence of the two super-powers. Only the United States and the Soviet Union have the military capacity to destroy each other – and the rest of us in the process. Their mutual deterrence has so far prevented a third world war and, barring an accident, should continue to do so. Despite the frosty nature of the relationship today, it must remain a prime ambition of both to maintain and widen the basis of this overriding common interest.

A second factor was the need to reconcile the former enemies in Western Europe and to repair the material devastation of the most ruinous war in history. Another factor was the dismantling of the former colonial empires. This led to a wide diffusion of power to a multitude of centres, some of which are politically insignificant but which nevertheless cannot be ignored. The political emancipation of the hundreds of millions of inhabitants of the old colonies has focused attention – and rightly so – on their poverty and social deprivation, and has raised in the international forum sensitive issues of race, creed and culture which can provoke prejudice, envy and fear.

The United Nations also deserves mention. Although unquestionably an improvement on its predecessor, the League, the United Nations has nonetheless not fulfilled the high expectations of the original signatories of its Charter. This is not due to any serious defect in the Charter itself, which has stood well the test of time. The failures of the UN have been the consequences either of deliberate frustration of the Organisation, or abuse of its procedures by individual member states or groups of states. Sadly, the disillusion that has followed has dissuaded most member states from investing either the political will or the human talent which are indispensable if it is to have any chance of fulfilling its purpose. Despite occasional setbacks, the UN has achieved some success in containing violence through, for instance, its peace-keeping activities in parts of the Middle East, Cyprus and elsewhere. Today the most valuable function of the UN is to provide a forum where the problems can be discussed which divide the affluent North from the nations of the deprived South. The great debate in which the international community has been engaged, especially since the oil price rises of

1973 and 1979, introduced entirely new considerations into the international economic equation and these have highlighted the fact of our interdependence which is fundamental to any understanding of contemporary diplomacy. Although some Western leaders are reluctant to accept the fact, there is no longer a first, second or a third world. There is only one world.

*   *   *

Three other characteristics of the post-war period are also relevant. First, in individual nations the state has greatly expanded the sphere of its activities. The Communist regimes are of course based on the supremacy of the state. But it is also true that the overwhelming majority of the new states which have come into existence since the late 1940s have one-party systems; and even in the parliamentary democracies of the industrial West there has been more state intervention than ever in the affairs of the citizen, whether on ideological grounds or for reasons of expediency. Although many Western governments, including our own, are trying to reverse this tide, it has to be accepted that inter-state relations today cover a much wider range of issues, and most of these were rarely if ever the subject of diplomatic exchanges in the past.

Secondly, groups of adjacent nations with common interests and problems have thought it to their advantage to coordinate their policies and, in some cases, to pool their sovereignty. The European Community, whose unique characteristics distinguish it from all other groupings of states, is the outstanding example. But there are others, less ambitious perhaps, for instance the Association of South East Asian States (ASEAN) and the Caribbean Common Market.

The third characteristic is a more recent and entirely different phenomenon. This is the sponsorship and, in some cases the actual conduct by governments of terrorism. The so-called 'Cultural Revolution' in China, the iniquities inflicted on the people of Kampuchea by successive regimes, the atrocities of Idi Amin and Khomeini and the relentless hunting-down of his opponents by Qaddafi pose new problems for those states which still regard the principles on which inter-state relations have been conducted hitherto as a bulwark against a descent into international anarchy.

*   *   *

If these are the main developments in international relations over the past thirty or forty years, how has the nature of diplomacy been affected?

The purpose of diplomacy remains to protect and further one's interests through dialogue and negotiation. But, given the diffusion of political power and influence, the proliferation of regional groupings of states, the unprecedented improvement in communications, the steady approximation in many parts of the world of standards, mores and of aspirations – given all these, the scope for bilateral diplomacy is becoming more limited. The Falklands War and the recent successful conclusion to the long and hard negotiations over Hong Kong naturally enough attracted wide public attention. This is precisely because these are as readily comprehensible as any contest between two protagonists. But this obscures the fact that far more time and energy are devoted today to multilateral than to bilateral diplomacy. And, while the major international issues still concern the security of the state and the protection of its inhabitants – and there remain difficult problems in this area and others will surely arise in future – international exchanges are today much more concerned with issues which are not purely political, notably in the economic and commercial fields, transport, the environment, human rights, and so on. Although the modern equivalent of the gunboat is still far too much in evidence, the tariff, the quota and the exchange rate have become powerful instruments of foreign policy.

Economic interdependence – the dominant feature of today's world – is matched by an unprecedented inter-relation of problems which complicates the task of the diplomatist. Take the European Community. Even if we have made some headway in checking inflation, our growth rate is still too low and unemployment too high. Without growth how can we deal with the divergence between different parts of the Community which is greater now than when the Treaty of Rome was signed? How can we reduce unemployment when many of our industries are under attack from the highly competitive producers in the newly industrialising countries? And when we protect our vulnerable industries, we affect the interests of our major trading partners, the United States and Japan, and contradict the stated objectives of our policies towards the developing world.

Perhaps the most significant characteristic of the issues which face present-day diplomatists is their intractability. In the past the cataclysm has been the main instrument of change. Happily, humanity seems to be more skilful in avoiding world wide disasters of the kind from which we have suffered twice this century. So we have to find other and infinitely preferable ways of removing the causes of tension and the sources of grievance. But these fleeting opportunities are not easy to recognise, and even when they are perceived, the will to act may be lacking.

A notable exception was the decision by the United States to launch the Marshall

Plan in 1947 to stimulate the economic recovery of Europe – an initiative which sprang as much from an imaginative concept of American self-interest as from a generosity of spirit which marks this out as one of the most noble actions in the history of international relations. Since then too many opportunities have been missed. In 1973 there was a moment during a meeting between the British Prime Minister and Chancellor Willy Brandt when a major initiative towards economic and monetary union in Western Europe might have been taken. The advocates of caution prevailed and the opportunity slipped away.

*   *   *

My own experience as head of a diplomatic mission illustrates some of these points. In 1969 I took up my post as British ambassador in Libya ten days after Colonel Qaddafi and his colleagues staged their revolution. The identities of the leaders other than Qaddafi himself were unknown, as were their intentions towards foreign interests in Libya. In some parts of the country law and order had broken down. Foreign nationals, including a number of British subjects, were being molested and property damaged. My first duty was to send to London as early as possible my best assessment of the character of the new regime, the strength of their support in the country, the likely direction of their policies, and the implications of all these for British interests. At the same time I had to do all I could to protect and reassure the British community, which numbered five thousand souls, and to advise those of them who were in Libya in business on the best course to follow.

Over the next several months each succeeding day brought its bad news. Assets were sequestrated, private companies were nationalised without any immediate prospect of compensation. Offices and houses were searched without warning, British subjects were detained arbitrarily and had their passports removed. Information was laid against individuals by persons nursing real or imagined grievances. Restrictions were placed on a whole range of innocent activities and, in due time, there took place the ostensibly spontaneous, but in fact carefully organised, attack on our embassy. Gradually the apparatus of the police state was set in place.

Despite this it was possible for me to do business with the regime. We negotiated the successful and safe evacuation of our people, their equipment and their stores from the military bases at El Adem and Tobruk, and gradually British firms began to resume their legitimate activities. In those uncertain days, as so often happens, ranks were closed. The sustained courage of individuals in adversity was an example to all. And we found comfort in the solidarity of the Diplomatic Corps and the expatriate community, and inspiration and solace through our prayers.

When I arrived in New York as the United Kingdom Permanent Representative to the United Nations in August 1973, the Middle East was about to enter one of its ritual periods of crisis. The Israelis had forced down a Lebanese airliner and within two days I found myself sponsoring a Resolution in the Security Council condemning this action. Soon afterwards the Yom Kippur war broke out, the Arabs embargoed the supply of oil to certain Western countries, the price of oil increased five-fold and, as some said at the time, the post-war era came to an end. In due course the Security Council achieved a cease-fire and set in train the process which led, on the one hand, to reconciliation between Egypt and Israel and, on the other, to the disintegration of the state of Lebanon.

Unlike the General Assembly of the United Nations, where soap-box oratory is too often the order of the day, what happens in the Security Council matters. For years it had been the habit of successive Secretaries-General to invite the fifteen members of the Security Council to lunch once a month. We sat round the same table –the American, the Russian, the Chinese, the Europeans, the representatives of the developing world. We exchanged neither pleasantries nor generalities. Rather we discussed the serious issues of the hour. I never left those lunches without having experienced – if only for a moment – a sense of shared responsibility around the table for the safety of our world.

A similar sense of shared responsibilities binds together the Permanent Representatives in Brussels of the member states of the European Community. When I arrived in Brussels in 1975, the Referendum and the so-called 're-negotiation' of the terms on which the United Kingdom had entered were behind us and I looked forward to Britain's playing a more positive role. Things turned out otherwise. First, the controversy over the fisheries policy, then the growing scandal of the Common Agricultural Policy and, finally, the problem of the United Kingdom's contribution to the Community budget, gave my staff and me a hard row to hoe.

The Office I headed in Brussels is unique among British diplomatic missions abroad. 60% of the senior staff were drawn from home departments, the rest from the Diplomatic Service. The Office is a microcosm of Whitehall. This reflects the fact that the Community embraces virtually every aspect of public affairs except defence, which is the responsibility of NATO, whose headquarters are also in Brussels. My staff worked as a homogeneous team; different origins and backgrounds were largely irrelevant; and all but a few who carried their prejudices with them to Brussels jettisoned them before they returned home.

The 'construction of Europe', as it is called in Brussels, occupied us day after day, and sometimes night after night. It is a slow, painstaking and often frustrating process, given the range of conflicting interests to be reconciled. I gradually came to appreciate that solutions to seemingly intractable problems become feasible when common perception of the issues involved reaches a certain level. This being so, the key to progress lies in improving the analysis and understanding of the problem.

It is in this respect that the Permanent Representatives have a crucial role to play. Their first allegiance is, of course, to their governments. But, since the member states share the same civilisation and are animated by the same liberal principles which spring from our Christian heritage, the Permanent Representatives have no ambition but to find solutions to problems. At our informal lunches every Thursday, when we could talk frankly as members of a college, time and again inspiration enabled us to devise ways of raising the level of our collective understanding.

*   *   *

The lesson I learned in Brussels is one of general application. In dealing with the complex problems of today's world, there is no alternative to the relentless search for that level of common comprehension of the issues and the interests involved which will permit agreement. The process is often long drawn out; the agreement, when it comes, may either fall short of expectation or be too complex to be readily explained. There is a risk, especially when the differences between states have been exaggerated, that public confidence in the effectiveness of modern diplomacy will be diminished. This risk must be avoided. The issues of today are certainly less precise. Only rarely are the solutions finite. There is seldom cause for a bear hug of satisfaction in the Foreign Secretary's office overlooking St James's Park. But the task of the diplomatist is no less important today; and it cannot be accomplished successfully without faith and constancy.

V

A TIME FOR NEW ATTITUDES

THE NORMAN ANGELL LECTURE
BALL STATE UNIVERSITY, MUNCIE, INDIANA – OCTOBER 1985

Six months after the attack on Pearl Harbour I landed at Bombay to join the Indian Army. What followed changed my life. In 1942 Japanese forces had overrun Burma and stood on the threshold of India. The leaders of the Indian nationalist movement had initiated a campaign of civil disobedience. Mahatma Gandhi and others were in jail. In the main cities the atmosphere was tense. But my own thoughts were occupied otherwise. I was overwhelmed by the sheer size of India and by the apparently infinite variety of its landscape and peoples. I had not imagined cities groaning under such a weight of population. I had never seen such disparities of wealth. I learned what was meant by grinding poverty. My formal education had been largely oriented towards Western Europe and what I now saw of the civilisation of the Indian sub-continent was a revelation. Over the next few years I began to discover the genius of the people. I saw no reason why they should not be entrusted with responsibility for their own affairs. In this respect, though I did not know it at the time, I was on Roosevelt's side in his argument with Churchill. I shared with my Indian colleagues the conviction that when the war against Japan had been won an independent India would make its way in the world.

The British decision to quit India in 1947 set in train the process of dismantling the colonial empires. The partition of the sub-continent into the two states of India and Pakistan was the occasion for atrocious massacres. In Indo-China, Indonesia and Algeria the struggle for independence was long and bloody. In other cases the transition was peaceful. Over the next ten years the empires were replaced by scores of new states in Asia, Africa and Central and South America. Today the only vestiges of the old empires are small outposts such as Puerto Rico, Tahiti, or Gibraltar where, for one reason or another, the inhabitants wish to retain their dependent status. The membership of the United Nations, which stood at 55 in 1946, has trebled.

Many of the leaders of the new states realised that the achievement of independence was no more than the beginning of a fresh struggle to consolidate their sovereignty and to develop their economic and social potential. In a world by now dominated by the two super-powers, they found that they shared many preoccupations and ambitions. They believed, not unreasonably, that their objectives might more easily be achieved by concerted action. Under the inspiration of Pandit Nehru, President Tito and Gamal Abdul-Nasser, the leaders of 29 Asian and African states came together at Bandung in Indonesia thirty years ago – in April 1955. This Conference, which was viewed with much scepticism in Western capitals, conferred a personality on a new force which came to be known as the Third World or, more recently, the South. The motto of this force was 'positive neutrality', subsequently redefined as 'non-alignment'. The new movement had three objectives. First, to support liberation movements; second, to resist the formation of military alliances dominated by either of the super-powers; and, third, to stimulate the economic and social development of the new nations. In a recent account of the birth of the Non-Aligned Movement (which was formally inaugurated in 1961) Ali Sabri who, as Nasser's right-hand man, played a key part in the early negotiations, argues that the third objective of economic and social progress was from the beginning the dominant aim and that the other two were in the nature of prerequisites. While this may well have been in the minds of some leaders at Bandung and the conferences which followed, the rhetoric at the time gave the impression – unfairly perhaps – of a political movement wishing a plague upon the houses of the industrialised countries – be they democratic or communist.

It is to the credit of the Non-Aligned Movement that the first of its objectives has been achieved, even if some of those seeking independence were pushing at an open door. As regards the second, the movement can also rate it a success that the membership of the two main military groupings – the North Atlantic Alliance and the Warsaw Pact – has not spread into the developing world – at least in a formal sense. There are however in the Third World states which have a close military relationship with one or other of the super-powers, or their allies.

In the field of international politics the coordinated efforts of developing countries have also had an impact. Amongst the 55 original members of the UN the industrialised world was heavily represented and the only notable contingents from the Third World were the Latin Americans and the Arabs. The UN at that time more often than not performed the will of the Western powers – and particularly the United States – except when this was frustrated by a Soviet veto. The arrival of new members in the 50s and 60s changed the balance in the UN. The developing countries formed their own coalitions and gradually took control of the General Assembly and exercised strong moral pressure in the Security

Council. Outside the UN the proliferation of centres of power made it more difficult for larger states – including even the super-powers – to further their interests either through political domination or persuasion, except where they
maintained a military presence.

As regards economic and social development, the story is more complex. Over the
years the Third World has put forward a number of specific demands. Some of
these were prompted by suggestions in the 50s that economic development was
being hindered by what were regarded as unfair terms of trade between industrialised countries and the Third World. The case for change was put forward at the
first Conference on Trade and Development in New Delhi in 1964, where the
developing countries formed the Group of 77 through which they sought to
improve their situation by joint action. This Group, which now numbers 126, has
continued to press the case for reform of the arrangements for trade at successive
Conferences. The latest of these, the Sixth, was held in Belgrade in June of this
year.

Demands concerning other aspects of the economic relationship have been made
from time to time. At the fourth summit meeting of the Non-Aligned Movement
in Algiers in 1973 a programme was drawn up for a New International Economic
Order. This owed much to the thinking of the Algerians and the Mexicans. Latin
American economists belonging to the so-called 'dependency school' had for
some while argued that the main constraints on development were external. Not
only were trading arrangements biassed against developing countries, the same
was true, they claimed, of the terms on which capital and technology had to be
imported. These ideas no doubt influenced the Algiers programme which articulated the desire of the Third World for a fairer share of the earth's resources and
the products of man's ingenuity, as well as their dissatisfaction with the operation
of the world economic system over which they had too little control. The programme called for a radical restructuring of the world economic system.

This demand for a New International Economic Order was given a powerful
impulse by the oil crisis of 1973 and 74. The OPEC, established in 1960, has
unquestionably been the most influential grouping of developing countries. Its
policies have not only brought enormous wealth to its members, but they were the
first to have a palpable impact on the life of ordinary citizens in the industrialised
world. Until 1973 Americans had not had to wait in line at gasoline stations.

Part of the motivation for these attempts by developing countries to coordinate
their policies and activities was their perception of the solidarity of each of the

two blocs which constituted the industrialised world. They had no illusions about who called the tune in the Warsaw Pact and who dictated the policy of the Council for Mutual Economic Assistance (COMECON). As for the democracies, developing countries were inclined to regard NATO as an unavoidable evil, the OECD as an all too effective instrument for the protection and advancement of the interests of the industrialised world, the International Monetary Fund as a severe but indispensable disciplinarian, and the World Bank as well-meaning but close-fisted. The creation of the European Community and its progressive enlargement aroused hopes in the Third World on two grounds. First, the Community, while a part of the Western comity of nations, was not directly involved in the superpower confrontation; and, secondly, it included countries such as the United Kingdom, France, the Netherlands and Belgium, which had strong historical links with the developing world and therefore a fund of knowledge and understanding. For these same reasons the accession of Spain and Portugal to the Community next year will be warmly welcomed in Latin America.

To regard the efforts of the industrialised and developing worlds to co-ordinate their respective policies as processes entirely separate one from another would be to leave the picture incomplete. One could be misled, however, if one relied on the declarations and communiques issued after meetings of the Non-Aligned Movement on the one hand and on the other of the OECD, the Economic Summits of the seven major western powers, or COMECON.

These understandably reflect the point of view of the participants and are therefore bound to seem introspective, if not narcissistic. Rarely do these documents mention – let alone stress – the interests which industrialised and developing countries share. For this one must look to the meetings of Commonwealth Heads of Government, the Organisation of American States or the successive Lomé agreements between the European Community and its 64 partners among the states of Africa, the Caribbean and the Pacific. Apart from the countless commercial, professional, academic, cultural and private links, the great programmes of assistance for development acknowledge the obligation on the part of industrialised countries to help the less advanced by transferring resources, expertise and technology. The Marshall Plan, though primarily aimed at the reconstruction of Europe, was one of the first to embrace aid for development. Point Four and its successors, the Colombo Plan, the European Development Fund, International Development Assistance are outstanding examples. The numerous bilateral and regional programmes must be added to the list. Together all these links constitute a comprehensive multi-faceted relationship between North and South.

If we take stock of the results of the policies pursued and the actions taken over the past 30 to 40 years, what would be revealed?

First, how have the countries of the South fared? The political map shows a mixture of regimes. Most developing countries are either one-party states, or dictatorships in which the military often play a key role. A sense of insecurity has led in many cases to the suppression of all opposition. Some countries, especially in Africa, are rent by tribal rivalries. In others, political extremism has taken the form of religious fanaticism. In a few tragic cases, the hapless inhabitants have fallen victim to a reversion to barbarism. Some of the more ineffectual leaders live in an unreal world which they try to talk into existence with rhetorical declarations. Faced with this dismal catalogue what would be the verdict of Gerald of Wales, who said 800 years ago: 'The hilarity of liberty makes men capable of honourable actions'? Perhaps he would point to those developing countries whose destinies have been guided by some of the most intelligent, courageous and articulate leaders of the present day. Perhaps he would point to India — the jewel in the crown of parliamentary democracy.

What about relations between developing countries? Here again the picture is of uneven quality. If the nuclear weapon has preserved an uneasy, if at times tense, peace between the super-powers it has not prevented regional wars. It has been estimated that in the 150 wars since 1945 some 20 million people have died, virtually all of them in the developing world. These include 2 million Vietnamese and 1 million Algerians. The virus of war continues to spread. To the long series of conflicts between India and Pakistan and between the Arabs and Israel have recently been added wars between Iraq and Iran, Somalia and Ethiopia, Uganda and Tanzania, Vietnam and China and the atrocious civil wars in Lebanon and Nicaragua.

Apart from these open conflicts there are serious political differences within the Non-Aligned Movement. This is to be expected in an organisation whose members include Cuba, Vietnam and the Afghanistan of Babrak Karmal on the one hand, and Singapore, Zaire and Jamaica on the other. But, having said that, it is only fair to note the remarkable fact that for the most part the countries which became independent after the Second World War have remained within the frontiers they inherited and have tried to preserve the administrative structures which the colonial powers had put in place. This is true even in Chad and Uganda, the break-up of which has been confidently predicted more than once.

There are grounds for some encouragement. Regional groupings of like-minded states have solid achievements to their credit. The Association of South-East Asian States is an example. Coordination of policies both internally and externally on the basis of common interest, tradition and political outlook is steadily lifting its members out of the ranks of developing states into those of the New Industrialising Countries – the NICs. Progress on similar lines is being made in South America by the members of the Andean Pact and in the Caribbean through the Caribbean Community and the Free Trade Area. There have recently been signs that the more relaxed relationship between Kenya and Tanzania might revive interest in the East African Community, which was established in 1967 but broke up ten years later in some acrimony.

How successful has the South been in its efforts to develop its economic and social potential – the third of the objectives the Non-Aligned Movement set itself twenty-five years ago?

It is a sad fact that the situation of many developing countries is worse today than it was at the time of independence, in spite of social and structural change and increases in output and incomes. Today up to 1 million people in these countries live at or below the poverty line and suffer malnutrition or starvation. The flow of aid, whether in the form of finance or technology, has not matched the needs of its recipients. Much of it has been misdirected, some of it misappropriated. At the other end of the scale, the New Industrialising Countries have emerged as a powerful economic force. Of equal significance is the steady advance of countries such as Brazil, India and the Philippines and the accumulation of vast financial reserves by some of the oil producers in the Gulf.

The more far-seeing leaders of developing countries accept that the attempts of the South to bring about structural changes in the world economic and trading systems have not proved successful. Where countries of the Third World have acquired a dominant position, as for example in the General Assembly of the United Nations or in the agencies of the UN, and have pressed their demands in resolution after resolution, the principal western industrial powers have progressively lost interest and sought to negotiate agreements in other fora. Not even the Arab members of the OPEC were able to use their virtual stranglehold on the West in the early 1970s to secure satisfaction for the Palestinians. And the international economic order which has come into existence since 1973 is new in two unintended respects: the emergence of the New Industrialising Countries and the wealth of the Gulf oil producers have magnified the differences between developing countries and so weakened their solidarity, and the Southern horizon has come to be dominated by one major feature – the accumulation of debts, which amount this year to US $90 billion.

To many people in the West none of this may seem to matter. Why not leave the countries of the Third World to sort out their own affairs in their own good time? Insofar as we need their raw materials, have they not a corresponding need to sell them to us? Are they likely to cut off their noses to spite their face?

For a number of reasons I believe this view is profoundly mistaken. In the first place, we cannot ignore the fact that the Soviet Union, which we know to be tirelessly opportunistic, will turn to its advantage any development in the Third World which could adversely affect Western interests. There are no sufficient grounds yet to believe that the new leadership has moderated Soviet long-term ambitions. We must not lose hope that they will, and we should give them every encouragement to do so. This entails allowing as few opportunities as possible to arise in the Third World for the Soviet Union to exploit to our detriment – a considerable test of Western diplomacy.

The second reason is this. To those who interpret non-alignment as actual disapproval of the First and Second Worlds we must strive constantly to convey the message, through actions as well as words, that our way of life and our political systems are superior. As that far-sighted American, Herbert Agar, wrote in 1943: 'It is impossible to hold moral convictions without believing that they must be expressed in action.'

There is also a strong material argument – the interest we and developing countries share in a growing world economy. More economic activity means higher growth, higher employment, more purchasing power, more trade. In the industrialised world we cannot hope to maintain our prosperity exclusively by taking in each other's washing. The Third World represents the fastest growing and potentially the largest market for our goods. Tomorrow's standard of living, as Willy Brandt has pointed out, depends largely on increased trade with the developing countries. That presupposes that their economies must also prosper.

There is another consideration – perhaps the most important–common humanity. In January 1918 President Woodrow Wilson concluded his message on the Fourteen Points with these words: 'An evident principle runs through the whole programme I have outlined. It is the principle of justice to all peoples and nationalities, and their right to live on equal terms of liberty and safety with one another, whether they be strong or weak. Unless this principle be made its foundation no part of the structure of international justice can stand.' Would anyone in the Western democracies reject that 'evident principle' today?

Common interest and common humanity should constitute a sufficient basis for a relationship. If this is accepted do common interest and common humanity not also justify a joint effort to improve the situation we face today? What, then could and should be done?

My answer would be: a great deal. But attitudes will need to change. Rhetoric and prejudice should be set aside, the realities of the present day should be faced and there should be applied to the current problems of world development that imagination and generosity of spirit which characterised Western policies in the immediate postwar years. Should you wonder what that might mean in practice, I have a number of specific suggestions to make.

First, we might revise the current vocabulary, convenient though it may be as shorthand. To talk of the South as though it were a political or economic entity is to ignore the enormous disparities between different parts of the world outside the OECD and the communist bloc, in regard not only to their economic condition but also to their preoccupations and ambitions. It is equally unrealistic to conceive as an objective for the international community the notion of bringing countries of the Third World up to the standard of the OECD. The late Shah tried to turn Iran into a modern state comparable with France, or the United Kingdom within a generation; the world still suffers from the consequences of this lunatic enterprise. The fact is that each developing country is a particular case. Many have special strengths and valuable cultural and religious traditions on which it would be sensible to lay the foundation of future progress.

There is, moreover, a political aspect to this question of definition. In the West we tend to be scornful of one-party systems and suspicious of dictatorships, whether of the left or the right. There may be good local reasons why such a system has been adopted in a particular country and why radical policies are being pursued. Should these have Marxist characteristics this may mean that the government concerned is acting under the direct inspiration of Moscow or one of its surrogates. But this is not invariably the case. Over the past thirty years there have been numerous examples of early radicalism being modified in the harsh light of experience. On the other hand, to suggest that East-West rivalries have no impact on North-South relations would be absurd. But it is important to keep this aspect of the matter in proportion and to treat the case of each developing country on its merits. A misjudgment or a miscalculation by the West can provide an opening for our adversaries and, before long, inflict misery on the people or the country concerned.

Next, we might look at the fora in which North/South relations are discussed. The only honest verdict is that neither successive UN Conferences on Trade and Development, nor the Special Assemblies of the UN convened to discuss the demand for a New International Order, nor the Conference on International Economic Cooperation called by President Giscard d'Estaing of France in 1975 to discuss energy supply and development, nor the UN Committee of the Whole which undertook so-called Global Negotiations in 1981 – none of these has produced the results developing countries desired. Much the same can be said for those international agencies which stray from the important technical issues which are their stock-in-trade into the field of development. For one thing the demands of developing country participants in international conferences have often represented the most extreme view amongst them and have been expressed in strident terms. For another, developed countries, over-impressed perhaps with the effects of industrial restructuring and recession at home, have not been in a generous mood these past ten years or more. Another disadvantage is the size of these fora. The highest common factor among 150 participants – especially when these are professional representatives of their governments and not themselves decision-takers – is likely to be so low as to be barely visible above the horizon. The problem is not solved by arbitrarily reducing the number of countries participating in these meetings, as President Giscard did in 1975 and as happened again at Cancún in 1981; political leaders speak only for themselves and cannot commit their partners or allies. Where progress has been made, attendance has been restricted to those directly concerned and the agenda has been specific. The European Community's negotiations with the ACP states and the periodical rounds of negotiations under the GATT are examples. The moral seems to be that exchanges of platitudes and rhetoric in gatherings where the entire international community is represented may enable participants to air grievances and vent their frustration, but practical progress is more likely to be made in more restricted meetings where precise proposals are discussed and all concerned are prepared to contribute to success on the basis of common interest.

For this and other reasons many developing countries now accept that their demand that the world economic system should be dismantled and rebuilt is impractical and that the best they can hope for is change by evolution. Even the well-argued proposals for new institutions, such as a World Development Fund and an amalgamation of the UNCTAD and the GATT which were put forward in the first report of the Brandt Commission, have not found favour with industrialised countries. In this situation perhaps developing countries should play a bigger role in the study of ways of adapting existing institutions to take fuller account of their interests.

So far as the actual processes of development are concerned, the change in attitudes required should be inspired by the successes which have been achieved in various parts of the world. The emergence of the New Industrialising Countries – NICs – and the spectacular progress of Brazil, India and others can be attributed in part to the special circumstances of these countries and, in particular, their natural and human endowment. But there are lessons of wider application to be drawn and other developing countries might usefully apply these in a form adapted to their own conditions.

Of course each developing country is a special case and it is unwise, as well as unfair, to generalise. Yet, any survey of the developing world shows clearly where errors have been made. First, there is the question of priorities. Where economic conditions are worse today than on independence, it is evident that the ordering of priorities has been wrong. Much of today's wretchedness in Africa can be attributed to the growth of population. Large families are a tradition. These allow for a high rate of infant mortality and provide a work force that will sustain the parents in their old age. Improved midwifery and hygiene have drastically reduced infant deaths. In Malawi half of the population is under 14 years of age; the population of Kenya will double within 20 years. Where this is not already the case population control should head the list of priorities in these and similar countries.

The other side of the population coin is more local food production, and secure water supplies – for drinking, irrigation and waste disposal. These are the two clear lessons of the appalling famine in Africa. Then, the development of indigenous energy supplies – wherever possible from renewable sources such as solar and small-scale hydro projects and vegetable waste – biomass.

In some countries considerations of prestige have had a baleful influence on development policies. The 'cathedrals in the desert', of which Edgard Pisani, the former European Commissioner for Development, complained, do exist. Large-scale projects for the generation of power, flood protection and communications are indispensable. But these should not blind planners to what can be achieved by smaller-scale projects, especially for the supply of energy and water. These can immediately improve the quality of life at village and district level. And, if the local population are involved in the construction and maintenance, further benefits flow.

In many developing countries too little attention has been paid to improving what is already there. Most of these countries, including the poorest, inherited basic road, railway and telecommunications systems. Through lack of investment and maintenance some of these are unusable. Upgrading these is less expensive than new projects. But then they have to be kept in order and this means efficient management. Michael Manley, the former Prime Minister of Jamaica, makes this point in clear terms: 'The real race is to create within a society like ours developed human beings at a rate equal to the growing management requirements of the infrastructure.' Effectively operated public services which meet demand not only contribute to economic and commercial activity, but also attract the foreign entrepreneur. At a World Telecommunications Development Conference at Arusha in Tanzania last May a spokesman for the Economic Commission for Africa underlined this point: 'Regardless of the source' he said, 'funds will not flow to inefficiency.'

Lack of money is widely believed to be the main obstacle to development. It is true that the most disadvantaged countries will need aid in the form of concessionary finance for many years to come. But other developing countries do not need this kind of help. When a particular economic activity can be shown to be actually or potentially profitable – and telecommunications is an obvious example – the funds needed for investment should be available from internal or external sources on a normal commercial basis.

Another substitute for aid is access to markets in the industrialised world. This has been a persistent demand of developing countries, and especially those whose development is progressing. The logic of their case is compelling. If developing economies are stimulated through the transfer of resources and technology – whatever the channel may be – they need an outlet for their products to maintain the cycle and earn foreign exchange to finance further investment and pay off their debts. Apart from this, some of the more successful developing countries have found that the promotion of exports brings wider benefits than import substitution. But two are needed to play this particular game.

The counterpart to the demand for better access to industrial markets is the desire of foreign entrepreneurs and investors to see more open and secure markets for their investment in developing countries. Prejudices on both sides have to be broken down and anxieties allayed. Western industry has shown its ability to adjust to new circumstances. For steel, ship-building and agriculture, for example, the experience has been painful. To survive, industry must continue to adapt and it is difficult to believe that our economies cannot absorb a reasonable level of new imports from the Third World, particularly when this means increasing their ability to buy from us. For their part, more developing countries should draw the conclusion from the success stories in South East Asia, for example, that multinational corporations are not the ogres neo-Marxist propaganda makes them out to be. They should also have it in mind that de-regulation and the retreat from state involvement in manufacturing and the utilities, which has occurred in Japan and the United Kingdom and elsewhere, has enhanced the role of the private sector which now has to carry responsibilities in the international field which previously rested on the shoulders of governments.

There is a message here for Western governments. If private corporations are to perform this role effectively they could be assisted by better co-ordination between donor countries. Fortunately there are signs that governments are more willing to consider this. It would be foolish, of course, to pretend that politics and commercial advantage play no part in aid. But competition in this field can be wasteful and cause delays. Recipient countries may be tempted to exploit rivalries between industrialised countries in order to secure what they may regard as the best deal. But equipment or services acquired simply because the terms of the financing are attractive rather than on grounds of suitability, technical merit, delivery date and so on, may not represent the best deal in the context of a country's development.

In one other field which bears indirectly on development I should like to see attitudes change. When it was suggested at the first United Nations Conference on the Human Environment at Stockholm in 1972 that developing countries would be well advised to avoid the pollution and general spoliation of the environment which accompanied industrialisation in the developed world, representatives of some developing countries reacted with vigour. This, they argued, was a barefaced attempt to maintain their backwardness. Since then, oil pollution, the destruction of forests for paper and fuel, the advance of the deserts have made governments more aware of the dangers. There is a strong case for protection of the environment to be accorded higher priority in development planning.

These, then are the areas where I believe a change in attitudes would bring great gains: treating each developing country on its political and economic merits; encouraging regional cooperation in the developing world; discussing development issues in as small a forum and in as specific terms as possible; and, so far as the actual processes of development are concerned, placing fresh emphasis on the ordering of priorities; the control of population; the stimulation of local food production; the provision of secure supplies of water and energy – and renewable energy in particular; the improvement and efficient maintenance of the existing infrastructure; the opening up of markets in the industrialised world for developing country products; the encouragement of investment in developing countries; better coordination of aid; and protection of the environment. This is a daunting programme. For a start we might change the context in which we regard the relationship between industrialised and developing countries. Lee Kwan Yew, the Prime Minister of Singapore and one of the most perceptive statesmen of our age, has raised the issue in this way: 'In the world the West has created,' he has said, 'change has been imposed upon certain societies in an abrupt and unsympathetic manner. There is no escape from the need to adjust to this world, because it is one inter-dependent inter-reacting world with swift transportation and instantaneous communication. But it is a change which must be made primarily by the Third World societies themselves and their leaderships. This can be frustrated or assisted by the attitudes and policies of the developed world.'

The international community will do no more than pay lip-service to this interdependence so long as it clings to established notions of sovereignty. In Britain we have in the past willingly accepted limitations on our sovereignty. For centuries we worked with others to prevent the domination of continental Europe first by Spain, then by France, then by Germany. We learned much about the machinery of alliances and of the concessions which have to be made to one's partners in order to sustain a coalition. During the Second War cooperation between Britain and America reached unprecedented levels. The period which followed was remarkable for the extent to which nations were prepared to set sovereignty on one side in facing the problems of reconstruction, reconciliation and securing the peace. Is it not possible to do the same today in order to confront hunger, poverty, disease and ignorance and to promote economic progress and social well-being across the world.

I paid my most recent visit to India last April when I led a British team for informal talks with an Indian group on issues in which we have a common interest. On our side we expressed our admiration for India's economic achievements and outstanding debt record. On theirs the Indians looked for an increase in British investment and of joint ventures involving a transfer of high technology suited to India's needs. We discussed regional and global issues. We concluded that 'there was much more in common between the two countries than the differences that seemed to arise from time to time. New India and new Britain presented a fertile field for greater cooperation and reducing past differences.' If sentiments of that kind were to become fashionable, relations between North and South would flourish, to their mutual advantage.

VI

INDO-BRITISH RELATIONS

ANNUAL DINNER OF THE INDIAN CIVIL SERVICE ASSOCIATION LONDON – OCTOBER 1985

One of my masters at school said that India was a geographical expression. That seemed a clever observation. However, I did not appreciate how apt it was until I saw for myself. I arrived in India at the moment in 1942 when the Congress leaders were jailed and when, as readers of *The Raj Quartet* will recall, Daphne Manners was falling in love with Hari Kumar in Mayapore.

For each of us the name 'India' evokes a picture – the teeming cities; the Moghul splendours on the banks of the Jumna; the lush forests of Assam; the towering white clouds of the monsoon evenings in Kerala; the cool, crisp, smoke-scented air of the Himalayan foothills; the shimmering plains of Rajasthan. Earlier this year I had no need to make do with an evocation. To my delight I found myself for three days in one of the enchanting towns of Himachal Pradesh.

A year earlier, when they met in New Delhi, the Prime Minister and the late Mrs Gandhi decided to revive the arrangement whereby, once a year, unofficial discussions on the whole range of Indo-British relations took place between two groups representing different backgrounds, interests and disciplines. The hope was that such discussions might nourish the unofficial relationship between our countries. Last autumn I was invited to form the British group, my Indian counterpart being T N Kaul, an intimate of the Gandhi family, a former Indian ambassador to the United States and the Soviet Union and Foreign Secretary at the Ministry of External Affairs.

Tiki Kaul and I agreed that the first meeting of what was to be called the Indo-British Colloquium should be held in India. We were determined that, rather than exchange platitudes, we should deal with practical issues and should, if possible, formulate recommendations which we might make to our respective governments. The subjects we thought appropriate were foreign policy, economic and commercial relations, cooperation in the field of culture, science and technology; and the role of the media. The composition of our two teams reflected this agenda.

The British group contained an economist, a banker, a scientist, a journalist, two educationalists and a Member of Parliament. I accepted the Indian side's proposal that the meeting should be held in April at the Indian Institute for Advanced Studies in Simla. This is the former Viceregal Lodge – that astonishing combination of neo-Moghul and Scottish baronial.

All members of the British group felt that the moment had been well chosen to resume a dialogue of this kind. For one thing, in the short space of a few months, India had had to endure three calamities – the tragedy of the Golden Temple at Amritsar, the disastrous gas leak at Bhopal, and the murder of Mrs Gandhi and the ensuing violence in the capital. We were keen to learn at first hand with what tolerance, absorptive capacity and resilience the people of India had coped with these events. Apart from that, here at home, the flood gates of nostalgia had opened. Paul Scott and John Masters were turned into films and radio plays. Richard Attenborough had made *Gandhi*, David Lean had made *Passage to India* and *Far Pavilions* had made a fortune. Indian food had leaped from the high street on to our television screens. Indian music and art had found a new group of admirers.

Yet this revival of interest in India and things Indian disguised the fact that on issues of direct concern to us in this country ignorance was widespread and profound. One of our members, Andrew Rowe, had been involved in the work of the Committee of Inquiry into the education of ethnic minority children. This, he told us, had found that teachers in schools with large proportions of children from the sub-continent claimed that their pupils spoke either 'Indian' or 'Pakistani'. Many vigorous supporters of integration assumed that every Indian in Britain was either a professional or a small businessman. The truth is of course that the great majority of immigrant families are unskilled workers and disproportionately unemployed.

Within the immigrant community itself the numerous sub-groups which mirror the diversity of the sub-continent jostle for position and respond often in unexpected ways to events 'back home' in India. Those individuals whose work brings them into direct contact with immigrant communities are aware of these currents and cross currents. But, so far as the public at large is concerned, they have passed unnoticed – at least until the assassination of Mrs Gandhi, when a tiny minority of Sikhs in Southall caught the attention of a wide audience by their disgraceful exultation over an international calamity.

Before leaving for India the British team were warned by the Foreign and

Commonwealth Office to expect sharp criticism over what was seen in India as inadequate efforts to curtail the activities of the leader of this group, Chauhan Singh. We were carefully briefed on what is and is not possible under our law. This warning was repeated by the UK High Commissioner when we arrived in Delhi on the morning of 10 April. It was therefore with some apprehension that we joined our Indian colleagues and boarded the air-conditioned coach which was to take us to Simla.

Except that we were not going to Simla. We learned that T N Kaul, who had gone on ahead, had doubts about the accommodation at Simla and that we were now to meet at Chail, where the facilities were superior. And so, having rested briefly after our flight from London, we set off shortly before noon. Someone had said that the journey took five or six hours by car and suggested that we should allow another two hours or so for the journey by coach. After a short stop for lunch we sped through towns and villages and mile after mile of prosperous grain fields. Then, a strict security check on entering Punjab and another on leaving. We stopped for a late tea and to stretch our legs. The scent of the blossom was heavy on the air. By now it was getting dark. A few hours later we stopped again for fuel and a fresh supply of cool drinks. Iqbal Singh, the editor of *India Weekly*, said: 'I know this place. Chail is three hours from here'. It was now 8.30. Precisely at 11.30 our coach drew up outside the former palace of the Maharajah of Patiala – now the Palace Hotel – which was to be our home for the next few days. Iqbal Singh, the timekeeper, was the first to get down. 'It was worth it', he said. Above us, as we drew our first breath of mountain air, was a myriad of stars. Surely a good omen.

The members of both groups had put the shared adventure of our twelve hour journey to good use. The floor of our coach was littered metaphorically with broken ice and the air was conditioned with embryonic *bhaibandis*. And so, when we began our talks the following morning we penetrated to the heart of the matter without delay. For our part, we explained the objectives of British foreign policy and what these meant in practice – not that every member of our team agreed on every detail. In return we were advised not to expect any radical shift from the India of Rajiv Gandhi. The Indian position in international affairs during the period of his mother's ascendancy was a careful reflection of the Indian national interest. As one of our colleagues across the table put it, India was 'a hopeful democratic society surrounded by confident anti-democratic neighbours'. To survive, India had to maintain an area of economic tranquility for itself by keeping a balance between these neighbours. The Soviet Union was the only power able to cancel out the nearest threats – from China and Pakistan –

and, given United States support for Pakistan, the most convenient and cheapest source of armaments. The price India had to pay, so we were invited to deduce, was not exorbitant – public support in international bodies for the Soviet position. But in almost every other respect, it was made clear, India would go its own way – with a mixed economy, a leading role in the Commonwealth and countless valuable economic links with the West. It was stressed more than once that there was nothing exclusive about India's relationship with the Soviet Union.

On our side we noted that, apart from being the world's largest parliamentary democracy, India was the United Kingdom's most important market in the developing world and we understood that there was a large reservoir of affection and admiration for Britain. This, together with the language factor, made Britain India's easiest and most durable point of contact with the West. That was reason enough to keep the relationship in good repair.

So we went on to identify various ways in which this could be done – by taking better advantage of the commercial opportunities, by stimulating investment, by wider cooperation in specific fields of science and technology, by increasing and diversifying cultural exchanges and by improving language training. We also discussed without inhibition the problems created for each of us by the other's press. As one of the Indian team said: 'In India you will find anything you wish' – a subtle rebuke to some of the less responsible reporters of the Indian scene. And it was in this context that the British side – not the Indians – at length raised the issue of Chauhan Singh. We deplored the licence he had been given by the BBC but urged that more be done by Indian spokesmen both in India and in Britain to put across the Indian point of view about the Punjab's place in the Republic of India.

Apart from our formal discussions across the table members of the two groups had numerous opportunities for more intimate conversations – on our visit to Simla or our walks through the palace grounds. From these it emerged that there were many more subjects on which it would be useful to share experiences and opinions. Terrorism – that lethal combination of crime and fanaticism, whether Sikh or Provisional IRA – poses special problems for moderate governments attached to democratic principles and regard for human rights. Or drugs. Here Britain and India share an interest in exploring the tangled roots of the drug trade and in working to eliminate it. Or education. There is a variety of issues here in which we have a common interest. To take one example, the fact that too many children in this country, including the children of immigrants from the sub-continent, perform so badly that they leave school with little of value.

Another example. In India an increasing number of students educated to grade VIII or grade X find that their aspirations outrun India's ability to meet them. We have analogous problems in this country. Then there are the threats to family life and the problems faced by small businesses. Each of our countries faces difficulties in these areas and we can surely learn from each other's experience.

At the end of our talks we lunched under the trees as guests of the Himachal Pradesh authorities. This was the moment for the group photographs. We made Tiki Kaul sit in the middle flanked by Janet Morgan of our group and the statuesque Saryu Doshi. He slipped his arms round their waists. Andrew Rowe, who took the pictures, commented: 'This adds an entirely new dimension to the word Kaul-girls.'

The joint statement we issued at the end of our talks included this sentence: 'It was felt that there was much more in common between the two countries than the differences that seemed to arise from time to time. New India and new Britain presented a fertile field for greater cooperation and for reducing past differences'. That was not a platitude but rather a pointer to the agenda for our discussions next year in Hampshire.

At Chail we did not shake the earth. Our contribution to lubricating the machinery of the official relationship between our two countries was modest. But I am inclined to echo Iqbal Singh: 'It was worth it.'

VII

THE 'SPECIAL RELATIONSHIP'

BATH AND DISTRICT ENGLISH-SPEAKING UNION
THANKSGIVING DINNER – NOVEMBER 1988

Today, all over the world, Americans recall with thanks the first harvest gathered by the Pilgrims who landed from the *Mayflower* at Cape Cod in Massachusetts in the year of our Lord 1620.

Events of historical importance often inspire myths and this is no exception. It is pleasing to think of the Pilgrims as a group of simple, devout men and women who built themselves a ship and cast themselves on the ocean and the mercy of God. This is less than the truth. Of the 149 persons who sailed from Plymouth, forty-seven were officers and crew. Another forty were so-called Separatists, who had fled earlier to Holland to escape poverty and religious persecution at the hands of James I. The rest were from London and Southampton. They were a severely practical company. The Dutch party had had the good sense to engage a soldier of fortune, Captain Myles Standish, the leading Rambo of the day, whose military skills and ruthlessness were to see the Pilgrims through the privations of their first winter in the New World and defend them against the Indians.

The founding of the settlement in Massachusetts is a notable example of what is known vulgarly as the 'cock-up', as distinct from the 'conspiracy' theory of history. The Pilgrims were in fact making for Virginia, where a settlement had already been established at Jamestown, but the navigator was of such incompetence that *Mayflower* was beached at least two hundred miles north of what was the northern limit of Virginia. However, the Pilgrims turned their enforced isolation to advantage and seized their liberty. Through the bridgehead they created, further waves of refugees from oppression arrived to establish Puritan New England.

The Pilgrims' greatest achievement was to survive. They were, of course, English men and women under the Crown. Yet their endurance and eventual success made them, far more than their predecessors in Virginia, the true fathers of the American way of life. Following Independence, the new nation consciously developed its American characteristics as a means of asserting its own separate identity; and in this it succeeded splendidly. Nonetheless, common ancestry and common language have encouraged many to believe that there is something unique about the relationship between Britain and the United States. This is a proposition which I have come to believe one should approach with care.

* * *

During the Second World War cooperation between Britain and the United States reached an unprecedented level. President Roosevelt and Mr Churchill had absorbed the lessons of the First World War and, in particular, the need for an integrated military command and a coordinated industrial strategy. Petty jealousies among the more egocentric commanders in the field do not detract from the outstanding achievements of the Alliance, to which men like Eisenhower and Marshall on the American side and Alanbrooke, Tedder and Dill on the British made an invaluable contribution.

Planning for the post-war world took place in similar conditions of close understanding. Already in 1941, when America was still neutral, the two countries had set out their political blueprint in the Atlantic Charter. Plans were laid for the creation of the United Nations – an organisation into which the United States would be bound in such a way that the disasters of the 1920s and 30s, when America retreated into isolation, would be avoided. Equally important were the financial negotiations which laid the foundations for the international economic order which was to be put in place after the war. A yellowing piece of paper salvaged from the negotiations at Bretton Woods, which set up the International Monetary Fund and the World Bank bears these lines:

> In Washington Lord Halifax
> Once whispered to Lord Keynes:
> 'It's true they have the money bags
> But we have all the brains.'

If this mischievous little verse does less than justice to the brilliance of the American negotiators, it betrays sensitivity to the true balance between the two countries at that time.

It was not to be expected that the intimacy of this wartime relationship would endure when peace came. The Marshall Plan, which combined enlightened self-interest with remarkable generosity of spirit, helped Europe to arise from the ashes. In the process new patterns of relationships were formed and these were crystallised when, within a few years, NATO was formed to meet the new menace from the East.

It is seldom appreciated today that by 1945 the people of Britain were physically, emotionally and financially exhausted. And yet, at that very moment, we set our-selves two daunting tasks – to create a new social system at home and to dismantle the Empire in good order. Americans looked on the first of these processes with curiosity and mild concern. The second – decolonisation – of which the United States heartily approved in principle, placed an immediate and unexpected strain on Anglo-American relations.

In 1946 I found myself in Palestine, where British forces had the distasteful task of preventing the landing of Jewish refugees from Europe. The activities of the two ter-rorist groups – the Irgun Zvai Leumi and the Stern Gang – whose leaders were each to become Prime Minister of Israel, faced the British army with a new kind of threat – and one with which it has since become all too familiar. Ben Hecht, the American playwright, at a safe distance in New York from the agony of Palestine, said in a noto-rious interview: 'My heart leaps every time I hear of the death of a British soldier.' That kind of utterance those of us on the spot could treat with contempt. But Ernest Bevin could less easily resist President Truman's pressure to permit the refugees to land and, in the end, he felt obliged to recommend to his Cabinet colleagues a policy which he knew was fraught with danger for British interests.

Then, in 1951, Muhammad Mossadegh, the Prime Minister of Iran, nationalised the properties of the Anglo-Iranian Oil Company – the antecedent of British Petroleum. In so doing he paved the way for the oil price rises of the 1970s which plunged the economies of the industrialised world into recession. My wife and I were in Iraq at the time and felt the shock waves which spread throughout the Middle East. The atti-tude of the Americans to the crisis in Iran was ambiguous. On the one hand, they were nervous of the opening offered to the communists; on the other, they were not averse to a diminution of British influence in Iran. And there were commercial con-siderations too. In the end Mossadegh was removed by a *coup* organised by the Americans with British help, and the Anglo-Iranian Oil Company was replaced by a consortium which included American and other non-British participants.

Differences also arose further east. Preoccupation with communism dominated American policy towards China and South East Asia. The new Chinese Government appeared on the world stage for the first time at the Geneva Conference on Korea and Indo-China in 1954. When Chou en-Lai entered the Conference Hall at the head of the Chinese delegation, John Foster Dulles, the American Secretary of State, not only refused to shake his hand but would not even turn his head in Chou's direction. It was left to the British Foreign Secretary, Anthony Eden, to negotiate settlements of both conflicts which served Western interests, at least for a time. In order to achieve these agreements he had to hold in check the urge of the American Chiefs of Staff for drastic military intervention.

If Geneva 1954 was the zenith of Eden's career as an international diplomatist, Suez 1956 was its nadir. This disastrous episode not only placed a greater strain on Anglo-American relations than at any time since the Second World War but also, by cutting Britain's ambitions down to size, persuaded us, at long last, to focus attention on the far-reaching developments taking place across the Channel. Within a few years Britain, with the full-hearted support of President Kennedy, who wanted the Western Alliance to be based on two pillars – one on each side of the Atlantic, was seeking membership of the European Community. And, while the United States was playing the old imperialist role in Vietnam, Dean Rusk, the Secretary of State, was pleading with the British Foreign Secretary for just one company of the Black Watch as a gesture of solidarity. How quickly had the wheel turned.

*   *   *

If the United Kingdom is to influence the course of events, it is important, in my view, that we shed any illusions we may have about the nature of our relationship with the United States.

Barbara Kreutz, who is American, and Ellen Fleming, who is English, begin their book *Introducing America* with an important statement: 'America is different. This fact must be the starting point for any attempt to understand American diplomacy'.

In the first place, as is evident from the examples I have quoted, United States foreign policy, naturally enough, is often aimed at satisfying impulses and emotions fashioned by the American view of the world. Secondly, their attachment to personal liberty and individual enterprise has made Americans deeply distrustful of communism. So strong is this sentiment that Americans have found it harder than Europeans to accept neutrality or non-alignment. Black and white Stetsons distinguish the good guys from the bad; grey Stetsons are perplexing. This has often led the United States to support cruel and corrupt regimes because they were perceived as a bulwark against communism. It is disappointing, to put it no higher, that the United States has never enjoyed an easy relationship with the world's largest democracy – India. And it was maladroit of the Americans to exclude Syria for so long from their Middle East diplomacy, simply because they deemed Damascus to be a client of Moscow.

Successive United States Administrations have learned the hard way that solutions to diplomatic problems usually take time. Yet the American public is still inclined to feel frustrated when quick results are not perceptible. This is particularly so with issues which affect countries in the third world or involve international agencies, and the United Nations in particular. Things were different, they may feel, in the 1950s, when the United States dominated the United Nations and the developing world. This impatience encourages Americans to see peace and strength in military terms – a concept underpinned by the traditions of the frontier. When the Brazilian Foreign Minister told Henry Kissinger that small nations respected strength, Kissinger commented: 'Yes, especially in the strong.' In a leading article in 1984, *The Economist* put it this way: 'At one extreme, the United States ignores the world outside the Americas because it feels it neither likes it nor needs it. At the other it plunges into the world to put it to rights.' *The Economist* was less than fair. After all, the peace we in Europe have enjoyed these past forty-three years we owe in large measure to the commitment of the United States to the defence of its partners in the North Atlantic Alliance.

Like every other sovereign nation, the United States is entitled to base its foreign policy on its perception of its own national interest. The most sincere compliment we can pay our American friends and allies is to respect this right. We can count ourselves lucky that on the major issues our interests and those of the United States march side by side. But if, by hankering after a special relationship we expect the Americans to do things for us which conflict with their interests, then we delude ourselves. And if we believe that we play a special role in Washington, then a careful search for news and views about Britain in the American media will persuade us that this too is a delusion. Americans have their own preoccupations and they are immensely and rightly proud of their country. The freedoms enshrined in their democratic institutions lie at the heart of this pride. The belief of the Puritans of New England that theirs was God's own country because they were God's chosen people has been passed down from generation to generation and is now part of the American character.

Today's Americans and today's Britons share the view embodied in our Christian tradition that in any society the interests of the individual must be sovereign. This common conviction inspires our mutual respect, admiration and affection. It is this which makes our relationship special and, though our interests and diplomatic objectives may from time to time diverge, in the end that is all that matters.

VIII

THE CHRISTIAN AND THE COMMUNITY OF NATIONS

WELLS CATHEDRAL – OCTOBER 1989

Individuals derive comfort and benefit from living in a community. There is no reason why nations should not do the same. But, as the late Professor Joad would have said: 'It depends on what you mean by community, and by nation.' He would have been right. How the term nation has been defined in the past is one of the keys to our understanding of the present; and the way in which it is interpreted today will affect the prospects for humanity.

A nation is usually defined as a body of people distinguished by common descent, language, culture or historical tradition and the term *nation* is often regarded as synonymous with 'the people of a state'. Neat and tidy, one would say. The Japanese fit this description to perfection. They alone inhabit the Japanese islands; they alone speak Japanese; their religion, culture and historical tradition are unique. The Pyrenees and the Rhine – and their own fierce pride – mark out the French and the Spaniards as individual nations living within their natural boundaries. But, as we run our finger down the list, we soon realise how numerous are the exceptions to this rule. How many Sikhs in the Punjab accept that they belong to the same nation as the Hindus of Uttar Pradesh or the Tamils of Madras? What have the Moroccans and the Iraqis in common – the one at the western, the other at the eastern end of the Arab world? And, for that matter, who are the Iraqis? A short walk through the streets of Baghdad is an anthropologist's delight: the descendants of invaders who came from east, north and south, many bringing their slaves with them, mingle with latter-day Babylonians, Assyrians, Akkadians and Sumerians. When asked, Arabs, whether Moroccan or Iraqi, will say that an Arab is someone who speaks Arabic and regards himself as an Arab – a convenient and convincing definition. But Egyptians who, under Gamal Abdel Nasser, claimed leadership of the Arab world, would insist that they are *Egyptians*, even though they were proud of the fact that Arabic is their language and even more proud of their pre-eminence in the use of the modern idiom.

There are anomalies nearer home. On one of my first visits to Northern Ireland in the early 1970s, I asked my Protestant hosts whether they thought of themselves as Irish or British. With one of those indulgent smiles characteristic of the brave people of that province they replied: 'Well, if you really want an answer, how long have you got?'

For practical purposes we accept today that by *nations* we mean states in the international sense. The League of Nations was so called for a variety of reasons – the dignity, even pomposity, of the title reflected the high purpose of the organisation. Apart from this, to refer to states might have prejudiced issues still to be settled and could have implied a tendency towards federalism which would have been unwarranted. Similar considerations applied to the choice of the title United Nations in the 1940s.

The nations and states we recognise today represent the furthest limit of man's advance from the law of the jungle – the survival of the fittest. Fear created the need for security and this was found in the unity of the family, tribe or clan, and then in alliance with neighbours. If fear was a main motive in the formation of groups, success in the struggle to survive depended on native human qualities and, above all, on leadership. Leadership attracted loyalty by appealing to the common interest and common advantage of the led. But leadership, which had its own rewards, also attracted rivalry. So, success in confronting the enemy without often inspired the enemy within.

From earliest times the leadership of nations has been responsible for major human achievements. The Rome of Augustus, the Byzantium of Justinian, the England of Elizabeth the First, the France of Louis XIV are all regarded as products of a Golden Age. The contributions of other leaders have been equally notable for their negative impact – Attila, Genghis Khan, Tamerlane, Hitler, Stalin, Idi Amin, Pol Pot.

For a brief period during the Italian Renaissance in the sixteenth century hopes rose that a new way of life might be adopted, based on the principles of political freedom, public spirit and free enquiry. This, it was believed, would enhance man's awareness of God. The Council of Trent snuffed out the flickering flame and the opportunity to replace the idea of the state as the natural political and administrative framework was lost.

In the periods between wars in the following centuries relations between states and peoples were comparatively relaxed. Responsibility for public security and administration was widely diffused and, generally speaking, travellers went on their way without political let or hindrance.

The rise of modern nationalism, for which we are indebted largely to Napoleon and, to a lesser extent, Bismarck, focussed attention on sovereignty. Like others, we in Britain are attached to our land and property and our right to manage our own affairs. Yet we have accepted limitations on our sovereignty when this has served our interests. For centuries we have formed alliances with others in order to achieve our aims. The Charter of the United Nations, which acknowledges the equal rights of nations large and small, specifically permits regional arrangements for dealing with such matters as international peace and security.

Today the international map is cluttered with groupings of states of one kind or another. Sometimes these groups have been created in order to confront a threat, real or perceived, to the security of their members. The North Atlantic Treaty Organisation and the Warsaw Pact are obvious examples. Some, such as the Non-Aligned movement founded at the Bandung Conference in 1955 and the so-called Group of 77 – the membership today numbers 126 – which was established in New Delhi in 1964, have grown out of a shared sense of political and economic disadvantage. Common problems and preoccupations and a desire to encourage regional identity inspired the creation of the Association of South East Asian States – ASEAN – and the Organisation of African Unity – the OAU. The Organisation of American States, which on the face of it seems to be a similar body, serves a different purpose. The OAS provides a forum where Latin America can meet the North Americans on an equal basis to discuss their differences. The states who created the Arab League in 1944 had a variety of motives. They wanted to align their policies in preparation for the post-war settlement; they wanted to close ranks against the Zionist threat; and they wanted to emphasise their Arab identity based on common language and tradition. Other groupings, such as the Organisation of Petroleum Exporting Countries (OPEC) and CARICOM – the common market of Caribbean countries – have specific economic and commercial purposes.

The most ambitious and complex experiment in regional cooperation is, of course, the European Community. The Community differs from all other regional groupings in two important respects. First, it is a dynamic organisation motivated by the continuous dialectic between the Commission, which represents the interests of the Community as a whole, and the Member States. Secondly, this process aims at no fixed target but rather an 'ever closer union among the peoples of Europe'. The European venture has no precedent in human history.

The only universal, or nearly universal, groupings of states are the General Assembly of the United Nations and the international agencies which derive their authority from the United Nations – agencies such as the World Health Organisation, the International Labour Office, the International Telecommunication Union, UNESCO, the International Bank for Reconstruction and Development and the International Monetary Fund.

The United Nations has attracted much cynical comment. Clearly the original expectations were pitched too high. Nor did anyone expect the Russians of Stalin's era so blatantly to abuse the power of veto granted to the permanent members of the Security Council. But even so, that did not justify the tendency of some governments to dismiss the organisation as an expensive coffee shop. It is satisfactory that a more balanced view of the role the UN can play is taken today. This is due in part at least to the fact that, over the past two decades, the UN has performed the invaluable function of providing a forum where regional problems and the issues which divide developing and industrialised countries can be discussed objectively and dispassionately.

Many of the UN's *peace-keeping* operations have been quietly successful. *Peacemaking* is never easy if the protagonists do not want peace and the UN should not be blamed for the intransigence of individual member states. Sometimes progress is possible only when the optimum moment arrives. I was at the United Nations in New York when the Yom Kippur War broke out in the autumn of 1973. The then Foreign Secretary, Lord Home, gave me authority to work for a cease-fire. With the active support of the non-aligned members of the Security Council, my French colleague and I worked out a formula which we believed would be acceptable to both sides. We made several unsuccessful attempts to persuade the Arabs and the Israelis to discuss this in the Council. We were forced to the painful conclusion that the two sides were determined for the time being to continue the blood-letting. Eventually, after some weeks, reason returned and our draft Resolution instituting a cease-fire was passed by the Council virtually without argument or amendment.

* * *

How should Christians charged with responsibility in the field of international relations approach their task? I suggest that the starting point should be acceptance of the fact of our common humanity; our duty to love our neighbour; our acknowledgement of human fallibility; and our trust in the Providence which is eternally on hand to save us from our follies and errors – our faith in the Second Adam who, in Cardinal Newman's words, 'to the fight and to the rescue came'. From this starting point our destination, however great the intervening distance, is clear. We must aim for unity, peace and justice — the only sure basis for a community of nations of the kind Professor Joad would have accepted without qualification.

Unity, peace, justice. Easy to say; not so easy to achieve. Others do not start from the same position. Our aims are not universally shared. Others have objectives totally incompatible with our own. From what we know of human nature and human history, this is to be expected. What then should we do? As Paul told the Corinthians, we may be perplexed, but not in despair. We should turn aside from our perplexity and apply wisdom and patience to the task of analysing the impediments to the creation of a real community of nations.

The greatest of these impediments is distrust. Distrust begets fear, hatred and anger — the worst of counsellors. Sadly, in too many parts of the world distrust is so deep-seated that the best one can hope for is that the virus will not be allowed to spread while efforts continue to find a remedy. In some cases it is obvious that the passage of time, widely acclaimed as a great healer, has in fact fortified hostile attitudes and allowed new sources of distrust to be created or invented.

Another much discussed cause of international tension is the disparity between the affluence of industrialised countries and the deprivation of a majority of developing countries. Although the more serious aspects of this problem, and notably the debt issue, are firmly inscribed on the international agenda, this will continue to arouse resentment and envy for decades to come.

Conflicting ideologies are another obstacle. It is not easy to bridge the gap between diametrically opposed views about the nature of man, the structure of human society and the role of the state. When overlaid with racial or religious prejudice, and intolerance which at times crosses the limits of reason to become fanaticism, ideological differences are even more difficult to reconcile.

Then there are the contemporary manifestations of the 'evil things' which Neville Chamberlain told us fifty years ago we would be fighting — tyranny, oppression, denial of human rights, systematic cruelty, genocide. These are still widespread today.

Despite these obstacles along the path towards greater international understanding, we can be grateful that for two generations there has been no global war and that the numerous regional conflicts, disastrous as these have been for those involved have been contained and in many cases brought to an acceptable end.

The most immediate threat to the security of the community of nations is international and domestic terrorism, frequently allied with highly organised criminal activity and carried out in the name of causes which are often so obscure as to be unintelligible. This is, in a sense, the Third World War.

* * *

There is no magic formula for removing these impediments. Each represents a separate problem requiring its own solution. Each has to be confronted as and when opportunity offers. It is seldom the case that right is all on one side in a dispute. Discovering where right lies is therefore a prime task and it is essential that the diplomatist should develop the relevant skills and techniques. He must then deploy these when facing problems of whatever kind with one overriding purpose — to identify the common ground which might provide a basis for an eventual solution.

An eventual solution. Realistically, that is usually the best one can hope for. But in the end progress will be made. In the recent past we have seen striking evidence of the virtues of patience and adherence to cherished principles. The changes which have taken place in Eastern Europe have taken us all by surprise. But we should not forget that our approach to the communist world for forty years has been based on our conviction that the political system behind the Iron Curtain was flawed and that in due time tyranny would be broken by the strength of the human spirit.

There have been hopeful developments in other fields. The North/South debate, conducted with much acrimony in the early 1970s, has identified new instruments for the transfer of resources and expertise which are not only more effective but also reflect a spirit of partnership, based on common interest and common humanity, more appropriate to the present day.

Concern for our environment transcends national frontiers, as indeed it must. Here at last is an issue, quite literally, of global concern. Pollution can also erode sovereignty. The community of nations must act in concert and, if this happens, the benefits could be felt in other fields. Good habits are just as easy to pick up as bad.

In another way which has attracted less public attention frontiers are being broken down. The satellite, micro-electronics and the merger of the technologies of the computer, communications and broadcasting have brought within range the comprehensive world communications network envisaged by Marshall McLuhan in the 1960s. The opportunities presented by these new technologies have coincided with changes in the structure of industry and the business market. Easy access to international sources of finance and labour have persuaded firms to offer both goods and services and to develop strategies for production and marketing on an international scale, many commercial undertakings can no longer be supported by purely national markets, And so, through their computer links, they reach out to their suppliers, their work units and their customers in whichever country they may be. In this way, without the intervention of governments or international agencies, economic interdependence between communities at different stages of development is giving way to inter-connection — a major step on the way to the creation of an integrated global market.

*   *   *

Any development which undermines traditional notions of sovereignty deserves to be encouraged by Christians. We must support actions which will replace distrust with confidence; fear with resolution; deprivation with sufficiency; prejudice with tolerance. We must persuade our political leaders that it is more productive to talk to their peers than to talk at them and, when they do, to feast together, as Paul advised his brethren in Corinth, with the unleavened bread of sincerity and truth.

At this point I hesitate. Fifty years ago the role of the Church was described in these terms: 'Not compromise for the sake of peace, but rather comprehension for the sake of truth'. This definition makes me uneasy. Nothing more may have been meant than that the Church should not settle for a quiet life. But if something else was intended, then I am puzzled by the antithesis. No relationship between states can be soundly based unless it is founded on a true appreciation by each of the legitimate interests, aspirations, strengths and weaknesses of the other. Nor, in my view, will any relationship between states endure unless proper account is taken of these.

Even so, this may not be enough to promote understanding and the going may be hard. When it is, we can comfort ourselves with the knowledge that the Second Adam is always at hand. Nearly twenty years ago I experienced one of the most difficult moments of my diplomatic career. I had had to tell Colonel Qaddafi that we were cancelling a contract to supply Libya with a large quantity of Chieftain tanks. He was not amused. A few months later I learned — and so did he — that the British Government were likely to respond favourably to a request from the

Israelis to supply them with Chieftains. The 5,000 British subjects scattered throughout Libya for whom I was responsible were understandably alarmed. I told London that if such a deal went ahead many of these people would be placed in jeopardy. London's reaction gave me no comfort; on the contrary. The volume of prayer that arose from British hearts in Libya the night before the British Government were due to take their decision must have been impressive. The following afternoon I learned that – for the time being at least–the sale would not proceed. Face was saved in London – and so were skins in Libya.

There were better moments. The painstaking and at times painful construction of the European Community in which I was closely engaged in Brussels for over four years, is often portrayed as a continuous wrangle over points of detail. This is not an inaccurate picture. But it is only part of the story. The phase of reconciling former enemies has long since ended. The creation of a Single European Market by 1992 is no more than the latest stage in the process of developing an 'ever closer union' which, to my mind, represents the most original constitutional and political concept since the American Declaration of Independence in 1776. This approach is based on common heritage, common interest and a common perception of the role of the individual in society. What is more, the Community functions in accordance with two principles which should command wide approval: comprehension for the sake of truth, certainly; but also compromise for the sake of progress.

The European endeavour will succeed and will be imitated by other groupings of nations to the benefit of mankind as a whole. It will succeed not only because there is no alternative to success, but also because this will be the best way to repay our debt to the earlier generations who gave their lives to preserve freedom and justice. A few days before we left Brussels in 1979, my wife and I visited the battlefield at Vimy. The autumn sun was slowly burning off the mist which hung over the village and the farms in the valley below. We stood on hallowed ground. Behind us rose a monument to one of the great tragedies in human history and on it were inscribed words which surely find an echo in the heart of every Christian who wishes to see the community of nations become a reality:

'Nations, soyez unies; hommes, soyez humains'.

IX

RING ROUND THE WORLD

THINKNET COMMISSION – PARIS – MARCH 1990

Over the past forty years the international community has become accustomed to certain seemingly constant factors. The Second World War and the development of the nuclear weapon created a world dominated by two super-powers. The clash of ideologies and mutual distrust led to the formation of two opposing military groupings whose existence preserved world peace and prevented a nuclear holocaust.

During the War much of the infrastructure in Europe and Asia was destroyed and the economies of Germany and Japan were gravely weakened. However, industrial regeneration on the basis of the state of the art ensured that these two economies again became dominant; the economic power of the United States declined in relative terms.

The Iron Curtain divided Europe into two apparently irreconcilable camps. In Western Europe determination to avoid another Franco-German catastrophe stimulated the movement towards closer integration. The countries of eastern Europe, on which communism had been imposed by force, laboured under varying degrees of tyranny while their economies stagnated.

Having secured their political independence, the peoples of the colonial empires faced unprecedented economic and social challenges. In most cases they were incapable of confronting these because they lacked the skills and experience required. The great programmes of financial and technical aid alleviated but did not cure their condition. Some of these countries believed that by uniting their political and diplomatic efforts they could change the world order and they persuaded others to act with them. When this failed developing countries pursued other policies. Some turned to regional cooperation, some to partnerships with foreign enterprises, some actively encouraged inward investment. In many cases these policies led to substantial economic advance. Others sought salvation in isolation.

In imperial days, when political power was effectively in the hands of a score or so of states, international problems were easier to comprehend and to manage, even if they were just as difficult to resolve. Today, the ambitions and aspirations of nations in every continent seem to be in contention. That there have been more victims of armed conflict since the Second World War than during it shows that such problems are no easier to settle by peaceful means.

Meanwhile revolutionary changes have been taking place in the fields of science and technology, for instance in travel, transportation and medicine. Less widely appreciated by public opinion but of deeper significance in the longer term are advances in the handling of information.

The emancipation of colonial peoples and scientific and technological advances have brought immense benefits. But to each of these achievements there seems to be a counter. Economic growth has raised living standards but in the process our environment has been jeopardised. Divergent growth rates have widened the gap between the affluent and the deprived. Advances in medicine have not emptied hospital beds; on the contrary. The assumption of responsibility has released new ideas and energies. But where it has been delegated to groups or nations ill-equipped to accept it, or eager to abuse it, new threats to international peace and law and order have arisen.

This is no new challenge. Human history is marked by a continuous conflict between the acquisition and application of knowledge and the preservation of values.

*   *   *

The rush of events in Eastern and Central Europe in the late 1980s is not the end of history, but rather the preface to a great and novel challenge which mankind is better placed than ever to confront. None of these events was unpredictable – only the pace of the change. Moreover, the governments concerned are conscious of the risks to be avoided as they adapt to the new situation. Furthermore there is available a range of techniques for managing change without jeopardising peaceful progress.

Prime responsibility for preserving world peace rests with governments. In the management of change international organisations and regional groupings of states have a role to play. But the most important contribution to effecting a peaceful and equitable transition from the twentieth to the twenty-first century will be made by those with the wisdom and skills to exploit the opportunities which flow from the revolution in methods of handling information. The advent of the satellite, micro-electronics and optical fibre and the junction of the communications and computer technology coincided with changes in the structure of industry and the business market. Through the evolution of a global communications service, these technological advances have made possible the development of 'networking' – the creation of series of interconnecting relationships from which each participant benefits.

The political, economic and social potential of networking on a world scale cannot be exaggerated. If the right conditions exist, networking can pave the way to an integrated global economy. How can the right conditions be created? The North Atlantic Treaty Organisation and the Warsaw Pact will have to maintain the peace. International agencies such as the GATT and the International Telecommunication Union must ensure that regulatory systems not only create fair conditions but do not impede the establishment of networks. The European Community and other regional groupings should see networking as a means of consolidating regional identity, increasing prosperity and of breaking down barriers world wide. Governments and parliaments will have to accept that the spread of networks will constitute a further erosion of national sovereignty.

If, unlike other advances of the past forty years, networking is to proceed without countervailing disadvantage another important condition has to be fulfilled. Unless developing countries can take part in networking on fair terms a new gap will open up. This would damage the interests of industrialised and developing countries alike and lead to be tensions in the future. What needs to be done was set out in *The Missing Link* – the Report of the Independent Commission for World Wide Telecommunications Development issued in 1985. Failure to ensure that developing countries can and do participate in networking would be to forgo the best opportunity the international community has had to stimulate economic and social development on a global scale and, in the process, to create a more equitable world system. The opportunity must not be lost.

X

INTERNATIONAL ORDER IN THE TWENTY-FIRST CENTURY: THE ROLE OF THE UNITED NATIONS

UNITED NATIONS ASSOCIATION: BATH
OCTOBER 1999

The search for an effective and generally acceptable system of international order has occupied most of the twentieth century. And it is inevitable that the process will continue for many years to come.

For much of the latter part of the nineteenth century the major European powers were engaged in a contest to colonise what we now call the developing world. Following the unification of Germany in the latter part of that century a new force appeared on the international stage. Under vigorous and ambitious Prussian leadership, the new Germany sought to dominate Europe. The young Kaiser Wilhelm, anxious to emerge from behind the towering figure of Bismarck, skilfully played off one rival for power in Europe against another. He built up Germany's military and naval strength . The threat this posed to peace in Europe was recognised too late and the German invasion of Belgium in August 1914 marked the beginning of the war which did not end all wars – the first of the cataclysms which have characterised the history of this wonderful and dreadful twentieth century.

For over two and a half years the United States stood aside while the carnage continued on the Western Front. It was not until April 1917, when Germany broke its undertaking to refrain from attacking American merchant ships carrying supplies to Europe, that President Woodrow Wilson decided that the United States should enter the conflict. Up to this point he had played the role of leader of the neutral states. He now assumed the mantle of moral leader of the world. He set out his peace aims on 8 January 1918 in his Fourteen Points. These included the evacuation and restoration of territory which had been occupied by the German armies; the free, open-minded and impartial adjustment of colonial disputes; autonomy for the subject peoples of Austria-Hungary and the Ottoman Empire; open diplomacy; and freedom of the seas. President Wilson also proposed a 'general association of nations' which would guarantee their political and territorial integrity in the future. Three days after the Fourteen Points were published, the British Prime Minister, Lloyd George, issued a statement on similar lines.

President Wilson's personal instincts were honourable; his ambitions for the future structure of the world were idealistic. Until 1914 it was generally acknowledged that peace in Europe had depended on the balance of power. After the Russian Revolution in 1917, the defeat of Germany in 1918 and the exhaustion of France and Britain, there was no balance of power. It was recognition of this fundamental change that inspired Woodrow Wilson's concept of an association of nations.

The new reality was clear. In 1918 Europe ceased to be the centre of the world; the continent was dwarfed by two world powers – the United States and the Soviet Union. Each of these powers had its own idealism by which the notion of 'One World' would come into existence. For the Soviet Union the instrument was communism; for the United States liberal democracy, as set out in shorthand in the Fourteen Points. This would replace the balance of power as the guarantor of peace.

* * *

The first item on the agenda of the Peace Conference which began its work in Paris in January 1919 was 'the creation of an international organisation for the peaceful settlement of disputes between states'. A special commission headed by President Wilson drafted a covenant for a league of nations. This was approved by the whole conference in the following month. The Covenant was adopted as the first twenty-six articles of the Treaty of Versailles which was signed in June. The treaty was ratified in January 1920 and, at this point, the League of Nations came into existence.

The objects of the League were 'to promote international cooperation and to achieve international peace and security'. The League was to act through an assembly, consisting of representatives of all the members and a council, which would have five permanent members and others elected by the assembly. It was intended that the permanent members would be representatives of the 'principal allied and associated powers' – namely, the British Empire, France, Italy, Japan and the United States. However, the United States, daunted by the wide commitment implicit in the language of Article 10, which required members 'to respect and preserve against external aggression the territorial integrity and existing political independence of all members', refused to ratify the Treaty and so did not become a member of the League, despite the fact that it was the brainchild of its President.

The absence of the United States, Germany and Russia and the admission of a number of smaller states prevented the League from acting as the sole directing body in world affairs. Isolationism in the United States, the general fear of communism and the drastic terms of the peace treaties meant that there was little prospect of general agreement on the means whereby the League would perform its main task of promoting international peace and security. In practice, the major problems that arose were handled through direct negotiation between the parties concerned. Nevertheless, in the first four years of its existence the League did succeed in settling a number of disputes which were relics of the war, such as the future status of the Åland Islands between Finland and Sweden and of Vilna and Memel in Lithuania.

If there were any golden years in the League's history these were in the late 1920s. Germany became a permanent member of the Council of the League in 1926 and cooperated closely with Britain and France in the main task of the day – preparation of the proposed Disarmament Conference. During this period disputes between Greece and Bulgaria and between Britain and Turkey over the future of the vilayet of Mosul in Iraq were satisfactorily settled. In 1928 the signatories of the Pact named after its two architects – Frank Billings Kellogg, the US Secretary of State, and Aristide Briand, the French foreign minister – pledged to dispense with war except for certain limited purposes such as defence of the Pact itself, of the Covenant of the League, the British Empire and the Monroe Doctrine, promulgated in 1823, which prohibited any further colonisation or other interference in the Western Hemisphere.

The real tests came in the 1930s. The Sino-Japanese war led to Japan's withdrawal from the League in March 1933. In October of the same year Germany withdrew on the ostensible grounds that the Disarmament Conference had not fulfilled its purpose. Italy defied the League over its invasion of Abyssinia and, having completed its conquest, resigned its membership at the end of 1937. The final act of the League was to condemn the Soviet Union for its invasion of Finland in 1939 and, in 1946, it ceded its functions to the infant United Nations.

* * *

When German forces invaded Poland in September 1939, once again the United States stood aside. Once again it was not until it was itself the victim of aggression – in December 1941 – that the United States entered the war. However, his country's neutral status did not prevent its President expressing his views about the post war world. In August 1941 Roosevelt and Winston Churchill, whose leadership during the Battle of Britain in 1940 had won him acclaim throughout the free world, signed the Atlantic Charter. In this document the two leaders, on whom the mantles of Woodrow Wilson and Lloyd George had fallen, sought to outlaw territorial or any other aggrandisement as well as territorial changes against the freely expressed wishes of the people concerned. They looked forward to 'a peace, after the defeat of the Nazi tyranny, which would allow all nations to dwell in safety within their own boundaries, and enable all men in all lands to live out their lives in freedom from fear and want.'

As regards the form of a post-war world organisation for securing peace and security, both Roosevelt and Churchill favoured a regional pattern. However Stalin's lack of confidence in the intentions of the Western allies and his own ambitions led him to advocate an organisation with unrestricted sovereignty. He won the argument. In October 1943 the foreign ministers of the three allies met in Moscow. They endorsed the principle of the sovereign equality of all states and proposed a global organisation.

The United Nations which came into existence in 1946 was a revised version of the League. While the Charter did not proscribe war, it went a long way towards banning it except in defence of the obligations in the Charter and it authorised the Security Council to determine whether a given situation constituted a threat to international peace. If the Council did so determine, then all member states would be required to act against the delinquent state; whether force was to be used would be decided by each member. However, such an arrangement would be effective only if the major powers were in agreement and if a sufficient number of member states were prepared to provide the military forces required.

The late 1940s were overshadowed by the readiness of the Soviet Union to use its veto. Other members complained that this practice breached the spirit if not the provisions of the charter. This prompted the Soviet Union to boycott meetings of the Security Council. This had an unexpected beneficial effect. In the absence of the Soviet Union the United Nations was able to act decisively when war broke out in Korea. The Security Council voluntarily transferred part of its authority to the General Assembly which responded to the challenge by passing the Uniting for Peace Resolution which was adopted by 50 votes to 5 with two abstentions. This resolution provided the basis for the UN's action against North Korea and was again used in 1956 when British and French forces attacked Egypt. This procedure was challenged by the Soviet Union, but the International Court ruled that, while the Security Council had primary responsibility for peace-keeping, this responsibility was not exclusive.

Wrangling in the Security Council seriously damaged its prestige and encouraged members to devise alternative methods of dealing with threats to peace. The interventions of the UN in Palestine and Suez had the characteristics of mediation. In Cyprus the role of the UN was both mediatory and military. In Kashmir the UN succeeded in negotiating a cease-fire in 1949, but failed to secure the withdrawal of Pakistani or Indian troops and, fifty years later, the Kashmir dispute is no nearer a solution. The intervention in Korea was in sharp contrast to the failure of the League of Nations to act in Manchuria twenty years earlier. The action taken in the Congo removed the Belgian presence and prevented intervention by either the Russians or Americans. Only medium states were asked to supply combat units and the Secretary-General himself was given executive control. The growth of the Secretary-General's power was unwelcome to the major member states. But the inescapable fact was that unless the UN was allowed to act in defence of international peace and security, they would have had to carry out the task themselves.

The aggressive actions of Argentina and Britain in support of their irreconcilable claims to sovereignty over the Falklands in 1982 and the United States naval and air assault on Libya in 1986 were technical violations of the obligations accepted by all signatories to the UN Charter.

When the cold war ended it was hoped that the UN might at long last be able to act as originally intended when the Charter was signed. The Iraqi invasion of Kuwait was the first test. The Security Council authorised military action under Chapter VII. But the Council went further. In a landmark decision – Resolution 688 – the Council described the situation inside Iraq as a threat to international peace and demanded access for humanitarian organisations to parts of Iraq where the rights of minorities were being abused. For the first time this focused attention on the conflict between the obligations in articles 1(3) and 55 to respect human rights and the prohibition, in article 2(7), of intervention in the essentially domestic affairs of a member state.

From the late 1980s onwards demands on the UN increased rapidly. The reason was that the UN was not merely involved in stopping wars but also began to assume a measure of responsibility for domestic order where disorder threatened international peace, or where human rights were under serious threat. This increase in the scale of the UN's activities inevitably led to a sharp rise in its costs.

While much of the UN's work at this time was well conceived and on the whole effective, its intervention in Somalia in 1992 was disastrous. Following the overthrow of the ruler the country had descended into anarchy. Contrary to the wishes of the Secretary-General, a force was formed to intervene in the crisis, but this was given no authority to disarm the warring factions. More serious, it was unclear whether UNOSOM, as it was called, was a United Nations or a United States operation. In December 1995 a group set up to investigate this operation issued its 'Comprehensive Report' on the lessons to be learned. Reading this is a chilling experience. Paragraph after paragraph is a statement of the obvious. A catalogue of fifteen of the most elementary mistakes and shortcomings is revealed. For example: 'There is a need for a clear and practicable mandate'; 'Mandates must be matched with the means to implement them'; 'Integrated planning is essential in order to deal with the multidimensional problems in peace-keeping operations'; 'The timely deployment of well-trained personnel is essential'; and so on.

The United Nations became involved in Yugoslavia in September 1991 following the intervention by the European Community. Its first step was to place an embargo on the supply of arms. A mediation effort was mounted and a force – UNPROFOR – was formed and despatched to the region with the principal tasks of assisting victims of the fighting and protecting aid workers in the worst affected areas. A notable innovation was the decision by the Security Council in 1993 to establish an *ad hoc* tribunal to hear charges of serious violations of international humanitarian law in Yugoslavia since the outbreak of hostilities in 1991.

* * *

The end of the cold war was seen by many as an opportunity to remedy the short-comings of the United Nations. In January 1992 the Security Council met at the level of Heads of State and Government to discuss the way forward. At the conclusion of this meeting the Secretary-General, Boutros Ghali, was invited to prepare for circulation to all member states an 'analysis and recommendations on ways of strengthening and making more efficient within the framework and provisions of the Charter the capacity of the United Nations for preventive diplomacy, for peace-making and for peace-keeping'.

In June 1992 the Secretary-General delivered his response, to which he gave the title 'Agenda for Peace'. In describing the context in which he approached his task, Boutros Ghali set out a number of home truths about the state of the world. While the concept of peace was easy to grasp, he argued, that of international security was more complex. He pointed to the widespread accumulation of arms, the rise of new racial tensions, the technological advances which had altered the nature and expectations of life – these, as well as the persistence of poverty, disease, famine, oppression and despair. It followed that, if the United Nations was to build peace and security, it had to encompass matters beyond military threats in order to break the fetters of strife and warfare which had characterised the past. Since the United Nations was created in 1945 over one hundred major conflicts had left some 20 million dead. And 279 vetoes had rendered the United Nations powerless to deal with many of these.

Boutros Ghali then put forward detailed proposals for the role the United Nations might play in preventive diplomacy, peacemaking, peace-keeping and peace-building. In performing these functions the United Nations should also address the deeper causes of conflict – economic despair, social injustice, political oppression and denial of human rights on ethnic, religious, social, or linguistic grounds. Against this background he recommended a number of steps for reinforcing the role of the International Court of Justice.

The Secretary-General went on to point out that, since the end of the era of abuse of the veto, demands on the United Nations had surged. At the time of his Report the annual cost of approved peace-keeping operations was estimated at nearly $3 billion. Unpaid arrears towards these costs stood at over $800 million. This constituted a debt to the states which had contributed troops to these operations and vividly illustrated what the Secretary-General called a stark fact: the financial foundations of the organisation daily grow weaker, debilitating its political will and practical capacity to undertake new and essential activities. There was one inescapable necessity, he said: 'Member States must pay their assessed contributions in full and on time. Failure to do so puts them in breach of their obligations under the Charter'.

In July 1997, six months after he had succeeded Boutros Ghali as Secretary-General, Kofi Annan submitted to the General Assembly a Programme of Reform under the title 'Renewing the United Nations'. In this he did not confine himself to radical administrative reforms such as establishing a new leadership and management structure; creating a new post of Deputy Secretary-General; integrating twelve Secretariat entities into five; setting up a new Emergency Relief Coordination Office; effecting a major shift in the United Nations public information and communications strategy and functions; and reviewing the charter and legal instruments of the specialised agencies. He also addressed a number of the critical political issues facing the Organisation. For example, he created a Revolving Credit Fund to assure financial solvency; he promoted sustained and sustainable development as a central priority; he improved the Organisation's ability to deploy peace-keeping and other field operations more rapidly and strengthened its ability for post-conflict peace-building. He also extended the scope of the Organisation's activities in the field of human rights. And, as a final flourish, he designated the General Assembly in the year 2000 a Millennium Assembly.

* * *

In 1905, the Spanish-American philosopher George Santayana wrote: 'Progress, far from consisting in change, depends on retentiveness . . . Those who cannot remember the past are condemned to repeat it.' Objective observers of the performance of those who have wielded political power in the field of international relations throughout this century might conclude that they have been intent on confirming the truth of Santayana's dictum. As we approach a new century we must hope that the lessons of the past will not only be learned and inwardly digested, but also acted upon.

Through their clear thinking and the reforms they stimulated, both Boutros Ghali and Kofi Annan have made significant contributions to the search for an effective and generally acceptable system of world order through the Agenda for Peace and the Programme of Reform. Today there is in place a more secure platform than has existed in the past. The question now is whether the leaders of the Member States will have the wisdom, will and courage to build upon this platform policies, procedures and programmes relevant to the needs of the next century.

One of the first tasks should be to identify the new challenges the United Nations will face in the future. The recent increase in the number of small scale conflicts, many of them within states, as for example in Yugoslavia and central Africa, has created new problems. The causes of these conflicts are often deep-seated and, to the outsider, irrational. In most cases those who suffer most are innocent civilians. Their plight poses a moral challenge. For those in authority whose thinking is still conditioned by the cold war, the appropriate response is not always obvious and, in the end peace-keeping efforts in support of humanitarian aid tend to be limited in scope. The more far-sighted have already accepted the rationale behind Boutros Ghali's *Agenda for Peace* and Kofi Annan's *Programme of Reform* and concluded that more effort should be devoted to preventing such conflicts. Apart from the obvious benefits in human terms, timely preventive action, combined with longer term efforts to build peace, will be far less costly than military and humanitarian intervention. The need for such an approach was recognised in Article 1 of the UN Charter and Article 99 places on the Secretary-General responsibility for bringing to the attention of the Security Council any matter which could threaten peace and security. We should expect to see more instances of this prevention strategy in operation, beginning with early warning, then preventive diplomacy and preventive deployment and, at a later stage, preventive disarmament and peace-building.

Another important innovation is the proposal for practical collaboration over the prevention of conflict between the United Nations and regional organisations. Indeed, with the growth of regional consciousness across the world, the idea of delegating more tasks to regions might well be encouraged.

These developments certainly represent an important advance, but the United Nations should go further. Television has, quite literally, brought home to us all the suffering and distress inflicted on the innocent through disregard for human rights. The incompatibility between, on the one hand, the injunctions in Articles 1(3) and 55 of the Charter and the prohibition in Article 2(7) on the other must be addressed. One is entitled to ask whether public opinion across the globe today is content to regard the outrageous effects of wholesale or, as in the case of Burma, particular disregard for human rights as 'essentially within the domestic jurisdiction' of the state authorities responsible. The recent creation of the post of UN High Commissioner for Human Rights and the appointment to this post of Mary Robinson will have been welcomed by all people of goodwill. This extension of the United Nations' sphere of responsibility follows the setting up of the International War Crimes Tribunal for former Yugoslavia in The Hague and the signature in Rome in July of last year of the Final Act of the United Nations Diplomatic Conference on the Establishment of an International Criminal Court.

A number of comparatively minor figures responsible for atrocities during the hostilities in former Yugoslavia have been tried and sentenced by the War Crimes Tribunal in The Hague. However, the deterrent effect of the Tribunal and the new Criminal Court when it has been set up will not be felt until those charged with instigating the atrocities have been brought to trial and sentenced. It is a scandal that Radovan Karadzic and Ratko Mladic are still at large. Unless those communities which have suffered so grievously at the hands of these criminals can see that justice has been done, their children will be tempted several years hence to exact their own revenge. If the international community has any pretensions to being civilised, devising means of ensuring that indicted war criminals are brought to justice must be an urgent task for the next century. Thought might be given to imposing selective sanctions, such as cutting off certain critical supplies – fuel, for example – to those states which give sanctuary to such individu-

als. Another possibility would be to ban travel beyond their own borders by specified categories of citizens of such states until those indicted have been surrendered. A solution to this human and moral problem must be found and the events
of the past several weeks in Yugoslavia should provide a spur.

History will record that, on the instructions of the President of the sovereign state
of Yugoslavia, Serbian military and paramilitary forces in the province of Kosovo,
began to expel the ethnically Albanian Muslim inhabitants, who constituted the
majority. The methods used were barbarous and hundreds of thousands left to
take refuge in neighbouring nation states. The members of the North Atlantic
Alliance called on the Republic of Yugoslavia to stop its atrocious actions and
withdraw its forces so that the refugees could return under international protection to their homes. Yugoslavia at first refused but acquiesced after an eleven-
week bombing campaign had caused enormous damage to the infrastructure of
Yugoslavia. At this point the United Nations Security Council endorsed the terms
laid down by the Alliance. The actions of the President of Yugoslavia, who has
meanwhile been indicted for crimes against humanity, contravened Articles 1(3)
and 55 of the UN Charter. Inasmuch as they constituted interference in the
internal affairs of a sovereign state, the actions of the North Atlantic Alliance contravened Article 2(7) of the Charter.

On several occasions the Secretary-General of the United Nations has expressed
his concern. Addressing leaders of the North Atlantic Alliance at the end of
January he said: 'The bloody wars of the last decade have left us with no illusions
about the difficulty of halting internal conflicts – by reason or by force – particularly against the wishes of the government of a sovereign state. But nor have they
left us with any illusions about the need to use force, when all other means fail.'
He suggested that the success of the NATO-led mission operating under a UN
mandate in Bosnia should be a model for future endeavours. On 24 March he
reminded the international community that, under the Charter, the Security
Council has primary responsibility for maintaining international peace and security and that this was explicitly acknowledged in the North Atlantic Treaty. It followed that the Council should be involved in any decision to use force.

It due time it may emerge that events in Yugoslavia have effectively amended the
UN Charter by bridging the gap between those provisions which, on the one hand
call for respect for human rights and, on the other, preclude intervention in the
internal affairs of a sovereign state. But meanwhile the question will be asked:
Why was endorsement by the UN Security Council not sought before rather than
after the event?

*   *   *

If one were to conclude that, on balance, the prospects for the United Nations in the years ahead are somewhat better than they have been in recent years, one must also recognise that obstacles still have to be overcome. For one thing the notion of preventive action has not yet been generally accepted; indeed some states might argue that this constitutes unwarranted interference in their internal affairs. Then again, the Organisation remains seriously underfunded. But the most serious constraint on the development of the United Nations into the effective guardian of world order is the lack of political will. All those who have personal experience of work with the United Nations are acutely conscious of the inescapable truth. The United Nations can do only those things which its members allow it to do. The failures of the United Nations are the failures of its members. Equally, its members deserve credit for its successes.

A change of attitude in the United States could transform the outlook overnight and the European Union might have a role to play in this respect. After years of sterile debate, the members of the Union have at last taken the step which will enable it to exercise real influence in world affairs. The appointment of Javier Solana as the Union's *High Representative* with responsibility for coordinating foreign and defence policy will in due course raise the question of the way in which the Union is represented in the United Nations, and on the Security Council in particular. Meanwhile, it will fall to Britain and France, as permanent members of the Security Council, to encourage and support the developing role of the United Nations. The example the newly articulate European Union would set were it to adopt a more positive attitude, could encourage the United States to do the same, both in its own interest and as a means of improving its relationship with the depressingly unstable Russia and with China, a super power of tomorrow. Support by all the major powers for an effective and respected United Nations as we enter the new century would be a fitting sequel to the dismantling of the Berlin Wall.

XI

THE NATION STATE AND WAR

BATH ROYAL LITERARY AND SCIENTIFIC INSTITUTION
MAY 2000

In the beginning there was man; there was also woman. They created a family. Then there were other families. These families devised a means of communicating one with another; this became their language. They had the same hopes and fears. They became a tribe. The tribe needed a leader. The leader acquired and exercised power. The leaders of some tribes were wise, others foolish; some were modest, others ambitious; some were generous, others greedy.

In such elemental happenings we can trace the origin of the political systems which our ancestors have created with varying degrees of success over the centuries. In recent times the dominant actor on the international stage has been the nation state. It has claimed an identity and has acquired a legal status. Both its identity and its legitimacy have been recognised by other nation states. The state we acknowledge today is the product of history – and notably European history.

*   *   *

The process by which nation states have been created has varied according to circumstances. In some cases it was long-drawn out, in others surprisingly swift. The earliest example of note was the city of Rome, which became an empire. Poor communications and inadequate means of supplying its outposts were the main reasons for its decline. Yet, until the middle of the 15th century, the pretence was maintained that the Roman Empire continued to exist in Eastern Europe. In Western Europe the Roman Empire was the inspiration for Charlemagne and the Roman Empire of the German Nation, which we in Britain have always called the Holy Roman Empire. The spiritual successor to the Roman Empire in Rome was the medieval Papacy. But both the Holy Roman Empire and the Papacy had passed their peak by the middle of the 19th century. The successor in Europe was the nation state.

As Peter Calvocoressi, the noted writer on international affairs, has pointed out, the state in Europe was originally what we would now regard as a piece of real estate owned by its lord or king. When Louis XIV said: 'L'état, c'est moi', he was uttering a truth. However, when the king could no longer levy contributions from his subjects for the maintenance of the state except in exchange for promises or concessions, his rule had ceased to be absolute. The consequence was that the nature and characteristics of the state became less clear; the nation state was no longer an attribute – or a property – of the lord or king, but simply what the people said it was.

In the eastern world events followed a similar pattern. Any ambition nourished by Dar ul-Islam (the Household of Islam) – the Islamic community which was formed as a result of the teachings of the Prophet Muhammad – to establish undivided dominion was dashed when the schism occurred in the 7th century over the succession to the Prophet, and what came to be known as Shi'a Islam dissociated itself from the Sunni mainstream. Islam, like Christianity, has survived into the contemporary political order, but the Muslim world – from Nigeria to Indonesia – is fragmented into states which assert their individual sovereignty in the same way as the secular states of Europe.

The story of the Spanish nation state begins with the marriage of Isabella of Castile to Ferdinand of Aragon in 1469. When Ferdinand acceded to the throne of Aragon ten years later, he recognised Isabella as Queen of Castile and thereby created a union between two states whose histories, interests and policies had diverged widely. In 1492 the new union mounted an assault on Granada which ended with the reconquest of the territory occupied for centuries by the Moors. This enabled Spain to take her place among the nation states of Europe.

The union of the crowns of England and Scotland in 1603 and of the parliaments in 1707 created a new nation state. While this was widely accepted, the attachment of many Scots to the Stuarts provoked an act of gross irresponsibility by Charles Edward Stuart in 1745 which led to the tragedy of Drumossie Moor.

The French nation, which did not emerge until the Middle Ages, was the product of prolonged co-habitation, during which linguistic differences disappeared. The Revolution in 1789 and the subsequent campaigns of Napoleon Buonaparte consolidated the sense of national identity.

At the beginning of the 19th century Italy was divided into a number of political units, many under the rule of foreign princes. The opposition of these princes prevented earlier unification. Germans also lived under a great number of different rulers but faced the additional problem that there were no clearly defined frontiers. The prerequisite for membership of the German nation was the German language. Germany set the tone for European nationalism in the 19th century and by 1920 most of Central Europe up to the Russian frontier had been divided into states claiming to be national. The exception to the general rule was the Union of Soviet Socialist Republics, where there was no basis for unity and nationhood other than common acceptance of the communist creed.

*   *   *

These processes all had their own characteristics. Yet the leaders of the day were motivated by similar ambitions and responded to certain common sentiments. These have been the subject of detailed study over the centuries.

It is generally accepted that Roman tradition, both temporal and spiritual, lingered on through the Dark Ages and early Middle Ages, not eliminating national consciousness but blunting it. It has also been acknowledged that there exists among human beings a powerful and peculiar sense of solidarity with some of their fellows – called for want of a better term national feeling – for which a common sovereign political organisation is not a prerequisite. However, where such an organisation has existed it has stimulated national sentiment. John Stuart Mill believed that this sentiment arose from 'the identity of political antecedents, the possession of a national history, and consequent community of recollections, collective pride and humiliation, pleasure and regret connected with the same incidents in the past'. Some German scholars took a broader view. They believed that only a long historic process would stimulate 'national consciousness'. It followed, they argued, that true nations were the product only of a modern age and an advanced stage of civilisation. Some conclusions drawn from study of the process were less reassuring. It has been claimed, for example, that, as distinct from patriotism, nationalism contains elements of the vanity and egotism found in the individual and is, therefore, a half-way house on the road to chauvinism and imperialism. This immediately brings to mind *Rule Britannia* composed in 1740, the *Marseillaise* inspired by the French Revolution and *Deutschland über Alles*, one of the early products of German nationalism written in 1841. Other scholars have taken a more charitable view; they maintain that the pride and justification of a state should be that, whatever its basis, it satisfies the national feeling of its citizens.

*   *   *

One conclusion to be drawn from historical experience has not been seriously challenged. This is that the significance of the nation state depends essentially on notions of sovereignty and identity.

Interpretations of sovereignty have varied through the ages. For Aristotle sovereignty rested on the law. As philosophy became increasingly divorced from religion, the idea that the ruler should be seen as under God and the law was questioned. The extreme example was Macchiavelli's *Prince*, who believed that he could exercise absolute power by any means, without regard to traditional and moral judgments. The 17th century English philosopher, Thomas Hobbes, argued in his magnum opus *Leviathan* that, with one qualification, the ruler had unlimited power. The exception was that his subjects had the right to defend themselves against him. In due course the philosophical pendulum swung. In the *Social Contract*, published a hundred years later, Jean-Jacques Rousseau placed sovereignty in the community; what he called 'popular sovereignty' rested on the general will. In the 19th century growing nationalist self-confidence, together with parliamentary reform in the United Kingdom, raised doubts about the legitimacy of monarchies. This found expression in the theory of *constitutionalism*.

Nation states have applied the concept of sovereignty in a variety of ways. While French opinion was still arguing over Rousseau's *Social Contract*, Thomas Jefferson and his colleagues were drafting what was to become the *Declaration of Independence of the United States*. This placed sovereignty unambiguously with the people. Under the Constitution sovereign power was to be exercised by both the federal and the state authorities, any residual power being retained by the people themselves. In theory, and to a great extent in practice, sovereignty in the United States is widely distributed.

In the mid-1940s these considerations among others may have been in the minds of the allied powers occupying that part of Germany not overrun by the Red Army when they invited a group of leading German experts to draft a new constitution. The allies were determined to exclude the possibility of a centralised Fourth Reich with supreme unrestricted power as had been the case under the Nazis. The result – the Basic Law of 1948 – was a masterly response to the challenge. Substantial powers were assigned to the regions – the *Länder* – which, in addition to their own identity, were accorded their own parliaments and it was only on issues of truly national importance, such as defence, foreign and macroeconomic policy, that power was reserved to the Federal Government. When the Berlin Wall came down in 1989 and Germany was once again united, it was with little hesitation that this constitution was applied to the former East Germany.

More recently similar arrangements have been introduced in Spain. In response to strongly expressed regional sentiments, a system of regional autonomy was introduced. And here in the United Kingdom, with the creation of the Scottish Parliament and the Welsh Assembly and the prospect of a return to devolved government in Northern Ireland, we have set out along a similar path. However, our historical experience has been exceptional. Britain is one of the few countries which has, in its time, enjoyed virtually absolute sovereignty. This island nation has not been invaded or defeated in war for almost a millennium and this has engendered in many a sense of separateness. It is too easy for the British – or some of us at least – to feel that they are not like the people of other countries. However, this has not prevented us from accepting limitations on our sovereignty when circumstances required. When national survival is at stake it is natural that the demands of any alliance to which a state has adhered should predominate. And during the Second World War cooperation between the United Kingdom and the United States reached unprecedented levels.

The period immediately after that War was notable for the extent to which nations were prepared to share aspects of their sovereignty in order to face the problems of reconstruction, reconciliation and securing the peace. The Bretton Woods Agreement, the Charter of the United Nations and, later, when the division of the post-war world became a reality, the North Atlantic Treaty, were all based on the conviction that only by collective action could agreed objectives be achieved.

* * *

In the eyes of many the creation of nation states has been a stimulus to conflict. The Wars of the Spanish and Austrian Succession, the Napoleonic Wars, the two calamitous World Wars, as well as the persistent hostilities between India and Pakistan and between the Arab States and Israel would appear to substantiate this view. But in a number of cases it could be argued that it was not the creation of a nation state that provoked conflict, but rather that an ambitious and ruthless ruler saw the nation state as an effective instrument for the pursuit of whatever might be his overriding objective.

This reasoning would suggest that the creation of a nation state by itself is not necessarily a belligerent action. While the history of each nation state in today's world is unique, many similar influences contributed to the process. In the same way alliances between nation states have several common features, whether they be traditional or opportunistic arrangements. However, while experiences shared by allies confronting a common threat undoubtedly strengthen relationships, they do not necessarily diminish the sense of nationhood in each member of the alliance.

Whatever link there may be between the nation state and war, the children of the 20th century are all too familiar with the causes of conflict – lust for power or revenge (whether justified or not); boundary disputes; economic ambition; ethnic and religious animosities; clash of doctrines or political ideologies. In many cases conflict has not resolved the original dispute which has erupted once more into violence a generation later. Some quarrels between nation states seem insoluble because the parties, for particular reasons, cannot agree to differ.

The two World Wars of the 20th century stimulated efforts by the states involved to devise means of preventing a recurrence. For well-known reasons the League of Nations failed to fulfil its purpose. The Charter of the United Nations signed by 51 states in 1946 was a substantial improvement on the Covenant of the League, even though it had to accommodate the supremacy of the sovereignty of the nation state; while Articles 1(3) and 55 placed an obligation on all member states to observe and respect human rights, Article 2(7) prohibited intervention in the internal affairs of member states. The Charter did not proscribe war, but it virtually banned it except in defence of the obligations in the Charter. It authorised the Security Council to determine whether a given situation constituted a threat to international peace. If the Council did so decide, then all member states – and today they number 188 – would be required to act against the delinquent state.

The early years of the United Nations were marked by the readiness of the Soviet Union to use its veto. When war broke out in Korea in 1950 the Security Council bypassed the Soviet veto by transferring part of its authority to the General Assembly. The Assembly responded by adopting the Uniting for Peace Resolution, which provided the legal basis for the UN's action against North Korea.

The following decades were dominated by the Cold War. The resolve of the North Atlantic Alliance under firm American leadership together with mutual nuclear deterrence prevented a catastrophic third world war in the 20th century. But there were other dangers and the best endeavours of the United Nations during the decades of the Cold War did not prevent conflicts from breaking out in different parts of the world. Nor were the efforts to find solutions to the animosities which prompted the resort to force invariably successful. In many cases these disputes were of long standing. The Kashmir problem and the periodic resort to war in the Middle East spring to mind. The wars in Angola, the Congo, Ruanda, the

Sudan, Sierra Leone and Sri Lanka, for example, seem interminable. The Korean peninsula remains divided. The most disastrous of these conflicts was the war in Vietnam. The obsession of Washington with what was perceived as the threat posed by China to the whole of South East Asia led the United States into a war it could not and did not win. Ignoring the advice of the British whose strategy in Malaya had successfully suppressed a rebellion, the United States employed methods which caused their armed forces to suffer needless casualties. This conflict had two important consequences. First, the long-suffering people of Vietnam were reunited and their country took its place among the nation states of the world. Secondly, the willingness of the American people to see their service men and women committed to military operations in which they might suffer casualties was gravely undermined.

Meanwhile, the nature of human conflict was changing. But not everyone perceived this. An exception was Edward Heath. When he addressed the UN General Assembly in New York in October 1970 – four months after becoming Prime Minister – he said: 'We must recognise a new threat to the peace of the nations, indeed to the very fabric of society. We have seen in the last few years the growth of a cult of violence, preached and practised not so much between states as within them. It is a sombre thought, but it may be that in the 1970s, civil war, not war between nations will be the main danger we will face.'

*   *   *

It was hoped that the end of the Cold War in 1989 would usher in a new era of peace and stability. But, almost immediately the resolve of the international community was put to the test. When Iraq invaded Kuwait in 1990 the UN Security Council authorised military action under Chapter VII of the Charter. But it went further when it determined that the situation inside Iraq obliged it to demand access for humanitarian organisations to parts of the country where the rights of minorities were being abused. This was a landmark decision in that it sought to overcome the inconsistency between the prohibition in Article 2(7) and the obligation to respect human rights.

The time had come for new thinking about the role of the United Nations. In January 1992 the Security Council invited the Secretary-General, Boutros Ghali, to prepare an 'analysis and recommendations on ways of strengthening and making more efficient within the framework and provisions of the Charter the capacity of the United Nations for preventive diplomacy, for peace-making and for peace-keeping'.

In June 1992 the Secretary-General delivered his response, to which he gave the title *Agenda for Peace*. Boutros Ghali began by pointing out that, while the concept of peace was easy to grasp, that of international security was more complex, witness the widespread accumulation of arms, the rise of new racial tensions, the technological advances which had altered the nature and expectations of life, as well as the persistence of poverty, disease, famine, oppression and despair. It followed that, if the United Nations were to build peace and security, it had to address matters beyond military threats in order to break the fetters of strife and warfare which had characterised the past. Since the creation of the United Nations in 1945 over one hundred major conflicts had left some 20 million dead. And 279 vetoes had rendered the United Nations powerless to deal with many of these.

Boutros Ghali then put forward detailed proposals for the role the United Nations might play in preventive diplomacy, peacemaking, peace-keeping and peace-building. In performing these functions the United Nations should also address the deeper causes of conflict – economic despair, social injustice, political oppression and denial of human rights on ethnic, religious, social, or linguistic grounds. Against this background he recommended a number of steps for reinforcing the role of the International Court of Justice.

The Secretary-General then described the financial position. Unpaid arrears towards the costs of peace-making operations stood at over $800 million. The financial foundations of the Organisation grew weaker every day, debilitating its political will and practical capacity to undertake new and essential activities. There was one overriding necessity: Member States had to pay their assessed contributions in full and on time; otherwise they were in breach of their obligations under the Charter. The United States is the principal defaulter.

In July 1997, six months after he had succeeded Boutros Ghali as Secretary-General, Kofi Annan submitted to the General Assembly a *Programme of Reform* under the title *Renewing the United Nations*. In this he did not confine himself to radical administrative reforms; he improved the Organisation's ability to deploy peace-keeping and other field operations more rapidly and strengthened its ability for post-conflict peace-building. He also extended the scope of the Organisation's activities in the field of human rights.

These imaginative initiatives called for a serious response relevant to the challenges the United Nations will face in the future. The increase in the number of small scale conflicts, many of them within states, as for example in Yugoslavia,

Central and West Africa and East Timor, has created new problems. The causes of these conflicts are often deep-seated and, to the outsider, irrational. Those who suffer most are innocent civilians; their plight poses a moral challenge. For those in authority in the international community whose thinking is still conditioned by the cold war, the appropriate response is not always obvious and, in the end, peace-keeping efforts in support of humanitarian aid tend to be limited in scope and often late. The more far-sighted have already accepted the rationale behind Boutros Ghali's *Agenda for Peace* and Kofi Annan's *Programme of Reform* and concluded that more effort must be devoted to preventing such conflicts. Apart from the benefits in human terms, timely preventive action, combined with longer term efforts to build peace, will be far less costly than military and humanitarian intervention. The need for such an approach was recognised in Article 1 of the UN Charter, and Article 99 places on the Secretary-General responsibility for bringing to the attention of the Security Council any matter which could threaten peace and security. We should expect to see more instances of this prevention strategy in operation, beginning with early warning, then preventive diplomacy and preventive deployment and, at a later stage, preventive disarmament and peace-building.

*   *   *

On several occasions the Secretary-General of the United Nations expressed his concern over the response of the international community to the conflict in Kosovo. Addressing leaders of the North Atlantic Alliance at the end of January of this year he said: 'The bloody wars of the last decade have left us with no illusions about the difficulty of halting internal conflicts – by reason or by force – particularly against the wishes of the government of a sovereign state. But nor have they left us with any illusions about the need to use force, when all other means fail.' He argued that the success of the NATO-led mission operating under a UN mandate in Bosnia should be a model for future endeavours. Though he did not say so, this was a vast improvement on the intervention in Somalia in 1992, which was a barely mitigated disaster. Two months later Kofi Annan reminded the international community that, under the Charter, the Security Council has primary responsibility for maintaining international peace and security and that this was explicitly acknowledged in the North Atlantic Treaty. It followed that the Council should be involved in any decision to use force.

East Timor was a different story. The breakdown of law and order following the referendum on the future of the territory confronted the international community in general with formidable challenges. Kofi Annan played an important role in the negotiations which led to the agreement between Portugal, the former colonial power, and Indonesia, the occupying power, on the modalities for the ballot on the future of the territory and on the security and supervision arrangements. This led to the despatch of the UN Mission to East Timor (UNAMET) last year. He also stimulated international pressure on Indonesia to accept the deployment of an international force to restore law and order in East Timor after the atrocious violence by the militias – with the complicity of the Indonesian armed forces – against the majority who had voted for independence. This enabled the Security Council to take action under Chapter VII of the Charter. When authorising the deployment of a multinational force in Resolution 1244 of 10 June 1999, the Council also demanded that those responsible for the acts of violence be brought to justice. The Report of the High Commissioner for Human Rights on her visits to the region last September is a grim account of what Mary Robinson describes as 'a deliberate, vicious and systematic campaign of gross violations of human rights'.

In due time it may emerge that the Security Council's response to events in Iraq, in former Yugoslavia and East Timor has gone some way towards modifying the prohibition on intervention in the internal affairs of a sovereign state. If so, this would be a welcome erosion of the power of the nation state.

* * *

The international, political and social certainties of the early years of the 20th century belong to another world. The pace, extent and depth of change have no historical precedent – if one leaves Noah out of account. The forces at work have been various. Many are the product of human ingenuity, others of human wisdom and generosity. But many are the consequences of wickedness. Our tasks on the threshold of this new century and new millennium are, first and foremost, to recognise – and seek to appreciate – the significance of these changes and, secondly, to turn them to the advantage of humanity.

Scientific and technological skills have improved the lives of many of our fellow citizens, and have provided opportunities not previously available to us. But many have been shown to carry dangers which were not foreseen, and were indeed unforeseeable. Environmental pollution, catastrophic floods interrupted by equally catastrophic droughts are notable examples. Population growth has far outstripped previous forecasts and, in many parts of the developing world, has also outstripped the capacity of the land to feed all the new, hungry mouths.

The marriage of the technologies of the computer and communications has already changed many aspects of our daily lives. The information society, and in particular the INTERNET and its broadband rival, are making a reality of the global village – a concept first articulated by the Canadian Professor Marshal McLuhan in 1968. Many of the benefits are already clear and widely appreciated, notably the instantaneous access to information of all kinds as well as the contact with the like-minded which the INTERNET enables citizens all over the world to enjoy. But what is less sure is the extent to which the independent existence of this novel means of communication will suck real power away from governments, the media and the international commercial sector. It has been said that the digital world is new terrain which can be a power for infinite good, or for infinite evil.

An undoubtedly beneficial trend in the second half of the past century has been the proliferation of regional organisations. These resulted from increased aware-ness of common interests and recognition of the advantages of collaboration not only in the regions themselves but also in the wider international community, where a combined voice carries additional weight. The League of Arab States, the Organisation of African Unity, the Association of South-East Asian Nations, the North American Free Trade Area, the Asia Pacific Economic Cooperation, have all established their place in the international order. The most significant of these is of course the European Union which, by the end of this decade might be com-posed of 26 or 27 member states with a total population of some 480 million.

In parallel with the development of regional cooperation, power has been pro-gressively devolved within states. The demand by citizens, especially in Europe, for more say in those matters which affect them directly has somewhat belatedly been recognised by most political leaders who make a virtue of necessity when they proclaim their determination to bring government closer to the people. The fact is that sovereignty is divided not vertically to coincide with national frontiers, but horizontally, major decisions being taken at the top level and the rest at the lowest effective level – down to the parish.

In the light of these various trends it is reasonable to conclude that the principal casualty in the 20th century has been the nation state which, in many respects, is now little more than a legal fiction.

*　　*　　*

Although its nature has changed, armed conflict remains the curse of the human race. As we saw in the latter part of the last century, wars within states are the new norm and international terrorism, often in pursuit of the most obscure causes, is now one of the principal manifestations of the evil in man. Nor can we ignore the suffering and distress inflicted on the innocent through disregard for human rights across the world. The problem of Article 2(7) of the Charter must be addressed. Is public opinion across the globe today content to regard the outrageous effects of wholesale or, as in the case of Burma, particular disregard for human rights as 'essentially within the domestic jurisdiction' of the state authorities responsible? The creation of the post of UN High Commissioner for Human Rights and the appointment to this post of Mary Robinson will have been welcomed by all people of goodwill. This extension of the United Nations' sphere of responsibility follows the setting up of the International War Crimes Tribunals for former Yugoslavia and Ruanda and the signature in Rome in July 1998 of the Final Act of the United Nations Diplomatic Conference on the Establishment of an International Criminal Court.

A number of comparatively minor figures responsible for atrocities during the hostilities in former Yugoslavia have been tried and sentenced by the War Crimes Tribunal in The Hague. However, the deterrent effect of the Tribunal and the new Criminal Court when it has been set up will not be felt until those charged with instigating the atrocities have been brought to trial and sentenced. It is a scandal that Radovan Karadzic and Ratko Mladic are still at large. Unless those communities which have suffered at the hands of these criminals can see that justice has been done, their children will be tempted several years hence to exact their own revenge. If the international community has any pretensions to being civilised, devising means of ensuring that indicted war criminals are brought to justice must be an urgent task for the new century. Thought might be given to imposing selective sanctions, such as cutting off certain critical supplies – fuel, for example – to those states which give sanctuary to such individuals. Another possibility would be to ban travel beyond their own borders by specified categories of citizens of such states until those indicted have been surrendered. A solution to this human and moral problem must be found and recent events in the Balkans and East Timor should provide a spur.

There is one arena in which the nation state has retained its power and that is in the array of international organisations and, in particular, the United Nations – in addition, of course, to the Olympic Games. This is true especially of the permanent members of the Security Council, who still number no more than five. This Council retains sole authority to determine threats to peace and international security and, when the individual members of the Council cast their vote, they do so as representatives of their nation state. However, when hostilities arise within states the Security Council is still handicapped by the conflict between Articles 2(7) and 55.

*   *   *

Through their clear thinking and the reforms they stimulated, both Boutros Ghali and Kofi Annan have made significant contributions to the search for an effective and generally acceptable system of world order. Today there is in place a more secure platform than has existed in the past. The question now is whether our political leaders will have the wisdom, determination and courage to build upon this platform policies, procedures and programmes relevant to the needs of the 21st century.

Formidable obstacles have to be overcome. For one thing the notion of preventive action has not yet been generally accepted; indeed some states might argue that this constitutes unacceptable interference in their internal affairs. Then again, the Organisation remains seriously underfunded. Other member states should follow the example set by the United Kingdom and France last June when they signed separate memoranda placing forces on permanent stand-by for emergency UN peace-keeping operations. The British and French contingents are appropriately trained and equipped. But the most serious constraint on the development of the United Nations into the effective guardian of world order is lack of political will. All those who have personal experience of work with the United Nations are conscious of an inescapable truth: the United Nations can do only those things which its members allow it to do. The failures of the United Nations are the failures of its members. Equally, its members deserve credit for its successes. All concerned should have in mind the verdict H G Wells handed down nearly fifty years ago: 'Human history becomes more and more a race between education and catastrophe'.

A change of attitude at the highest political level, and notably in the United States, could transform the outlook, and the European Union might have a role to play in this respect. After years of sterile debate, the members of the Union have at last taken the step which will enable it to exercise real influence in world affairs. The appointment in 1999 of Javier Solana as the Union's High Representative with responsibility for coordinating foreign and defence policy will in due course raise the question of the way in which the Union is represented in the United Nations, and on the Security Council in particular. Meanwhile, it will fall to Britain and France, as permanent members of the Security Council, to encourage and support the developing role of the United Nations. The example

a newly articulate European Union would set, were it to adopt a more positive attitude, could encourage the United States to do the same, both in its own interest
and as a means of improving its relationship with the depressingly unstable
Russia and with China, a super power of tomorrow. It would be essential of course
that such encouragement be offered by the Union in a way which neither undermines the resolve of the United States to contribute to the maintenance of peace
and security in Europe, nor ignores the contribution Russia could make to the
same cause. That being clearly understood, the effort should be made. The prize
to be won is beyond price. Support by all the major powers for an effective and
respected United Nations as we advance into the new century would be a fitting
response to the evaporation of the influence of the nation state.

And, as for us here in Britain? Yes, as Dean Acheson bluntly reminded us in 1962,
we lost an empire – the greatest the world has known. But in doing so we did not
shed our responsibilities as members of the international community and the
human race. Our actions today and in the future should honour our noble
heritage.

CHAPTER FOUR: **THE HOME FRONT**

In the early 1970s I became involved in domestic controversies for the first time. The government's public relations are continually under scrutiny. The way in which the health service reacts to new challenges is invariably of general concern. And disillusion with politics and politicians has raised questions about our system of government. In recent years I have been called upon to comment on these issues and their wider implications.

I

GOVERNMENT AND PUBLIC: THE PROBLEM OF COMMUNICATION

STEPHEN TALLENTS MEMORIAL LECTURE, LONDON – SEPTEMBER 1971

I had been Chief Press Secretary to the Prime Minister for about a year when I was invited to address the Institute of Public Relations in London on the Government's perception of the role of the press. A decade later I was asked to comment on changes in the relationship between government and the media.

Successful statecraft lies in combining soundly judged policies with the courage and determination to carry them out. A government's prime duty therefore is to devise the right policies and put them into effect. But it also has a secondary duty; that is to explain these policies to the public.

There are various ways in which a government in this country can communicate with the public. It is our practice in Britain that important statements of government policy are made in the first instance in Parliament. But of course these statements are not directed solely towards Members; they are intended to be conveyed through the Parliamentary Press Gallery and *Hansard* (the official Report) to the public.

The government may address the public direct. Policy decisions may be set out in White Papers, which are Parliamentary documents. A government's proposals may be published in Green Papers. Both White and Green Papers can be bought by the public through the Stationery Office. Departments of State may address the public through advertisements in the press or on television. Important developments are often the subject of a ministerial broadcast. And hardly a day passes when some member of the government is not making a public speech. The public may also be informed of governmental decisions through press releases issued through the government information services or through press conferences and press briefings.

The press (in which I include television and the radio) is clearly the principal channel through which the government communicates with the public. But the press also has a duty on behalf of the public to question a government's judgment and to expose its inadequacies.

The criticism voiced by the Opposition in Parliament is to a great extent predictable because, in the nature of things, it is expressly partisan. The press on the other hand is able to perform its critical function from a much wider range of standpoints than the parliamentary opposition. Except therefore when there is a crucial debate or a crucial vote in Parliament, governments are inclined to regard the press as their more effective and persistent critic.

The government, and the public, expect the press to play an additional role. Only the press, with its access to unlimited sources of information, can perform the indispensable task of holding up a mirror to society – a mirror which will reveal facts and reflect public opinions and attitudes.

From the government's point of view therefore the press has a triple identity. First, it is the channel through which the public is informed about Government policies; secondly, it is a critic; and, thirdly, a mirror. The press for its part regards government as a source of information about government policy and an object for observation and criticism.

In carrying out their respective roles the government and the press assume certain obligations. For its part a government must be as frank and forthcoming as circumstances permit. This must be the aim of ministers when they make statements, answer questions, or speak in debates in the House of Commons. This must also be the aim of the government information services, and in particular the press officers in the departments of state whose task it is, through their day to day contact with the press, to complement what is said in Parliament.

They should do this in a number of ways. They must inform the press of the factors surrounding the issues of the day and, when a decision has been announced, of the considerations which led to that particular conclusion being reached. They must inform the press of the general direction of government thinking so that the press will understand the background to decisions yet to come. They must be able to answer coherently and authoritatively the whole range of questions put by the correspondents of the national, provincial and foreign press in Britain.

But above all the government information services, and ministers when they speak in the House, must not mislead. Otherwise government policies will suffer. They will cease to be credible. The government will forfeit the confidence of the press and the public. And if such a state of affairs were to continue over a long period, the fabric of our democratic system would come under threat.

The press for its part has a corresponding obligation to perform its triple function as channel of communication, critic and mirror as fairly, effectively and competently as possible. If it does not, a government will have reasonable grounds for complaint.

No government is ever likely to be wholly satisfied with the way the press carries out its obligations. It is equally unlikely that any government will be totally dissatisfied. What is more important is that, if a particular newspaper, agency or broadcasting organisation is neither fair, nor effective, nor competent, its influence on the government's thinking and policies will diminish correspondingly.

These then are the respective obligations of the government and the press as I see them in the matter of informing public opinion about government policies.

* * *

Mr Harold Evans, the Editor of the *Sunday Times* recently described the relationship between government and press as one of tension. I believe that this definition is apt. To suggest that the tension arises solely from the desire of the press to find out more than the government is prepared to disclose on the one hand, and on the other from a desire on the part of government to conceal, would be an oversimplification. As that doyen of journalists, Lord Ardwick, has pointed out, ministers and public servants are only too anxious to talk about their work.

I would go further than this. In my experience governments may not always be as concerned about the disclosure of certain types of information as is widely supposed. The premature publication of a ministerial decision or an important appointment may cause inconvenience, or embarrassment on the personal level. But these are not matters of great national consequence. Nor, in my experience, do governments resent as deeply as is sometimes claimed the uncovering of some scandal. Indeed governments, who cannot possibly know all that is happening everywhere all the time, regard it as an important part of the responsibilities of the press to shine a bright light into dark corners. The press as watchdog is an integral part of our democratic system.

There are however certain fields where the interests of government and press may come into conflict — where the press may want to know and publish more than the government is prepared for the time being to reveal. The most important of these is that which is generally known as 'national security' or 'the interests of the state.' The precise requirements of national security cannot be scientifically defined and the phrase 'the interests of the state' has been abused so often by totalitarian regimes that even in a democratic society it has an arbitrary air about it. And so it is only reasonable to expect questions to be raised when a government calls 'national security' in aid when refusing to disclose a particular item of information.

At the same time the fact must be faced that we are a committed state, a member of the Western Alliance, and our national security is threatened in a variety of ways. Some people would like us to abandon our allies and become non-aligned. They would argue that we should have no military secrets. But so long as it is British policy to be aligned we will have military secrets.

The points at issue then are these: which so-called secrets really are secret? And how long should those which really are secret remain so? On these two questions the attitude of the press and the government may well differ.

*   *   *

Another difficult area is that in which the right of an individual to privacy may be involved. The government machine is concerned with many aspects of the life of the individual — taxation, health, social services, the issue of licences and so on. In any one of these fields an incident may occur — say, an instance of maladministration — which the press rightly believes is a matter of public concern. The government must accept this. But the government may reasonably ask that the interests of any individual citizens who may be innocently involved should be consulted. The borderline between public and private interest in some such cases is not easy to delimit, but common sense is the wisest counsellor.

A conflict of interest might also arise if, in the course of an investigation, the press were to interfere with proper administration – the efficient working of the government machine. In such a case the distinction between what is and what is not reasonable intervention by the press is generally fairly clear and disagreements are usually easily resolved.

I do not wish to suggest that governments would claim that where national security, the rights of the individual and proper administration are concerned there are permanent divisions between what they are willing to see published and what they would prefer not to be disclosed. This would be absurd. Neither the requirements of national security nor the dictates of proper administration are immutable.

Ideas about the rights of the individual may well have more permanence. One sensible and effective way of deciding where to draw the dividing line is that which is followed as regards national security. This particular problem is the subject of periodical discussions between representatives of the government and the press. None of these are easy issues and to my mind undue tension between government and press could best be avoided and the interests of the community best served if the collective wisdom of both government and press were applied to them.

* * *

How do the government and the press carry out their respective roles?

So far as the government information services are concerned, I have already stated the golden rule: they must never mislead. Observance of this rule is only the beginning. The press offices of the departments of state must be readily available; in the larger departments this means maintaining a 24-hour service. The information and guidance they give to the press must be prompt and authoritative. This means that the staff of the press offices must keep themselves fully informed about the major problems with which their department is dealing; and they must have ready access to the minister in charge and to the senior administrators whose confidence they must enjoy. The press office staff must also be conversant with the needs of the press and its methods of work. And they must be articulate. Selection of the right people to staff press offices is therefore essential.

While there are obviously many common features, the work of the Information Divisions in Whitehall differs widely. These variations reflect the differences in the role of the departments of state in the life of the country and in their relationship with the public. The Departments of Employment and of Health and Social Security, for instance, could not perform their functions unless they had large numbers of staff in direct contact with individual citizens all over the country. Yet neither of these departments will receive anything like the volume of inquiries which pour into the Foreign and Commonwealth Office from the national and provincial press. A large part of the work of the Information Division at the Ministry of Defence is concerned with recruiting for the armed forces. Recruiting for the police forms a much smaller but still important part of the work of the Home Office Information Division. Given these differences, and the fact that the most authoritative source of information on a particular subject must be the department of state dealing with that subject, the scope for centralising the issue of official information is limited.

None the less, if the relevance of a new decision by one department to the work already set in hand by another and to the government's strategy as a whole is to be understood, then close coordination of the public presentation of that decision is called for. Coordination is also an essential part of the management of any crisis in which more than one department is involved. An example of this was the hi-jacking of the three airliners to the Jordan Desert a year ago in which the Home Office, the Foreign and Commonwealth Office, the Ministry of Defence, the Department of Trade and Industry, and the Law Officers were all closely and continuously involved. We do not pretend that the service offered by the information divisions is perfect. But I can say that we are constantly looking for ways to remedy our shortcomings.

*　*　*

As for the criticisms which are made from time to time of our press, I inevitably set these against the background of several years spent in countries where all means of mass communication operate under the direction of the government. This experience has sharpened my appreciation of our national good fortune in having a free press.

The most common criticism of our press is that it tends to trivialise public affairs, to personalise the great issues and, more generally, to sensationalise. I suppose it would not be too difficult to find examples of each tendency. Many of the political storms which the headlines foreshadow turn out to be of teacup rather than epic proportions. No reasonable person can expect these tendencies to be abandoned overnight. But I have no doubt from discussions I have had with proprietors and editors and with the radio and television authorities that they pay heed to the criticisms which are made and do seek to improve their performance.

*   *   *

There are three particular observations I should like to make on the functioning of the press.

First, what above all causes governments concern in press reporting is factual inaccuracy. The reason is not simply that inaccurate reporting may constitute an injustice or cause misunderstanding. There is more to it than that. It is notoriously difficult for any correction to catch up with an error once broadcast and next to impossible for that correction to erase such false conclusions as may have been drawn from the original inaccuracy. That there is a need to find a remedy here was recognised in an important comment made by the Press Council on 5 August last. In upholding a complaint that a newspaper had put out uncorroborated statements and assumptions which it had taken no steps to verify, the Council expressed the view that confidence in the press would increase considerably if newspapers showed their readiness to admit their own errors.

My second comment relates to reporting of the way in which major political issues are handled. Most of these reports are both readable and well founded. A recent example was the penetrating analysis of the situation in Northern Ireland by the Deputy Editor of the *Guardian*. But others tend to portray complex issues in terms of black and white, whereas for those whose responsibility it is to take the decision the choice all too often lies between two shades of grey. Some published anatomies of particular crises might lead us to believe that our political leaders are motivated solely by considerations of power or personal rivalry and are indifferent to the effects of their decisions on individual members of the community. One reason for the propagation in all seriousness of such notions may be that relatively few commentators today have had personal experience of the government machine. During and after the Second World War many journalists worked in government departments and agencies. Some came to hold positions of high responsibility. On returning to Fleet Street or Broadcasting House in the late 40s or early 50s they could draw on the insights they had gained into the work of government. A new generation of commentators has arrived on the scene who have had no such opportunity to acquire personal knowledge of government. It might be worth considering whether some opportunity for this should not be created. If the youthful irreverence of some political reporting were tempered by experience of administration, it might become more authoritative and correspondingly more influential.

My third comment concerns the role of the specialist correspondent. This has developed steadily in recent years and has improved the quality of the reporting of public affairs. Like the BBC and the television companies, most newspapers have correspondents who specialise in international affairs, industrial affairs, science, education, medicine, the arts and so on. Given the complexities of modern life the services of specialist correspondents could well be said to have become essential if the public is to remain in touch with developments in all these fields. This is especially necessary at a time when professional jargon daily becomes less intelligible to the layman.

At the same time the risk must be recognised that over-specialisation could blur the whole picture — the totality of our national and individual effort. Were this to happen the strategy of the government could be obscured. And damaging assumptions might be made that, for example, the teaching of techniques was the same thing as education and that technological prowess was the same thing as civilisation. Professor John MacMurray once wrote: 'The preoccupation of the modern spirit with the development of science has meant that its energies have been withdrawn from the appreciation of the world to knowledge of it.' It would seem to me helpful therefore if over and above their examination of specialist problems, the press could take more frequent opportunities to discuss the problems of the nation in the round.

A notable recent example of such a general survey of our affairs was the series of leading articles published in *The Times* last April and May. In some respects of course the preparation of this kind of commentary is not only an exercise in judgment but also an essay in courage; it requires the writer to make the kind of broad assumptions which are easy to criticise. I for one should hope, however, that commentators would not be deterred by criticism from setting out their views on our national condition from time to time.

* * *

It could be argued that if both government and press strove conscientiously to discharge their respective obligations in presenting public affairs to the nation, and worked together to remove the tensions from their relationship, then there would be no communication problem. Indeed, it could reasonably be claimed that for a variety of reasons communication between government and public should be more free and easy today than ever before. For one thing, systems of communication have improved greatly in the recent past, especially through military necessity and the exploration of space. For another, the standard of education in this as in other advanced societies has been rising steadily. Awareness of public affairs should therefore be wider and deeper than in the past. Again, the Civil Service as a whole is more conscious of the connection between the prompt, clear and full presentation of government policies and their effectiveness. All this may fairly be claimed. But in my view communication between government and public in Britain is today far from free and easy. I believe that public opinion is peculiarly unreceptive to what the government has to say. The reason for this, to my mind, lies in the fact that we have been and still are living in a period of change. To many people, and indeed to a society as a whole, change can provide stimulus and refreshment. But for most people change is unsettling to a greater or lesser degree. And the more radical the change, the greater the disturbance.

Some of these changes are worth examining in some detail.

Those which have occurred in our national circumstances have been radical enough. In 1939 we lived the comfortable life of a *rentier*. The interest on our overseas investments enabled us to pay our way. We were still the greatest imperial power the world had known. In 1945, however, we took on three daunting tasks. First, we began earning our living. Secondly, we set about dismantling our empire. Thirdly, we laid the foundations of a system of social and health services aimed at eliminating the misery of the 20s and 30s of which collectively we had become deeply ashamed.

Any one of these undertakings would have taxed our resources, our skills and our patience. Yet within a generation we have virtually accomplished all three. Our balance of payments on current account is in surplus; a Commonwealth relationship has replaced the empire; and a comprehensive structure of health and social services has been established. By any standards this is a remarkable achievement. But the process of adjustment has been neither easy nor agreeable. It has presented challenges of many kinds. We have seen a sudden reduction in our international circumstances and have striven to establish our status as a leading power of the second rank. To earn our living we have built up new export industries and penetrated new markets. We have adapted our methods of furthering our legitimate interests abroad to the new conditions. Throughout this process we have been obliged to devote a high percentage of our national product to our defence. It has not helped that the threat to our national security is both complex and subtle; a conflict of state interests presents a more palpable challenge than a clash of ideologies. This transition from imperial power to our present status has been a rapid process and it has left many people confused.

Further confusion, if not disillusion, has resulted from the obstinacy of the problems in such areas of the world as the Middle East, Southern Africa and the Indian sub-continent, which have adversely affected our interests and which we, and the international community as a whole, have seemed powerless to settle. Moreover, the immensity of the problems confronting the developing nations is as difficult for most people to envisage as the cost and sophistication of the programmes for the exploration of space. And the relevance of each to our own situation is even harder to understand.

The rapid change in our international status and the intractability of so many current international problems have created in the minds of many people uncertainty as to the role which this country can and should play in the world. The government's foreign policies are therefore neither as readily understood nor as acceptable as in the days when both our international role and the issues themselves were more clear.

Important changes have also taken place in another quite different sphere — in public attitudes to authority. As we all know, there is a division of opinion in this country as to how far the government should assume responsibility for the affairs of the individual. But I had something else in mind. In recent years we have seen power and responsibility concentrated increasingly in the top ranks of organisations, whether these be the government, industrial or commercial organisations, or academic institutions. To some extent this is a by-product of the improvement in systems of communication, to which I have already referred. All lines of communication now tend to lead into the boss's office, not to mention his penthouse, his Rolls or his executive jet.

Within living memory the pro-consul, the defender of some outpost of Empire, was obliged to deal with any immediate crisis as he thought best. He accepted that control of the situation might well have slipped from his grasp by the time his headquarters had reacted to any request he sent for guidance or instructions. Now, however, it has become far too easy for those in the lower echelons to refer problems upwards for a decision. However, one must acknowledge that the same perfection of our systems of communication has made it easy for the boss, if he so wishes, to interfere in the work of his subordinates.

The effect of this concentration of responsibility at the top has been to reduce the number of layers in the hierarchy which are actively involved in the process of deciding. In consequence the gap has widened between the governors and the governed, between those who give the orders and those who are meant to carry them out.

This is a widely recognised problem in all advanced societies and conscious efforts have been made to tackle it both by planned delegation of responsibility and by providing wider opportunities for participation by members of a community in community affairs. Nonetheless, alienation of the majority of those affected by the decisions of a diminishing minority can only impair the regard in which those who wield power are held.

This tendency towards concentration of power and responsibility has coincided with a steady increase in the influence of the younger generation. Their scepticism and iconoclasm have already provoked important new thinking, especially as regards the environment and higher education. It is imprudent to generalise about the views of any particular generation. But I believe it can be said that some sections at least of the present young are disillusioned with politics. Either, as Dr Joseph Luns remarked two months ago, they set up their individual judgment in forceful challenge to a democratically chosen policy, or they decry all authority without advocating any particular alternative. The blanket disapproval which this section of the younger generation has expressed in the vividly irreverent terms to which we have become accustomed has also had its own particular influence on public attitudes towards authority.

Perhaps the most significant changes of the past 25 years have taken place in the social sphere. Thanks to the reforms instituted by successive governments in Britain there is today infinitely more social mobility. Our society may still be stratified. But the dividing lines are blurred and less significant. Few young people can say today that the circumstances of their birth disqualify them from achieving wealth, fame or power.

In addition to this domestic change, our society has been deeply influenced by world developments during the past quarter century. The political emancipation of the peoples of the developing world, which has affected relationships between the races, the establishment over large parts of the world of one-party states, in many cases dedicated to materialism, and the growth of subversive movements which seek by any means, including violence, to overthrow the existing order have all coloured public attitudes.

The combined effect of social changes at home and radical political developments abroad has been to call in question the whole range of established concepts. No aspect of life is immune from critical scrutiny. The result is a ferment of new ideas about religion, morality, marriage, crime and punishment, education and so on. Traditional notions about almost every form of human relationship have been put in the crucible. Social experiments have been carried out which earlier generations would have found it impossible to imagine. Under the same impetus of fundamental change, the limits of artistic expression have been pushed beyond what was generally acceptable only a few years ago.

These social changes and the volatility of opinion which has resulted have created new opportunities, stimulated new appetites and created new fears. And in the process questions have been raised about the values by which, as individuals, we should seek to regulate our lives. There was less doubt on this score when the main challenge to our well-being came from poverty, misery, ignorance and disease. But our society seems not yet to have come to terms with the challenges of comfort, leisure and affluence.

You may think that in making these observations I have strayed rather far from the problem of communication between government and public. But to my mind there is a direct link. Any government has two main tasks. First, to provide for the security of the nation; and secondly, to offer all citizens the opportunity to improve the quality of their life. Without these two aims politics are meaningless. If individual citizens are so uncertain as to the kind of society they wish to live in that they cannot exploit the opportunity a government may provide for them, then the line of communication between government and public has broken down at a critical point.

*   *   *

May I sum up my thesis in these terms? As a nation we have been passing through a period of comprehensive change. The pace has been rapid. No one can yet say when the process will be complete. I have tried to suggest that a steady improvement in the working relationship between the government and the mass media will not by itself ensure effective communication between government and public. Until as a nation we have made up our minds about the three major issues to which I have referred – the role we can and should play in the world; the part we wish government and authority generally to play in our society; and the kind of society we wish to see created in Britain — until we have cleared our minds on these three issues we should not expect communication between government and public to be free and easy.

I also suggest that individual citizens and the press as well as our political leaders have a contribution to make towards deciding these issues. The German philosopher Nietzsche said: 'We are born to do our duty and we can be thankful when we know where our duty lies.' As regards what that duty might be, few would disagree with the proposition put forward by the Director-General of the BBC that each of us, and each of our institutions, ought to be dedicated to the creation of a better life in a better society.

II

CHANGING RELATIONS BETWEEN DOWNING STREET AND FLEET STREET

CENTRE FOR JOURNALISM STUDIES, UNIVERSITY OF WALES, CARDIFF
– FEBRUARY 1992

On 21 June 1970 I received a message from the head of the Foreign and Commonwealth Office instructing me to leave my post as ambassador in Libya and return immediately to London. Edward Heath, the new Prime Minister, whose spokesman I had been during the United Kingdom's first attempt to enter the European Community in the early 1960s, wanted me to head his press office at Number Ten.

To be invited to join the staff of the Prime Minister was not a common honour. Yet my enthusiasm was qualified. My dealings in the past had been mainly with diplomatic correspondents, who are not noted for their passion for party politics or the House of Commons; the parliamentary Lobby would be different. However, having worked occasionally with previous press secretaries at Number Ten, I had a modest acquaintance with some members of the Lobby.

I flew to London the following morning. As I entered Mr Heath's sitting room at Albany that afternoon I was both excited and apprehensive. The Prime Minister began by saying that he was glad that I would be joining his staff. 'You know the job,' he said, 'get the facts out.' We readily agreed that my spell of duty at Number Ten would be treated like a normal posting and that after, say, three years, I would return to the Diplomatic Service. In the discussion that followed, the Prime Minister made it clear that he wanted a radical change in the way Number Ten handled its press relations and, as I discovered the next day, the Lobby correspondents had already been told that changes were on the way.

My problem was where to begin. I had no secretary. The room I occupied had to be cleared each morning so that members of the Lobby could come in for the eleven o'clock briefing, perch on the arms of chairs, lean against the wall, or the door if it was a busy day, and make their notes. It seemed to me that the amenities of the Prime Minister's official residence carried the British cult of amateurism and obsession with tradition to absurd lengths.

These were minor problems and fairly easy to resolve. I moved to a more convenient office and recruited as my assistant a member of the Downing Street staff who had been not especially usefully employed with archives on an upper floor. The more serious challenge was that at the start I had to operate within the system I had inherited.

Like many aspects of life in Britain, tradition, convention, practice and that virtue with which we believe we are uniquely endowed – common sense – have governed relations between Downing Street and the press. There are no formal rules, there is no statutory framework. The chief government spokesman, unlike his or her counterpart in the United States or elsewhere, operates for the most part out of public view. In 1929, George Steward, who served as press secretary to Ramsay MacDonald and his two successors as Prime Minister, decided arbitrarily to brief members of the Parliamentary Lobby every day. In 1932, Steward told members of the Lobby that, in addition to acting for the Prime Minister and the Treasury, he would thereafter act also for the Government as a whole on matters of a general character. The actions of this shadowy figure inaugurated the Lobby briefing system which operates today.

*   *   *

For many years the Foreign Office News Department has held a press conference at 12.30 every day. On this occasion announcements and statements are made 'on the record' and are attributed to a 'Foreign Office spokesman'. Following this press conference informal exchanges take place between members of the department and the journalists present – mostly representatives of the news agencies, evening papers and the broadcasters – it being clearly understood that what is said then is not for attribution to the department. Each afternoon groups of journalists call at the Foreign and Commonwealth office for non-attributable briefing. However, if need arises, the department may issue an on the record statement at any time of day or night – and in these days of non-stop news coverage on television and radio this happens only too frequently – and members of the department will be available subsequently to brief journalists non-attributably by telephone.

This procedure had seemed to me both convenient and sensible. I realised of course that the need not to infringe the rights of Parliament was one reason why Lobby briefings were entirely non-attributable. However, as time passed I found the pretence that these occasions did not take place increasingly absurd, especially when some of the afternoon briefings in the House of Commons were attended by upwards of sixty correspondents.

I was more concerned however that even the most straightforward statement of fact could be presented in the press the following day in a variety of forms, some quite unfair to the government. Apart from the disadvantage to the government, this product of Lobby briefings was a disservice to the public. Surely they were entitled to know what the government's position actually was before being told what to think about it. Accordingly, in 1972 I suggested to the Lobby that, as far as possible our briefing sessions should in future be 'on the record' but that, where appropriate and by mutual agreement, we would move to a non-attributable basis. This proposal was rejected by the Lobby. I therefore decided that any formal statement we would normally have made to the Lobby would in future be issued as a press release which would be carried by news agencies and broadcasters and so find its way on to the desk of every news editor in the country. News editors love quotes. From then on we made extensive and successful use of this procedure.

Mr Heath is a master of detail and an extempore speaker of the most lucid English. Other than in his periodical radio and television interviews, this talent was not displayed to the public. To exploit these skills and to enable him to address the public direct, we decided to arrange Prime Ministerial press conferences. At the first of these, in 1971, Mr Heath reported on progress towards membership of the European Community. At the second, in January 1973 and also at Lancaster House, the Prime Minister announced the measures the government intended to take in Stage II of its pay and prices policy. At the end of each set of negotiations between the government and representatives of the Confederation of British Industries and the Trades Union Congress leading up to this announcement, agreed tripartite statements were issued. Later sessions of the talks were followed by on the record press conferences, normally chaired by the Chancellor of the Exchequer. Transcripts of these press conferences, which we circulated without delay, were often reproduced in full by *The Times, The Guardian* and the *Financial Times.*

In these various ways we tried to convey government messages direct to the public.

In my first year at Number Ten I maintained close touch with Lord Whitelaw, then Lord President of the Council, one of whose tasks was to coordinate government information. Later, responsibility fell to me. I arranged for a senior administrator of Assistant Secretary grade to join the press office at Number Ten to ensure effective coordination with and between Whitehall departments. This was carried out through *ad hoc* groups composed of the information officers directly concerned. Notable examples were Northern Ireland, once direct rule from London had been introduced, and the pay and prices negotiations. Coordination on Northern Ireland involved, in addition to the Number Ten press office, the Northern Ireland Office, the Ministry of Defence and the Foreign and Commonwealth Office; the coordinating group on pay and prices included the heads of information at the Treasury and the Departments of Employment and of Trade and Industry.

Throughout my three years as his press secretary, I had access at all times to the Prime Minister. He ensured that I for my part had access to all the information I needed and attended all important meetings other than meetings of the Cabinet. He understood the shortcomings of the Lobby system. He expected me to find remedies and never failed in his support. I could not have asked for more.

*   *   *

Since I first acted as a spokesman it had seemed to me that the relationship between government and the media belonged to the same family of issues as, say, law and order. It exercises endless and undue fascination and can arouse strong feelings. Like relations with foreigners and the selection of the national football team, it is also a subject on which large sections of the population regard themselves as expert and which, in their exasperation, they are inclined to think other societies manage better.

The reality, of course, is far from glamorous. In our society the media have a number of different roles to play. First and foremost as reporter – as the recorder of current events. Then, as articulator of public attitudes, anxieties and preoccupations; as commentator, critic, advocate, opinion former. Finally, and not least, as watchdog on behalf of the public, as investigator, as shiner of light into the darker recesses of the state machine and of society in general. To perform these functions the press requires, among other things, a full and regular flow of information from the government and as much insight as possible into the factors which lie behind government policies, decisions and actions. Ensuring that this service was provided was how I interpreted the cryptic instruction the Prime Minister had given me at Albany.

The significance of the role the press has played in our political history is well documented and the lessons to be drawn are clear. No government can expect its policies to succeed if these are neither understood nor accepted by a substantial body of public opinion. It follows that a government should devote as much care to presenting its policies as to formulating them in the first place. There is another consideration. In our type of society no amount of powerful and sustained advocacy can persuade opinion to acquiesce indefinitely if the government embarks on a wrong-headed course of action. Lincoln's dictum about not fooling all of the people all of the time is a basic truth about democratic societies. Successful and effective government therefore depends, first, on wise policies and then, to an important extent, on the manner in which these policies are presented not merely to Parliament but, more important, through the media. The role of the press secretary at Number Ten should be judged in this context.

If this is a fair account of the key elements in the relationship between media and government, there appears on the face of it to be some common ground, or at least a measure of interdependence. Such a proposition, I know, is not universally popular.

* * *

Relations between Downing Street and the press, constructed as they are on the modest base of the Lobby system, are open to a range of influences which change their nature from time to time. However, certain enduring characteristics give the relationship its unique substance and form.

In the first place, the relationship is and always will be uneasy. The press want more information than the government can give. On some occasions the government is inhibited from conveying to the press information which, under our system, Parliament is entitled to receive first. Most of the media understand this. But some sections of the Lobby are convinced that it is an objective of government to withhold information. I recall an assertion in one of the leading national dailies some years ago that the relationship between government and press was 'a continuing battle between those who deem it necessary to keep things secret and those who want to prise those secrets out'. That this is a grotesque misrepresentation is evident from the extensive and generally well-informed political coverage in the broadsheets and current affairs programmes on radio and television. In my experience ministers, other politicians and senior government servants are only too ready to talk to journalists about their current concerns and intentions. Nonetheless the suspicion persists that by their very nature governments are less than forthcoming. For its part, Downing Street will seldom if ever feel satisfied with the way in which the press reports. Frustration on both sides creates constant tension.

Secondly, because it is ostensibly founded on the principle of confidentiality, the relationship between the press and Downing Street can arouse the curiosity, suspicion, envy and distrust of many of those who are excluded from it, whether these be non-Lobby journalists, parliamentarians, or others whose profession it is to follow public affairs. These attitudes are reinforced by the fact that the Lobby is self-selecting and takes pains to preserve its privileges and defend its perceived status.

Then there is the wide range of interests represented in the Lobby – the national dailies, the provincial press, the evening papers, the broadcasters, the news agencies. Many of these interests conflict. Moreover, the Lobby will always contain comparative novices. Others have been in the business for many years and are on intimate terms with ministers and parliamentarians. These journalists have their own sources of authoritative information, and their accumulated knowledge and well developed antennae lend authority to their reports.

Another factor, common to most democratic societies, is the variety of points of view reflected in our press. For some correspondents their daily task is to expose the latest outrage or folly perpetrated by the government; for them any modification of policy, even when it is a sensible reaction to an external event, is a U-turn or a climb-down. Other journalists are on the lookout for a wise decision to acclaim, or a mistake to excuse.

Many Lobby journalists, regardless of the political orientation of the organisation they serve, tend to subscribe to the 'conspiracy', rather than the 'cock-up' theory of government. Not surprising; conspiracies are more interesting and have a longer shelf life. Nonetheless it is a weakness in our system that few political correspondents have experience of work in government and appreciate that most political decisions entail a choice between shades of grey.

On a more positive note, three axioms may be added to the list of permanent factors in the relationship between Downing Street and the press. First, the freedom of the press within the law is not an issue; second, those who speak for the government must not mislead; third, non-attributable briefing of the press has a valuable part to play in a sophisticated society such as ours.

* * *

These are the more or less constant factors in the relationship. What about the variables?

Neither government nor press is impervious to shifts in public attitudes, for example towards authority, law and order, civil liberties, taste and decency, social services, market forces and even Parliament and politicians. Over the past ten or fifteen years many attitudes have changed markedly, but the full impact of such changes on relations between government and press may not yet be apparent.

So far as the press is concerned, the principal variable factors are the economic health of the writing press, radio and television; changes in the structure and policies of newspapers and broadcasting organisations; and the development of new techniques, or new idiosyncracies in the treatment of news and current affairs.

Following the trauma in the newspaper industry in the early 1980s competition intensified. Today some of our serious newspapers seem less serious and their international standing has declined. Some political reporting is even more blatantly partisan than before. Pressure groups have increased their influence. The tendency to editorialise political reporting is widespread. Because they carry some security classification, leaked documents, of which there has been a rash in the past few years, are treated as trophies of wars regardless of their intrinsic importance, or more often unimportance. Their publication usually confuses rather than clarifies.

Meanwhile television continues its relentless advance. In addition to the current affairs programmes which offer political leaders a splendid platform, we now have quasi-impromptu televised press conferences in the street outside Number Ten. Much television coverage compares with the best in the world, though sadly from time to time the BBC offers us a concoction of editorialising, uninspired comment and speculation instead of the Nine o' Clock News. In this respect BBC Television could learn from BBC Radio. Following the recent re-distribution of franchises, commercial television faces a period of turmoil which could result in poorer service to the viewer, Since, quite literally, it puts a face value on politicians, television inexorably reinforces the trend towards the personalisation of national issues and exaggerates the confrontational aspect of British politics.

* * *

Changes in Downing Street can immediately affect relations with the press – changes in personality and style; in attitude to the media; in relations between the Prime Minister and other members of the Cabinet; in the mandate given to the press secretary and in the relationship between the Prime Minister and the press secretary; in addition, of course, to any change in policy.

Answering a Parliamentary Question in June 1981, Mrs Thatcher said: 'We are committed to making available as much information as possible and are doing so'. In substance, not unlike Mr Heath's instruction to 'get the facts out'.

Much has been said and written about Mrs Thatcher's eleven years in office and the role of Sir Bernard Ingham. The way in which press relations were conducted from Downing Street during those years, which had no precedent and is unlikely to be repeated, is not hard to explain. A strong leader, inclined towards a presidential style, quite by chance found in her experienced and talented press secretary a devoted supporter and advocate. As time went by the self-confidence and authority of each increased at the expense of tolerance and patience. For a press secretary eleven years in a position of power and influence must take their toll. Understandably, at certain stages things were said and done which ought not to have been said or done. Perhaps there was merit in a three year term.

III

HEALTH EDUCATION AND OCCUPATIONAL MEDICINE

JAMESON PARKINSON LECTURE, BRISTOL – JULY 1989

In the late 1980s and early 90s the Health Education Authority, of which I was then chairman, had to deal with a number of politically sensitive issues. These called for patient exposition. But the Authority was not alone. It received support from other organisations both inside and outside the National Health Service.

The state of the National Health Service and its prospects for the future featured prominently in the last General Election campaign. Today, the Government's proposals for improving the performance of the Service and making it more responsive to the needs of the people have aroused the wrath of important sections of the medical profession. Battle has been joined. However, it cannot be contested that it makes sense, after forty years, to review the way the National Health Service – the NHS – has been operating, especially since, in the past decade or so, many new ideas have been aired about the structure and management systems of large organisations.

One notable feature of the White Paper and of its predecessor, *Promoting Better Health*, issued last year, is the emphasis placed on the prevention of disease. For many years the NHS has recognised the importance of prevention rather than cure, but what has been done in this field has not had the impact we all desired. A commitment to prevention needs not only additional resources but also a political accolade. The incentives and targets for general practitioners in screening, immunisation and child care and the wide range of health promotion activities which are envisaged in the White Paper indicate political endorsement of what is no less than a fundamental and timely change of direction. We must welcome this opportunity for the Service to advance with more audacity into the field of health promotion. Others in the Service can draw inspiration from occupational medicine, which understands the benefits of prevention and how these can best be obtained.

*   *   *

As you know, the Health Education Authority was set up in 1987 as a Special Health Authority within the National Health Service with the purpose of helping the people of England to achieve and maintain good health. The Authority is required to undertake certain specific tasks. These include providing information and advice about health direct to the public so that they can make informed choices; supporting other organisations and staff who provide health education to members of the public; and advising the Secretary of State for Health on matters relating to health education.

Last month, together with other Members of the Authority and our senior staff, I retreated to Torquay for our annual conference. This year the Retreat had special significance. Since the Authority came into existence it has been working on the basis of annual Operational Plans. We are due to submit our Strategic Plan for the next five years to the Secretary of State later this year. At Torquay we assessed our progress to date, reviewed our objectives and, where appropriate, re-ordered our priorities as a basis for our Strategic Plan.

A high proportion of the Authority's budget is devoted to our AIDS programme. In October 1987 the Authority was given national responsibility for the prevention of HIV/AIDS through public education and health promotion. Since AIDS is a global problem, international collaboration is essential to the success of any strategy designed to prevent, or control infection. We therefore maintain a close dialogue with the World Health Organisation's Global Programme in Geneva and have been developing bilateral links, most recently with our French colleagues who visited us last week. Here at home we work in concert with those concerned in Scotland, Wales and Northern Ireland, with Regional and District Health Authorities, local authorities and the numerous voluntary organisations active in this field. It is not our intention to spread alarm about HIV/AIDS; equally we understand the dangers of complacency. Given the sensitivity of the issues raised, this programme calls for special skills and qualities.

We are confident that the other programmes on which we will be concentrating our efforts will, if carried out effectively, make a major contribution to the prevention of disease and the enjoyment of healthy family and individual life in this country. We will underline the need not only to curtail the use of substances which adversely affect health, but also to reduce the incidence of premature death and disability from the major causes of disease. While the messages we address directly to the public will be the more visible part of our activities, we will be strengthening our links with others in the public and voluntary sectors as well as professional bodies such as yourselves. We will operate in particular in those settings which offer the best opportunities for successful health education. Schools and youth services, primary health care, public health services and community organisations are obvious examples of settings where our expertise can profitably be deployed. But it is in the workplace that you in your profession and we in the Health Education Authority have common aspirations and responsibilities.

*   *   *

The benefits of preventing disease and promoting health through education programmes in the workplace are clear. Let me mention three. Health promotion saves lives. Health promotion enhances the quality of life. In the long run, health promotion can reduce the cost of health care. The truth of these three statements cannot plausibly be challenged. But unfortunately in too many cases programmes aimed at prevention are the poor relation in the family of health care services in the workplace.

For sound practical reasons the workplace is a natural and advantageous setting for health education programmes. Any organisation whose staff enjoy better health and increased well-being will reap the benefits of high morale, fewer absences on sick leave and less turnover of staff. But health promotion programmes cannot become an accepted adjunct of occupational health services overnight. The ground has to be prepared. Managers have to be informed about the purposes and methods of health education and how these can best be applied in the workplace. Staff have to be persuaded that health education produces benefits that justify the diversion of effort and resources entailed. The Health Education Authority has learned the hard way that, like any new product seeking a large audience, health education has to establish its market through attractive packaging and a keen pricing policy.

Health promotion programmes are usually directed at physical fitness, smoking, misuse of alcohol and drugs, stress and other so-called lifestyle concerns, as well as specific health risks such as heart disease. The Look After Your Heart (LAYH) programme, which is promoted jointly by the Department of Health and the Health Education Authority, is one example. We owe you, in the Society of Occupational Medicine, a special debt. In 1986, the year before the campaign was launched, your Society circulated a draft outline of the programme to all its members. In so doing you provided us with the support of those whom we regard as key players so far as the campaign in the workplace is concerned. The success this programme has achieved in little over two years of existence owes much to this support and has encouraged the Authority to study possibilities for expanding the scope of the programme and exploiting our access to schools, primary health care and the workplace.

There are some 26 million people in full-time employment in England. For these 26 million reasons the workplace has been regarded as a critical setting for promoting messages and launching initiatives about the prevention of heart disease. Our aim is to secure the support of senior management in industry and commerce, the National Health Service, local authorities, government departments and agencies, and others. We invite organisations to undertake, in the early stage of the programme, three out of ten measures designed to encourage healthy living within their workforce and to implement the remainder in the longer term. For example, a firm might choose to provide smoke-free areas, to increase opportunities for physical exercise, provide a healthy choice of food in their canteen.

Our experience with the LAYH programme has demonstrated the numerous advantages of promoting better health in the workplace. First of all, the number of those who take advantage of such health services as are available in the workplace is much higher that at other locations, partly for reasons of convenience and partly because of the support and encouragement of peer groups. People and resources are concentrated at the workplace and employees seem inclined to presume that a programme sponsored by their company will be of good quality and relevant to their needs. Continuous contact is relatively easy in the workplace, as is mass communication.

We have been encouraged by the extent to which firms and organisations have sustained their interest in the LAYH Programme. Of the original 52 participants all but one – where the personnel and occupational health department of the company closed down – are still actively engaged. During the first two years of the programme the heads of 220 organisations, employing some two and a quarter million people, have pledged their support. We hope to cover ten million people by 1993.

We believe that this programme has established a firm base on which we can construct a longer term strategy. We intend that it should be increasingly recognised as a national programme for better health both by highlighting the problem and by helping individuals to make the changes which will reduce the risks to which they are exposed. The position of this country at the top of the coronary heart disease league is a national disgrace and I know that the Authority and the Department of Health can count on the continued support of your profession in the national effort to remedy this unacceptable situation.

As I mentioned earlier, the LAYH programme is a joint undertaking by the Department of Health and the Health Education Authority. The relationship between the Department and the Authority was recently the subject of reports in the media which misrepresented the situation and inevitably caused concern to those working in the field of health education. Since becoming Chairman of the Authority in the spring of this year I have learned two important facts: first, whatever other resources health education may lack, there is no scarcity of experts; and, secondly, even serious press and radio programmes seem ready to give prominence to the more exotic opinions on the subject. The facts, needless to say, are not exotic. On the contrary, they are rather dull. But for all that they are important.

In that its relationship with the Department of Health is based on the same principles, the Health Education Authority is no different from other health authorities. The Secretary of State for Health determines overall national policies and priorities and he is, of course, answerable to Parliament. But, while he has power to direct health authorities, or to set particular service or managerial targets, authorities themselves enjoy a large measure of autonomy in deciding how priorities can best be met.

There are, however, important respects in which the Health Education Authority's role differs from that of other health authorities. First of all, the Authority operates on a national basis. This covers England and, in some instances, such as the AIDS programme, the whole of the United Kingdom. An even more distinctive characteristic of the Health Education Authority is the specific obligation to advise the Secretary of State on matters relating to health education. It is in this field in particular that the Authority is able to exercise the 'sturdy independence' Mr Norman Fowler told the House of Commons in 1987 he hoped it would demonstrate.

Nothing occurred in the course of the recent Ministerial Review of the Health Education Authority to amend the relationship between the Department and the Authority which was enshrined in the Establishment and Constitution Order under which the Authority was set up in 1987. If any attempt to do so had been made, it would of course have been improper.

I should add this. If the Government had wished the Health Education Authority to lie down and do what it was told regardless of whether this was sensible or not, it appointed a highly unsuitable group of people to do its bidding. I am privileged to chair an Authority whose membership must be among the most eminent and experienced in the National Health Service. Is it really to be expected that such a body would be other than independent in expressing its views to the Secretary of State?

These then are the facts about the relationship. But it is also true that the replacement of the Health Education Council by the Authority in 1987 was not universally popular. There are those who take the global view – that health education programmes will be of no avail unless they encompass all the factors which can affect the health of our people. No doubt this opinion is sincerely held. But the suggestion that the major public health issues of the day are Hillsborough, Zeebrugge and Clapham Junction is surely the product of an imagination of unusual elasticity. No one would disagree that the health of individuals can be subject to a wide range of influences – the environment in which they live and work, their genetic inheritance, their general awareness, and so on. Under our sophisticated system of administration, responsibilities in different economic and social sectors are allocated to a wide range of departments, authorities and agencies and it would be wholly impractical for a single body to exercise responsibility over such a wide range. As it is, the Health Education Authority has quite enough to do.

And now I return to a point I made earlier. My colleagues and I are confident that, if it succeeds in discharging the obligations placed upon it, the Authority will make a significant contribution to a healthier life for our people. We are greatly heartened by the encouragement and practical help your Society has given us; and we hope that all those who sincerely share our ambition will be equally forthcoming with their support.

IV

THE ROLE OF THE PHARMACIST

ROYAL PHARMACEUTICAL SOCIETY 150TH ANNIVERSARY BANQUET CHESTER – SEPTEMBER 1991

This is a special occasion. I have been wondering these past months why you should have honoured me with the invitation to propose the Toast this evening to the British Pharmaceutical Conference and the Royal Pharmaceutical Society of Great Britain. It could be argued, after all, that if, over time, the Health Education Authority were to succeed in achieving its objectives of preventing disease and promoting good health, then the prospects for the pharmaceutical profession would be gravely impaired. Interesting speculation but, like much else, implausible. So I still have some doubt about your motive.

It may be that you had in mind our collaboration in the Pharmacy Health Care Scheme. This scheme involves six different organisations. It has presented your Society and the Health Education Authority with a valuable opportunity to work with a range of agencies operating in the field of pharmacy. These include the Family Planning Association, the Health Education Board for Scotland, the National Pharmaceutical Association, Boots the Chemists and the Department of Health and Social Services in Northern Ireland. We in the HEA are proud to be associated with this innovative and thoroughly practical scheme. Next year the scheme is expected to focus on smoking, HIV/AIDS and skin cancer – a sound selection of topics.

This scheme is of course only a minor element in the panoply of your activities. That concern with education would be a major preoccupation of your Society was evident from its earliest days when the teaching laboratory established under the direction of Professor Theophilus Redwood received its first intake of students. In this field today, your pharmacy degree courses play an essential role. By offering research grants and scholarships you assist some members of the profession to gain higher qualifications. Your diploma in agricultural and veterinary pharmacy offers a post-graduate qualification. The specialist member groups are an effective means of meeting the needs of different areas of practice. The Academic Pharmacy Group provides not only a forum for discussion but also a voice for the academic staff of schools of pharmacy. Recognising an important trend in health care, you have recently taken further steps to stimulate local activity.

These are all examples of the worldly wisdom, the spirit of enterprise and the vitality of your Society. Yet, I suppose, in the eyes of many of your admirers, and indeed for many of you, the library and the museum, both founded in the first year of your existence, and the annual British Pharmaceutical Conference which dates from 1863, are the three jewels in your profession's crown.

The breadth of the Society's current interests and concerns was no doubt beyond the imaginings of those chemists and druggists who met that Spring evening 150 years ago in the Crown and Anchor Tavern on the Strand and resolved to form the Pharmaceutical Society. It is relatively easy for us today to see in perspective Sir William Glyn-Jones and Sir Hugh Linstead – two towering figures in the later development of the Society – as they were men of the twentieth century. But what of Jacob Bell, who provided the initial inspiration, who insisted on the need to draw a distinction between the practice of pharmacy and the practice of medicine, who saw science as the foundation of pharmaceutical knowledge – what of Jacob Bell and his colleagues with their stove-pipe hats, extravagant neckties and assertive side-whiskers?

The world of 1841 is for many of us an historical middle ground between the rise of modern nationalism in the era of Napoleon and the carnage of the Somme and Flanders – between the last years of manual labour and the advent of the machine. To gain some insight into Jacob Bell's world I turned to the edition of *The Times* of 16 April 1841. It would be interesting, in any event, I thought to see how the Crown and Anchor resolution of the previous day had been reported. Nothing on the main home news page. But, a notice under the heading 'Music' lodged Jacob Bell neatly alongside his eminent contemporaries. This read: '*M.Liszt, the eminent pianist, will make his first appearance this season at Mrs A Toulmin's and Mr John Parry's concert on Friday evening, May 7, at the Hanover Square Rooms, commencing at 9 precisely. Tickets, 10s 6d each, stalls 15s, to be had at the principal music shops'.*

Still nothing about Jacob Bell on the next page. But I could not miss another item under the heading *'Amusing caper in Wales': On Saturday last, as the Hartford down mail was descending Rhyallt-hill . . . , the leaders were attacked by a ferocious dog, which sent them away at a runaway pace. On turning a sharp corner the coach was turned over, and shattered to pieces. The inside passengers escaped without much injury, but Mr. Watkins, of Llanfair, who was on the outside, as well as Davies, the driver, received some severe contusions.'* Indeed an amusing caper. One can almost hear Mr Watkins of Llanfair and Davies, the driver, laughing all the way to the infirmary.

Next page and still no reference to the Crown and Anchor. But there was an advertisement for nineteenth century health education in the form of Works by Dr James Johnson. These included *Pilgrimages to the Spas, in pursuit of Health and Recreation* and what was obviously Dr Johnson's pride and joy – a work entitled *Stream of Human Life – The Economy of Health; or Stresses of Human Life, from the Cradle to the Grave; with Reflections, Moral, Physical and Philosophical, on the successive Phases of Human Existence. Third Edition. Greatly enlarged.* Could one ask for more?

Another item seemed more promising. This read: *DR SCOTT's BILIOUS and LIVER PILLS, prepared without any mercurial ingredient from the recipe of Dr Scott of Bromley. These pills will be found an invaluable blessing to all who suffer from bilious and liver complaints, indigestion, wind, . . . giddiness, dizziness of the eyes, and many other symptoms, which none but a sufferer can describe . . . Prepared only by W Lambert, Chymist of 29 Jermyn Street, Haymerket, London, in boxes, . . . Be sure to ask for Dr Scott's Liver and Bilious Pills; if you ask for Scott's Pills, you will get quite a different medicine; if you ask for bilious and liver pills, you will get a spurious compound, which, if taken, will not have these beneficial effects. Take down the particulars – Dr Scott's Bilious and Liver Pills: they are a square green package.* Who said knocking copy was a new phenomenon?

The history of your Society in the intervening years was lucidly summarised in a supplement to *The Pharmaceutical Journal* earlier this year. It is a story of justifiable professional pride, of ambition to raise standards and to spread knowledge. It is a story of a succession of important achievements; at times you were running with the wind, at others seemingly in the doldrums. Such is life. But, above all, it is the story of a profession with a clear and honourable purpose.

The Society marked its centenary in the darkest days of the Second World War. You are more fortunate today. It is a happy coincidence that you should be celebrating your 150th anniversary in a year which has seen what I believe could be the most important development in the history of the National Health Service. This was the publication by the Secretary of State for Health in June last of the Green Paper *The Health of the Nation*. If implemented with vigour and determination, the strategy outlined in this document will profoundly affect the well-being of future generations, if not the shape of our society. Prevention of disease and the promotion of health are now taking their rightful place alongside treatment and care.

Most of us think of the National Health Service as concerned with tending the sick and injured. This is how, almost invariably, the Service is portrayed by the media. Whatever view one takes of the recent reforms, there is no disputing their purpose. This is to improve the management – and so enhance the value and effectiveness – of the magnificent asset we have in those who devote their working lives to the Service. While these reforms are being carried through, it is entirely appropriate that the emphasis should shift from 'better health care' to 'better health and better health care'. What is now proposed in the Secretary of State's Green Paper is a concerted assault on the major causes of early death, disease, or disability and a combined effort to bring about substantial improvements in health and well-being. Responsibility for implementing the national strategy will be widely distributed. Yet, in the end, its success will depend on individual citizens taking a positive decision to improve their health. This will inevitably place a heavy burden on those, especially in primary health care, who are in most frequent contact with the public and will also test the efficacy of health education.

The going will not be easy. Those who work in the fields of prevention of disease and the promotion of good health face serious obstacles. Amongst the most formidable are ignorance, complacency and prejudice. Ignorance can be overcome by education. Complacency is more difficult to dispel. We are all inclined to assume that misfortunes befall other people. Heightened awareness among the sexually active young of the risks of HIV infection has not been translated into major changes in behaviour. Many young people prefer to believe, despite the evidence put before them, that they themselves are not at risk. Where HIV and AIDS are concerned, thinking 'Not Me' could be a tragic delusion.

Prejudice creates intractable problems. For reasons which are deeply embedded in our culture, health education in this country often arouses criticism, if not outright hostility. This may be because health education calls for change – change not only in attitudes and in habits, but in those numerous aspects of our daily life over which we can exercise control and which affect our well-being. Opinion in this country, reflecting our spirit of tolerance, our attachment to individual liberties and our irreverent attitude to authority, is scornful of what is generally portrayed as 'nannying' or 'blaming the victim'. Here we encounter a notably British paradox. We are often reluctant to acknowledge the obverse side of our virtues – to accept that we are at times too slow to face unpleasant facts, too quick to identify extenuating circumstances where none exist and too prone to extol liberty above common sense.

The charge of 'nannying' assumes that health education seeks to deny the right of individuals in a free society to behave as they would like. By supporting health education the Government is held to be interfering with individual liberties. 115,000 deaths in the United Kingdom each year from smoking and 28,000 from alcohol misuse are tragic proof of the falsity of this accusation. Health education does not deny any individual rights. On the contrary, it honours an important right – the right of individuals to be made aware of essential facts so that they can make informed choices about the way they live their lives. In a different context, the remarkable events in central and eastern Europe these past two years have reminded us that knowledge of the truth opens the gates to the fields of liberty.

The accusation that health education amounts to 'blaming the victim' expresses a point of view which is one step away from capitulation and two from despair. Because – so the argument runs – improvements in health are impossible without an all-embracing programme of social and economic change, any attempt to educate those destined to have poor health because of the conditions in which they live and work is considered unacceptable, even harmful. This argument, which Lewis Carroll would have been proud to invent, contradicts the basic concept of equity in health enshrined in the original Beveridge Report – the concept that no citizen should be debarred from achieving their full potential for a healthy life. Indeed, those who experience social and material disadvantage need even greater access to education and, in particular, education about their health.

* * *

Health education has a vital role to play in providing individuals with the knowledge, the skills, motivation and self-assurance to make positive changes in their lifestyles. The combined effort now under discussion could well lead to the emergence of a five-point code for healthy living which individual citizens would consider it in their interest to adopt. This would cover: not smoking; using alcohol sensibly; following a balanced diet; taking regular exercise; and learning to manage stress. A code of this kind, together with the relentless campaign to check the AIDS epidemic, would address the most serious avoidable causes of premature death and morbidity in this country.

The HEA is well placed to formulate a simple message of this kind. Your Society can also make an important contribution. The potential for developing your role in health promotion is evident from the fact that six million people visit chemists or pharmacists every day – a high proportion of the population. Pharmacists are trusted, well respected members of their communities. They are perceived as unbiased and highly professional, available for informal discussion on health matters of general concern and, at the same time, ready and able to offer advice to our fellow citizens.

In saying this I am not telling members of the Royal Pharmaceutical Society anything they do not already appreciate. We in the HEA are eager to work closely with you in fashioning our respective contributions to the national strategy for health. Does there lie here, Mr President, the answer to the question I raised in my opening remarks? Perhaps it was a kindred thought in your mind that prompted you to invite me to propose the toast this evening, which I now do with great pleasure. I wish your Society every success over the next 150 years.

V

HIV AND AIDS

BBC ENGLISH SUMMER SCHOOL, LONDON – JULY 1993

You may be surprised to learn that the Health Education Authority, widely known as the HEA, was established in 1987 in response to a specific challenge – the AIDS epidemic. In November 1986 a Cabinet Committee on AIDS was formed under the chairmanship of the Deputy Prime Minister. In the same month the House of Commons debated this issue for the first time. In opening the debate the Secretary of State for Health Mr (now Sir) Norman Fowler recalled that there were no known cases of AIDS before 1981 and that the first case of transmission by blood transfusion had been reported in the United States in 1983. Mr Fowler stressed the importance, alongside other measures, of a campaign of public education. He quoted the conclusion of a report of the Institute of Medicine of the National Academy of Sciences in Washington. This read: 'For at least the next several years the most effective measure for significantly reducing the spread of HIV infection is education of the public, especially those individuals at higher risk. People must have information on ways to change behaviour and encouragement to protect themselves and others.' He went on to quote a telling comment by the United States Surgeon General: 'Information is the only vaccine we have.'

Mr Fowler then announced the start of an advertising campaign designed to convey two messages: 'Stick to one partner, but, if you do not, use a condom.' And for drug misusers: 'Do not inject drugs; if you cannot stop, do not share equipment.' He echoed the American message: 'What we must all achieve is a change in people's behaviour – everyone taking responsibility for his own actions.' Advertising, he said, would have to go into detail and would have to use language that would be easy to understand. Some, he accepted, could be offended by this; but the greater danger was that the message might not get across. He acknowledged that the infection was still virtually confined to a few relatively small groups. But he warned that, unless action was taken, the infection could spread into the heterosexual population, as had happened elsewhere. So a balance had to be struck; everyone had to be warned of the risks without unnecessary panic being caused.

The Secretary of State then announced the Government's intention to establish a new body to devise and carry forward the education campaign for the good reason that the challenge posed by AIDS was bound to continue. Accordingly, he said, the Health Education Council would be replaced by the Health Education Authority – a special health authority within the National Health Service. In addition to conducting the AIDS campaign, the new Authority would continue the wide-ranging health education programmes already being undertaken by the Council. So far as the AIDS campaign was concerned, the Authority's geographical responsibility would cover not merely England but the whole of the United Kingdom. The HEA inherited the mandate of the Council on 1 April 1987 and in October of that year its responsibilities were extended to include the prevention of HIV infection and AIDS through public education and health promotion.

Meanwhile, the first AIDS campaign in the United Kingdom foreshadowed by Mr Fowler had begun in March 1986. This took the form of advertisements in the press. These were followed by television advertisements in January 1987 and an 'AIDS Television Week' in February, in which all the TV networks cooperated in showing programmes on AIDS – an unprecedented instance of network collaboration. This campaign – under the slogan 'Don't Die of Ignorance' – was followed by a further series of television advertisements and posters aimed at drug users. The theme was: 'Don't Inject AIDS'.

At the end of 1986 a National AIDS Helpline was inaugurated to provide an information service for listeners to BBC Radio One during a week-long campaign called 'Play Safe – AIDS and You'. The primary function of the Helpline today is to provide a free, confidential 24-hour information and counselling service. It receives between 10,000 and 20,000 calls each week.

*   *   *

The aim of the AIDS programme in the newly constituted HEA was to enable people to avoid infection and maintain good health. It is difficult to imagine anything easier to say than to do. This aim was to be achieved in three ways. First, by advising and informing the public through advertisements, posters and leaflets; secondly, by helping others engaged in health promotion, and especially those working for the National Health Service in the field, in local authorities and in voluntary organisations; thirdly, by advising the Secretary of State.

If this approach was to be successful certain conditions had to be met. The most effective preventive practices had to be identified and then developed; those involved throughout the country had to be trained and briefed regularly; and essential research had to be undertaken.

The HEA's first press and television campaign was launched in February 1988 under the title 'AIDS. You Know the Risks. The Decision is Yours.' In June of that year a campaign was directed at holidaymakers, with posters at airports and other travel sites. In December the main effort was intensive work with the press. The advertisements posed the question: 'What is the difference between HIV and AIDS?' To which the answer was, of course, 'Time'. Another striking full page advertisement showed a young woman above the caption: 'If this woman had the virus which leads to AIDS, in a few years time she could look like the person over the page'. The second page showed an identical photograph: the caption read: 'Worrying, Isn't It?'

The evaluation of these campaigns was positive. At the end of 1987 only about half of the population had noticed information about AIDS during the previous month. However, when the TV advertisements appeared, this rose to 70%. The use of condoms by the 18-24 age group rose from 23% in December 1987 to 30% a year later.

Inevitably our advertising campaign led us into controversy, but not of the kind we had expected. We had become increasingly concerned about the risk to young heterosexual people and, in April 1989, we decided that addressing this risk should be a major element in a mass media campaign towards the end of the year. We knew it would not be easy to devise a message advocating safer sex. We believed then, as we do now, that a caring relationship is the proper context for a sexual relationship. But we had to accept that many young people have a different attitude. The responsible minister in the Department of Health at the time defined the problem this way: '. . . we have to give practical advice based on behaviour patterns we know about, not necessarily behaviour we approve of.' The particular problem we faced in preparing the television campaign was to compose a message which would, on the one hand, alert young people to the risk without alarming them and, on the other, place this message in a context which would not appear to condone, or be readily misrepresented as condoning, promiscuity.

In July and October 1989, following our normal practice, we conducted research into the effectiveness and acceptability of our proposed television advertisements. The findings, while generally satisfactory, did not give us the clear guidance we wanted. It was evident that, while many young people were indeed concerned about the risk, there was doubt about the effectiveness of the message in the form proposed. We concluded that we had to do further work on this material.

That, however, was not our only problem. First, the press reported – correctly as it turned out – that the Prime Minister, Mrs Thatcher, had intervened to stop plans for a £1million national survey of sexual behaviour for which the HEA had undertaken a pilot study. This news was followed a week later by a report that the Cabinet Committee on AIDS had been disbanded. Then a campaign against the AIDS programme was mounted by influential sections of the press. On 7 November, an article was published in the *Daily Mail* under the headline 'Phoney Face of the War on AIDS'. The author, Sir Reginald Murley, a former President of the Royal College of Surgeons and a sponsor of an organisation called the Family and Youth Concern Group, argued that it was wrong to address the general population. He disclosed that he had advised Mrs Thatcher that only drug users and gay men were at risk. On 16 November, Lord Kilbracken claimed in the House of Lords that 'the chance of catching AIDS from normal sexual contact is statistically invisible'. Not surprisingly, this statement gained massive coverage in the media.

These events combined with a lack of dramatic statistics about the spread of HIV infection and the incidence of AIDS to create an atmosphere of scepticism in which our proposed message would run the risk of being discounted. Ministers in the Department accepted our advice that the launch of the TV campaign should be deferred; if our messages to the target audience were to be both effective and acceptable, the level of public awareness of the risk to heterosexuals had to be raised.

We acted without delay. On 24 November the Department of Health and the HEA jointly hosted a symposium attended by over 200 delegates in The Queen Elizabeth II Conference Hall in Westminster. This was addressed by six eminent figures in the field of public health. In her opening remarks, Mrs Virginia Bottomley, then Minister for Health, set out the four main strands in the government's strategy – to stem the spread of HIV infection; to increase understanding of the nature of HIV; to help those affected by the virus; and to foster informed, sensible and caring attitudes within society in order to create conditions in which action could be effective. Mrs Bottomley noted that the symposium was taking place at a time of renewed public debate about the spread of HIV in the United Kingdom and, in particular, about the extent to which heterosexuals were at risk. 'No one,' she said, 'can afford the luxury of complacency. Even where, statistically, the risks of infection are small, the consequences for individuals and ultimately for society are disastrous . . .The essence of prevention is to act before a new and serious condition reaches epidemic proportions.'

The symposium and its stark message stimulated a lively debate, as we hoped it would. This debate did much to put the true situation before the public and, in turn, inspired a large number of mass media programmes on 1 December 1989 – World AIDS Day. The scene was therefore set for the HEA's television campaign in February 1990. In this campaign a number of experts, including some who had taken part in the symposium, set out the facts in straightforward and sometimes moving terms. We hoped that, for the moment at least, the tide of scepticism about the threat to heterosexuals had been stemmed.

The response to this campaign exceeded our expectations. The television advertisements regularly achieved 'prompted awareness' levels among sexually active young people of between 70% and 90%. We realised however that raising awareness of the threat of HIV infection was easier than achieving changes in personal behaviour. If people are to change their behaviour they must have a reason and a motive.

We saw no problem over the reason. The main way in which the virus is transmitted, world wide, is through heterosexual intercourse. Condoms and safer sex practices generally offer protection against HIV.

The critical task we faced was motivating people. Our response to this challenge was the personal testimony campaign which was shown on television from December 1990 to March 1991. Three women and three men told in their own words how they came to be infected. Their clear message was: 'This disease can happen to anyone.' The TV campaign was accompanied by advertisements in cinemas which used humour to convey messages about the use of condoms. The two parts of the campaign were well received. More than 80% of those interviewed recalled at least one of the 'testimony' advertisements and most of these thought the individuals featured were 'real and believable'. Two thirds said that the testimonies made them think about their own sexual relationships. Our research continued to show satisfactory levels of awareness both of the risks to heterosexuals and the means of reducing these. But the changes in sexual behaviour remained stubbornly modest. Accordingly, at the end of 1991, the Authority reviewed its strategic approach to the AIDS challenge and in March 1992 we discussed our provisional conclusions with a number of leading authorities in this field. This enabled us, in May 1992, to submit to the Secretary of State proposals for a revised strategy for the promotion of sexual health.

The problem we addressed was how to combat the combination of ignorance, lack of personal skills and confidence as quickly and as effectively as possible so as to enable sexually active young people to protect themselves and their partners. We were impressed by the fact that available evidence pointed to the high ethical values of the majority of young people, the loving nature of most early sexual relationships and the concern for the welfare of their partner by the sexually active young. This led us to conclude that that our strategy should not only recognise the known behaviour of young people and meet their needs but also take account of the moral values the young embrace. Our overall aim had to be to enable our young people to enjoy healthy safer sex and, through health education, to help to prevent the spread of HIV infection and other sexually related problems, including unwanted pregnancies. This approach has been discussed with Ministers and a revised strategy for meeting the AIDS challenge is emerging.

Meanwhile the HEA is laying its plans. The current campaign uses press advertisements and builds on editorial and other work carried out by the Authority's staff. During the preparation of this campaign the Department of Health released a major report on 'The incidence and prevalence of AIDS and other severe HIV diseases in England and Wales for 1992-97: projections using data to the end of June 1992'. This document was prepared by the Public Health Laboratory Service, but is widely known as the 'Day Report', after its author. The document indicated that the number of AIDS cases among homosexual men will soon plateau and that HIV infection is declining among drug users. At the same time, a steady increase is predicted in new cases of AIDS among heterosexuals and this will continue at least for the medium term. This authoritative report emphatically vindicated the policies followed in this country since the AIDS challenge was first recognised. Equally emphatically it confounds those who, for whatever reason, have persistently sought to deny the existence of any threat to heterosexual people. The United Kingdom now has one of the lowest estimated HIV prevalence rates in Western Europe and it is vital that we maintain this position. In France the rate is six times as high, in Spain four times, and in Italy three times as high as in this country.

*   *   *

What thoughts are provoked by our experience in confronting the AIDS epidemic?

First, sexual health, and AIDS in particular, arouse strong emotions – some far from noble – and these can influence people's readiness to accept the facts, especially those that are inconvenient.

Secondly, despite recent painstaking research, not enough reliable information about patterns of sexual behaviour is yet available.

Thirdly, while some sections of opinion deplore the intervention of government and the HEA in this area and the methods used, which they claim encourage promiscuous behaviour, others argue that guidance should be even more explicit. Whatever policies are adopted will be criticised.

Fourthly, we suffer from the absence in the past of thoughtful and responsible sex education in our schools. This has allowed ignorance and prejudice to flourish and deprived many of our young people of the skills and confidence they need to handle relationships.

And finally, despite these difficulties policies have been devised and actions taken which have both raised awareness and influenced behaviour to the extent that the impact of the epidemic has been manageable. While there remain no grounds for complacency, a modest victory against heavy odds can be proclaimed.

VI

THE HEALTH OF THE NATION

TRADES UNION CONGRESS / HEALTH EDUCATION AUTHORITY CONFERENCE LONDON – SEPTEMBER 1993

In the late 1970s one of the prominent members of the European Commission in Brussels was a talented Belgian diplomatist, Viscount Davignon. One day, when the Council of Ministers was making heavy weather of a Commission proposal of which he was the sponsor, he raised his eyes to the ceiling and said: 'May the good Lord save us from the complicators'. Divine intervention followed within the hour. But his appeal was a bit rich; the Belgian delegation was notorious in Community circles for its tendency to obfuscate to good effect when it suited them.

In the Health Education Authority we find that the effectiveness of our work is in direct proportion to the extent that we succeed in clarifying issues.

First and foremost, what is the challenge we face? A visit to any high street on a Saturday morning will provide part of the answer. The inhabitants of these islands come in many sizes and shapes. A few have a spring in their step; they look trim and alert, sometimes radiant. Others waddle. A fair proportion smoke, including many young women and even parents with children in push chairs.

Although health in this country today is better than ever, our people have a poor record compared with our neighbours in continental Europe. Our death rate from coronary heart disease, which incidentally loses us nearly 50 million working days each year, is one of the highest in the industrialised world. Forty-eight per cent of men and forty per cent of woman are overweight. A substantial proportion of deaths caused by fire, drowning, homicide, suicide and traffic accidents are attributable to smoking or alcohol misuse, or both.

The work in which the HEA is engaged, which is an essential element in health promotion, is one response to this challenge. Health education is not so much a science as an art and a practice. It is more than occasional AIDS or anti-smoking advertisements, or press photographs of celebrities sitting self-consciously on exercise bicycles, or cheerful kiddies holding balloons aloft at health fairs.

Education about health enables the public to acquire the knowledge and skills, motivation and confidence to lead healthier lives, provided they have decided that it is in their interest to do so. To have access to information about ways of avoiding disease and of enjoying good health on which individuals can base their choice is, in my view, just as much a right as any of those enshrined in the Citizen's Charter.

Our efforts in the HEA are inspired by profound respect for that right. For some years now we have been conveying information and advice on coronary heart disease, cancers, smoking, alcohol misuse, HIV/AIDS and sexual health, nutrition and family and child care through a variety of channels – through schools and colleges, primary health care and the workplace. Our collaboration with countless others in the field has, of course, been supported by our numerous publications and by advertising in the mass media through which we address the public direct. While sexual health and the prevention of accidents call for particular treatment, we have found that, for the rest, our message can be distilled into certain essentials: do not smoke, drink sensibly and enjoyably, follow a balanced diet, take plenty of exercise and learn to manage stress: a simple five-point code that we have so far kept out of the reach of the complicators.

*   *   *

Concern for public health in this country has stimulated a number of historic initiatives. In the early 1800s Jeremy Bentham articulated the philosophy of the 'preventive way' and made 'preventive medicine' a speciality. In 1840 Thomas Southwood Smith founded the Health of Towns Association. Edwin Chadwick's Report on the Sanitary Conditions of the Labouring Population led in 1848 to the creation of the General Board of Health. Administrative responsibility for public health became linked with the Poor Law function of local authorities in the mid-nineteenth century. In 1919 the Local Government Board became the Ministry of Health, whose main task since the Second World War has been administering the National Health Service which came into existence in 1948.

The White Paper, 'The Health of the Nation', published in July 1992, is intended to mobilise all relevant resources to confront the pubic health challenge on a national basis. The strategy set out in 'The Health of the Nation', if it is implemented effectively, could prove to be another milestone in the social history of this country, and not least because it aspires – not before time – to redress the balance between treatment and care on the one hand and the prevention of disease and the promotion of health on the other.

Easier said than done. Imagine the cultural change this entails – no more 'Casualty', no more 'Dr Finlay's Casebook'. But change is essential – and for two good reasons. First, in a society such as ours it cannot be right that any of our fellow citizens, for reasons beyond their control, should lead other than the healthiest lives possible. Secondly, as everyone recognises, like other nations, we are finding it hard to afford the cost of the National Health Service. The facts that the population is ageing and that novel treatments for hitherto incurable conditions are constantly being discovered only add to the problem. In the end, the immense financial burden will be lightened and waiting times for hospital beds shortened only when the incidence of avoidable ill-health is reduced. This is the irrefutable fact which needs to be protected from the complicators.

If the targets for improvements in health set out in the White Paper are to be met, action at various levels and in different spheres of activity will be needed. Healthy alliances are well established in many centres throughout the country. There already exists a great reservoir of knowledge and experience of health promotion in the workplace. Well over 900 organisations of various kinds, covering four million employees, have joined the Look After Your Heart programme. For the past five years the HEA's special unit at Oxford has been providing advice on health promotion as well as practical assistance to those who work in primary health care. So we do not start from scratch. There is no need for the wheel to be re-invented, nor for the existing literature to be needlessly extended.

Progress can best be made if the challenge is approached systematically. In industry and the corporate sector generally, as in the military, strategic objectives are attained through a series of operational plans which set out in clear terms the tasks to be accomplished, by whom, in what time scale and by what means progress will be monitored and coordinated.

Where health promotion in the workplace has been approached in this way, the results have been encouraging. This is good news because people spend up to 60% of their waking hours in their places of work. But places of work also provide an environment in which information and guidance about healthy lifestyles can be readily disseminated. In the first few months of 1992 a survey of places of work was conducted on behalf of the HEA. The subsequent Report – *Health Promotion in the Workplace* – published earlier this year makes interesting reading. Naturally enough, the survey confirmed that no two workplaces present the same problems and offer the same opportunities. Different firms have different interests and concerns, and derive different benefits from their workplace policies. But the general conclusion can be drawn that, where the workplace is organised in such a way as takes full account of the interests of the employees, not only is health measurably improved but also productivity, morale, loyalty and the public image of the organisation.

In this enterprise the role of the unions in achieving the results we all desire is critical. The HEA shares your concerns and admires your enthusiastic approach to the challenges. I wish you success today and hope that in this conference you will reach clear conclusions and keep the complicators at bay.

VII

THE STATE OF THE NATION: A PERSONAL VIEW

WESTMINSTER COLLEGE, OXFORD – SEPTEMBER 1996

From time to time I have been asked to share with others the conclusions I have drawn from working abroad and in different forms of public service.

When the Second World War ended over fifty years ago a kind of contentment settled on the people of this country. Though wounded, exhausted and impoverished by an experience without precedent, we embarked on a social revolution. We set about rebuilding our economy and dismantling the greatest empire the world had known. We consciously embraced a programme of radical change both at home and abroad. We thought we knew where we were going – even if we were not sure who was going with us.

Today we are an inward-looking society. The catalogue of public concerns is forbidding – crime and fear of crime; drug abuse; unemployment and fear of unemployment; disparities in wealth; homelessness; the divorce rate; threats to our environment; disillusion with politics and politicians.

If our national self-confidence has faltered there are sound reasons. It has not been easy to adjust to the changes which have affected us directly. While opening our eyes to the realities of the world, television has provided those on the other side of the screen with an instrument with which we can be subjected to powerful influences in our own homes. The transistor and the micro-chip have enabled each section of society and each generation to remain constantly in tune with the culture of its choice – and to exclude others. The contraceptive pill has offered women a wider role. Innovations in medical treatment and care, and changes in lifestyle, have altered the demographic structure. The advent of the intelligent machine has changed the nature of work. Through advances in telecommunications and the means of processing information, we are more than ever part of a global community and cannot live in isolation from events and opinions elsewhere. Yet many factors which influence our lives remain within our control and, as enfranchised citizens, we cannot escape responsibility for the consequences of the choices we make in the political field.

In the 1970s organised labour enjoyed too much power. When this was abused, the economy suffered and the nation decided, after the winter of discontent, that enough was enough. Different theories, adapted from the teachings of eighteenth century thinkers, began to affect our lives. Responsibility, it was argued, rested with the individual, not the state. Market forces would determine the conditions of trade. Competition would increase efficiency. Greater efficiency would generate greater rewards. The greater wealth created would trickle down to all levels of society.

After an initial period of economic turmoil, this prescription seemed to be curing the patient. Then doubts arose. Allowed free rein, market forces and competition – in themselves admirable concepts – looked like the survival of the fittest, otherwise known as the law of the jungle. In the same way, the profit motive, undoubtedly a powerful incentive, began to look like greed. This was not what was intended. Had some ingredient been omitted from the prescription? Experience suggested that the insistence of the classical economists on social justice as a prerequisite for the proper functioning of the market had been overlooked. The missing ingredient was adequate provision for the effects of the economic prescription. It was not clear what would be done with those who proved not to be the fittest; nor what would happen to those unable even to enter the competition – the deprived, the less well endowed, those less able to fend for themselves. What Abraham Lincoln meant at Gettysburg was that all men had equal rights, not that they were equally capable of exercising those rights and enjoying their fruits.

Given our differing aspirations in the different parts of these islands, we cannot re-create the national solidarity of the 1940s. But we can surely strive for greater social justice. Who imagined fifty years ago that home for any of our fellow citizens would be a cardboard box, or a blanket in a shop doorway? Who imagined that elderly invalids would be obliged to sell their homes to pay for their care? Who imagined that, meanwhile, other sections of society would be earning what are wittily called telephone number salaries and bonuses. How does all this make us feel?

We have no choice but to draw on our reserves of patience. Even if we start now, it will be many years before our way of life can be reformed and our place in the world re-defined. Today we can at least identify some of the tasks which will have to be undertaken if our self-confidence is to be restored.

*　*　*

For years our ills have been attributed to failings in education. It cannot be beyond our collective wit to put in place a system which ensures that none of our young people complete their formal education without acquiring the literacy and numeracy they will need in the new millennium, and a clear idea of our place in the world. Easing the bureaucratic burden could allow more time for schools, families, religious leaders, voluntary organisations and local communities to combine in setting those standards of personal conduct which will, in the end, reduce the level of crime and misbehaviour which blights our cities and towns, and causes such misery to those affected.

Education is not the sole cause of dissatisfaction. Anxiety about threats to our environment and our heritage has still to be translated into comprehensive and effective policies, even though, in continental Europe and elsewhere in the world, the results of bold action have won public approval. More investment in energy efficiency and renewable sources of power; a coherent transport policy which makes the optimum use of our extensive rail network, our rivers and canals and the sea which surrounds us; encouraging the designation of traffic-free areas; and obliging us all to distinguish between ownership and use of a motor car – all these are obvious ways in which the detriment to the health of the nation, the quality of our lives and the fabric of our towns and cities can be checked. We await decisive action.

Developments in other fields also cause concern. It is not clear how, as a society, we will absorb the intensified bombardment by the media, how we will adapt to the INTERNET, nor resist the temptation of instant gratification provided by multi-channel television. Each of these questions deserves to be the subject of national debate, but that will be possible only when opposition from the influential vested interests has been overcome. However, one issue affecting our society transcends all others in importance since it holds the key to progress. This is the system of governance in this country which, more by accident than design, has perpetuated a political, social and economic hierarchy which discourages consideration at political level of the longer term. It is naive to think that our relative economic decline can be stemmed once and for all so long as we continue to be governed as we are today. Constitutional reform should not only remove the public's sense of alienation from parliament and government, but also restore respect to the notion of service to the public.

*   *   *

The most serious issue facing this nation is our role in Europe. The relationship with our neighbours across the Channel and the North Sea has perplexed us for some time. From the moment in the sixteenth century when Mary Tudor ceded Calais to the French, it has been a cardinal principle of English – and later British – foreign policy to prevent the domination of continental Europe by any single foreign power. In hostile hands, such a concentration of authority on the land mass beyond our shores could threaten our vital interests.

For centuries this policy was pursued with skill and vigour. We became the supreme architects of strategic alliances and we begat a succession of brilliant military commanders. The Spaniards were humbled by Francis Drake, the grand designs of Louis XIV were thwarted by Marlborough, Napoleon's dreams were destroyed by Wellington. Twice this century the ambitions of Germany were frustrated by coalitions in which the United States and the British Empire played dominant roles. Later the threat came from the east. The resolve of the North Atlantic Alliance and the steady penetration of truth into the Soviet heartland combined to end the cold war.

What seems to be a long-running success story requires closer scrutiny. The record of those who governed this country at times of impending crisis is instructive. In the early years of this century, it was obvious to all that the irascible and impetuous German Kaiser had inherited the ambitions of Bismarck. He built up the German navy and, through a mixture of blandishments and threats, sought to prevent his rivals in Russia, Austria, France and Britain from forming coalitions to keep him in check. Successive British governments, still mesmerised by our imperial role, awoke too late to the danger and the world slid into 'the war to end all wars'.

The lesson was not learned. The advent to power of Adolf Hitler in 1933 divided opinion in Britain. This split persisted even when Hitler dissolved the German parliament, suppressed all political parties except the Nazis and began to persecute Jews and intellectuals; even when he withdrew from the disarmament conference and the League of Nations; when he began to re-arm Germany in 1935; when he re-occupied the Rhineland in 1936; when he invaded Austria in 1938. In the mid-1930s Winston Churchill's persistent warnings about the threat posed by German re-armament earned him the accolade of 'warmonger'. Scarcely credible, but true.

There is material here for an A-level essay, or even a doctoral thesis. The question might be put in this way:

In the field of foreign policy, what element in the British character or British society induces influential sections of opinion from time to time to ignore evidence apparent to the vast majority and to vilify their opponents? Is it excess of tolerance bordering on indifference? Is it an inevitable consequence of our short-term political cycle which discourages the long-term view? Or is it merely self-deception, arrogance, myopia, xenophobia, stupidity; or a combination of some or all of the above? Discuss.

Until we in this country have established our place in the European Union beyond doubt, we cannot clearly define our role in the wider world. There is no need for some post-imperial syndrome to deter us from drawing on the experience and skills which equip us to play a leading role in peace-making and peace-keeping. However, as far as the deprived peoples of the developing world are concerned, we seem in recent years to have echoed Cain when he asked: 'Am I my brother's keeper?' and to have forgotten that his question was answered centuries later by the Samaritan on the road to Jericho.

* * *

My generation did not intend that our legacy to the young who stand on the threshold of a new millennium should consist of so many problems unresolved and so many daunting challenges. One must hope that they will draw inspiration from the principles, beliefs and values on which our civilisation and culture are based. We will observe their efforts with close interest.

What new concepts for living and governance will they devise?
How will a more just, self-confident, generous and secure society be created?
Will a better balance be struck between individual rights and individual responsibilities?
How will our environment and heritage best be protected?
What role will this country play in Europe and in the world?
How will the wealth of nations be harnessed and distributed for the general good?
What law of nations will preserve the peace?

Since in the end the human spirit always prevails, I do not doubt that new generations, drawing on the unique genius of this nation, will find answers to these and other questions.

VIII

GOVERNANCE & DECISION-MAKING:
WHERE DOES POWER LIE?

COUNCIL HOUSE, COLLEGE GREEN, BRISTOL – APRIL 1998

The result of the General Election a year ago was unusual in a number of respects. First, the successful party's majority was the largest for two generations. Secondly, it brought into power a political leadership of whom only very few had experience of government at national level. Thirdly, this leadership was supported by a phalanx of political advisers who had devised methods of work which had proved effective for a party in opposition, but which were not necessarily suitable for a party in office.

The early decision to restore responsibility for exchange rate policy to the Bank of England and publication of the proposals for a Scottish Parliament and a Welsh Assembly created an immediate impression of a decisive government. In other respects the new government has performed reasonably well. However, as time passed the handling of its public relations suggested deficient coordination and, incidentally, disregard of the convention which symbolises the sovereignty of Parliament. Earlier this month Betty Boothroyd, the Speaker of the House of Commons, was moved to break with tradition. In a television interview she disclosed that she had complained to certain ministers that individuals in their departments, whom she called 'apparatchiks', had been leaking policy announcements to the press before these were made in the House. She appreciated that when in opposition it was the aim of these individuals to seek maximum publicity; but they had to behave differently in government. Indeed, had these political advisers consulted the civil servants in their departments, they would have been warned that to breach the tradition that policy statements should be made first in the House of Commons would invite criticism and gain no obvious advantage. The respective responsibilities of ministers, their political advisers and their civil servants are no doubt better understood now than they were a year ago.

*   *   *

My experience over many years in the public, private and voluntary sectors in this country and in international organisations has led me to a spectacularly banal conclusion. This is that the respective roles of ministers and civil servants and the relationship between them are much the same as one finds in other organisations with a hierarchical structure.

First, some facts. The duties and responsibilities of ministers contain no mysteries. They formulate policy collectively and individually. Once determined, policies may be vouchsafed to the public in a number of ways. The most obvious are the successful political party's manifesto issued before a general election, statements at the governing party's annual conference at the end of the summer recess, and the Queen's Speech, in which the government sets out the legislative programme for the forthcoming session of Parliament. At any other time policy decisions may be announced, as I have said, through statements in Parliament, to which ministers are accountable, or in answer to parliamentary questions. When parliament is in recess, policy statements are issued through the media.

Cabinet ministers give general direction to the work of the department they head. They speak for their department in parliament and before the press; and they speak for the United Kingdom at international conferences convened to discuss issues arising in their area of responsibility. This means, among other things, that they occupy the United Kingdon seat at relevant meetings of the Council of Ministers of the European Union. They receive representations on particular policy issues from interested parties and single issue pressure groups. A minister's life is burdensome; learning to cope with fatigue is essential.

The function of the civil service is equally clear. This is to support ministers in all these various roles. In the early 1850s, Sir Charles Trevelyan, the Permanent Secretary at the Treasury, and Sir Stafford Northcote, a former civil servant in the Board of Trade, were charged by William Gladstone, then Chancellor of the Exchequer, with a task to which he attached special importance and which he felt was long overdue. He required them to recommend reforms of the public service which at that time was widely regarded as incompetent and tainted with a nineteenth century version of 'sleaze'. In their report, published in 1854, Northcote and Trevelyan advocated that a civil service hitherto appointed by patronage and influence should give way to a highly qualified non-political administrative class. In other words, recruitment to the civil service should be determined by merit and not connection. The Northcote-Trevelyan reforms gave this country a public service which, for nearly a century and a half, has been admired throughout the world. The method of recruitment to the civil service today is based on the same principle – quality not patronage.

* * *

Naturally enough, the substance of the work undertaken by civil servants varies from department to department. Some tasks are common to all, as are methods of working. The senior civil servant in each department – the permanent under-secretary – is the accounting officer. As such, he is directly responsible to parliament for the proper management of the public funds put at the department's disposal by parliamentary vote. Once a year he is required to explain and defend his stewardship to the Public Accounts Committee of the House of Commons. This is invariably a serious occasion.

Civil servants provide the minister in charge of the department and the junior ministers who help him carry his burden – the ministers of state and parliamentary under-secretaries – with a range of services. These include the drafting of legislation, speeches and replies to correspondence. In their routine briefings of the media, civil servants in the departments' press offices draw on policy statements by the government as well as specific guidance given to them by ministers in response to a particular development, or press inquiry. They also arrange press conferences and interviews. The civil servants throughout the department ensure that ministers receive a flow of relevant information from a variety of sources and are given an objective assessment of the importance of each item.

The civil servants' most important function is, of course, to offer advice on policy issues. This advice may be spontaneous – an idea originating in the mind of one or two civil servants in reaction to some development of concern to the department. Or it may be advice commissioned by the minister. Whatever their inspiration, formal submissions to ministers will be drafted after consultation with other departments of state concerned, with other relevant bodies, official and non-official, and, when necessary, with legal advisers. The submission to the minister may begin by defining the issue to be resolved and go on to rehearse the background to the problem, analyse the options available, state the pros and cons of each of these and, finally, recommend a course of action.

In the end it is for the minister to decide on the course of action to follow. In reaching that decision he or she will have to balance a number of considerations. The civil servants who advise the minister are fully aware of government policies relevant to the issue. They will also be sensitive to any other factors which may be in the minister's mind. Nonetheless, they will base their recommendations as far as possible on objective considerations. It is essential that even the most unpalatable advice can be offered and accepted or rejected without rancour. And when the discussion, and perhaps the argument, is over, the civil servants will loyally defend the minister's decision, whatever their private misgivings.

Unlike the harlot in Rudyard Kipling's famous dictum, ministers exercise power and shoulder responsibility. Civil servants, the faithful advisers and supporters, exercise influence. If their advice is shown to be sound, their influence will grow. This is not an official secret; it is a truism.

*   *   *

In a number of ways the system of government at the centre has been changing over the years. For example, many senior posts in the civil service and the diplomatic service are advertised when they fall vacant. This has brought a number of talented people from other walks of life into the public service. For many years now, ministers have been introducing political advisers into their own offices. The first such adviser I worked with was John Harris, now Lord Harris of Greenwich, whom Michael Stewart brought with him when he became foreign secretary in 1965. John Harris was especially interested in the presentation of policy. At that time I was head of the Foreign Office News Department and it was feared by some that there might be a clash of interests. In fact there was none because we each understood the sphere in which the other had to work. Years later, when I became permanent under secretary at the Department of Energy, I invited the secretary of state's political adviser to join the steering group I set up. This young man accepted with enthusiasm and made a valuable contribution to our work. His name was Michael Portillo. Once again there was no clash of interest because the line dividing official advice and political advice was clearly drawn. This is the secret of the success of the French 'cabinet' system; in Paris the private offices of ministers contain a mixture of politically neutral permanent staff and advisers drawn from the minister's political party. Similar arrangements are now quite common in Whitehall and the fears expressed by some of the more excitable commentators about what they termed the 'politicisation' of the civil service have proved to be unjustified.

A more substantial change in the structure of the civil service was set in train nearly ten years ago. Since then nearly one hundred and fifty executive agencies have been created. This represents three-quarters of the entire civil service. Each of these agencies performs administrative tasks in accordance with guidelines which are laid down annually by the minister, to whom the chief executive of the agency is responsible, and which are published. The agencies do not make policy. One of the unexpected advantages of this development is that ministers have been obliged to pay more attention than previously to those in their charge who are engaged in activities other than policy-making. The disadvantage is that the remaining quarter of the service, who work at the centre and are close to the source of the department's power, run the risk of developing elitist characteristics. The system is not yet perfect and there is a case for further clarification of the lines of public accountability between secretaries of state and chief executives of agencies.

* * *

The processes of government at the centre are seldom as orderly or as controlled as this brief account may suggest. In practice, government consists to a great extent of responding to today's bad news and choosing between options of barely distinguishable shades of grey. It is in addressing these situations that the relationship between ministers and their senior advisers is put to the test. In many cases the outcome will be the least unsatisfactory from the point of view of the government, and only rarely will the national interest be damaged. However, if ministers ignore the robust and urgent advice they are given and take a decision which is based not on rational argument but on dogma, prejudice, or considerations of expediency, then the results may be of a different order. The great European beef war of 1996 and the concession on tobacco sponsorship to the motor racing industry are recent examples.

The success of the British system of government does not depend only on the competence and dedication of ministers and civil servants. The essential element is a relationship of mutual trust and respect between ministers and those who serve them. Sadly this was affected in recent years by systematic denigration of the notion of public service. Morale and, with it, standards of performance and conduct fell. The basic truth was overlooked that for hundreds of thousands of our people the public service is not a sinecure but a vocation, and the national interest is best served when this is acknowledged.

* * *

Thanks to meticulous preparation, Whitehall adjusted at once to our entry into what was then the European Economic Community in January 1973. However, as Lord Nolan pointed out in his Radcliffe Lectures eighteen months ago, the same cannot be said of Westminster. 'A serious debate about Europe is needed', he said. He went on: 'What is not needed, and what demeans us as a nation, is our constant tendency to regard foreigners as inferior, to disparage their institutions, and to believe that the oldest must necessarily be the best. If the world around Parliament is changing, Parliament must look at how it can best contribute to and influence the good government of Britain in that changing world and should not rule out the possibility of radical changes in its role and procedures.' Well spoken, M'Lud.

The methods by which the interests of the United Kingdom are furthered and protected in the European Union are dictated in the first instance by the unique constitution of the Union. It is often forgotten that the preamble to the Treaty of Rome, which was signed in 1957, set as the objective 'ever closer union among the peoples of Europe'. In 1973, Andrew Shonfield captured the essence of this concept in his Reith Lectures, to which he gave the title *Journey to an Unknown Destination*. The Treaty provided that each step towards that ever closer union would be taken only with the agreement of all member states. The process would be never-ending and it would be advanced by a continuous dialectic between the Commission, representing the interests of the Community – now the Union – as a whole, and the Council of Ministers, representing the interests of the member states. Under the treaties, the Commission has the duty to recommend policies which the Council of Ministers may accept, amend or reject. The Commission proposes, the Council disposes. It is by this procedure that the whole corpus of European law has come into being.

* * *

Because of the peculiarities of the law-making system in the European Union, which appears unduly complicated to the outsider, and the fact that much of the business done in Brussels is concerned with detail, the media have inevitably tended to concentrate in their reports on the contentious issues which arise from time to time at political level. However, below the surface work proceeds at an intense pace from September to July. In August the various institutions of the Union pause for breath.

British contributions to the work of the European Union are prepared in London by a special committee in the Cabinet Office, and in Brussels by the Office of the United Kingdom Permanent Representative. The task of the Cabinet Office committee, which embraces civil servants from all the government departments concerned, is to coordinate the United Kingdom position on all issues under discussion in the institutions of the Union in the light of policies determined by the Cabinet and Cabinet committees. This committee submits advice to ministers collectively and individually. The staff of the United Kingdom Representation in Brussels – known for convenience as UKREP – is drawn from a range of home departments in addition to the Foreign and Commonwealth Office. Members of UKREP represent the United Kingdom at the various levels of the continuous negotiation.

The structure of this office in Brussels reflects the diversity of the work of the Union. The different sections deal, among other things, with agriculture, economics and finance, external trade, industry and energy, transport and the environment, regional policy and the Union's relations with developing countries. Other members of the staff, such as the legal adviser and the press officer, serve the needs of the entire office.

The senior body in Brussels representing the member states is the Committee of Permanent Representatives, known as COREPER. This committee is divided into two parts. Part I, which is composed of the deputy permanent representatives of the member states, handles the more technical subjects which are to come before the Council of Ministers for decision. Part II, composed of the ambassadors, handles the rest, including those issues which are the most sensitive politically. Agriculture is the province of the separate Special Agriculture Committee. Senior members of the Commission staff and of the Secretariat which services the Council attend meetings of both parts of COREPER and of the Special Agriculture Committee.

COREPER normally meets twice a week – the ambassadors on Thursdays and the deputies on Fridays. The principal function of these committees is to prepare material for meetings of the Council of Ministers and of the European Council, which is composed of the heads of state and government of the fifteen member states. Members of COREPER scrutinise proposals put forward by the Commission and, where necessary, amend those aspects which their governments are unlikely to accept. The arguments put forward by members of COREPER on behalf of their governments are based on initial reactions to Commission proposals in their respective capitals. These in turn will have taken into account comments and advice from permanent representatives themselves. In most cases Commission proposals, whether amended or not, are agreed at this level and the resultant draft legislation is presented to the next convenient meeting of the relevant Council of Ministers for formal adoption without debate. The substantive items on the agenda of the Council will be those on which COREPER has been unable to agree, or are of such importance that they merit debate at ministerial level. The dossiers which come before the two parts of COREPER are the result of preliminary examination in the appropriate working groups. The composition of these groups matches that of COREPER and the Council of Ministers.

What may sound like bureaucratic indulgence and a procedural extravagance is neither. Should a problem arise unexpectedly, or an opportunity be perceived which requires swift attention, the issue can pass from Commission to working group to COREPER without delay and the Council can then be presented with a proposition which has undergone all the usual checks and will have been refined and no doubt improved on the way. The weightier and more complex issues which require detailed attention and debate by ministers inevitably take time.

When the staff of UKREP are not representing the United Kingdom point of view in a working group or at COREPER, they will be gathering intelligence for London about the intentions of the Commission and the attitudes of other member states and advocating the British point of view. They will also offer informed advice to others with a stake in the European enterprise, such as Members of the European Parliament, the Economic and Social Committee and those with business or other professional interests in Europe.

*   *   *

The United Kingdom Representative visits the Cabinet Office in London every Friday to amplify orally the reports he will have sent overnight on the meetings of COREPER, and to discuss the following week's business. He may take the opportunity to brief the minister who will be occupying the United Kingdom chair at the next meeting of the Council of Ministers.

Meetings of the Council often take place on Mondays. Ministers and their advisers arrive from their capitals the previous day. Over a working dinner the London and Brussels teams will review the agenda for the following day's Council. The ambassador will relay the latest news about the attitude of the Commission and other member states and the minister will explain any amendments he has made, or wishes to make, to the briefs prepard by the Cabinet Office committee. After this the tactical handling of the major items will be debated – which of the minister's colleagues might usefully be lobbied in advance, what alliances might be forged, what trade-offs might be considered when the negotiations become serious.

Over the years a cadre has been created within the foreign service and the home departments which consists of talented officials with first-hand experience of the workings of the Union. This pool of knowledge has proved of great benefit to ministers and there can be few better examples of team work between ministers and their advisers than that evident at meetings of the Council of Ministers, and especially during the six months when the United Kingdom holds the Presidency of the Council.

*   *   *

The theme for today is 'Governance – where does power lie?' To answer this question it is necessary to address two persistent allegations. The first is the theory propagated by many political commentators that, for their own purposes, senior civil servants seize every opportunity to manipulate ministers. 'Yes Minister' is satire and not to be confused with the real thing.

There is a variant to this argument. When things go wrong, these same commentators look for a conspiracy, whereas those in the front line know that 'cock-up', rather than 'conspiracy' is almost always the explanation. A notable exception was the Suez affair in 1956, which was both a conspiracy and a cock-up.

The other persistent charge, nourished by the so-called Eurosceptics, is that, having surrendered our sovereignty through our membership of the European Union, we are now ruled by twenty unelected bureaucrats in Brussels.

I hope that what I have said both about life and work at the heart of government in Whitehall and in Brussels has persuaded you that these two allegations border on the absurd. Both here and in the European Union, power lies with democratically elected ministers. Where the confusion is genuine, one reason may be that, in both cases, the critics have been aiming at the wrong target. A European Union of twenty-one, twenty-five, or even thirty member states cannot be administered in the same way as a Community of Six. So, as the European Union is enlarged, the principle of subsidiarity, first advocated by the then President of the Commission in 1975 and eventually enshrined in a treaty at Maastricht in 1991, will have to be rigorously applied. This will entail a dispassionate review and revision of the powers of the European Commission. The rules for decision-taking will have to be amended. The proceedings of the Council of Ministers will have to be more transparent. But none of that will affect the truth that ultimate power in the Union rests and, as was intended from the beginning, will continue to rest, with the Council of Ministers.

*   *   *

In recent years regard for politics and politicians, not only in this country but also in other long-established democracies, has declined. This is not solely because of misbehaviour in high places, or of televising the yah-boo of Question Time in the House of Commons. There are more serious concerns. Is our parliamentary system democratic? Is the House of Commons truly representative? How often since the Second World War has a British Government been voted into office by a majority of the electorate?

There are anxieties of wider significance. We live in an increasingly inter-connected, interdependent world. Have we yet given sufficient thought to the impact of the INTERNET, which has been cogently described as a power for infinite good or for infinite evil, not only on society but also on contemporary systems of governance?

One aspect of the information society has already caused widespread concern. This is the extent to which the media are increasingly controlled by one or two individuals accountable only to their shareholders. As yet no remedy has been suggested at political level. Is this a case of hesitating to bite the hand that feeds one?

*　　*　　*

The overwhelming victory of New Labour last May raised hopes that many of our concerns would be addressed. Those who deplored the relentless centralisation of power in recent years may hope that, apart from changes being made in existing structures, the establishment of a Scottish Parliament and a Welsh Assembly and the new arrangements for the government of Northern Ireland will lead to further constitutional changes in the United Kingdom. This is not uncharted territory. Those who believe that more respect should be paid to regional identities so that new energies can be released, can find inspiration in systems of governance which have proved their worth elsewhere. An outstanding example is the system devised for Germany after the Second World War. The Basic Law of 1948, which established the Federal Republic and granted considerable autonomy to the Länder, has served Germany well for fifty years. It was extended with enthusiasm to the former East Germany when the Berlin Wall came down. In more recent years Spain has successfully adopted a system of regional autonomy.

However, if the high expectations of May 1997 are not to be disappointed, the way in which the electorate is informed day by day of government policies will have to be improved. When chiding ministers for allowing their 'apparatchiks' to reveal new policies by means of leaks to the press, Madam Speaker was not merely defending the prerogative of Parliament; she was also speaking for the electorate, who are entitled to be presented with lucid and authoritative statements of policy

by the ministers responsible. If the new policies which have been under preparation for several months are announced by their authors in clear terms, the point
will be made that power lies with elected ministers and not with apparatchiks.
Careful coordination in Whitehall and sensitive anticipation of public reaction
are the keys to securing acceptance of government policies. And, when you stop
to think of it, that is not too difficult.

From the moment in 1942 when I joined an Indian Division whose objective was to defend the oilfields in Iraq and Persia, I have been in no doubt about the international significance of energy. The knowledge I gained then and during the years I spent later in Iraq, Egypt and Libya and at the United Nations in New York was invaluable when I served as the permanent under secretary at the Department of Energy in the early 1980s.

I

ENERGY POLICY: THE WIDER CONTEXT

INSTITUTE OF PETROLEUM: LONDON – MARCH 1981

You have a reputation in this Institute for foresight. I have noticed that the Institute of Petroleum Technologists, as you called yourselves then, was set up before the First World War. Your predecessors showed remarkable prescience when they decided that the need had arisen for a society to be formed to bring together the knowledge, experiences and diverse interests of those engaged in the various branches of the burgeoning oil industry for the benefit of all. It is as important today that your knowledge and experience – and your various interests – should be joined with those of governments and other sectors of industry in finding solutions to the immense problems which face us in the energy field.

If the original members of your Institute were the odd men out, the world as a whole took the supply of energy for granted; and continued to do so until quite recently. To be fair, there seemed to be little reason why energy as a vital resource should not be taken for granted. Transitions had been made without undue disturbance from one source of energy to another – from wood and wind to coal and then to oil. The transitions occurred not because the older sources of energy were running out or becoming too expensive. Very obviously not. But newer sources became available which were more convenient, and in some cases more efficient. Oil, because of the ease with which it can be handled, moved and stored, became the energy source of paramount importance. It was readily available and cheap and so the demand for it grew. Historians of the future may well argue that oil was too cheap for too long and that a much earlier appreciation in its price might have prevented the major industrialised nations of the West becoming so dependent on imported supplies. That, as I say, is a point for the historians. We have to deal with the situation as it is today; we have to deal with the consequences of the sudden and massive price rises and the disruption of supplies in 1973/4.

In working out policies to deal with the energy crisis, it is only right that we should keep in mind the situation of the non-oil producing countries of the Third World. It is not only the affluent North which has problems. Many developing countries are more sorely afflicted, especially those who have only one or perhaps two resources which they can trade in order to pay their way in the world. For them additional expenditure on oil means increasing the burden of debt which they may be already barely able to service. Yet if they are to develop their potential they need to increase their consumption of energy – which in practice means oil in most cases – more rapidly than those countries which are further along the road of economic progress.

It is not only governments, our society and our economies which have felt the wind of change over the last decade. You know as well as anyone that the world oil industry has under-gone a continuous transformation since the beginning of the oil crisis in 1973. One of the objectives of certain members of the OPEC at that time was a transfer of power from the major international oil companies to the governments of the producing countries. I recall one of my first impressions of a major oil company. On language study in Southern Iraq in the Spring of 1947 I was invited to see something of the operations of the Basra Petroleum Company – the southern sister of the Iraq Petroleum Company which handled Kirkuk and Mosul. What I saw on the ground was of course of interest, especially in the light of the great discoveries which were to follow. But what impressed me more was the influence the Company enjoyed and the extent of the services the Company provided to the local community through education, from the basics to what we now rather pompously call transfer of technology, through medical and other social care, transport, recreation and so on. As the pale grey BPC buses took the BPC shift-workers, with their BPC pay packets in their pockets, back to their BPC accommodation, I realised the extent to which the Company was a state within a state, with all that that implied. Those were, I suppose, what some would call the 'good old bad old days'.

Over the past several years most of the power which the integrated international oil companies used to exercise over the oil production of member states of the

OPEC has been removed by one means or another. The most radical method was of course full-scale nationalisation which brought the role of the concessionaire companies to a complete end. In those OPEC countries where the major oil companies, as well as other foreign enterprises, still operate; they no longer have the power to set production levels, to determine production capacity or to decide when and where to set exploration in hand. By the mid-1970s all of these functions had been transferred to the national oil company of the producing country, or to some other state agency. The international oil companies were obliged to assume a new role. The essential policy decisions were out of their hands. So they became purchasers of oil, contractors and technical consultants in one form or another.

What matters in regard to these developments in the recent past is not whether they were for better or for worse; what matters is that the role the companies have to play now and in the future will be different.

The companies, like governments, have to form a view of what that future is likely to be. The forecasts do not agree; that is to be expected. So far as petroleum is concerned some predict a shortfall while others suggest that supplies will exceed demand. In the real world, of course, supply and demand balance. It is common ground amongst the forecasters that resources of oil are finite and diminishing and that demand for oil must also diminish.

One of the main uncertainties which have to be taken into account, whether in companies or in governments, by those to whom it falls to take decisions concerns the level of future oil production. Some believe that production of freely flowing oil might plateau in the 1990s and decline thereafter. Others take the view that production will peak around the year 2000, or perhaps even later. There are a few who argue that world oil production may already have peaked. A major factor in predicting future world oil production levels is the judgment one forms as to the policies of the OPEC. Amongst the members of the OPEC only the Gulf States have the potential to increase production rapidly from their own resources. However, given the pressure on the governments of these states to pursue prudent depletion policies and the prospect that they will continue to accumulate large current account surpluses, it must be unlikely that oil production in these countries will increase significantly above the current levels. Production in the other OPEC countries will be constrained by their relatively low reserves. This leads one to suppose that production from the OPEC as a whole is unlikely to increase substantially, if at all; and there is always the possibility, if not the likelihood, of significant cutbacks in production.

*   *   *

The level of oil production is only one of our preoccupations. Price is another. If oil follows the precedent set by other resources then, as reserves dwindle, the real price will increase. Whatever the precise levels at which oil is produced we can be reasonably certain that oil prices will rise. And the amount and pace of the price rises will have an important effect on the world economy as our experience over the past few years has taught us. Our aim must therefore be to ensure that the gradual decline in oil reserves and the associated rise in prices is such that they cause the minimum economic detriment.

It seems to me that there are three particular aspects to this problem. First, while economies seem able to adjust fairly readily to a smooth and predictable increase in prices associated with a gradual decrease in resources, recent events have shown that sudden unexpected increases can have a severe and long lasting effect on the world's economy, in particular the economies of the oil importing developing countries. It might be argued that this results from attempts by governments to control the pricing of oil, and that these interventions by governments have distorted the natural fine tuning mechanism of the market. At the same time it must be acknowledged that, whatever actions governments have taken, companies still retain significant powers. The plain fact is that market expertise does not lie within governments, but within companies. You have, and will continue to have, a vital role to play in the control of price increases.

Closely linked is the second consideration – the most efficient use of remaining reserves. If oil prices rise too rapidly, funds will be diverted to the development of cheaper alternative sources, and oil reserves will be left unexploited. If on the other hand prices are depressed below realistic levels, reserves will be exhausted before alternatives have been developed. It is essential, therefore, for the best use of our resources, that oil should be priced realistically. Here again, I suggest, the companies have an important role.

Thirdly, we must do all we can to ensure that the transition from oil is managed as efficiently as possible. There will be a transfer from oil to non-oil substitutes in the main bulk fuel market – industrial boilers, power stations, etc. This will mean that the remaining oil supplies will be concentrated increasingly on meeting demand in the premium sectors, and notably transport and petrochemicals.

The transition away from oil will not be smooth unless we handle the exploitation of our reserves with care. It is to be expected that the major oil companies will be in the forefront of any new oil discoveries. I recall a study commissioned by the International Bank for Reconstruction and Development in 1978, which covered

70 developing countries. This study concluded that, of 23 countries with high or very high national petroleum reserves, only seven had been explored adequately. A curious phenomenon. It is possible, provided the circumstances are right, that more attention will be paid to non-conventional oil sources such as oil shale and tar sands. Oil prices are now probably within reach of the sort of levels at which exploitation of these unconventional oil sources might be economically attractive, although there are of course other technical problems still to be overcome. As governments exercise increasing control over the crude end of the operation, and as demand moves towards the lighter end of the barrel, you may pay more attention to the downstream end of the operation – petrochemicals and so on. You may also be thinking of diversifying out of oil into other parts of the energy sector such as coal or the renewables. You may even be thinking of diversifying right out of energy.

The governments of the main western industrialised nations recognise that the development of our energy reserves must be controlled with special care. The European Community is committed over the next ten years to reduce to 0.7 the average ratio for the Community's rate of growth in primary energy consumption to the rate of growth in GDP. At Venice last June the seven participants in the Economic Summit agreed to double their collective production and use of coal by 1990. Greater use of coal implies a reduction in oil-burning in power stations and in industry. And we must persist with the development of nuclear power. Nuclear power is indispensable to any adequate re-structuring of energy economies.

Then there is the other source of supply – conservation. In 1977 the International Energy Agency adopted a set of principles for energy policy. One of these was a commitment to allot a higher priority to the conservation of energy. There is a very long lead time on major supply investments. For example, it takes about ten years from the initial investment for a nuclear power station to come into operation. Therefore, for the rest of this decade conservation will have to be the major tool of ensuring reasonable balance in the energy markets.

*   *   *

Reciting these elements in the energy strategy of the industrialised world does not by itself make one sanguine about the future. There are significant political, institutional, social and environmental constraints to be overcome if the objectives of this strategy are to be achieved and not remain pious hopes.

The international dimension is critical. Energy is an important component of the relationship between the industrialised nations represented in the OECD, the members of the OPEC and the rest of the developing world. The present may not be an opportune moment to open any formal dialogue on energy issues. But we can build on the informal bilateral exchanges which have been taking place and which continue. These exchanges constantly widen the area of mutual comprehension. And perhaps we saw the first beneficial results of this process when the other producers in the Gulf area, and Saudi Arabia in particular, increased their production to mitigate the effects of the revolution in Iran in 1979 and of the Gulf War last autumn when oil exports from Iraq and Iran ceased for a time.

We should draw encouragement from that. But the challenge in the energy field which faces the major international organisations, governments, companies and individuals alike, remains. Change is inevitable. That change may be gradual and beneficial, or it may be sudden and destructive. All of us must contribute to the process so that the transition is as painless as possible. If we do so, the challenge will be well met.

II

ENERGY IN INTERNATIONAL RELATIONS

HARVARD UNIVERSITY, USA – OCTOBER 1982

In a memorandum addressed to his management committee in 1921 Sir Charles Greenway, then the Chairman of the Anglo-Persian Oil Company, wrote the following:

> '. . . the geological information we possess at present does not indicate that there is much hope of finding oil in Bah-rain or Kuwait . . .'.

This illustrates a truth which had become evident much earlier, namely that there is an international dimension to energy issues. So far as the Europeans are concerned there has always had to be such a dimension, given the size and nature of Europe's energy resources. And the history of the expansion in the production and consumption of energy, and of oil in particular, over the past 150 years bears ample testimony to this.

This period was characterised by a series of bold initiatives by Governments, as for instance, the British Government which in 1839 acquired the Port of Aden not only as an extension of its political influence but also as a coaling station for the Royal Navy; and again in 1914, when it bought a controlling interest in the Anglo Persian Oil Company – and by individuals. Prominent amongst these was Baron Julius de Reuter, the founder of the news agency, who in 1872 took out a mineral concession in Iran. But the mercantile acumen of Calouste Gulbenkian is perhaps the outstanding example of individual enterprise in the international energy field.

The other notable characteristic of this long period was the remarkable pace of the expansion in energy supply and demand, which seems to have matched and almost at times to have outrun developments in industry and transport. And, as so often in history, war provided a major stimulus. One statistic illustrates the point. The British Expeditionary Force arrived in France in 1914 almost entirely dependent on horses for transport. In 1918 it was equipped with nearly 80,000 motor cars and 34,000 motor cycles. No wonder Lord Curzon, a senior member of the British Cabinet, was able to declare in November 1918, with fine disregard for specific gravity: 'The Allies floated to victory on a wave of oil'.

This whole period of development and expansion was remarkable in these and other respects. But what is perhaps most surprising is the comparative indifference of lay opinion in our societies to the problems entailed in securing our supplies of energy, and especially of oil. In the Cabinet rooms and the Chancelleries, in the Board Rooms of the energy industries and, naturally enough, on the Stock Exchanges much attention had been devoted to the question of access to and control over sources of energy. That the public was on the whole inclined to take energy for granted, whether as a source of light, heat or power, is perhaps a tribute to the wisdom of successive Governments and the enterprise and skill of the leaders of the industries concerned.

*   *   *

The shock when it came in 1973 was all the greater. When individuals are touched in their pocket or their fuel tank, or both, they react. Compare the relative indifference of the previous century with the vigour, if not ferocity, of the public debate about energy which opened then and which, despite the more relaxed oil market of the past two years, continues unabated today.

There are numerous elements in this debate. For one thing we are now all OPEC-watchers, and events in the Middle East are today far more widely recognised to be of direct concern to our well-being in the western industrialised world. For generations the Europeans have acknowledged the people of this region to be their next door neighbours. In 1973 in America too people had to form lines at the gasoline stations. For this and other reasons this special sense of involvement in what happens in the Middle East is now fully shared by the Americans and Japanese and others. On our side of the Atlantic we welcome this. The Camp David agreement, the Habib mission, the presence of US servicemen in Sinai and Lebanon are evidence of American determination to sustain progress towards a Middle East settlement. The close relationship between the TJS and Israel is a key element here. But it must also be borne in mind that the Arabs, so eloquent on many issues, are reticent about certain of their preoccupations and resentments arising from their different religious, cultural and social traditions. These too need to be understood if an enduring settlement is to be achieved. Only such a settlement will bring stability to the region. And stability is the best guarantee of an uninterrupted flow of oil.

This is perhaps the most important constituent of the energy debate. But there are others. As soon as one recognises the extent of the dependence of western economies on imported oil one naturally focuses on alternative sources of energy and on ways of using energy more efficiently. So this subject too is avidly discussed.

Then again, appreciation of the finite nature of the world's resources of fossil fuels has aroused interest in renewable sources of energy – wind, solar, geo-thermal and so on – which, however exotic they may be, are usually good these days for a half page spread in our more serious newspapers. The renewables seem to be accorded a special nobility.

In the course of the public debate preoccupation with future supplies of energy has occasionally collided with the already lively concern for our environment. This latter is a worthy cause; anyone who cares about the condition in which we pass this earth of ours into the 21st century must acknowledge the strength of the arguments about, for instance, the disposal of spoil from deep mining and the emission into the atmosphere of noxious substances such as lead or sulphur dioxide. Where to strike the balance between the economics of energy and the protection of our environment will long be a matter for dispute, both domestic and international.

A sensitive issue revived by the energy debate is safety, especially in regard to nuclear energy. When this subject is raised emotions are readily touched, and a facile link can be established between nuclear power for generating electricity and nuclear weapons. It is a pity that so often on this subject the debate is con-ducted with more passion than respect for facts. In the United Kingdom we have always encouraged open debate based on full exposure of the evidence about the operation and safety of nuclear power plants. This has, I believe, led to a wider acceptance of nuclear power by the general public than in some other western countries; perhaps there is a moral here to be drawn.

There is of course an international aspect to the public debate about energy and about nuclear power in particular. The reason is clear. For one thing, as the much quoted John Donne pointed out, no man is an island. Nor is every nuclear station a Three-Mile Island, and that is just as well. Indeed, if there is to be general accep-tance by our societies of the benefits of nuclear power there must be no more Three-Mile Islands. The nuclear industry in all our countries must operate with scrupulous attention to safety and to legitimate public concern.

*   *   *

You will deduce that, while welcoming the wide discussion of energy issues, I should prefer this to be conducted in a rational way. May I illustrate this point with a recent example from our own experience in Britain? Some commentators sought to link the despatch of our Task Force to liberate the Falkland Islands with the oil potential of the waters that surround them. I cannot speak for the motives of the Argentine authorities. But I can say that whether hydrocarbons exist or not in that region played no part in our decision.

For many years we have been concerned about the future economic development of the Islands and surrounding waters. To date information about the presence or absence of hydrocarbon-bearing strata in the area has been limited. Further detailed seismic surveys and drilling will be needed before any conclusion can be drawn. Despite this, in April and May of this year some commentators had identified huge oil deposits in the waters of the South Atlantic. The future may prove this to be so. But there is no evidence to support this at present, and the link made between this speculation and the despatch of our Task Force was momentarily unhelpful in clouding what was from our point of view a clear issue.

*   *   *

The public debate about energy over the past decade has been part of the context in which Governments have had to deal with the issues raised by the events of 1973-74.

In the first months following the Yom Kippur war the western industrialised nations scrambled to a rough and ready stabilisation of the situation. I was at that time involved at the London end in preparing the United Kingdom's brief for the long and complex negotiations which led, in the end, to the establishment of the International Energy Agency. I retain a vivid impression of the prolonged *tour de force* by Vicomte Davignon, to whose determination, intellectual ingenuity and powers of persuasion as Chairman of the Coordinating Group the establishment of the IEA is largely due. I have to add however that the satisfaction we felt at the outcome was diminished by regret at the absence from the enterprise of one important member of the European Community.

The IEA seldom hits the headlines these days. This does not mean that it has outlived its usefulness. On the contrary. The very existence of the Agency and the fact that it meets from time to time to review its arrangements has been a major factor in our recovery from the crisis of the early 1970s. The Agency is right to avoid ambitious initiatives when there is no call for these. It is also right, when the oil market is slack, to warn Western Governments and public opinion against the dangers of complacency.

The effort devoted by eight of the then nine Member States to the negotiation setting up the IEA undoubtedly distracted attention from the task of developing an articulate and distinctive European Community response to the energy crisis. The slow and occasionally painful progress it made over the succeeding years is characteristic of the way in which the Community reconciles important conflicting interests and can in the end evolve a generally acceptable approach. In this case as in others the Community, once it had determined its policy, was able to exercise important if not decisive influence on its major partners in the industrialised world.

When I arrived in Brussels in the autumn of 1975 I found ideas about a Community approach to the energy crisis still unformed. The British proposal at the end of that year for a minimum safeguard price for oil to protect and underwrite the huge investment in the North Sea provoked a conflict of views which highlighted the differences in the Member States' approach: the British were arguing for oil support (at a price of $7 a barrel – how absurd this seems today); France was committed to an extensive nuclear programme; and Italy to the development of alternative sources of energy. In this situation the European Commission recommended a centralised approach to a Community energy policy which, as it turned out, sat ill with the more relaxed international climate that had developed meanwhile. Energy prices had stabilised; economic growth had resumed, and the incentive for concerted action, which had been so obvious 18 months earlier, had diminished.

The idea of a centralised approach to a Community energy policy was therefore progressively discarded.

It was thought right instead to see what could be constructed on the basis of the national energy policies of the individual Member States. This more empirical approach to Community policy was reflected in the lecture Mr Roy Jenkins, the then Chairman of the European Commission, delivered in Florence in October 1977.

This lecture attracted widespread attention for its advocacy of a European monetary system. I myself felt at the time, as I still do, that the prescription in that lecture for the process of constructing Europe might prove in the end to be more significant. Mr Jenkins said then: 'We must only give to the Community functions which will, beyond reasonable doubt, deliver significantly better results because they are performed at Community level. We must fashion a Community which gives to each Member State the benefits of results which they cannot achieve alone. We must equally leave to them functions which they can do equally well or better on their own'.

The message in the Florence lecture was taken to heart in Community discussion of energy problems. The formula was developed that the Community's energy policy should consist of the sum of the Member States' national energy policies plus those elements, for example research and development and the setting of objectives for reducing our collective dependence on imported oil, which could be done better on a Community basis.

By the end of 1978 the Community as a whole had recognised that its own efforts would be ineffectual if they were not concerted with those of the United States and Japan, given the importance of these two countries in the international oil market. The need for closer collaboration amongst the industrialised countries was in any event reinforced by the oil supply difficulties which followed the revolution in Iran in 1978. Some 6 million barrels a day were lost to the market as oil production in Iran came to a halt. Not all oil companies, not all consuming countries were directly affected; but they all shared the same anxiety. The supply of oil seemed once again vulnerable to interruption. This meant high prices and further recession. Pressure grew at Brussels for Community action.

The Community took a decisive step at Strasbourg in June 1979, when the European Council – that is to say the European Heads of State or Government – drew up a broad response to the latest challenge. One week later, at the Economic Summit at Tokyo, the European leaders persuaded the Americans and the Japanese to join them in their approach. At Tokyo objectives for the western world were defined and, a year later, in June 1980, the policy options for achieving these objectives were agreed. From Venice there emerged a strategic framework for reducing the demand for energy without hampering consuming countries when they realised the implications of the extent of their dependence on imported oil have combined with the effects of the long drawn out economic recession to produce a market situation which no one could have expected in 1973. The oil producing countries have seen the demand for their product drop from some 30 million barrels a day (mbd) to 16 mbd in March of this year. Few forecasters see demand for OPEC oil climbing much above 24 mbd within the next two years.

Inevitably this new perspective of the oil market, with most commentators seeing slack conditions for several years to come, has influenced attitudes towards investment in alternatives and the production of oil from very high cost areas. It will pay us in this situation to avoid complacency. Once bitten, twice shy should be our motto. Were we to react on the basis of premature conclusions we could well find ourselves once again in circumstances as difficult as those of 1973/4 or 1979.

Moreover, we should understand the problems present conditions pose for the

OPEC. From time to time the suggestion has been made that the consumers – perhaps the OECD itself – should establish a dialogue with OPEC. I find this a somewhat naive idea. For almost a decade now it seems to me there has been a dialogue between western industrialised countries and members of OPEC through our manifold contacts at all levels. Through this process we have a better understanding of OPEC's attitude to this finite source of wealth and to the investment of their earnings. For their part most members of OPEC have long since understood the harm that can be done to their interests by shocks, whether over the supply or the price of oil, administered to western economies. I wonder whether it is fanciful to suggest that the remarkable efficiency with which the international Community coped with the effects on the oil market of the outbreak of the war between Iraq and Iran in 1980 was due at least in part to this dialogue.

We in the United Kingdom and the European Community conclude from our experience that our present method is the right way to conduct the dialogue and we give this appropriate priority. Nor do we neglect the political dimension. As I suggested earlier, we regard any threat to the stability of the Middle East as a threat to our own prosperity as well as to the prosperity of the people of the region. We therefore attach equal importance to the dialogue with the States of this sensitive region on the more political issues and for this reason we warmly welcome President Reagan's recent proposals for a Middle East settlement. We will play our part in the sustained effort which will be needed to achieve this.

* * *

There is another group of countries whose interests we will increasingly have to bear in mind. The great majority of developing countries, numbering about 100, depend in varying degrees on imported oil. Already these countries account for some 20% of free world demand. Despite the most recent indications this proportion is bound to increase; not only will the populations of these countries continue to rise faster than the populations of industrialised countries, but their progressive economic development will raise the level of their *per capita* consumption.

Oil imports place a heavy burden on these countries. Between 1980 and 1981 the current account deficit of oil importing developing countries increased by some $70 billion. Why, it may be asked, should this concern us? It seems to me there are at least three reasons.

First, any improvement in the way these countries use energy and any diversification of their sources of supply will help to ease the energy situation in the free world as a whole. This will maintain the present relaxed state of the oil market to the general benefit, and postpone the day when increased demand by these countries will have an important influence on the price of oil. The second reason is economic. If the constraints on the consumption of oil by these countries were lessened, their economies would advance more rapidly; this in turn would benefit world trade. The third reason is political. If the economies of these countries declined owing to high import bills they could become prey to influences hostile to our ideals in the free world. To these three reasons we must add our humanitarian concern that the struggle against poverty in the world should have been hindered by violent movements in the oil market.

There is no single solution to this problem. Developing countries hold the key to their own progress by adopting policies which encourage investment. The industrialised countries can help by more efficient use of energy, by reducing their demand for oil and by relevant aid policies. Companies, banks and OPEC countries with surpluses to invest can all play a role. We believe that an Energy Affiliate of the World Bank could help, provided it attracted genuinely additional finance. Even so, I believe the energy problems of developing countries will represent a continuing challenge. And we should be alive to new remedies.

*   *   *

Up to this point I have not mentioned the Soviet Union. For sound reasons the Russians have been virtually excluded from the international arrangements for handling the energy crisis. But they are now involved through the affair of the West Siberian gas pipeline which has become a regrettable irritant in an otherwise generally healthy transatlantic relationship.

In Britain and the other states of the European Community we share American concern over the tragic developments in Poland. We believe that the Western response to these events should be closely coordinated; and that it should also be the most effective that can be devised. We have to bear in mind, amongst other things, that the Soviet Union has 40%: of the world's proven gas reserves, 9% of oil reserves and perhaps half the world's known reserves of coal. This immense geological endowment is bound to influence the balance between world supply and demand for energy. The West's relations with the Soviet Union in the energy field are part of our wider economic, commercial and political relations, and it is within that framework that we should seek to work out a solution to the problems which have arisen over the gas pipeline.

I am confident that the difficulties over the pipeline will be resolved before long and that, on both sides of the Atlantic, we will reaffirm the importance of close understanding and consultation for the good health of the Alliance. This surely is the paramount common interest.

*   *   *

What conclusions can be drawn from the way we in the western industrialised world have handled the energy crisis over the past decade? I suggest the following.

First, the international dimension to the problems we face in the energy field is real and cannot be ignored. The interdependence of energy producing and consuming nations is a demonstrated fact. If the market is to be the dominant factor in balancing supply and demand it follows that we should accept that supply and demand will be continually affected by decisions over which we have little or no influence. So our individual and collective energy policies must be seen as part not only of our economic policies but also of our foreign policies. We must therefore ensure that the energy aspect of our relations with the energy-producing nations – and particularly the oil producers – including those in eastern Europe as well as the developing world, is kept in proper perspective.

Secondly, we must sustain our efforts to avoid a repetition of the difficulties we encountered in 1973/4 and again in 1979. Complacency is the enemy. And the strategy developed at Venice is still the best prescription. We should adhere to that strategy; and we should keep our crisis arrangements in the International Energy Agency in good repair. This does not mean however that if the oil market remains slack for a prolonged period we should not turn the better terms on which we obtain our supplies of oil to the advantage of our economies and our peoples.

Thirdly, we should recognise that the emerging countries in the developing world represent an increasingly significant market for oil. It is in the general interest that they should be enabled to meet their growing needs.

Finally, the Venice strategy – like all the best-laid schemes of mice and men – is not impregnable. A major disturbance in an important oil producing region could have critical consequences. The Middle East is one such region. How best to contribute to a Middle East settlement must therefore continue to be a major pre-occupation for the western nations.

III

THE SIGNIFICANCE OF OIL TO THE MIDDLE EAST

ROYAL COLLEGE OF DEFENCE STUDIES, LONDON – JUNE 1984

Until a few weeks ago the phrase 'renewed tension in the Middle East' would have suggested that the lamentable state of affairs in the Levant had in some respect become even worse. But the spread of hostilities from the territories of Iraq and Iran into the Gulf proper and the involvement of nationals of other countries have shifted the focus of our attention; Middle East oil is now a major international issue.

Over the years the rest of the world has looked on this subject with varied emotions. A year ago, we wondered whether it was too soon to congratulate ourselves on having established comparative stability in the international oil market. In 1982 the world-wide glut of oil dominated our expectations. A year earlier, in the spring of 1981, the possibility of yet another rise in the price of oil following the outbreak of the war between Iraq and Iran was causing anxiety. In 1980, and indeed in 1979, the spectacular rise in world oil prices precipitated by the revolution in Iran was our chief worry. And the previous year – 1978 – we were all optimistic about the prospects for both the supply and the price of oil.

Energy is a subject to which certain myths are attached; so one or two facts have to be recorded at the outset. First, oil is not the same thing as energy. The importance of a single fuel that satisfies a substantial part of the world's total demand for energy cannot be questioned. But it should not be overlooked that other fuels, as well as influences on the demand side of the equation, also make an important contribution – and not least coal. Secondly, oil does not mean only the Middle East producers. Over the past few years the Soviet Union has become a significant exporter of both oil and gas; the United States remains a major producer, and others outside the Middle East and outside the Organisation of Petroleum Exporting Countries – OPEC – have been satisfying an increasing part of world demand. Thirdly – but this is a point of more potential than actual importance – the Middle East contains major reserves of gas in addition to oil.

*   *   *

It is as well at the outset to see the importance of Middle East oil in its historical context.

When Sir Charles Greenway, then the Chairman of the Anglo-Persian Oil Company, told his management committee in 1924 '. . . the geological information we possess at present does not indicate that there is much hope of finding oil in Bahrain or Kuwait . . .' he was, apart from perpetrating a howler of major proportions, illustrating the truth that there is an international dimension to energy issues. So far as Western Europe is concerned, there has always had to be such a dimension, given the size and nature of our energy resources. The British Government acquired the Port of Aden in 1839 not only as an extension of its political influence but also as a coaling station for the Royal Navy. In 1914 the British Government bought a controlling interest in the Anglo-Persian Oil Company.

The most notable feature of the story of energy over the past century has been the remarkable pace of the expansion of supply and demand which seems at times to have outrun developments in industry and transport. As so often in history, war provided a stimulus. In 1914 the British Expeditionary Force arrived in France with less than 900 motor cars and 15 motor cycles. In 1918 it was equipped with nearly 80,000 cars and 34,000 motor cycles.

Another characteristic of this period was the comparative indifference of lay opinion in our societies to the problems entailed in securing our supplies of energy, and especially of oil. In the Cabinet rooms and the Chancelleries, in the board rooms of the energy industries and, naturally enough, on the stock exchanges, much attention had been devoted to the question of access to and control over sources of energy. That the public was on the whole inclined to take energy for granted, whether as a source of light, heat or power, is a tribute to the wisdom of successive governments and the enterprise and skill of the leaders of the industries concerned.

After the Second World War the pace quickened. For a variety of reasons economic growth was accorded a high place on the international agenda. The very causes of the war – deeply rooted in stagnation, unemployment and depression – required the point to be made that democratic societies, based on the market system, could create jobs and rising expectations without the dislocation caused by monetary instability. Memories of the inter-war years tempered hope, but the results, when they came, far exceeded what had been expected. By any standard what was achieved was astonishing. Between 1950 and 1973 the gross national product of the United States increased two and a half times; that of Western Europe three and a half times; and Japan's ten times. There were many elements in this success – the Bretton Woods Agreement which stabilised the international monetary system, European integration, technological advance, and energy, and particularly oil.

From the 1950s to the early 1970s oil was readily available and cheap – some might say too cheap. The ease with which oil can be handled and stored enhanced its attraction as a source of energy. And so the demand for oil grew. But this was accompanied by another important trend. The role the oil companies played in the producing countries came under the scrutiny of the local governments who gradually increased the measure of their control over the world's most important reservoirs of oil in Africa, Latin America and the Gulf. By stages, these governments improved their ability to determine the price of oil. After a series of confrontations with the oil companies – of which perhaps the most significant was Libya's successful challenge in 1970, imitated a year or so later by the Shah of Iran – this process culminated in the dramatic price rises of 1973/4. A separate but associated sequence of events underlined the extreme vulnerability of the world oil market to international conflict when, to support the Egyptian military effort in the Yom Kippur war, the Arab oil producers imposed an oil embargo on certain states.

It is easy to see how the OPEC came to occupy the position which enabled them to act as they did in 1973. The energy economy of the United States in that year was 45% dependent on oil, of which 38% was imported; 75% of Japan's energy needs were met by oil, almost all of it imported; at that time we in the United Kingdom were 46% dependent on oil and production in the North Sea had not yet begun.

The reaction of the industrialised countries to the four- and then five-fold price rise and to the interruption in supplies had about it a flavour of 'sauve qui peut'. Having been forced brutally to realise the extent of their vulnerability, these countries sought by various means to reduce their dependence on imported oil. For example, the United States set a goal of energy independence, without having in place any machinery to achieve that goal. France tried to establish special relationships with particular producers such as Algeria and Iraq, and placed more emphasis on conservation and nuclear power. Japan practised much higher energy efficiency, while Germany relied on market forces to reduce demand for oil and to encourage diversification to coal, natural gas and nuclear. The United Kingdom pinned its hopes on production from the North Sea.

By early 1974 the sense of shock had worn off and consultations among the industrialised countries led in due course to the compilation of the International Energy Programme (IEP), which contained measures for dealing with any future supply crisis. The International Energy Agency was created within the Organisation for Economic Cooperation and Development (OECD) to implement the IEP and to promote other aspects of international cooperation. Unfortunately, for reasons of their own, the French declined to take part in this operation.

By 1976 the world oil picture had begun to change. Energy prices began to fall in real terms – by 25% in the United States, by 40% in Germany and by 50% in Japan. Economic recovery and these lower prices stimulated demand. By 1977 it seemed that some order had been restored to the world oil situation and confidence was still growing when the second shock occurred in 1978. This shock was different in character from the first. Industrial unrest in Iran briefly interrupted the flow of oil which then ceased altogether from the end of December 1978 to March 1979. This removed some 6 million barrels a day (mbd) – one fifth of OECD's imports – from the market. The effects of this relatively small cut in the supply of crude oil at a time of rising demand were exacerbated by fears on the part of refiners and consumers that oil supplies would once again become scarce, and by the failure of governments to act collectively. The result was a rise in price of 150% – an increase of $21 per barrel, compared with the rise of $8 pb in 1973/4. On this occasion the process was not initiated by any deliberate action by the producers, and it is widely accepted today that the 150% price rise was largely a self-inflicted wound on the part of the industrialised countries – the unedifying product of a faulty perception of events, panic by consumers and an inept response by their governments. Not surprisingly, even those members of OPEC inclined to take the longer term view were not unwilling on this occasion to take advantage of the turn of events in order to raise their export prices.

These developments provoked acrimonious exchanges amongst the industrialised countries; but they also gave fresh momentum to the policy of shifting away from oil. At the Tokyo economic summit in June 1979 objectives for the western world were defined and, a year later, at Venice, the policy options for dealing with these objectives were agreed. From Venice there emerged a strategic framework for reducing dependence on imported energy without hampering economic growth. The main elements were clear: a reduction in the consumption of oil; an increase in the production of coal; the development of nuclear power and renewable sources of energy such as solar, wind, hydro, and the development of indigenous hydrocarbon reserves. Central to the strategy was the economic pricing of energy, domestic prices being based on world prices.

* * *

Eighteen months later – in the autumn of 1980 – the supply of oil from the Middle East was interrupted once again when war broke out between Iraq and Iran. But on this occasion swift action by other producers, and notably Saudi Arabia, to make good part of the loss, and by the International Energy Agency (IEA), steadied the nerves of both governments and oil companies and prevented a major disturbance. It seemed that the international community had at last learned some important lessons.

Before long the economic recession was reflected in a drop in the demand for oil; demand was further reduced with the drawing down of oil stocks and by the response of consumers to higher prices, such as the more efficient use of energy. Between 1979 and 1983 demand for OPEC oil fell by nearly 44% – from 31 million barrels a day to 17½mbd. It seemed, eighteen months ago, that the oil producers were heading for a crisis against the background of speculation that the price of oil – then $34 pb – would collapse. After long and difficult discussions in London and despite the predictions of some commentators that OPEC would break up, the producers agreed in the spring of 1983 on a comparatively minor reduction in the oil price – a cut of $5 pb to $29 pb – and on production quotas. This agreement has been observed for over a year. Furthermore, large reserves of oil are held at present by members of the IEA and by Saudi Arabia and, three months ago, the US Secretary of Energy announced the readiness of the US to draw on the Strategic Petroleum Reserve in the event of major disruption of supplies. Work on ways of handling lesser crises has recently been resumed in the IEA.

* * *

This is all reasonably good news. The present is therefore a convenient moment to assess the impact and implications of this series of events and so to edge closer to the heart of the matter.

First, the effects on the industrialised countries in the OECD. It is often forgotten that world inflation was already gathering momentum in the early 1970s. From the point of view of the industrialised countries there was an unfortunate combination of factors – rising food prices, a commodity boom, declining productivity, the financing of the Vietnam war and increasing rigidity in the labour markets. The international monetary system was under pressure and, even in Japan, there was anxiety that its remarkable growth rate might be slowing down.

These trends have to be kept in perspective: the highly controversial action of President Nixon in introducing wage and price controls in August 1971 was a response to the inflation rate reaching the then dizzy height of 3.8%.

The oil price rises fuelled inflation in two ways. First, because oil plays such a pervasive role in the economy, these price increases affected the price index directly. They also bid up the price of alternative fuels and of palliatives, such as coal, home insulation and fuel-efficient motor cars.

The second main effect has been on economic growth. The oil price increases represented what the International Monetary Fund described as a 'real resource transfer of unprecedented magnitude'. The income of the population of the industrialised world was reduced; and so demand fell and with it the level of economic activity. This in turn raised unemployment. The impact on individual countries has been compounded by the fact that the economic recession was world-wide, affecting rich and poor alike. The transfusion service had run out of blood, and it is only over the past year that we have seen signs of economic recovery, notably in the United States.

Modern economies are dynamic; they adjust to new circumstances and new forces. The adjustment to the so-called oil shocks has been impressive; and it has taken various forms. First, there has been a significant diversification away from OPEC oil towards other sources of supply. Secondly, other fuels have been substituted for oil. Thirdly, energy efficiency – also known rather misleadingly as energy conservation; the link, previously considered inexorable, between the rate of economic growth and the rate of the expansion in energy consumption has been broken. These three forms of adjustment to the new energy situation echo the strategy adopted at the Venice economic summit.

* * *

If some in the industrialised nations feel that the impact of the 'oil shocks' has been severe, they should reflect on the plight of those developing countries which have no oil. The rise in real oil prices has placed great pressure on the balance of payments of these countries, many of whom are dependent for their earnings of foreign exchange on one primary product. And these are countries which have to grow at a far higher rate if they are to break out of their penury.

At the other end of the spectrum stand the oil producers and, in particular, the states of the Gulf. The events of the past decade have conferred on the thirteen members of the OPEC unprecedented financial and economic strength which, by itself, is a political fact of major significance. Wealth beyond the dreams of avarice has presented each of these countries with a wide range of policy options. These include the development of their domestic economy and social structure; aid to the like-minded but less fortunate; the pursuit of prestige and political influence; and even finance, encouragement and sanctuary for the practitioners of world-wide terrorism.

The process of absorbing this wealth has been neither smooth nor even, in some cases, benign. Whether Iran was already heading for revolution when the price of oil rose in 1973 and 1974 is for historians to decide. But the link between the two events is obvious. The Shah believed he had acquired the means to transform the social and economic structure of Iran in one generation. When at length, in 1976, he recognised his miscalculation, it was too late to retrieve the situation.

The Arab producers, and especially the Gulf States, have handled their affairs with more prudence. For one thing they seem to have calculated far more accurately than the Shah the capacity of their people to absorb economic and social advance. For another they have had to rely to a great extent on immigrant labour, largely from the surrounding area, to meet the immense demands of their construction programmes. In conditions of rapid change immigrant labour, which has so much more to lose, is easier to manage. Apart from this, the home countries of the immigrants have benefited from their remittances and from direct government-to-government aid. Egypt and Jordan in particular have been helped in this way.

The longer-term implications for the members of the OPEC of their acquisition of economic and financial power will vary from country to country. Because of their large populations and greater natural diversity of resources, Indonesia and Nigeria may well rise through the ranks of the new industrialising countries to wield significant regional power and influence by the end of this decade. The course the Gulf States follow may well differ. Some of them keep a large part of their revenues within the industrialised world as deposits or investments and thus have an important stake in the continuing economic health of those countries. Saudi Arabia – in so many ways the key element in this situation – has committed itself to development policies which entail a growing degree of international interdependence. This has been reflected in the gradual evaporation of the Saudis' reluctance to give a political lead to the forces of moderation in the Arab world and to improve the level of cooperation amongst the Gulf States.

The drop in the demand for oil over the past few years has had a profound effect on exports from OPEC countries, and consequently on their revenues. These were further diminished as the price cut agreed in 1983 took effect. Over the past three years OPEC's revenues have fallen by 40% and there may be a further slight drop this year. This has obliged the members of the OPEC to rein in their economies and to reduce their imports. Last year Venezuela reduced its imports from the larger industrialised countries by 52%, Nigeria by 40%, Indonesia by 21%. The Gulf producers on the other hand scarcely reduced their imports in 1983, but they are expected to make a cut this year. Saudi Arabia bore the brunt of the drop in revenue as its exports plunged, but its foreign assets still stand at $150bn. Kuwait earns almost as much from the interest on its foreign assets as from oil exports. Iraq is being sustained by Saudi subventions and trade credits from Western Europe. And Iran subsists on the immense foreign exchange reserves it built up in 1982 and 1983.

*   *   *

We may now have come close enough to the heart of the matter to draw certain conclusions. I suggest the following.

First, the international community has learned a great deal, in the painful way man seems to prefer, about the dangers of mishandling an issue as sensitive to the world economy as energy. Interference with the supply, or arbitrary manipulation of the price can cause havoc across the world.

Secondly, the producers, having faced the prospect of the collapse of their cartel, have had the courage to make the painful adjustments to their policies needed to maintain their cohesion and have coped successfully with the sudden and severe loss of revenue.

Thirdly, the western industrialised nations have been pursuing the long-term policies which alone will reduce their dependence on imported oil. However, these policies will become more difficult for consumers to sustain if the price of oil continues to soften. Meanwhile, the communist bloc continues to have little if any impact on the oil equation.

Fourthly, many developing countries, unless they can be helped to acquire alternative sources of energy and are relieved of the burden of their indebtedness, will continue to be severely disadvantaged economically for another decade or more.

* * *

The demand for oil is likely to remain volatile for as far ahead as one can see. There are too many imponderables. What level of economic growth will the industrialised west eventually settle for? How soon will the new industrialising countries become a significant determinant of demand? Will alternative sources of energy continue to be worth developing? Will the drive towards the more efficient use of energy be sustained? Where will individual countries strike the balance between economic and environmental considerations in the production and use of energy?

Reciting these questions recalls the basic facts I placed on the record at the beginning: oil is not the same thing as energy, nor does it mean only the Middle East producers. We in the West will be in trouble if we ignore these facts. The development of the new oil provinces should be encouraged. The move away from oil should be sustained. But even so, Middle East oil, and especially Gulf oil, will continue to be of prime importance for the foreseeable future. Some 60% of the free world's known reserves are in the Middle East and one-sixth of the free world's supply flows through the Straits of Hormuz. As oilfields elsewhere pass their peak production, the importance of the Gulf will increase.

The stability of the region is therefore of major importance. It is worth remembering that all the states of the Gulf, from Kuwait southwards, are ruled by the same families as were in power when oil began to be exploited. They clearly possess special skills and wisdom. But they are right to be vigilant. Regional rivalries, militant Islam, internal dissension stimulated by the Soviet Union all pose a threat. Yet there is one development more than any other which could reinforce the authority of the moderate regimes: and that is a fair settlement of the Arab-Israel problem.

A final word. The appropriate mood for today? Calm, alert, but not complacent.

CHAPTER SIX: SIGNPOSTS TO THE GLOBAL VILLAGE

The Missing Link, *the Report of the Independent Commission for World Wide Telecommunications Development which I chaired, was published in 1985. This focused attention on the immense information gap between industrialised and developing countries. The Commission's analysis and prescription for addressing this global problem are still seen as relevant today.*

I

BRIDGING THE MISSING LINK

AFRICA TELECOM 86, NAIROBI, KENYA – SEPTEMBER 1986

The claim is frequently heard these days that the world stands on the threshold of the information society. This assertion is based on the remarkable pace at which micro-technology has been developing over the past decade or so, and in particular on the junction of the technologies of communications and the computer. Great volumes of information can be processed and transmitted across the world accurately and instantaneously. What is more, ways in which this astounding facility can be applied multiply daily. In the so-called advanced societies the impact of these developments is felt not only in industry, public administration and the service sector, but also in the life of the community and even the family.

Many people in the industrialised world are inclined to take these developments for granted. But in the minds of others anxieties have been aroused. Manufacturers of micro-electronic equipment are concerned about the future market for their products. Social scientists and some of the more far-sighted political figures recall how the agrarian revolution gave man the capacity to feed himself and how the industrial revolution expanded his physical capabilities, but in each case the revolution created as many problems as it solved. They wonder today how society will accommodate to the expansion of man's intellectual capacity which the micro-electronic revolution is making possible. Human history is marked by a continuous conflict between scientific and technological ingenuity and the demands of the spirit – between the inexorable acquisition of knowledge and the preservation of values. So those in the industrialised world who are anxious today about the implications of advances in micro-technology face an age-old problem in a new guise.

These preoccupations must seem supremely irrelevant to those, especially in the least developed countries, who grapple with problems of poverty, disease, hunger and ignorance and who have no prospect, except in the longer term, of enjoying the fruits of the information society. Many of these countries, as we know only too well, do not possess a telecommunications system capable of offering even a rudimentary service. We also know that the gap between the two ends of the chain is growing wider. The need to set in place the missing link becomes daily more urgent.

For this and other reasons, the organisers of this Forum are to be congratulated on their choice of theme. They have courageously assumed that the existence of the telecommunications gap between industrialised and developing countries is widely acknowledged. And so they have rightly sought to focus attention on how to bridge it.

There is no call today to rehearse the various recommendations in the Report of the Independent Commission for World Wide Telecommunications Development. At Arusha in May 1985 these were examined in detail and, in its concluding Declaration, the Conference 'endorsed the broad thrust of the Commission's conclusions and recommendations', as did the Administrative Council of the International Telecommunication Union when it met in July 1985. In subsequent conferences and seminars as far afield as Japan and the Caribbean, the Commission's Report has been subjected to critical scrutiny. Even as we meet here in Nairobi, the International Institute of Communications at its annual conference at Edinburgh is discussing the problem of telecommunications and development.

If the existence of the telecommunications gap is acknowledged and the Commission's proposals for bridging it have been broadly endorsed, that is good news. It is also gratifying that developing countries such as China and India, as well as others smaller and less populous, have identified the telecommunications sector as one deserving higher priority. The bad news is that this enlightened attitude is not yet widely spread throughout the developing world. There is one commanding reason for this: in too many countries the key role telecommunications can play in economic and social development and in enhancing the quality of life is not sufficiently appreciated at the highest political level. This is the missing link we have to bridge.

Easier said than done? Perhaps; but not impossible.

Let us begin with two contrasting scenarios. First of all, let us assume that the international community as a whole sees merit in the idea of a joint effort by governments, international agencies, operators of telecommunications systems, manufacturers of equipment and finance houses aimed at bringing all mankind within easy reach of a telephone by the early part of next century. This combined operation would be carried out in stages. It would entail a higher priority and the allocation of more funds – both public and private – for investment in the telecommunications sector; it would require that existing networks be made more effective and expanded; and it would call for more effective international cooperation in this field.

In due time a joint effort on these lines would transform the telecommunications map of the world. In the early stages one might expect the systems in urban areas of developing countries to be upgraded to the point where they generated suffi-cient revenue not only to pay for the investment but also to fund the extension of the network into rural and other remote areas. An effective and comprehensive world telecommunications system which meets demand would consist in the first instance of a variety of systems, exploiting the versatility of all the technologies available – analogue, digital, open wire, co-axial cable, optical fibre, satellite, micro-wave, cellular, and so on – and such others as may be devised and produced in the future. There is no technological reason why such a world wide system should not be in place by the early years of the 21st century.

The present network is already the largest machine in the world and the service it provides is of immeasurable value. A digital global network, transmitting voice, text, graphics, images or video would constitute a hyper-efficient world wide nervous system. Surely there is something here to touch the imagination. And it is not too soon to consider the consequences of progress towards such a world network.

Many developing countries already have extensive networks operating at reason-able levels of efficiency. More effective management and supervision, better train-ing and the allocation of more resources to this sector would enable these countries before long to develop their full potential. New technological skills would be generated, local manufacture of equipment would be encouraged and telecommunications would take its place as an industry in its own right and as another engine of growth contributing an increasing share to the gross domestic product.

In other countries — especially the poorest — a greater effort, funded at least in part by external concessionary finance, would be required if over time a service adequate to meet basic needs were to be established.

The process of improving and expanding telecommunications systems world wide would serve the common interest of industrialised and developing countries alike. It is evident from a number of encouraging events over the past year or two that many operators, suppliers of equipment and finance houses in the industrialised world regard those developing countries which give higher priority to telecommunications and which create conditions which attract foreign enterprise and investment as an important market of the future. They are right to do so and others should follow their example.

The benefits available to developing countries do not begin and end with the contribution telecommunications make to economic and social advance. An effective telecommunications system can be a channel for education and this in turn can enrich national culture and strengthen the social fabric. The linking of the more remote areas with urban centres reinforces the infrastructure, encourages self-reliance and contributes to national cohesion.

These are only the immediate local benefits. Suppose that instantaneous communication were possible between the great commercial centres — New York, Tokyo, London — and any small provincial town, or even a remote village, in Paraguay, Mali or China. The world would be a single market place — its components interdependent in commerce, manufacture, agriculture, banking and numerous other services. Telecommunications would be the new trade routes. New commercial partnerships would be formed. Demand for new goods and services would be stimulated. Standards would have to be set with the world market in view. Design would have to take account of a wider range of physical conditions, usage, aptitude, taste and tradition. Language barriers would have to be overcome. As this happened, ideas about social conditions, wages and the rights of the individual would be freely exchanged and hallowed notions about systems of governance would be eroded.

*   *   *

The trouble with this scenario is that it is too good to be true. For one thing, not all governments would welcome the free flow of information across frontiers and, on ideological or political grounds, they would doubtless prefer to forgo the economic and commercial advantages of full participation in a growing world network. Then again, within developing countries the benefits would not be absolute. High technology systems which increase productivity can aggravate problems of unemployment. The demand for new skills to operate, maintain and exploit an expanded and up-graded system could strain a country's educational resources. It is also hard to believe that all developing countries would be willing or able to increase investment in this sector. Economic and social objectives differ from country to country. High technology is expensive and many countries' finances are already under strain. In practice therefore the world network is likely to develop in an uneven, untidy fashion and this will inevitably increase disparities in economic growth. While the New Industrialising Countries, the oil producers in the Gulf and prosperous economies in South and South-East Asia and parts of Latin America continue their advance — aided by a more efficient and comprehensive telecommunications network — their growth will inevitably outstrip that of the less developed, who will still be struggling to make their existing systems operate at a minimum level of efficiency.

Such a state of affairs would be no more acceptable than the present. It is in the interest of no one that gaps in economic and social wellbeing should widen, or new disparities arise. What then is to be done?

I realise as I address you today that, if I am the preacher, you are the converted. You do not have to be persuaded that telecommunications have a key role to play in the development process, nor that more attention must be paid to this sector than in the past. Can the same be said of all of those who occupy the highest political positions or control the purse strings? In posing the question I intend no disrespect. But, as night follows day, the gap we all deplore will be bridged only when those at the highest political level appreciate the benefits of an effective network and—more impressive perhaps — the dangers to their nation of neglecting this sector while others forge ahead.

How can this simple message be delivered to the right address? May I offer a suggestion? The next Plenipotentiary Conference of the International Telecommunication Union will be held in Nice in 1989. It is not too soon for ministries and agencies in the member states to begin preparing for this occasion. The Report of the Independent Commission will be on the agenda. Representatives of industrialised countries will point to the role they played in the successful launch of the Centre for Telecommunications Development. They will have determined the measure of their future support for its activities. They will come prepared to face questions about their longer term contribution to the expansion of telecommunications world wide.

For their part, those who represent developing countries at Nice may well be asked to report to the Conference on their Government's response to the Commission's recommendations. In anticipation of this occasion they might think it prudent to warn their ministerial colleagues now that they are likely to be faced with the following questions.

First, have we accepted it as a principle that none of our development programmes will be balanced, properly integrated or effective unless we include in them a full and appropriate role for telecommunications?

Second, in reviewing our development plans have we ensured that adequate priority is being given to investment in telecommunications?

Third, have we taken steps to make our network more effective and progressively self-reliant and to ensure that new technologies are exploited to our benefit?

Fourth, are we meeting our training needs?

Fifth, have we explored with our neighbours the possibilities for regional co-operation in research and development, local manufacture and procurement?

Sixth, have we established a programme for extending our network into the more remote areas?

Finally, are we taking advantage of the pre-investment services provided by the Centre for Telecommunications Development?

If the Plenipotentiary Conference at Nice hears affirmative replies to these seven questions, then a major step will have been taken towards bridging the missing link. And the credit will belong to those in the highest political positions who authorised the right answers.

II

COMMUNICATIONS: A PATH TO ONE WORLD

CHELSEA CHURCHES UNITED NATIONS LECTURE; OCTOBER 1988

The subject of this lecture combines the elemental and the cosmic. Communication is an endless source of wonder. Smoke signals, whether from a hill-top in Wyoming or a chimney in the Vatican, the pealing of bells, the beating of drums, the lighting of beacons – all quicken the pulse. I recall my excitement when, as a young army officer in Waziristan, I read a message sent by a heliograph seventy miles away.

Sometimes the means of communication assumes special importance. Robert Browning's sense of romance so overcame him that he omitted to reveal what good news it was they took from Ghent to Aix. The truth is that communication and information are linked – as Dr Crippen discovered to his dismay when he was met on arrival in Canada by a detective from Scotland Yard. Facts have a value even when in the possession of only one person. When they are shared limitless possibilities are opened up. Facts exchanged become commerce – in its original sense. Facts accumulated become knowledge, power, opportunity.

Communication has never been an end in itself. Pheidippides did not run the 140 miles of rough road, goat track and scree-covered slopes from Athens to Sparta because he needed the exercise. He ran in order to convey information. The frontiers of ancient Greece were closely set and the runner was an efficient and reliable means of communication. The Roman Empire survived for so long largely because of its network of roads. The printing presses of Gutenberg and Caxton allowed ideas to spread. Faraday's discovery of magnetic induction, subsequently adorned by Hertz, Marconi, Bell and others, opened the way to the electronic communications of today.

Throughout history the pace of advance has quickened. Time-scales have shrunk: ten generations for the industrial revolution and the first agrarian revolution – the second has already begun; one generation for the information revolution. Twenty years ago the pocket calculators and video cassette recorders we take for granted today were curiosities.

The information revolution to which we are indebted for these and more important blessings has been driven by two forces — technological advance and the dispersal of economic power. The satellite, micro-electronics and the merging of the technologies of the computer, communications and broadcasting have transformed the original telegraph and telephone systems with which we were all familiar. We now have within our range the comprehensive world telecommunications network envisaged by Marshall McLuhan who, in the late 1960s, conceived the notion of the 'Global Village'.

We do not need a filing clerk to remind us that information can be generated, stored, retrieved, processed and transmitted. The technological advances of the past generation have revolutionised the way in which these functions are performed. This revolution is still in progress. The micro-chip, which lies at the heart of the revolution, will continue to be reduced in size every year at least until the end of this century. TAT-1, the name given to the trans-Atlantic cable laid in 1956, carried 36 circuits for the transmission of messages; TAT-9, which embodies the technology of optics — that is to say, glass fibre — and is expected to be in operation in 1991, will carry 68,000. The technology of satellites advances at similar speed. Early Bird, the first satellite launched in 1964 by the international organisation known as INTELSAT, carried 240 voice channels and one television service; INTELSAT VI, which should be in orbit next year, will accommodate more than 80,000 voice channels and two television services. Consumer equipment too is being transformed. Mobile telephones are now commonplace and are replacing multi-coloured umbrellas as the yuppies' trade mark. The original facsimile machine, which sends texts by telephone, transmitted a sheet of A4 in three minutes. The latest model transmits a sheet in three seconds.

By the application of computer technology to communications, the essential elements in the telephone system, namely switching and transmission equipment, have been converted from the long-serving analogue technique to digital. In the analogue system fluctuations in the voltage of a transmitted signal represent changes in volume of sound. Apart from their superior quality, digital systems (which transmit at a constant level messages composed of the combinations of zeros and ones which make binary mathematics a mystery to the older generation) are able to carry a wide range of so-called value-added services such as data and video. By the end of this decade most industrialised countries will have begun to introduce the integrated digital network — ISDN — which is destined to become the world telecommunications system of the future.

These various technological developments contain interesting paradoxes.

Communications systems today are more complex, but the customer demands — and gets — greater simplicity at the point of use; the push-button instead of the dial on the telephone, for instance. Micro-electronic capabilities have increased — greater volumes of information can be stored, information can be transmitted at higher speeds; and yet the components are smaller. Then again, the sensible pursuit of common international standards, which is the only way of ensuring that one piece of equipment is compatible with another, marches side by side with demands for equipment designed to meet special needs, such as telephone exchanges which can withstand the dust-storms of Arabia as well as the heat and humidity of West Africa.

The telecommunications network we have today is the largest machine in the world. And it is the nearest thing to a global nervous system.

The technological advances I have described have coincided with changes in the structure of industry and in the business market. As the older industrial processes on which we used to rely for the generation of wealth have been wound down, corporations have made organisational changes to match changes in the market. Costs of certain basic elements of industrial activity such as training, research and development and marketing have risen. At the same time access to international sources of finance for investment as well as human capital has become easier. A British company, for example, might raise funds through an American investment bank to finance manufacture in South East Asia of a product to be marketed throughout the developing world. This easy access to finance and labour has persuaded firms to offer services as well as goods, virtually without distinction, and to develop strategies for production and marketing on an international, rather than a local or even a national, basis.

The impact on commerce has been similar. Purely national markets are too small to support many businesses today. It is not only the commercial giants such as British Petroleum or Unilever that are multinationals today. As business becomes increasingly globalised, access to an efficient telecommunications system becomes essential, rather than merely important or desirable. To satisfy their customers and to remain competitive, firms must link the computer systems which have transformed the way business is done and reach out to their customers, their suppliers and work units in whatever country they may be. And to do this they must use telecommunications nationally and internationally.

*   *   *

These technological, industrial and commercial changes have had significant effects. For those who operate the telecommunications systems – whether they are state-owned administrations called PTTs (Posts, Telegraph and Telephone) or have been privatised, like British Telecom here in the United Kingdom or BT's Japanese equivalent, or de-regulated as in the United States – for these operators and for the manufacturers of equipment, telecommunications and information technology have become big business. In 1986 the world spent US$100 billion on telecommunications equipment – a doubling of expenditure over five years. In the United States, which dominates the world market, telecommunications ranks fifth in the business league after energy, transportation, merchandising and real estate. In the United Kingdom one million people provide information equipment and services – three times the agricultural work force. For many years telecommunications has been recognised as an engine of growth; today it has become a major industry in its own right.

What about those who use telecommunications systems? The shift from small-scale trade and the processing of materials to activity connected with the flow of information has made commerce, industry and the finance houses major players in the information economy. Here I have in mind not only the communications component of production, but also the information content of products themselves. These include design, market research, financing, advertising, transfer of technology, training and collaborative ventures between corporations over research and development.

These changes in the strategies and operating procedures of industrial and commercial enterprises have had two important effects on the pattern of telecommunications services. First, public service use of the network – that is the normal person-to-person telephone call we all make – has declined, while the use of other services of relevance to industry and commerce, such as the transmission of data, video and other so-called value added services, has increased. Secondly, the demand for international services has risen sharply.

A more spectacular consequence of the information revolution has been the proliferation of privately-owned telecommunications networks. These are independent of the PTTs and the international carriers. Some of these networks have been put in place by privately-owned telecommunications operators. The American Telephone and Telegraph Company (AT&T), one of the Titans of the information technology world, is constructing what it calls the 'World Intelligent Network' in collaboration with domestic monopoly operators in other countries. Cable and Wireless are creating a 'Global Digital Highway' in cooperation with partners who have no international facilities of their own. Both AT&T and Cable and Wireless are confident that their private networks will prove attractive to business customers.

There are other privately-owned systems. These are called Inter-Organisation Networks. For many companies in the service sector of the economy the number of messages sent and received is so great that processing by computer is essential. American Express authorises half a million transactions each day through its own network. International Business Machines (IBM), the other Titan of information technology, General Motors and Reuters are other examples of corporations who operate extensive global communications systems. Japanese conglomerates have created similar networks; some of these allow 100,000 messages to pass daily between parent company and subsidiary. Until the mid-1970s few would have regarded banking and air transport as connected with telecommunications. But these sectors have been compelled to set up dedicated networks outside the scope of the national monopoly systems. The best known of these specialist networks are the International Society for Aeronautical Telecommunications (SITA) and the Society for Worldwide Interbank Financial Telecommunications – a rather clumsy title which, however, produces the elegant acronym SWIFT.

There was a time when those engaged in trade regarded telecommunications as a useful adjunct to the postal service. Today the increased use of telecommunications, amounting in many cases to virtual dependence, has made the relationship between trade and telecommunications a key international trade issue.

This new factor has economic as well as political implications. For one thing, governments have to accept the link between the development of their telecommunications network, economic dynamism and international trade. That the network has a significance beyond inter-person communication has to be recognised. Priority has to be given to the development of the network in such a way as will enable all economic opportunities to be exploited. It will also be necessary to devise new ground rules encompassing the use of existing and newly developed networks. At this point we can discern some of the challenges which the international community will have to face if global communications are to develop in an orderly fashion.

The origins of the global network we have today lie in the enterprise and imagination of those who, over many decades, developed local, national, regional and then international telegraph and telephone systems. A remarkable spirit of co-operation was demonstrated by all those responsible. For the most part circuits and switches were compatible one with another and basic standards and specifications transcended national boundaries. Pockets of resistance remain, however, where attachment to national methodology and equipment stands in the way of acceptance of general principles. In Western Europe there are three standards for cellular car telephones. In some countries old and new equipment cannot be connected.

Four years ago the European Community, realising that the time had come to put its house in order, launched a common telecommunications policy. The main aims of this policy were to create a common market in telecommunications services and equipment as part of the programme for a single internal market in 1992 and to establish common specifications. In the various initiatives it has taken since this approach was endorsed, the European Commission has had in mind the need to secure the Community's competitive position, *vis-a-vis* the United States and Japan in particular, as regards both services and equipment.

The issue of standardisation is of course of global significance and an opportunity to take a major step forward is about to arise. A World Administrative Telegraph and Telephone Conference is to be held in Melbourne in December to work out a new set of International Telecommunication Regulations to take account of the changing environment. The International Telecommunication Union, the oldest agency of the United Nations, exists to promote interconnection. The intergovernmental agreement at Dresden in 1850, the International Telegraph Convention which established the Union in 1865, and the Preliminary Conference on Wireless Telegraphy in Berlin in 1903 all had this aim. The main concern of delegates at Melbourne will be whether recent technological advances call in question the principle of universality of international telecommunication services on which the regulatory functions of the Union have been based hitherto. Should the new Regulations be restricted to the basic services – telephone and telex – or should they apply also to all other international services – the transmission of data, new text services, specialised services, and so on?

A second United Nations agency is concerning itself with these matters. The future international framework for telecommunications will be discussed in the current Uruguay Round of Multilateral Trade Negotiations being conducted by the GATT – the General Agreement on Tariffs and Trade. The issue here will be what sort of rules should govern trade in telecommunications equipment and services. There must be a risk that the GATT and the International Telecommunication Union could find themselves in dispute over the dividing line between trade and communications issues.

*   *   *

It might be opportune to reflect for a moment on the implications – and the practical effects – of the advances in micro-technology. Great volumes of information can be processed and transmitted across the world accurately and instantaneously. Ways in which this facility can be applied multiply daily. Industrial and commercial strategies and methods of operating have been transformed. The market place is now the globe. Interdependence has ceded place to inter-connection. Events can be influenced by decisions taken almost by instinct by industrial, commercial or financial entrepreneurs in almost any part of the world. In the wake of the Stock Market crash in October of last year, Sir Eric Sharp, the Chairman of Cable and Wireless, said 'The power of Presidents and Prime Ministers, and even Finance Ministers, is confined within national boundaries while the financial world is fast becoming an integrated global network inter-communicating across national boundaries. If Presidents and Prime Ministers are to influence the financial world of today and tomorrow they will have to adopt global policies.' Thus Sir Eric Sharp. Where, we may ask, does this leave arguments about national sovereignty?

It is not only the political consequences that deserve our attention. It is as well to recall how the agrarian revolution gave man the capacity to feed himself and how the industrial revolution expanded his physical capabilities; but in each case the revolution created as many problems as it solved. How will society accommodate to the expansion of man's intellectual capacity which the micro-electronic revolution is making possible?

*   *   *

Such concerns do not preoccupy those, especially in the least developed countries, who grapple with problems of poverty, disease, hunger and ignorance and who have no prospect, except in the longer term, of enjoying the fruits of the so-called 'information society'. Many developing countries do not possess a telecommunications system capable of offering even a rudimentary service. In large tracts of territory there is no telephone service at all.

The uneven distribution of telecommunications across the world represents one of today's major challenges. The statistics are stark. Three quarters of the 670 million telephones in the world are in eight industrialised countries. Developing countries, which contain 70% of the world's population, own only 7% of the world's telephones. There are more telephones in Tokyo than in the entire

African continent. In Los Angeles there are 92 telephones per 100 people. In Brussels there are 70. The figure for Ethiopia is 0.3. The situation is worse than these facts suggest. Only some 30% of the inhabitants of developing countries live in towns and cities where they have access to a reasonable telecommunications system. In India, for example, 75% of the population live in half a million villages. So far the telephone service has reached only 35,000 villages.

The dangers in this widening gap between industrialised and developing countries, which is acceptable on grounds neither of common interest nor of common humanity, were recognised by the General Assembly of the United Nations in 1981. The following year the Plenipotentiary Conference of the International Telecommunication Union decided to charge an Independent Commission with the task of proposing ways of stimulating the expansion of telecommunications in the developing world.

The Commission began its work in the autumn of 1983. There were seventeen of us, representing different backgrounds and disciplines. Five of us came from industrialised countries, two from Eastern Europe and ten from different regions of the developing world – Latin America, Africa, the Middle East and South and South East Asia.

We began by noting the key role telecommunications play in public administration, commerce and other economic activity, in emergency and health services, and in enhancing the quality of life. We concluded that no development programme was likely to be effective unless it included an appropriate role for telecommunications; investment in telecommunications should therefore be seen as an integral part of economic advance. Next, we examined the shortcomings which had led to the poor state of communications in many developing countries: lack of appreciation of the key role telecommunications play in the life of a nation; competing priorities; lack of trained personnel and especially those with managerial skills; poor standards of maintenance; lack of resources, particularly foreign currency; inhospitable geographical and climatic conditions.

The most encouraging aspect of the Commission's debates was our common perception of the interest which industrialised and developing countries share in an expanded and more efficient world network. The actual process of expanding and improving existing systems in developing countries will create a major market for manufacturers of equipment and operators. A more comprehensive world system would increase international telephone traffic. Trade and other contacts would benefit.

The Commission saw no single remedy – for the good reason that there is none. A range of actions at different levels would be needed. The objective we set of bringing the whole of mankind within easy reach of a telephone by the early part of next century would be achieved only if all those who carried responsibility in this field were to join in a common effort which would have four main aims: to ensure higher priority for investment in telecomunications; to improve and expand existing networks through better planning, management, training, pro-curement of equipment and maintenance; to take account of the foreign exchange problems of developing countries; and to make international co-operation more effective. It seemed to members of the Commission that the chances of progress in this field were enhanced by the distinguishing character-istic of telecommunications, namely that they are inherently profitable. As soon as a telephone is installed in a remote village and the inhabitants begin to use it, the telephone administration begins to earn money.

The Commission's Report was unanimous. It was published in January 1985 and its broad thrust was endorsed later that year by the International Telecommunication Union. It has been discussed at numerous conferences in various parts of the world. There is progress to report. More developing countries now recognise the critical importance to their development plans of investment in telecommunications and of the risks of neglecting this sector. China and India are giving telecommunications privileged treatment. In Latin America, Africa and South East Asia programmes have been drawn up for taking telecommuni-cations to the more remote areas. Training opportunities have increased. And mutually beneficial deals are being struck for the provision of investment finance and the transfer of technology.

Yet much remains to be done to convince governments, operators, equipment manufacturers and finance houses in industrialised and developing countries alike of the interest they share in creating an effective global communications system. There are no grounds for denying developing countries the means to accelerate their economic and social progress and raise their quality of life. There are no grounds for denying ourselves the benefits of enhanced exchanges of all kinds with developing countries.

The development of the global communications system is changing the balance of economic activity, the content of commercial exchanges and the structure of organisations. More generally it is breaking down barriers between peoples and philosophies at a pace neither governments nor international agencies can hope to control. An eminent American engineer, Professor Simon Ramo, has pointed out that political, economic and social issues intersect, and issues of technological advance are at the centre of every intersection. Sometimes these cause problems. Sometimes they offer solutions. Now and then they offer world society the chance to rise to new, higher levels of productivity, satisfaction and happiness.

Professor Ramo is right. There is no technological hindrance to the creation of an effective and comprehensive global network. Nothing more needs to be invented. Nor is lack of finance a constraint, except in the poorest developing countries. The administrative and logistical problems are all soluble. The main obstacle is political. This stems from failure to recognise the opportunity our inventiveness and ingenuity have presented for narrowing the gap between industrialised and developing countries and taking a giant stride down the path towards one world. The children of the twenty-first century will judge us harshly if we fail to seize this opportunity.

III

THE PRIZE TO BE WON

ASIA-PACIFIC TELECOMMUNITY, BANGKOK – 4 AUGUST 1994

In August 1941, on a warship off Newfoundland, Franklin D Roosevelt and Winston Churchill drew up what Churchill later described as a 'rough and ready war-time statement' of the common aims of the United States and Great Britain. Since at that time the United States was not at war, the eight principles enshrined in what came to be known as the Atlantic Charter were not expressed in specific terms, nor was reference made to tension in the Pacific region. The significance of these principles lay in the fact that they inspired a series of pronouncements which found their final shape four years later in the Charter of the United Nations.

One of the principles in the Atlantic Charter – the sixth – looked forward to a peace 'which will afford assurance that all men in all lands may live out their lives in freedom from fear and want'. Four months after this encounter off Newfoundland, the United States was at war. In a message which he sent soon afterwards to the United States Congress, President Roosevelt added a postscript to this principle. He declared that the post-war world would be founded on four freedoms: freedom of speech and expression, freedom of religion, freedom from want and freedom from fear. Few would disagree that these Four Freedoms still constitute the essential basis for a stable world order.

Moments of crisis in human history tend to produce personalities who have the talent to shape our destiny. Was it indeed a mere coincidence that Roosevelt should have been President of the United States and Churchill Prime Minister of Britain at that moment of extreme danger over fifty years ago? Was it merely a stroke of good fortune for the long-suffering people of South Africa that Nelson Mandela and FW de Klerk were on hand to step forward and steer the Republic from disaster to the calmer waters of Good Hope? Whatever the reason, we should all be grateful.

It is an equally reassuring circumstance that major advances often follow in the wake of some cataclysm. Experience this century has shown that war is an effective spur to technological innovation. In 1914, at the outset of the First World War the British

Army had a total of 47 motor trucks at its disposal; three years later this same Army required the delivery of 350 new vehicles every week. But this, of course, is as nothing compared with the advances which have been made since the Second War. Within two generations the world and man's place in it have been transformed. The speed and scale of the change have no precedent in human history.

Today we take for granted overnight travel by air from east Asia to the cities of western Europe or crossing the Atlantic at twice the speed of sound. Personal mobility, now regarded virtually as a right, has been conferred through widespread ownership of motor vehicles, or at least bicycles.

Just as remarkable have been the advances in medical science. New drugs have virtually eliminated such diseases as smallpox and poliomyelitis. The transplanting of organs and replacement of joints have alleviated suffering and prolonged life.

Better methods of industrial production have reduced costs and brought the price of desirable consumer goods for the first time within the reach of the lower paid. Likewise, improvements in agricultural science and techniques have made possible dramatic increases in food production. Energy is generated and used far more effectively.

The extent and depth of the changes which have occurred in the political field could not have been imagined by the two wartime leaders when they promulgated the Atlantic Charter. Fifty-one sovereign states were represented when the General Assembly of the United Nations met for the first time in New York in 1946. Today membership of the Assembly is approaching 180.

*   *   *

It would be a matter for great satisfaction if all these developments were seen as successes for humanity. But we know that to make such a claim would not only be unjustified but would also contradict the lessons of history. Our own personal experience has shown that, more often than not, each step forward seems to be followed by one step — and sometimes two steps — backwards.

Examples of the perversity of the ways of the world abound. Economic development has raised living standards, but in the process our environment has been jeopardised. The skill of the medical and pharmaceutical professions has reduced morbidity but has also, inadvertently, added to the burden imposed on many societies by ageing populations. The freedom conferred by more convenient methods of contraception has raised questions about the validity of traditional relationships.

The same unwritten law seems to apply on a global scale. The process of decolonisation begun in the late 1940s was a fulfilment of one of the obligations assumed in the Atlantic Charter. Those immediate post-war years were characterised by a remarkable generosity of spirit on the part of the United States. Not only was help on a massive scale provided for the reconstruction of the ravaged continent of Europe, but the United States also took the lead, soon followed by the United Kingdom, in devising programmes of aid to developing countries. In Washington and London, at least, it was recognised that political emancipation did not necessarily bring economic freedom, let alone prosperity.

The intention was honourable, but in practice the aid programmes seldom achieved the results desired or expected. At times these were ill conceived – the cathedrals in the desert of which one French Minister for Development complained – do exist. At other times major projects appeared to serve the interests of the donors as much as, if not more than, the recipients. In some cases aid funds were misapplied. More generally the amounts disbursed fell far short of the need and across the world wide gaps remain to be bridged.

It was only natural that when the world emerged in 1945 from the great mid-century cataclysm, hopes should have risen. The issues then were clear. Virtue had triumphed over evil. The moment seemed ripe for a new beginning. Today we recognise that expectations then were too high. As we approach the end of the century and note that in many parts of the world the mood is one of pessimism, scepticism and apprehension, should we not ask ourselves whether current anxieties about the future are indeed justified? Fifty years on are we making the opposite mistake – are we setting our expectations too low?

We cannot, however, ignore the evidence; and many aspects of our contemporary situation understandably command attention. The end of the cold war, which had occupied centre stage in international politics for so long, has removed the threat of global conflict, but it has created areas of conflict and instability in central and eastern Europe. The European Union, poised to admit new members, is undergoing a crisis of self-confidence. The political and economic dominance of the United States has been gradually eroded as the significance of such countries as Japan, China, Korea, Indonesia, Mexico and Brazil has grown. The African continent inspires both despair and hope. The transition to majority rule in the

Republic of South Africa was accomplished in peace and with dignity that won the admiration of the world. Democracy has at length arrived in Malawi. But what are we to think of events in Liberia, the Sudan and Rwanda?

Meanwhile, economic recession and high rates of unemployment in industrialised countries have produced unwelcome social effects. In some societies immigration has provoked racial tensions. Crime and the drug traffic aggravate the problem. Here and there Semtex and the Kalashnikov play a sinister role, sometimes in the name of causes so obscure as to be barely intelligible.

Within societies the higher levels of prosperity which have reduced hardship have not proved unmixed blessings. The abundance of consumer goods has raised expectations. When these cannot be fulfilled, frustration and dissatisfaction ensue. Steady internationalisation has greatly enhanced the influence of the media, especially in the political and social fields, and the implications may not yet be fully appreciated. Has this, for example, contributed to the low esteem in which political leaders in many parts of the world are now held? Has it stimulated doubts about the validity of political systems, or undermined traditional ideas about the role of the family in society. And, perhaps more insidiously, have the imaginative powers of that generation of children who have been exposed to explicit depiction of violence and sex in what they read, see on television and video and in the cinema been impaired?

On the basis of this analysis one might modestly conclude that new phenomena are always disturbing and, when they manifest themselves in abundance, the disturbance, at least on the surface, is all the greater. It has not been easy, therefore, for the ordinary citizen to detect the underlying trends.

The world at the end of the twentieth century is in transition not simply because of the dismantling of the former empires and the end of the cold war. The principal causes are the changes which are taking place in the structure and nature of the world economy and in the role and power of governments.

Ease of travel, shifts in social attitudes, increased cultural interchange and, above all, the revolution in the way information of all kinds is conveyed and stored have drastically reduced distances and have facilitated the creation of an inter-connected global economy. The financial sector, the great international trading enterprises and the operators of telecommunications networks and manufacturers of telecommunication equipment have all played pioneering roles. To their credit, governments have not stood in the way of these developments and have instead chosen the path of lowering or removing obstacles in the way of closer economic and commercial ties through multilateral agreements. Imperfect though the results of the successive rounds of negotiations under the General Agreement on Tariffs and Trade may have been, they have combined with the exploitation of technological advances to maintain the momentum towards closer integration. But governments, under pressure from their electorates, remain reluctant to accept the diminution of national sovereignty this process entails and are therefore inhibited from turning their minds to the foundations on which the international community of the next century will have to be constructed. Serious issues will have to be addressed sooner or later – and the sooner the better. Should all barriers to trade be removed? Should the concept of national sovereignty give place to new patterns of relationships between groups of nations based on a balance between common principles and respect for diversity?

* * *

This, it seems to me, is the global context in which the Asia-Pacific Telecommunity has set the agenda for this Seminar. Over the next three days you will be discussing reforms and opportunities in the telecommunications sector, the achievement of critical objectives in a competitive environment and the changing role of international and regional organisations.

In the fifteen years of the Telecommunity's existence remarkable progress has been made. In many respects this region has set the pace – and there is no reason why it should not continue to do so, since the economic activity on which the remarkable growth rates of the past decade have been based owe much to the availability of high quality and effectively managed systems for handling information as well as for telecommunication, and especially facsimile services and mobile telephony. The statistics tell their own story. While particular problems remain to be overcome, for example in Cambodia, Laos and Mongolia, the penetration of telephones in Singapore and Korea already ranks with rates achieved in the countries of the Organisation for Economic Cooperation and Development – the OECD – in the region. And it is notable that the speed at which networks are being extended has been accelerating. These success stories provide models for other countries and other regions facing the same challenges. There are important lessons to be learned, not only in this Asia-Pacific Telecommunity itself, but also further afield.

One of the more important legacies of the Thatcher years in the United Kingdom is the transformation of telecommunications. In 1981 the postal and telephone services were divided when two separate nationalised corporations – the Post

Office and British Telecom – were created. Three years later, while the American Telephone and Telegraph monolith was being dismantled in the United States, British Telecom was transferred to private ownership. The motive was not merely to raise much needed funds for the Exchequer. It was held to be essential to release British Telecom from the financial straitjacket of Treasury control over investment, which for years had done so much to stifle enterprise, and to expose the management of the organisation to the disciplines of the market. In the ten years that have passed since then, many other major operating entities in different parts of the world have been privatised. Efficient regulation, especially where competition has not been introduced, has been one reason why the experience has been beneficial. The other side of this coin is that many of those telecommunications systems which are still state monopolies have been unable even to meet existing demand for services let alone the demand for those which are likely to become available in the future.

A significant by-product of the success achieved through privatisation and the introduction of competition has been the extent to which the interest of latter-day merchant venturers has been aroused. Ten years ago the opinion was expressed in *The Missing Link* that developing countries would do well to create a climate generally conducive to inward investment including adequate assurance of creditworthiness. *The Missing Link* also stressed the essential truth that an effective telecommunications system which meets demand not only is inherently profitable but also generates wealth; as soon as a telephone is installed and comes into use, it begins to earn revenue for the operator and contributes to economic activity. These *obiter dicta* have been justified by experience during the intervening years.

The interest of the merchant venturers is important in another respect. Recession, unemployment, heavy social charges, debt and budget deficits make it difficult today for governments of most OECD countries to show the generosity of spirit that characterised the 1940s and 50s. Developing countries do well therefore to look increasingly to the private sector for investment, not only in telecommunications systems but also in related sectors. Foreign investors are alert to the opportunities, and mutually beneficial arrangements will increasingly be the pattern of the future. Joint ventures have already proved their worth in other industrial sectors and there is no reason why this success should not be repeated in the field of telecommunications. In this region there may well be opportunities to capitalise on the experience of Build-Operate-Transfer schemes in Indonesia and Thailand. In due course joint ventures may become more sophisticated, encompassing not only reciprocal investment but also joint investment in equipment, training and management in third countries.

* * *

Later this year the historic city of Kyoto will receive delegates to the Plenipotentiary Conference of the International Telecommunication Union. In capitals all over the world briefs are being prepared for the debates which will determine the role of the Union as we approach the next century. The challenges are daunting: telecommunications lie at the heart of the globalisation of economic activity and of improvements in international commerce; telecommunications facilitate the international division of labour and stimulate consumers' expectations. These challenges raise the obvious question: how can the ITU regulate a global system essential to the future prosperity of industrialised and developing countries alike, when national telecommunications systems are owned and operated by both state enterprises and private sector corporations? The answer will be as clear, or as obscure, as the approach of individual member governments.

Of more immediate concern to the Asia-Pacific Telecommunity will be the answer to another topical question: what should be the role of the ITU in promoting telecommunications in developing countries? Although good progress has been made since *The Missing Link* was published, there are still serious disparities in the distribution of telecommunications world wide. The advent of new technologies and new services could increase these disparities. As catalyst, the ITU should continue to collect and disseminate information about best practice. It should continue to encourage regional cooperation in all aspects of telecommunications development and, in particular, the acquisition of skills. It should consider practical ways of harnessing the enthusiasm of private merchant venturers, both within and outside regions, who see advantage in investment in this critical sector. It is from regions such as yours that the most beneficial initiatives will flow.

The high level of cooperation among members of the Asia-Pacific Telecommunity and the pertinence of your debates are an example to others. The topics chosen for discussion at this seminar show that success has not made you complacent. Perhaps than you might care to raise your eyes from your immediate preoccupations and consider the contribution you can make in the future.

It is common ground that the telecommunications and information technology sector is exceptional, not merely in terms of growth but also because it has been the instrument that has shifted the world economy from a condition of interdependence, through inter-connection to the edge of globalisation. The great technological advances of the past – the railroad, the steamship, the motor car, the aeroplane, splitting the atom, antibiotics have all changed life on earth. But sadly not always for the better. In the past enthusiasm for new inventions seems not to have been matched by a cautious and objective look at their potential and their implications.

A telephone within easy reach of all mankind by the early part of next century will bring obvious benefits. But, as we progress towards the era of multi-media, two considerations should give us pause. First, we should recognise that the influence that broadcasting, and especially television, can wield over mass opinion is such that robust systems of regulation will be required – systems which strike an appropriate and acceptable balance between the rights and obligations of those who own this powerful medium. Secondly, we cannot forget that our global village will include, among others, Liberia, the Sudan and Rwanda as well as the Republic of South Africa. So, although more than fifty years have passed, we should do well to take a fresh look at President Roosevelt's Four Freedoms – freedom of speech and expression, freedom of religion, freedom from fear and freedom from want. An issue of high political importance is at stake here. Should we not resolve that, as technological advance continues and the gap begins to close, the benevolent characteristics of telecommunications – its infinite power to do good – must be preserved and exploited with vigour, imagination and responsibility in order to assure the enjoyment by all mankind of these four freedoms? Perhaps one day the people of the Asia Pacific community might proclaim their commitment to this principle in their own aptly named Pacific Charter.

IV

THE NEW CHALLENGE

WORLD TELECOMMUNICATIONS DEVELOPMENT CONFERENCE
VALLETTA – MARCH 1998

It was with special pleasure that I received the Secretary-General's invitation to take part in this important conference. He suggested that my personal appreciation of the performance of the International Telecommunication Union – the ITU – in responding to *The Missing Link* and my vision of the future of telecommunications would assist the work of this conference. I will do my best to respond to that challenge.

In May 1983 the Administrative Council of the ITU charged the Independent Commission with the task of recommending ways of stimulating the expansion of telecommunications across the world. My colleagues and I interpreted the term 'telecommunications' in that mandate to mean public telephone systems because we felt that improving and expanding these would bring the greatest benefit to the greatest number of people throughout the world. The gross imbalance in the world wide distribution of telephones appalled us. That was not our only concern. We knew even then that technical innovation would provide inhabitants of the industrialised world with the benefits of the emerging information society before the end of the century.

That was more than thirteen years ago. The situation we face on the threshold of the new century presents us with equally daunting challenges. One of these is of direct concern to this Conference. Decades ago the late, great Koji Kobayashi, who was to play a distinguished role in the Independent Commission, determined to devote his talents and energies to promoting the marriage of the technologies of communications and the computer. The information society and, more recently, the INTERNET have satisfied Koji Kobayashi's ambition and, at the same time we are making a reality of Marshal McLuhan's vision of the global village.

The importance of this development cannot be exaggerated. It raises fundamental questions which affect each one of us – questions about the international division of labour, about the structure of corporations, the future of work, the nature of human society, the individual's sense of identity, systems of governance and the meaning of sovereignty in an interdependent, interconnected world. This is no secret. But it is a curious fact that, at the political level throughout the world, there has been marked reluctance to address these issues. The outstanding exception is Vice-President Al Gore, who identified himself with the concept of the Global Information Infrastructure as the foundation of the future information society when he addressed the Buenos Aires Conference in 1994.

*   *   *

It is legitimate – indeed essential – thirteen years after the Independent Commission submitted its Report, to ask whether the link is still missing – whether the gap the members of the Commission found unacceptable has been narrowed. The answer must be that, while there has indeed been some narrowing of the gap at least in basic services, disparities persist, not only between industrialised and developing countries but also within countries, and within regions, between urban and rural areas. And there is an additional problem. The advance of the information society and, more recently, the expansion of the INTERNET, have led to the opening up of a new gap – between 'information rich' and 'information poor' societies. This disturbing trend seems to have been largely unaffected by other developments during the restructuring of the telecommunications sector, such as the separation of operational and regulatory functions, privatisation and the liberalisation of segments of the market.

Were a new Independent Commission to be established today, its mandate would be significantly more complex, but no less daunting. In its initial survey of the world scene, the new Commission would soon appreciate the main preoccupations of those who labour in this sector.

The members of the Commission would become familiar with the debate over the rival merits of 'universal access' and 'universal service'. They would examine different approaches to the liberalisation of telecommunications systems and assess the importance of competition in this process. This would lead them to compare methods of regulation.

The perennial problem of funding the expansion and improvement of networks in the poorer developing countries would occupy much of their time and thought.

They would wish to assess the performance to date of the Development Sector – that especially important department of the Union – and to consider whether and, if so how, this might be enhanced. This would lead the Commission into the especially important area of partnerships between industrialised and developing countries.

The Commission would be compelled early on in its work to form a view on the impact of the World Trade Organisation Agreement on Telecommunications Services which has recently come into force.

These and other issues would occupy the time and thoughts of the members of any new Commission, and the international telecommunications community would hope that in the end they would point the way forward. However, there is no need for a new Commission. Over the next several days the knowledge, experience and wisdom assembled at this conference will be applied to these issues and, when your work is done, the way ahead will be clear.

Your starting point might be the Declaration issued at the conclusion of the Buenos Aires Conference in March 1994. This reminded Members of the ITU that telecommunications is an essential component of political, economic, social and cultural development. However, the evolving information society will either hasten the closing of the gap between developing and industrialised countries, or inadvertently widen it. This is the great challenge of today and you may well consider that it would be right for the ITU to ensure that the malign as well as the benign implications of the information society are understood at the highest political level by the member states you represent.

As regards the contribution the ITU itself can make in confronting this challenge, you may conclude that the best course is to apply the long-standing military principle of reinforcing success. Since its establishment in 1992 the Development Sector has done sterling work. It is well understood that the circumstances of each developing country are unique. This means that progress can only be made case by case. For this reason you may take the view that the scope of partnerships – or alliances as they are sometimes called – might be widened and that they should embrace not only financial cooperation but also the sharing of knowledge and experience and the transfer of expertise. You may also conclude that these partnerships will not be productive if they are short term; the experts concerned need adequate time to learn and understand the specifics of the markets so that they may offer appropriate guidance to officials and operators in the host country. The fact that the resources available to the Development Sector are limited suggests that the private sector should be given further encouragement to play a more significant role in this field. Discussion of this aspect of relationships with developing countries may lead you to stress the importance of the training of managers and other senior staff and to point to the substantial benefits that have been shown to flow from this.

Then there is the whole range of funding issues. One such issue which calls for close attention is the impact of the process of liberalisation on accounting rates. In some cases this could inadvertently prejudice revenue flows and, in consequence, the prospects for investment in developing countries. In this context you may consider that the ITU's admirable programme could be strengthened by new emphasis on regulatory and commercial strategies to enhance revenue and tele-density, particularly by providing targeted advice to specific countries.

There is also the question of universal access which, now that the United Nations has enunciated a right to communicate, is no longer seen as a technical issue for the ITU but one of high political importance. Until now it has been assumed that the shift from state-owned to privately-owned telecommunications systems would lead to more rapid development of the network as well as lower prices. In many cases this has proved to be true, but there have been notable exceptions where privatisation has not been followed by the introduction of competition. In any case, you will wish to examine this question in the light of the recent WTO Agreement on Telecommunications Services. I am confident that this Agreement will soon prove its worth. Renato Ruggiero, the Director-General, was right when he said that, since it will make access to knowledge easier, the Agreement 'gives nations, large and small, rich and poor, better opportunities to prepare for the 21st century'. That surely is a good enough reason for developing countries to subscribe to it. But there is another reason. By openly undertaking the obligations the Agreement contains, in whatever way and at whatever moment is most opportune, developing countries can, at a stroke, enhance their attractiveness to potential investors with an assurance of regulatory certainty.

* * *

Some here today may recall the comment in the Introduction to *The Missing Link* on the disparity in the distribution of telecommunications services across the world: 'Neither in the name of common humanity nor on grounds of common interest is such a disparity acceptable'.

The striking technological advances of the past decade have made the elimination of this disparity a practical possibility. The funds can be secured; after all, compared with the construction of roads, railways and airports, the expansion and improvement of telecommunications networks is cheap. The technology is proven and versatile. The expertise and skills are readily available. There is a wealth of relevant experience to draw on. What is at stake – what is within our grasp – is beyond price.

As we leave behind this wonderful and dreadful twentieth century, universal access to one of the most valuable products of human ingenuity could at last link members of the human race across the globe. All that stands in the way is reluctance to appreciate the significance of either the challenge or the opportunity, and, above all, lack of political will.

I for one hope that the ITU, in its wisdom, will feel able, in the course of this year, to adopt the measures which are needed to clear the way ahead.

ENVOI

It would be foolhardy to attempt to draw precise conclusions from the accounts in the preceding chapters of developments in the international and other fields in the second half of the twentieth century. Circumstances differ from case to case and any lessons to be drawn from past experience need to take that factor into account. This does not mean, however, that on my own journey through these past decades I have not formed my own impressions. Some of these I have discarded or amended in the light of subsequent experience; others have been confirmed.

The Second World War not only changed the balance of power in the world but also precipitated the end of the colonial empires. Cataclysms are not wholly without benefit. The defeat of communism in Europe, so dramatically signalled by the demolition of the Berlin Wall, was also bound to stimulate great change and to offer new opportunities. It was appropriate therefore that the Secretary-General of the United Nations should have been asked to set out his own ideas for the organisation's role in the new situation. However, the reaction of the United States in particular to the perceptive and well-balanced prescription in the *Agenda for Peace* was unenthusiastic. The sad truth is that the United States has never enjoyed an easy relationship with developing countries, who for decades have constituted an overwhelming majority in the organisation. In the absence of new thinking about the role of the United Nations, it was no surprise that the response to the intra-state conflicts which broke out in the 1990s was flawed. In other respects it has seemed that the international community, having heaved a collective sigh of relief, was reluctant to appreciate the full significance of the seismic change in Europe. And Russia ten years on is unstable, insecure and apprehensive, and the attitude of Europe and the United States towards the old enemy appears to lack confidence, coherence and vision.

There remain other causes for concern – the accumulation of weapons of mass destruction, international terrorism and traffic in drugs. Here and there age-old enmities – some racially motivated, others sectarian – persist and in most cases defy the conscientious efforts of others to effect reconciliation. Elsewhere tyrannical regimes have emerged, notably in Iraq, Burma and parts of Africa, which show no regard for the human rights of their citizens. The atrocities committed by regimes in Africa, Asia and the Balkans in the final years of the twentieth century disgrace the perpetrators who shelter behind the denial in the UN

Charter of the right to intervene in the internal affairs of member states. If they are to succeed, the efforts which are at last being made to overcome this obstacle, will need wide international support.

Reactions to developments in other fields have also lacked urgency. Many years have passed since the threats to public health and the environment from pollution of the atmosphere were first perceived and informed public opinion has been looking for an effective response at high political level. Yet the programmes of internationally agreed counter-action, which will be effective only if they have the support of developing and industrialised countries alike, seem heavily qualified and, rightly or wrongly, give the impression of being unduly influenced by vested interests in certain industrialised countries.

More serious is the reluctance to address the implications of the information revolution and, in particular, the advent of the INTERNET. Few aspects of modern life will remain unaffected and systems of governance will not be immune. One wonders how long political leaders in the parliamentary democracies will be content to see a steady rise in the power and influence of multi-national organisations in the financial, economic and media and other fields at the expense, no doubt, of their own. Global inter-connection can be exploited for a wide range of purposes and in the end the prospect before the political leaders of the day may be either enhanced world order or descent into anarchy.

A major source of encouragement is the growth of regional cooperation across the globe. The Arab League, the Gulf Council, the Association of South East Asian Nations, the Organisation of African Unity, the Organisation of American States, the North American Free Trade Area, the Asian Pacific Economic Cooperation forum, the European Union and the most recent initiative in the Far East involving both China and Japan - these among others exemplify realisation by the governments concerned that the sharing of interests and ambitions rather than the pursuit of purely national policies reinforces their efforts to ensure peace, security and prosperity for their peoples.

This is a welcome trend. But, in observing the running tide of history since the end of the Second War, I have derived most encouragement from the skill, wisdom and dedication of those with whom I have been privileged to work in different fields and in different countries and regions. The presence across the world of such human quality is the best reason for looking to the future with confidence.

INDEX

Abbasid Dynasty, 2
Abdulillah, Prince, 43-44
Academic Pharmacy Group, 258
 see also pharmacists
Acheson, Dean, 230
Aden, 4, 297
Afghanistan: Soviet invasion, 36
Africa, 108, 181, 308, 329
Agar, Herbert, 178
Agenda 2000, 128
Agenda for Peace, 213, 223-225, 345
AIDS/HIV, 253, 261, 262, 264-270
al-Din, Salah see Saladin
al-Rashid, Haroun, 2
Alanbrooke, Field Marshal, 191
Algeria, 63
Ali, Muhammad, 4, 38
Allenby, General, 4-5
American Express, 325
American Telephone and Telegraph Company
 (AT&T), 324-325
 see also telecommunications
American University of Beirut, 14
Amr Pasha, 164-165
Andean Pact, 177
Anglo-Iranian Oil Company, 192
 see also oil industry
Anglo-Iraqi Treaty, 30
Anglo-Persian Oil Company, 297, 307
 see also oil industry
Annan, Kofi, 212, 213, 224-226, 229
Antici Group, 121
Antonius, George, 32
Arab Awakening, (George Antonius), 32
Arab countries: armed forces, 17-18; British
 influence on, 13-14; economy, 9-10; and
 European Union, 88-92; fear of Israel, 20;
 general characteristics, 5-7; independence
 11-12; language, 22-25; nationalism, 5,
 14-21, 195; new Arabia, 34-35; relationship
 with West, 19, 21; Arab Revolt (1916), 14;
 Russian assistance, 157; society structure,
 7-8; view of Westerners, 14
Arab League see League of Arab States
Arab Maghreb Union, 89
Arabic language, 22-25
Ardwick, Lord, 233
ASEAN see Association of South East Asian
 Nations
Asia-Pacific Telecommunity, 335, 337
 see also telecommunications

Association Agreement, 102-103
Association of South East Asian Nations
 (ASEAN), 78, 82-84, 177, 197
Aswan Dam, 33, 41
AT&T (American Telephone and Telegraph
 Company), 324-325
 see also telecommunications
Ataturk, Kamal, 17
Atlantic Charter, 191, 209, 331, 333
Audland, Christopher, 54
Australia, 108, 111

Baath Party, 17, 44-45
Baghdad, 2
Balfour, Lord, 108, 155
Balfour Declaration, 5, 13, 27
Bandung Conference, 197
Bank of England, 280
Barclay, Sir Roderick, 54
Basic Law of 1948, 220, 289
Basra Petroleum Company, 292
 see also oil industry
Belgium, 99
Bell, Jacob, 259
Bentham, Jeremy, 272
Beveridge Report, 262
Bevin, Ernest, 31, 164-165, 192
Bidault, Georges, 131
Boothroyd, Betty, 280
Boots the Chemists, 258
Bosnia, 225
Bottomley, Virginia, 267
Brandt, Willy, 178
Brandt Commission, 180
Brazil, 163, 194
Bretton Woods Agreement, 132, 157-158,
 191, 221, 308
Briand, Aristide, 76, 208
Britain: cotton industry in Egypt, 14;
 developing relations with Middle East, 21;
 end of relations with Libya, 47; expansion
 in Eastern Mediterranean (19th century), 3;
 forces in Egypt, 39-40; foreign policy, 154-
 163; imports/exports, 159; independence
 of Iraq, 43; influence on Middle East,
 13-14; interests in Persian Gulf, 4; oil
 dependency, 308; order for Skybolt
 weapons from USA, 55-56; Owen Falls
 Dam, 164-165; Pilgrims, 190-191;
 relations with India, 185-189;
 routes through Middle East, 12;

telecommunications, 324; trade with Middle East, 12; Treaty of Alliance with Libya, 46; Treaty of Rome, 109; wartime relationship with USA, 191-193
see also European Union
British Expeditionary Force, 297
British foreign policy see Britain
British Petroleum, 4
British Pharmaceutical Conference, 258-263
British Telecom, 324, 336
Brown, George, 35, 113
Build-Operate-Transfer schemes, 336
Bulgaria, 137
Byzantium, 1-2

Cabinet Office, 285
Cable and Wireless, 324-325, 327
see also telecommunications
Caliphs, 2, 42
Callaghan, James, 105, 124
Calvocoressi, Peter, 217-218
Camp David Agreement, 298
Canada, 108, 111
Caribbean Community, 177
Carrington, Lord, 36, 107
Central Policy Review Staff (CPRS), 162
Centre for Telecommunications Development, 320
see also telecommunications
Chadwick, Edwin, 272
Chamberlain, Neville, 199
Charter of the United Nations see United Nations
Chauhan Singh, 187, 188
Chile, 142
China, 161, 316, 329
Chirac, Jacques, 116
Christian approach to international relations, 198-202
Chou en-Lai, 192
Churchill, Winston, 110, 191, 208-209, 278, 331
Citizen's Charter, 272
civil service, 281-284
Coal and Steel Community, 97
Cold War, 89-90, 93, 127, 222, 223
College of Commissioners, 133
Colombo Plan, 175
COMECON (Council for Mutual Economic Assistance), 117-118, 175
Committee of Permanent Representatives see COREPER
Committee of the Whole, 180
Common Agricultural Policy, 75-76, 79-80, 136, 163
Common Fisheries Policy, 79-80, 163
Common Foreign and Security Policy, 137
Commonwealth: and European Union, 109-

115; origins of the term, 108-109
Commonwealth Conferences, 55, 113
Commonwealth Heads of Government, 175
Commonwealth Relations Office, 110
Commonwealth Sugar Agreement, 114
communicating with the public, 231-243
see also Downing Street and the press
community of nations, 195-202
Conference on the Human Environment, 183
Conference on International Economic Cooperation, 180
Conference on Security and Cooperation in the Mediterranean, 89
Conference on Trade and Development, 174, 180
Congress of Vienna, 108, 165
COREPER (Committee of Permanent Representatives), 119-125, 165, 286-287
Council for Mutual Economic Assistance see COMECON
Council of Ministers, 86-87, 90, 95, 101, 104, 106, 114-115, 127, 287
Council of Trent, 196
Council of Western European Union, 113
Couve de Murville, Maurice see de Murville, Maurice Couve
CPRS see Central Policy Review Staff
Crimean War, 108
Crosland, Anthony, 124
Crossman, Richard, 31
Curzon, Lord, 297
Cyprus, 128, 135
Czech Republic, 128, 135

Daily Mail, 267
Davignon, Vicomte, 58, 271, 300
de Chardin, Teilhard, 146
de Gaulle, President: Britain entering the European Community 50, 52, 53, 57, 94, 113; Britain's dependence on USA, 56; collapse of Britain's EU negotiations, 58-60
de Klerk, FW, 331
de Murville, Maurice Couve: Britain's application to EU, 51, 52, 53, 54, 56-58, 60
de Reuter, Baron Julius, 297
Declaration of Independence of the United States, 220
Dehaene, Jean-Luc, 136
Delors, Jacques, 98, 133
Denmark: public opinion on EU, 80-81
Department of Employment, 236
Department of Energy, 283
Department of Health, 236, 254, 256, 267, 269
Department of Health and Social Services (Northern Ireland), 258
d'Estaing, Giscard, 83, 107, 133, 180

Deutschland über Alles, 219
Dill, Field Marshal, 191
Diplomacy, 164-171
Disarmament Conference, 208
Disraeli, Benjamin, 108
Dixon, Sir Pierson, 51, 52, 53, 56
Dominions Office, 110
Doshi, Saryu, 189
Doughty, C.M., 6
Downing Street and the press, 244-251
  see also Government and the media
Dulles, John Foster, 192

Early Bird (satellite), 322
East African Community, 177
East India Company, 4
East Timor, 225-226
East/West relations, 149
Eastern Question, 3
Eban, Abba, 27
Economic and Monetary Union, 127, 132,
  133, 134
Economic Commission for Africa, 182
Economist, 194
Eden, Anthony, 33, 41, 110, 192-193
EEC *see* European Union
EFTA *see* European Free Trade Association
Egypt: Anglo-French intervention (1956) 12;
  assault on Israel, 35-36; background,
  37-38; British forces in Canal Zone, 39-40;
  cotton industry, 14; declared a
  Protectorate, 5; nationalism, 195; Nile
  Waters negotiations, 165; Owen Falls Dam,
  164-165; severing the past, 40-41; Treaty
  of Alliance (1936), 19-20
Eisenhower, General, 191
EMS *see* European Monetary System
EMU *see* Economic and Monetary Union
energy: general policy, 291-296;
  international aspect, 297-305
  see also oil industry
ERM *see* Exchange Rate Mechanism
Establishment and Constitution Order, 256
Estonia, 128, 135
Euro-Arab Dialogue, 88
  see also Arab countries; European Union
European Assembly, 127
European Coal and Steel Community, 130,
  131
European Commission, 86, 95, 128, 135-137
European Community *see* European Union
European Council, 123-124, 134, 137, 302
European Defence Community, 79, 131, 137
European Development Fund, 175
European Economic Community *see*
  European Union
European Free Trade Association (EFTA), 50
European Monetary System, 70, 94, 133

European Parliament: elections, 65;
  malpractice allegations, 135
European Union: and the Arab countries,
  88-92; first British application, 50-55,
  56-58; British staff structure, 285-288;
  Budget, 74-76; and the Commonwealth,
  108-115; creation of, 85-86; criticisms of,
  95-96; development and growth, 62-67, 70,
  77, 132-137; economic/social divergence,
  69-70; effect of oil crisis (1973), 62; effects
  of recession, 62, 68; energy crisis,
  300-303; evolution, 86-88; first
  achievements, 76-77; German attitudes,
  81; Greek application, 102-107;
  Independent Review Body, 133-134;
  influence of Christian faith, 72;
  integrating new members, 62, 80-81;
  International Energy Agency, 300-301;
  Lord Nolan's lecture, 284-285; problem
  solving, 78-80; relations with ASEAN,
  82-84; sovereignty, 96; telecommunications
  policy, 326; Third World views, 175;
  world identity/obligations, 70-71; younger
  generation's views, 81-82
Evans, Harold, 55, 223
Exchange Rate Mechanism, 134

Faisal, King, 43, 44
Falklands War, 210, 299-300
Falluja, 39
Family and Youth Concern Group, 267
Family Planning Association, 258
Farouk, King, 40, 164-165
Fatimids, 2
Fayat, Henri, 57
Financial Times, 246
Fitzgerald, Dr Garret, 103
Fleming, Ellen, 193
Foreign and Commonwealth Office, 162,
  236, 245
Fourteen Points, 178, 206
Fowler, Norman, 256, 264-265
France: HIV prevalence rates, 269;
European
  Union, 99-100; oil dependence, 308,
  309
France, Pierre Mendès- *see* Mendès-France,
  Pierre
François-Poncet, Jean, 106-107
Free Officers, 34, 39, 40, 41
  see also Revolutionary Command Council
Free Trade Area, 177
French National Assembly, 79

Gandhi, Mrs, 185, 186
Gandhi, Rajiv, 187
GATT, 180, 326
General Agreement on Tariffs and Trade *see*

GATT
General Board of Health, 272
General Motors, 325
Generalised Preference Schemes, 71
Geneva Conference on Korea and Indo-China (1954), 192
Genscher, Hans-Dietrich, 106
George, Lloyd, 207
Gerald of Wales, 21, 176
Germany: armed forces, 131; Basic Law of 1948, 289; European Union, 95, 99-100; influence in 19th century Eastern Mediterranean, 3-4; late 19th/early 20th century, 206-207; oil dependence, 308, 309; reaction to Greek application to EU, 105; withdrawal from League of Nations, 208
Ghali, Boutros, 211-212, 213, 223-225, 229
Gladstone, William, 281
Global Digital Highway, 324-325
    see also telecommunications
Global Information Infrastructure, 340
    see also telecommunications
Global Negotiations, 83, 180
Glubb, Sir John, 6-7, 12
Glyn-Jones, Sir William, 259
Gore, Al, 340
Governance, 280-290
Government and the media, 231-243
    see also Downing Street and the press
Greater East Asia Co-Prosperity Sphere, 29
Greece: accession to EU, 66, 70, 102-107
Green Papers, 232
Greenway, Sir Charles, 297, 307
Group of 77, 174, 197
Group of Reflection, 99
Guardian, 237, 246
Gulbenkian, Calouste, 297
Gulf Cooperation Council, 89

Habib mission, 298
Hamid, Sultan Abdul, 4
Hansard, 231
Harris, John, 283
Hashemite, 4-5
HEA see Health Education Authority
health education, 252-257
Health Education Authority (HEA), 253, 254, 256-257, 258, 264, 265-270, 271-274
Health Education Board for Scotland, 258
Health Education Council, 257, 265
Health of the Nation, 260-261, 272
Health of Towns Association, 272
health promotion, 271-274
Health Promotion in the Workplace, 273
Heath, Edward: address to UN General Assembly (1970), 223; background, 49-50; European Union negotiations, 49-55, 56-58,

60, 82-83, 111, 112, 114-117; press relations, 244, 246
Hecht, Ben, 192
Hejaz, 1-2, 3
Herriot, Edouard, 76
Hitler, Adolf, 278
HIV/AIDS, 253, 261, 262, 264-270
Hobbes, Thomas, 220
Home, Lord, 198
Home Office, 236
Hungary, 128, 135
Hussain, Saddam: as head of state, 45; Palestine/Arab unity, 27
Hussein, grandson of Prophet Muhammad, 2, 42

IBM (International Business Machines), 325
Idris, King, 35, 46
IEP see International Energy Programme
Independent Commission for World Wide Telecommunications Development, 205, 315-320, 339, 340-341
India: independence, 29, 172-173; relations with Britain, 185-189, telecommunications, 316, 329
Indo-British Colloquium, 185
Indo-China, 131
Indonesia, 226, 312, 313, 336
Information Divisions (Whitehall), 236
Ingham, Bernard, 251
Institute of Medicine, 264
Institute of Petroleum, 291
Integrated Digital Services Network, 322
INTELSAT, 322
Inter-Governmental Conference, 135, 136
International Bank for Reconstruction and Development, 294-295
International Business Machines (IBM), 325
International Court of Justice, 212, 224
International Development Assistance, 175
International Energy Agency, 155, 295, 300, 305, 309, 310
International Energy Programme (IEP), 309
International Institute of Communications, 316
International Monetary Fund, 175, 311
International Society for Aeronautical Telecommunications (SITA), 325
International Telecommunication Regulations, 326
International Telecommunication Union, 316, 319, 326, 328-329, 337, 339-343
International Telegraph Convention, 326
International War Crimes Tribunal, 214
Internet, 227, 289, 339, 340
Introducing America (Kreutz and Fleming), 193
Iqbal Singh, 187

Iran, 158, 179, 296, 309, 312, 313
Iraq: background, 42-45; British influence,
  32; creation of, 30; invasion of Kuwait, 26,
  210, 223; overthrow of monarchy, 33-34;
  petroleum companies, 292
Iraq Petroleum Company, 4, 43, 292
Irgun Zvai Leumi, 192
Irish Free State, 108
ISDN, 322
Islam, 1-2, 3, 17, 218
Israel: Arab attitudes towards, 20; assault
  by Egypt and Syria, 35-36; formation of 5,
  26, 39
Italy, 45-46, 89, 99, 208, 269

Japan, 195, 208, 302, 308, 309, 325
Jay, Peter, 99
Jefferson, Thomas, 220
Jenkins, Roy, 97-98, 105, 107, 132-134, 301
Jews: post-World War I, 5
Joad, Professor, 195
Johnson, Dr James, 260
Joint Cooperation Agreement, 83-84
Jones, Sir William Glyn-, 259
Journey to an Unknown Destination (Andrew
  Shonfield), 95, 285

Karadzic, Radovan, 214
Karamanlis, Konstantinos, 106, 107
Kashmir, 210
Kaul, TN, 185, 187, 189
Khalifa see Caliphs
Kellogg, Frank Billings, 208
Kennedy, President: Skybolt order from
  Britain, 55-56; Western Alliance, 193
Kilbracken, Lord, 267
Kissinger, Henry: Egypt/Syria assault on
  Israel, 35-36; military strength, 194
Kobayashi, Koji, 339
Kohl, Helmut, 99-100, 116
Korea, 163, 209-210
Kosovo, 215, 225
Kreutz, Barbara, 193
Kuwait: income, 313; Iraqi invasion, 26,
  210, 223

Lake Victoria, 164
Latvia, 137
Lawrence, T.E., 4-5, 8
LAYH see Look After Your Heart programme
League of Arab States, 5, 26, 197
League of Nations, 43, 143, 144, 148, 196,
  207-208
Libya, 35, 45-47, 201-202, 210, 308
Life of Reason (George Santayana), 110
Lincoln, Abraham, 276
Linstead, Sir Hugh, 259
Lithuania, 137

Lloyd, Selwyn, 50
Local Government Board, 272
Lomé Convention, 63, 71, 113
Look After Your Heart programme, 254-256,
  273
Loucheur, Louis, 76
Luns, Dr Joseph, 241
Luxembourg, 99

Maastricht Treaty, 86, 87, 94-95, 98, 127,
  133, 134-135
Macmillan, Harold: background, 49-50;
  European Union, 50-51, 53-54, 111, 112;
  nuclear deterrents, 56
MacMurray, Professor John, 238
Madariaga, Javier Solana, 137
Maghreb, 89, 90
Malta, 137
Mandela, Nelson, 331
Manley, Michael, 182
Marlborough College, 37
Marseillaise, 219
Marshall, General, 191
Marshall Plan, 168-169, 175, 191
McLuhan, Professor Marshal, 93, 96, 227,
  322, 339
McNamara, Robert, 55
media relations with Government, 231-243
  see also Downing Street and the press
Mediterranean Policy, 102
Mehdawi, Colonel, 44, 45
Mendès-France, Pierre, 131
Mesopotamia, 3, 4
Middle East Centre for Arab Studies
  (Lebanon), 1, 22-25
Mill, John Stuart, 219
Ministry of Defence, 236
Ministry of Health, 272
Missing Link, 205, 315-320, 336, 339, 342
Mladic, Ratko, 214
Mongol invasions, 2
Monnet, Jean, 59, 95, 97, 111, 130-131
Monroe Doctrine, 208
Morgan, Janet, 189
Morocco, 63
Moslem Brotherhood, 39
Mossadegh, Muhammad, 192
Muhammad, Prophet, 1-2
Murley, Sir Reginald, 267

Nasser, Gamal Abder: after the revolution,
  40-42; Arab unity, 26; arms purchase, 33;
  background, 38-40; beginnings, 32; effect
  on nationalist movement, 14; Non-Aligned
  Movement, 173; revolution, 34; Suez
  Canal Company, 158
nation states, 217-230
National Academy of Sciences, 264

National AIDS Helpline, 265
  see also AIDS/HIV
National Health Service, 252, 265, 272, 273
National Pharmaceutical Association, 258
  see also pharmacists
national policy making, 161-162
nationalism, 195-202, 219
NATO 137, 156, 175, 191, 197, 225
Neguib, General, 40
Nehru, Pandit, 173
New Industrialising Countries, 177, 181
New International Economic Order, 174
New Labour, 289
New Zealand, 108, 111, 114
Newfoundland, 108
NHS see National Health Service
Nigeria, 111, 312, 313
Nile Waters negotiations, 165
Nixon, President, 311
Nolan, Lord, 100, 284
Non-Aligned Movement, 173, 174, 175, 177,
  197
North Atlantic Alliance, 73, 173, 215, 222,
  225
North Atlantic Treaty Organisation see NATO
North/South relations, 150-152
Northcote, Sir Stafford, 281
Northern Ireland, 195-196, 246-247
nuclear power, 299
  see also energy
Nutting, Anthony, 38

OAU see Organisation of African Unity
occupational medicine, 252-257
OECD (Organisation for Economic
  Cooperation and Development), 82, 155,
  175, 303, 309
oil industry: first discoveries, 4; effect of
  crisis on EC (1973), 62; growth, 35;
  importance in Middle East, 306-314;
  OPEC, 174, 177, 292, 293, 302-303, 308,
  310-313; price increases, 151; Western
  dependence, 12
  see also energy
OPEC, 174, 177, 292, 293, 302-303, 308,
  310-313
  see also energy; oil industry
Organisation for Economic Cooperation and
  Development see OECD
Organisation of African Unity (OAU), 197
Organisation of American States, 175, 197
Organisation of Petroleum Exporting
  Countries see OPEC
Ortoli, François-Xavier, 97, 119, 132
Ottoman Empire: background, 3-4; effects
  on Arab society, 8-9; end of rule, 30
Owen, David, 124
Owen Falls Dam, 164

Own Resources System, 79

Pakistan, 187-188
Palestine: Arab unity, 27; Zionist influence,
  31
Papaligouras, 105-106
Peace Conference (1919), 207
Permanent Representatives Committee, 104,
  171-171
Persia: background, 1-2; British interests in
  the Gulf, 4
Peyrefitte, Alain, 59
Pharmaceutical Journal, 260
pharmacists, 258-263
Pharmacy Health Care Scheme, 258
Pisani, Edgard, 181
Point Four, 175
Poland, 128, 135, 304
Pompidou, Georges, 59, 82-83, 114-115, 132
Poncet, Jean François- see François-Poncet,
  Jean
Poor Law, 272
Portillo, Michael, 283
Post Office, 335-336
Preliminary Conference on Wireless
  Telegraphy, 326
  see also telecommunications
Press Council, 237
  see also media
Prodi, Romano, 136
Portugal: accession to EU, 66, 70, 175
Programme of Reform, 213
Promoting Better Health, 252
PTTs (Posts, Telegraph and Telephone), 324
Public Accounts Committee, 282
Public Health Laboratory Service, 269

Qaddafi, Colonel: arms supply, 201-202;
  background, 46-47; oil industry, 35;
  revolution (1969) 169-170
Qassim, Abdul Karim, 44-45

Ramo, Professor Simon, 329-330
Reagan, President, 303
Redwood, Professor Theophilus, 258
Renan, Ernest, 22
Renewing the United Nations, 224-225
Resolution 242, 35
Reuter, Baron Julius de, 297
Reuters, 325
Revolutionary Command Council, 40, 41, 47
  see also Free Officers
Rhodesia, 156
Rippon, Geoffrey, 114
Robinson, John, 54
Robinson, Mary, 214, 226
Roll, Sir Eric, 51, 56, 57
Roman Empire, 217

Romania, 137
Roosevelt, President, 191, 208-209, 331
Rosebery, Lord, 108
Rousseau, Jean-Jacques, 220
Rowe, Andrew, 186, 189
Royal Pharmaceutical Society of Great
  Britain, 258-263
Ruggiero, Renato, 342
Rule Britannia, 219
Rusk, Dean, 193

Sabri, Ali, 173
Said, Nuri, 33, 44
Saladin, 2
Sandys, Duncan, 50, 54
*Sanitary Conditions of the Labouring
  Population*, 272
Santayana, George, 110, 213
Santer, Jacques, 135
Saudi Arabia, 296, 310, 312, 313
Schmidt, Chancellor Helmut, 105, 133
Schuman Robert (Schuman Plan), 85, 130
Scottish Parliament, 280, 289
Security Council, 35, 144-145, 156, 170, 209-
  210, 211, 225, 228-229
Select Committee on Foreign Affairs, 162
Seljuk Empire, 2
Sharp, Sir Eric, 327
Shi'a, 2, 3, 42
Shonfield, Andrew, 95, 131, 285
Simon, Lord, 136
Singh, Chauhan, 187, 188
Singh, Iqbal, 187
Single European Act, 86, 94, 127, 134
Single Market, 86, 97, 202
SITA (International Society for Aeronautical
  Telecommunications), 325
Six Day War, 35
Slovakia, 137
Slovenia, 128, 135
Smith, Thomas Southwood, 272
Soames, Lord Christopher, 50, 54, 83
Social Contract, 220
Society for Worldwide Interbank Financial
  Telecommunications (SWIFT), 325
  see also telecommunications
Society of Occupational Medicine, 254-255
Solana, Javier, 216, 229
Somalia, 210-211, 225
South Africa, 108
Southwood Smith, Thomas, 272
sovereignty, 96-101, 220-221
Soviet Union, 36, 127, 157, 159, 166, 178,
  187-188, 209, 304-305
Spaak, Paul-Henri, 57, 126
Spain: background, 218; accession to EU,
  66, 70, 175; cooperative project, 89; HIV
  prevalence rates, 269

Special Agriculture Committee, 286
Special Assemblies, 180
Spierenburg, Dirk, 133
Spinelli, Altiero, 98
Stalin, 209
Standish, Captain Myles, 190
state of the nation, the author's view,
  275-279
Statute of Westminster (1932), 108
Stern Gang, 192
Steward, George, 245
Strategic Petroleum Reserve, 310
Stewart, Michael, 283
Stock Market crash, 327
Suez Canal Company, 20, 33, 40, 158
Suez War, 41, 42, 193, 288
Sunday Times, 233
SWIFT (Society for Worldwide Interbank
  Financial Telecommunications), 325
  see also telecommunications
Sykes-Picot agreement, 5
Syria: assault on Israel, 35-36; relationship
  with USA, 193
Syrian Protestant College, 14

Tedder, Air Chief Marshal, 191
telecommunications, 315-320, 339-343
terrorism, 167
Thailand, 336
Thatcher, Margaret: AIDS campaign, 267;
  press relations, 251; telecommunications,
  335-336
Thesiger, Wilfred, 5
ThinkNet Commission: Gulf War, 26
Third World, 141-143, 158, 172-184
Thorn, Gaston, 61, 104
Times, The, 238, 246, 259
Tito, President, 173
Treaty of Alliance (1936), 19-20
Treaty of Amsterdam, 116, 127-128, 135
Treaty of Maastricht *see* Maastricht Treaty
Treaty of Paris, 109
Treaty of Rome, 61, 65, 69-70, 72, 74, 76,
  85, 109, 112-113
Treaty of Versailles, 207
Treaty on European Union and European
  Monetary Union, 94
Trevelyan, Sir Charles, 281
Trevelyan, Sir Humphrey, 44
Troutbeck, Sir John, 33
Truman, President, 192
Tsatsos, President, 107
Tunisia, 63
Turkey, 3-4, 104

Uganda, 164
UKREP *see* United Kingdom Representation
  in Brussels

Ummayad Dynasty, 2
United Arab Republic of Egypt, Syria, Yemen, 26
United Kingdom Representation in Brussels (UKREP), 285-286, 287
United Nations: agencies, 197-198; *Agenda for Peace*, 223-225; background, 143-145, 191; Charter, 97, 144, 197, 331; constraints, 229-230; failures and successes, 166-167; General Assembly, 332; General Assembly Declaration, 142; peace-keeping, 198; prevention of war, 222; role, 206-216; Soviet Union, 222; telecommunications, 326, 328; USA involvement, 194
United States of America: Agreement with Libya, 46; League of Nations, 207; Marshall Plan, 168-169; NATO, 156; oil market, 302, 308, 309, 310; Pilgrims, 190-191; Point Four Aid (Syria), 13; reaction to *Agenda for Peace*, 345; relationship with Soviet Union, 166; super-power status, 157, 166; supplying Skybolt nuclear weapons, 55-56; telecommunications, 324; United Nations, 194; wartime relationship with Britain, 191-193
Uniting for Peace Resolution, 209, 222
UNOSOM, 211
UNPROFOR, 211
Uruguay Round of Multilateral Trade Negotiations, 326

Venezuela, 313
Victoria, Queen, 108
Vietnam, 223
von Weizsacker, Richard, 136

Waldheim, Dr Kurt, 145
Warsaw Pact, 149, 173, 175, 197
Weizsacker, Richard von *see* von Weizsacker, Richard
Wells, HG, 229
Welsh Assembly, 280, 289
West Siberian gas pipeline, 304
White Nile, 164
White Papers, 232
Whitelaw, Lord, 246
Wilhelm, Kaiser, 30, 42-43, 109, 206
Wilson, Harold, 113
Wilson, Woodrow, 178-179, 206-207
World Administrative Telegraph and Telephone Conference, 326
World AIDS Day, 268
World Bank, 175, 304
World Development Fund, 180
World Food Programme, 144
World Health Organisation, 253
World Intelligent Network, 324
World Telecommunications Development Conference, 182
see also telecommunications
World trade, 159-160
World Trade Organisation Agreement on Telecommunications Services, 341, 342
see also telecommunications
World War I: Middle Eastern events during, 4-5
World War II, 109-111, 165-166, 203
Wormser, Olivier, 56

Yew, Lee Kwan 184
Yom Kippur war, 170, 300, 308
Yugoslavia, 211, 214-215